Joséphine *and* Emilie

Stars of the Bel Canto
in Europe and America
1823 - 1889

Joséphine *and* Emilie

Stars of the Bel Canto
in Europe and America
1823 - 1889

Dudley Cheke

JON CARPENTER
Oxford

First published in 1993 by
Jon Carpenter Publishing, PO Box 129, Oxford OX1 4PH
Tel/fax 0865 790715

Distributed in the USA and Canada by
Inbook, PO Box 120261, East Haven, CT 06512, USA

© Dudley John Cheke

ISBN 1 897766 08 4

Printed and bound by The Alden Press, Oxford

DEDICATION

To my late wife
Yvonne *née* de Méric

TO THE READER

Dudley Cheke died suddenly on 20 August 1993 while the book was still in production. He had corrected the proofs but unfortunately was not to see the finished book. The subsequent process has been supervised by his sons Anthony and Robert, who offer the publication of the book as a memorial to their father.

Many of the illustrations, culled from diverse sources over many years, are not in an ideal condition. Some were available to the author only as poor photocopies. Both publisher and printer have done their best to cope with the consequently variable quality of reproduction.

Contents

Foreword

BY RICHARD BONYNGE

DUDLEY Cheke's account of the soprano Joséphine de Méric and her daughter Emilie de Méric Lablache (mezzo soprano) brings to life two singers whose names have been unjustly forgotten. Both ladies pursued important careers in 19th century opera and performed with the greatest singers of the day.

Joséphine sang all over Italy as well as in Paris, Berlin and London in a repertoire which included *Semiramide*, *Ninetta* (La Gazza Ladra), *Amenaide* (Tancredi), *Elvira* (I Puritani), *Amina* (La Sonnambula), *Giulietta* (I Capuleti e 1 Montecchi), *Agata* (Der Freischütz), and *Gemma di Vergy*, as well as in operas by Ricci, Mercadante, Pacini and Vaccai.

She sang with Pasta, Malibran, Vestis, Cinti, Donzelli, and Tamburini and appeared on the same concert platforms as Paganini and Moscheles.

Her daughter Emilie had a most interesting career largely in London, Vienna and St. Petersburg. She sang for the Tsar, the King of Prussia, the Emperor of Austria and the King of Belgium. She appeared in "Cenerentola" with Lablache, "La Donna del Lago" with Grisi, Mario and Tamberlick, in "La Gazza Ladra" with Grisi, "Semiramide" with Grisi and Tamburini, in "Les Huguenots" with Grisi and Mario and "Rigoletto" with Tamberlick.

Mr Cheke gives us much fascinating information not readily obtainable elsewhere about the operatic and concert world of some seven decades of the 19th century and provides us with much contemporary criticism, sometimes quite hilarious.

This book is a most welcome and enjoyable addition to the history of Bel Canto and 19th century opera.

Preface

THIS is the story of two opera singers, mother and daughter, whose lives neatly spanned the whole of the nineteenth century. Each, in her day, achieved international fame. Both were exponents of that *bel canto* which is now enjoying a renaissance.

The mother, Joséphine de Méric, was gifted with a distinctive soprano voice, and played leading and secondary roles in most of the chief opera houses in Western Europe.

Her daughter Emilie, née Glossop, known after her marriage as Madame de Méric Lablache, made her reputation as a mezzo-soprano or contralto.

In this book an attempt is made to reconstruct the lives of Joséphine and Emilie against the background of that exciting nineteenth-century opera world which was then one of the few arenas where women made careers of their own.

In that period, music critics and reviewers usually stuck to their lasts, giving few if any personal details about the performers. On the other hand, successful singers were popular stars and the art of singing was taken very seriously. The newspapers and magazines of the day published such full accounts of operatic and concert performances that it is often possible, by balancing one against another, to arrive at a fairly clear assessment of a singer's achievements and of the reactions of the audiences.

Joséphine spent most of her career on the Continent of Europe, but she had two seasons in London, in 1832 and 1833. Emilie's long career took her from a *début* in Paris to London, St. Petersburg, Vienna, the British provinces, and, ultimately, to many of the major cities in the United States of America.

This book will have done a small service to operatic history if it has succeeded in disentangling Joséphine de Méric from her contemporary, the similarly-named soprano Henriette Méric-Lalande (1799 – 1867). There is no family connexion between the two. Henriette, née Lalande, married a horn-player at the *Opéra Comique* called Méric (not de Méric) and she added his name to hers.

Unfortunately, since Joséphine and Henriette were both sopranos and are frequently referred to without their Christian names, as Madame Méric, confusion has arisen. The mistake is to be found in highly-respected works of reference and Henriette has even been wrongly credited with being the mother of Emilie. Henriette sang in London in 1830 and 1831.

Some new light, it is believed, has been shed on the British impresario, Joseph Glossop, founder of the Royal Coburg Theatre which was to become the Old Vic. Through his first marriage, to the singer Elizabeth Féron, he became the paternal grandfather (despite the change of surname) of Sir Augustus Harris, the celebrated lessee of the Theatre Royal, Drury Lane, and of Covent Garden. However, Joseph Glossop's main rôle in this story is as the father of Joséphine's daughter Emilie. His colourful life deserves a biography of its own and contains several unsolved mysteries.

A biography should be written of Elizabeth Féron as well and a fairly full account of her life has been included here, not only as the wife of Glossop but also in her own right as an international *prima donna* and for the significant part which she played in popularising Italian opera in America.

A short chapter has been devoted to the career of the Italian tenor Timoleone Alexander, who became recognised as Joséphine de Méric's second husband.

Joséphine and her daughter had an international reputation. They held their own with many of the most celebrated of their contemporaries, and it is in that context that their performances are described in this work. At the same time, an attempt has been made to record audience reactions and reflect the fluctuations of public taste in music in the nineteenth century.

NOTE: Quotations, when not originally in English, are generally given in translation. For all except those in Russian, the versions are by the author (unless otherwise stated).

PART ONE *Joséphine*

Portrait of Joséphine by Vigneron.
(By courtesy of the Bibliothèque Nationale, Paris.)

CHAPTER 1

Joséphine de Méric in Strasbourg

'To the value and cleverness of Madame de Méric, as one able to carry out any part, whether it was one in Italian, or French or German, sufficient tribute has not been paid.'

Henry Chorley: 'Thirty Years Musical Recollections'

In her heyday, Joséphine de Méric was no stranger to fame. As many as seven operas (possibly eight) were written for her. Meyerbeer made an offer to write one for her, an offer which at the time she felt obliged to refuse.

Strasbourg

Enthusiastic Italian admirers in Ravenna acclaimed her in 1837 as *Prima Donna Assoluta* and wrote poems in her honour. One hails Joséphine as the new Euterpe, Muse of Dionysiac music and patroness of joy and pleasure, who could work marvels with her voice alone. Another speaks feelingly of the combination of nature and art by which her singing could evoke tears of delight.

Italian audiences are as free with brickbats as with applause and do not always take kindly to foreign performers, so the poets' praise for a non-Italian singer is significant.

Marie Joséphine Bonnaud Démeric (to give her name as in her birth certificate) was French. She was born in Strasbourg, in Alsace. The birth is recorded at the *Mairie* as having taken place at 4 p.m. on 2 Germinal (22 March) in the year IX of the French Republic (1801). Her father, Joseph, described as a musician, was living at No. 4, Marché aux Herbes, Strasbourg. The witnesses, both musicians domiciled in the city, were Joseph Jalliot and Gaspard Bach. Joséphine's mother, her father's second wife, was Marie Marguerite née Federlen. Joséphine was this couple's second child.

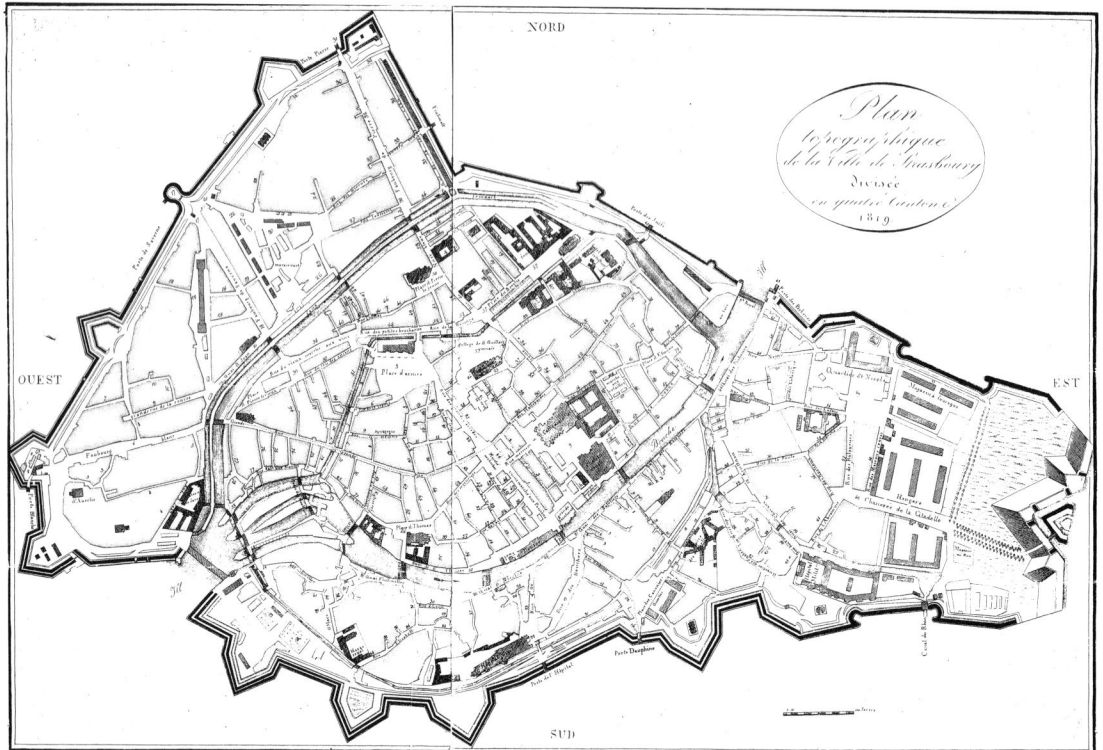

The record places Joséphine's birth in a musical setting, but in the disturbed atmosphere of the dying days of the First French Republic, and in a somewhat remote provincial frontier city under constant threat from the many enemies of revolutionary France.

Strasbourg, though then French, has always had strong ties with Germany, and Joséphine must have been accustomed from an early age to hearing both French and German spoken. When she was young, three quarters of the inhabitants were German-speaking. Her mother's family name, Federlen, suggests that she herself may have had some German blood.

In such a border town, the armed forces inevitably play a key role and Joséphine's family indeed had close connexions with the French Army. For much of his life, her father was employed by the Army and her brother Hector had a military career.

Strasbourg (1819), showing the fortifications – Josephine was born at No. 4 Marché aux Herbes, in the centre of the city.

Joséphine always regarded Strasbourg as her home city. By the time she was four, her father had moved to Toulon as musician with the 14th Regiment of Light Infantry. Her brother Hector Alexandre was born there in August 1804, but the family subsequently returned to Strasbourg, where two more brothers were born. By this time, Joseph had become a teacher of languages and mathematics and in due course he had charge of a *pensionnat* of his own.

Joséphine meanwhile had been receiving singing lessons which were sponsored by her father's friend Lieutenant-Colonel Braun, from the *ancienne garde*, a noted local musician. From the time she was in her late teens, she had been giving concert performances in Strasbourg and taking part in the musical evenings which were then very much *à la mode* there.

As recorded in the *Allgemeine Musikalische Zeitung (AMZ)*, 'Dem. Joséphine Bonnaud' was already well known in Strasbourg as an amateur singer as early as 1818. On 14 December of that year, she gave her first public concert, one for her own benefit. She took the part of the maiden in a lyrical drama called *The Vintage in the Vosges* (*Die Weinlese am Vogesus*), with a script by A. Launey and music by Maj. M. Braun. She also sang Weber's *rondo La dolce speranza* and a *polonaise* by Herr Braun. The reviewer described her as "full of promise, having a pure, rich, youthful voice." However, he added, "she lacked training, method, taste, expression and practice in roulades, though she had permitted herself a few shakes." All that having been said, the writer recalled the dilettante's youth and conceded that it was therefore unfair to submit her performance to rigorous criticism.

Joséphine was active as a concert singer in Strasbourg until the summer of 1822. The following record of some of the performances gives an impression of the kind of vocal music which was popular in Strasbourg at the time.

At a concert given by the *Gesellschaft des Musik Liebhaber-Vereins* in aid of the poor on 13 March 1819, Joséphine sang an aria by Portogallo, *Frenar vorrei le lagrime*, but "in a schoolgirlish way". She also took part in a quartet from Righini's *Jerusalem Delivered*.

In July 1819, an opera company from Karlsruhe gave performances in Strasbourg and Joséphine would have had the opportunity of hearing *Tancredi*, Paër's *Sophonisbe* and *Die Zauberflöte*.

Between 15 November 1819 and 22 January 1820, the *Connoisseurs' Society* in Strasbourg gave six concerts, under the energetic direction of the local piano-teacher and composer, Herr Berg. Mlle. Bonnaud was a regular performer, with a Mlle. Bonasegla. These two took the major parts in a rare full-scale performance of Haydn's *Creation* on 4 March 1820 and Joséphine sang the aria *La Tromba* by Elizabeth Féron's mentor and composer-friend Pucitta at a memorial service on 11 March.

A second society of *dilettanti* called the *Société d'Emulation* gave concerts every Monday, from 16 April 1820, under the direction of a Herr Nani. At a concert given for the poor, Joséphine was praised for her part in a scene with chorus from Paër's *Sargino*.

Of all the *soirées musicales*, none were more fashionable than those given by the Baronne de Pamphile de Lacroix who, as Joséphine's father said, had honoured his daughter with her protection. This will have been of great importance since the Baroness's husband was the Lieutenant-general in command of the 5th. Military Division in Strasbourg from August 1821 to the end of 1822.

In the Winter season (18 November 1820 - 3 February 1821) the audiences at the *Liebhaber-Vereine* concerts fell away. Mlle. Bonasegla had departed "and there was hardly a singer left except Joséphine". Things had been somewhat better in the *Emulation* concerts (25 Oct. 1820 - 2 April 1821) because Demoiselle

Bonnaud and Demoiselle Franville had been supported by several French and Italian *dilettanti*.

The AMZ of June 1821 reports that though the round of concerts had continued in 1821, these had not been reviewed because they had produced nothing new. On the vocal side, they had consisted of the usual, frequently heard arias, all sung by Mlle. Bonnaud. On 28 March 1821, for instance, she had given a concert in which she had performed the bravura scene from the age-old opera *Diana's Tree* (*Der Baum der Diana*), by Vincent Martin, and a *polonaise* by Maj. Braun. The critic credited Joséphine with an incredibly beautiful voice, but regretted that her artistry and technique (*Ausbildung*) were no better than they had been the year before.

What is described by the AMZ as the second *Dilettanten-Verein* gave twelve subscription concerts in the *Gasthof zum Geist* in Strasbourg between 28 October 1821 and 24 March 1822. These took place on Sundays, between 11 a.m. and 1 p.m. In an Extra-Concert on 5 December 1821, Joséphine sang two arias, by Mozart and Paër.

Mlle. Bonnaud herself gave a concert in the Strasbourg Theatre on 1 April 1822. This was a new theatre, built only the year before. She opened with the well-known duet from *Oedipe*, accompanied by Mezeria, a bass-singer from the French Opera. Joséphine's next offering was from Paër's *Sargino*, sung with the choir. The critic said that her pleasing voice had gained strength with the years, though not particularly in either technique or soul, and her pronunciation had remained careless. Later, she had sung really well in a duet from *Cenerentola*, with Pezzotti. Her finale was a cavatina from the *Barber*.

On Good Friday, 5 April, the cantor in the new Church had given a performance of Haydn's *Creation* in which Joséphine gave a good account of herself in the parts of both Gabriel and Eve. A political refugee from Italy, named as Madame Germany, gave some concerts in Strasbourg in mid-1822 at which Joséphine also sang. Though Joséphine had been applauded for an aria, with chorus, from *Tancredi*, there had been some uncertainty about whether she had been singing in Italian or in a German translation.

By 1822, Mlle. Bonnaud had become the leading soprano in amateur circles in Strasbourg, but the time had come for her to move to higher things, as Mlle. de Méric (or Demeric).

Joséphine's operatic début in Paris

Portrait of Joséphine de Méric by Wachsmut.

(By courtesy of the Bibliothèque Nationale, Paris, the Harvard Theatre Collection and the Civica Raccolta delle Stampe. A. Bertarelli, Castello Sfonzesco, Milan.)

IT was in November 1822 that Joséphine left Strasbourg for Paris, to embark on her operatic career. Both she and her father had shown some reluctance at first about her taking up singing as a profession. According to the letter which Joseph wrote to the Director of the *Académie Royale de Musique* on 22 October, she had set her face against doing so. If she had been willing to go on the stage in Strasbourg, he claimed, she could have been earning 10,000 francs a year ever since 1818, but she had refused to break her vow. However, these maidenly hesitations were overcome by the persuasiveness of the Baroness de Pamphile and of the talent scouts employed by the *Académie Royale de Musique*: Lieutenant-Colonel Braun and Monsieur Graziani.

The Baroness gave proof of her interest in Joséphine by herself going ahead to Paris early in November 1822 to make representations in person in Joséphine's favour. It was agreed that once a contract had been concluded, Joséphine would follow, accompanied by Mr. Graziani. Things moved quickly and on 10 November the *Engagement* was signed between the Director of the *Académie*, on the one hand, and Jacques [sic] Bonnaud de Méric and Joséphine Bonnaud de Méric on the other. The *Académie*, it should be noted, was in charge, administratively, of the Italian Opera in Paris.

Playbill announcing forthcoming début of Joséphine in Tancredi. Théâtre Royal Italien – Medea In Corinto.

(By courtesy of the Bibliothèque de l' Opéra, Paris)

THEATRE ROYAL ITALIEN
SALLE LOUVOIS.

Aujourd'hui jeudi 20 février 1823,

MEDEA IN CORINTO

(*MEDÉE A CORINTHE*),

Opéra seria en deux actes, musique de M. Mayer.

Acteurs : M rs Garcia, Bordogni, Levasseur, Deville ; M mes Pasta, Naldi, Rossi.

Les bureaux seront ouverts à 7 heures. -- *On commencera à 8 heures précises.*

Mardi 25, M lle DEMERI, débutera par le rôle d'*Amenaïde*, dans l'Opéra de Tancredi.

S'adresser, pour la location des Loges, au bureau de location de l'Académie Royale de Musique, rue Grange-Batelière, Hôtel-Choiseul.

C. BALLARD, Imprimeur du Roi, rue J.-J. Rousseau n. 8.

The contract was to run originally for one year from 1 December 1822 to the same date in 1823, but to be renewable for a second year at the discretion of the Administration of the *Opéra*. Joséphine undertook, in the standard form, to play, sing and recite in serious, semi-serious and comic (*buffa*) opera as *seconda donna, tenue à suppléer les premières.* Joseph had succeeded in insisting that his daughter should be paid 7,000 francs in the first year and 10,000 francs if the contract was extended for a second year. These can be regarded as terms favourable to Joséphine, as a *débutante*, and she probably had her father to thank for driving a fairly hard bargain. (In October 1823, Stendhal listed the annual salaries being paid to the singers at the *Théâtre Louvois*, where the 'Italians' were performing at the time, as follows: Mlle. Cinti received 15,000 francs and Mlle. Mori 10,000. Mlles. Rossi and Goria were paid only 5,000 and 4,000 respectively.)

On 10 November, when her father promptly returned the duplicate of the contract, he promised that Joséphine would arrive in Paris within a fortnight, accompanied by her mother. He wrote, he said, as one father to another, stressing his grief at being separated from the object of his most tender affections and imploring the Director to give his daughter his benevolent protection in the career on which she was embarking.

At the same time he gave a description of Joséphine which suggests that she had a good and fashionable figure and was a young lady of spirit. Though svelte, he said, she had a robust temperament, never suffered from *indisposition de boudoir* and loved her work. Her character had always won general esteem and he had every hope that it would be her ambition to deserve that of the Director. Certainly, Joséphine must have needed some spirit to decide to become a professional and to do so in the city which, with some justice, regarded itself as the capital of the operatic world.

In Paris, it seems, Joséphine received some training from both Paër and Garcia. Ferdinando Paër (1771 - 1839) had been Napoleon's *maître de chapelle* and succeeded Spontini as Director of the *Théâtre Royal Italien* in 1812. Manuel Garcia I (1775 - 1832), described by Rosenthal as probably the greatest teacher of singing of his day, had taught his own children, Maria (Malibran), Pauline (Viardot) and Manuel II. His pupils had also included Henriette Méric-Lalande, Nourrit and Géraldy. The *Administration* told Garcia on 26 November 1822 that permission had been granted for Mlle. De Meric to sing at his concert on the following day, and this may well have been Joséphine's first public appearance in Paris. Having been sponsored by no less a dignitary than Lauriston, *Ministre de la Maison du Roi*, Joséphine was on the books of the *Conservatoire* from 1 December 1823 to 1 October 1824. She received instruction in singing, Italian singing, lyric declamation and acting. Her teachers were Blangini, Bordogni, Plantard, Baptiste, Deshayes, St. Aubin and Ponchard. No record has been traced of any reports on her performance at the *Conservatoire* and she does not appear to have taken any of the examinations. She was an *élève externe*, i.e. not living in the *pensionnat*.

THÉATRE ROYAL ITALIEN
SALLE LOUVOIS.

Aujourd'hui mardi 25 février 1823,

Pour le début de Mlle DEMERI.

TANCREDI

(*TANCRÈDE*)

Opéra seria en deux actes, musique de M. *Rossini*.

Acteurs : Mrs Bordogni, Profeti, Deville ; Mmes Pasta, Demeri, Rossi,

Les bureaux seront ouverts à 7 heures.--On commencera à 8 heures précises.

S'adresser, pour la location des Loges, au bureau de location de l'Académie Royale de Musique, rue Grange-Batelière, Hôtel Choiseuil.

C. BALLARD, Imprimeur du Roi, rue J.-J. Rousseau n. 8.

Playbill announcing Joséphine's début in Paris. Théâtre Royal Italien – Tancredi.
(By courtesy of the Bibliothèque de l' Opéra, Paris.)

The promotion of their Mlle. Bonnaud to the opera stage in Paris naturally caused some excitement in Strasbourg. The *Journal des Dames et des Modes* of 16 January 1823 devoted a long paragraph to the subject:

> The *dilettanti* in Paris can talk of nothing but the discovery in Strasbourg of a young person called Mlle. B**, 18 years old [sic], who has a magnificent voice. Mlle B** has just been taken to Paris. Music-lovers who have heard her, say that her voice easily spans three octaves and that she can pass perfectly accurately, without transition, from the lowest note to the highest. The volume of Mlle. B**'s voice is such that she could be brilliantly successful even in the great Opera House, but we are assured that the new *virtuosa* will be making her *début* at the *Théâtre Italien*. According to the *dilettanti*, M. Paër will be directing the interesting singer of whom we

speak. He requires six months to make her worthy of an extremely critical public, a public which will take long to forget having heard Mme. Fodor. (Music-lovers in Strasbourg will immediately recognise that the reference is to Mlle. Bonnaud, whose charming talent and rapid progress have been a source of admiration and delight for us ever since her *début*).

Joséphine's *début* on the operatic stage took place at the *Théâtre Italien (Salle Louvois)* on 25 February 1823 as Aménaïde in Rossini's *Tancredi*. This was one of the most celebrated operas in the early nineteenth century, the hero's love-song *Di tanti palpiti* becoming a hit throughout Europe. The opera also contains a beautiful *andante* duet between Tancredi and Aménaïde in which, says Francis Toye, there is a feeling of tenderness exceptional in Rossini's music.

Joséphine clearly took Paris by surprise. There seems to have been no comment in advance of her arrival. She was just catapulted overnight from the provincial obscurity of concerts in Strasbourg to a spotlight on the operatic stage in the capital.

In the *Journal des Débats* of 5 March, the critic, the idiosyncratic Castil-Blaze, greeted the *débutante* in laudatory terms. As Aménaïde, he wrote, she had shown that she possessed, as a singer, qualities which were both rare and precious. Her voice was full, true and sonorous and encompassed two and a half octaves. In the performance of the graceful and sustained passages in *Tancredi*, she had displayed a fine musical sense. She was indeed a young lady who showed the greatest promise; and it must be a comfort to the *dilettanti* that her musical education was to be completed by the illustrious Paër, the *maestro* who had trained so many *cantatrices* who were the pride of both Italy and France.

So Joséphine received high praise when she made her *début*.

However, even thus early, there were signs that all would not be well in her relations with the *Académie Royale de Musique*. On 14 March, in the *Chronique Musicale* of the *Journal des Débats*, the critic, says that in making her début at the Louvois, Mlle. Demeri [sic] had chosen the one theatre in the world which could not encourage her talent or display her skills in the most favourable light. There, opera was being given second place to ballet. Many of the singers could sing extremely well, but they were denied the opportunities they deserved: the authorities insisted on repetitions of outdated 'gothic' music and, worse still, persisted with a system of vocal training which ruined both voice and talent and was even a danger to health. Finally, the singers were so miserably paid that those who ought to have become the glory and ornament of Paris were driven to seek fame abroad.

Critics such as 'XXX', while they inveighed against that respect for old music which resulted in the revival of outdated operas and demanded that modern French composers should be given the chance to show their mettle, nevertheless looked back with nostalgia to the 'sublime compositions of Gluck' and deplored the errors of the 'imprudent innovators' and 'ardent followers of Rossini' who set so much store by 'brilliant flourishes written for agile voices'.

Luigi Cherubini (1760-1842), after 'reforming his style from Italian traditions to those of Gluck' (Rosenthal) had achieved his great success in Paris with *Lodoïska* (1791) and (*Médeé*) (1797). In the view of 'XXX', it was in operas like those, as performed in the great days of the *Feydeau*, that Joséphine would shine. 'Her powerful, pleasing, sonorous, tender and majestic voice would re-create for us, to perfection, the curses of Medea, the lamentations of Calypso, the delightful airs of Ina and Lodoïska'. Alas, Mlle. Demeri was only being asked to sing parts in works where her most unusual talents would have no scope at all. She was being obliged to produce rapid runs to which her voice did not lend itself. Certainly, with a voice as beautiful as hers, she ought to be successful anywhere: but it was to be feared that in Paris the *dilettanti* would soon insist on having their *roulades* and would not be satisfied with that 'simple transformation of the scale into a perfect broken chord'.

Joséphine also had the misfortune to make her *début* at a time when the Italian Opera in Paris was itself in a crisis. After several years of prosperity it was threatened with mortal stagnation. Mlles. Naldi and Cinti were in poor health, so that almost the whole burden of the repertory fell on Mme. Pasta; but she could not be expected to play three times a week parts as tiring as Romeo, Tancred and Medea. So, it was asked, why not bring forward 'two young persons who had presented themselves'? Perhaps Mlle. Mori and Mlle. de Méric were the singers the critic had in mind.

The *Journal de Paris* (17 March) noted that Joséphine had made a successful *début* at the *Théâtre Italien* and that it was being said that she was to sing at the Paris *Opéra* itself. The critic hoped that she would face this test: the moment was propitious. Joséphine's voice had the range which an auditorium as large as the *Opéra* demanded. Since Mme. Branchu had retired, there could be no better chance to put on *Armide* (a five-act opera by Gluck), a revival which the lovers of opera were waiting for with impatience. This came to nothing, but in Holy Week Joséphine did take part in one of the Sacred Concerts which the *Académie Royale de Musique* gave in the *Salle de l'Opéra*. She found herself then in company with the leading male singers of the day: Zuchelli, Levasseur and Adolphe Nourrit. These concerts attracted a crowded and fashionable audience each night and their applause was 'the best testimony of the good taste of the selections and the excellence of the performers' (*Galignani's Messenger*).

The main work performed at the first concert on 24 March was Beethoven's oratorio *Christus am Ölberg* (Christ on the Mount of Olives) (1803). In the *Journal des Débats*, 'XXX' repeated that Mlle. Demeri had a magnificent voice, which was invaluable in the ensembles, but admitted that her inexperience and uneasiness detracted from her appeal in the solo parts. There was such magic, though, in the voice that she was entitled to risk all, as had been demonstrated in her singing of both *La Tromba* and the *Regina*.

The *Journal de Paris* commented on similar lines. Mlle. Démeri, who had made her *début, avec éclat*, at the *Théâtre Italien*, had sung the air *La Tromba* which Pucitta had composed for Catalani. She was a young lady who deserved to be watched. However, although her sonorous voice, effortlessly spanning two octaves and a half, easily filled the whole Opera House, she had not yet mastered the art of breath control. Fortunately, the tuition which she was receiving from an able master would enable her to make worthy use of the gifts which Nature had conferred on her. The critic considered that with her talents she should be destined to sing at the Opera and he commended this suggestion to the *Administration*.

The succeeding concert served to confirm the *Journal de Paris* critic in his opinions about Joséphine. The more one heard her, the more one recognised that her rightful place was at the *Opéra*. If her voice was somewhat lacking in lightness, 'a quality so precious at the Italian theatre', this mattered less on the premier lyric stage 'because our [French] declamation has more of prosody than the Italian'. The critic noted that it was Paër who was advising Joséphine. The concert had been well attended and even the most exigent connoisseurs had been liberal with applause.

In April, when *Tancredi* was performed again by the *Italiens* at the *Salle Louvois*, the part of Amenaïde was taken by Mlle. Naldi, presumably because she had sufficiently recovered her health. However, she gave only partial satisfaction, her *No, che il morir* having been received in expressive silence. (Later in the year, when *Tancredi* was revived, Joséphine was back and 'the duo in the second act between Mme. Pasta and Mlle. Demeri was uncommonly fine' according to *Galignani's Messenger*).

At the end of April, Joséphine had appeared as the Countess in the *Nozze di Figaro*. In the words of the *Messenger*, Mlle. Demeri's voice was powerful but lacked sweetness. Nevertheless, her *Dove sono* had delighted the critic, who hoped that after a few more performances she would be more at ease on the stage.

On 19 June, a revival of Cimarosa's comic opera *Il Matrimonio Segreto* met with its usual triumphant success. Based on *The Clandestine Marriage* by Colman and Garrick, this most popular of Cimarosa's works had so entranced the Emperor Leopold II when it was produced in Vienna in 1792 that he caused supper to be served to the whole cast before commanding a repeat of the whole performance.

The French critic 'XXX' had praised this opera as Cimarosa's *chef-d'oeuvre* and consequently that of the whole Italian School. Its first appearance in Paris had been in 1800, and a French version had been produced in Nîmes in 1817, but then it had been neglected for some years in favour of operas by Mozart and Rossini.

The 1823 revival at the *Louvois* was described by 'XXX' as being as brilliant as its Paris precursor of 1800. The theatre had been packed and the audience was as enthusiastic as if they had been offered something entirely new. The great rôle of the wealthy citizen Geronimo, in which Luigi Lablache became so famous, was taken by Barilli and that of his love-lorn daughter Carolina by Joséphine. In two respects, we are told, this part suited Mlle. Demeri particularly well: it was written simply and at a high pitch. The young singer had thoroughly deserved her applause. She had sung in the trio 'with much intelligence', happily supported by Mlle. Cinti and Mlle. Mori.

The critic in the *Journal de Paris* was such an enthusiast for Cimarosa that he thought Cimarosa's marble bust ought on no account to be replaced on its pedestal by the plaster bust of a Rossini. He had enjoyed Joséphine's rendering of the part of Carolina and it had indeed pleased even those whose memories went back to earlier first-rank performers of the part in Paris such as Mainvielle-Fodor. Joséphine had made palpable progress and all honour was due to Paër. *Galignani's Messenger* agreed that Mlle. Demeri was very much improved. She was far more at her ease and had sung uncommonly well. *Le Corsaire* noted that she was pretty, was the right age for Carolina and had electrified the audience with her voice.

In August, a benefit performance of *Il Matrimonio* was given for Joséphine and it is pleasant to speculate that this may well have been attended by the benefactors who had smoothed her path from Strasbourg to Paris. It had been announced on 31 July that Lieutenant-General Pamphile de Lacroix, having relinquished command of the 5th Division of the 2nd Corps of the Army of the Pyrenees, had that day arrived in Paris.

Il Matrimonio Segreto remained in the repertory until November 1824. Meanwhile, Joséphine's acting had not improved as much as had been expected of a pupil of Paër. In July, *Le Corsaire* had felt constrained to modify its earlier judgment that Cimarosa's beautiful work had never been better performed, that the three feminine rôles could not be entrusted to three prettier actresses or to three more skilful singers. Sadly, Mlle. Demeri had been acting less well as one performance followed another. Lapses of memory could be excused when they were caused by a silence from the orchestra, but Joséphine had not managed to recover herself. Her voice, normally so resonant and ringing, had seemed to fall flat. She had even been out of tune with Bordogni in the duet which, with Mme. Mainvielle, had never failed in its effect. Unfortunately, too, all the actors except Barilli and Pellegrini had burlesqued the dénouement of the opera, which should have been full of pathos. When Joséphine was on her knees before her father, she had been overcome by a fit of uncontrollable laughter which might have swept through the audience if Bordogni had not managed to bite his lips. The paper warned Mlle. Demeri not to presume too much on the indulgence of the public.

LE CORSAIRE,

JOURNAL DES SPECTACLES, DE LA LITTÉRATURE, DES ARTS, DES MŒURS ET DES MODES.

Aimez qu'on vous conseille et non pas qu'on vous loue.

(N° 65.)   SAMEDI 13 SEPTEMBRE 1823.   (Iere Année.)

THÉATRE FRANÇAIS.

CORIOLAN,

Tragédie en 5 actes, de Laharpe.

Coriolan	MM. Camille.
Volumnius	Saint-Aulaire.
Tullus	Dumilâtre.
Aufide	Lecomte.
Procule	Lafitte.
Véturie	Mmes Paradol
Flavie	Menjaud.

LES FOLIES AMOUREUSES,

Comédie en 3 actes et en vers de Regnard.

Albert	MM. Guiaud.
Eraste	Lecomte
Crispin	Lemelle.
Agathe	Mmes Brocard.
Lisette	Lebrun.

OPÉRA-COMIQUE.

LE SOLITAIRE,

Opéra-comique en 3 actes de M. Planard, musique de M. Caraffa.

Le Solitaire	MM. Huet.
Palzo	Henri.
Charles	Féréol.
Alberti	Darancourt.
Premier Soldat	Louvet.
Deuxième Soldat.	Belnie.
Un Paysan	Grangé.
Elodie	Mmes Rigaud.
Marie	Pradher.
Marceline	Paul.

JEAN DE PARIS.

Opéra-comique en 2 actes, de M. de Saint-Just, musique de M. Boïeldieu.

Jean de Paris	MM. Ponchard.
Le grand Sénéchal	D'Arboville.
Pedrigo	Desessarts.
Un Valet	Grangé.
La Princesse de Na-	

THÉATRE ROYAL ITALIEN.

LE NOZZE DI FIGARO,

(Le Mariage de Figaro.)

Opéra-buffa en 4 actes, de Mozart.

Il conte Almaviva	MM. Levasseur.
Figaro	Pellegrini.
Bartolo	Profeti.
D. Bazilio	Lodovici
D. Curzio	
Antonio	Auletta.
La Contessa	Mmes Demeri.
Susanna	Cinti.
Cherubini	Buffardin.
Marcellina	Goria.
Barbarina	Blangy.

SECOND THÉATRE FRANÇAIS.

THÉATRE DU VAUDEVILLE.

Un Dîner à Pantin. — MM. Armand, Guillemin, Victor, Justin. Mmes Minette Bras, Huby.

La Chasse au Renard, vaud. en un acte. MM. Hypolite, Isambert, Cossard. — Mmes Pauline-Geoffroy, Jenny Colon.

La Belle au Bois Dormant. — MM. Joly, Isambert, Guillemin, Justin, Platel, le petit Victor. — Mmes Pauline-Geoffroy, Clara, Dussert, Joséphine.

GYMNASE DRAMATIQUE.

L'Intérieur d'un Bureau.

La Maîtresse au Logis. — MM. Dormeuil, Gontier, Alexis. — Mmes Théodore, Dormeuil

Les Grisettes, tableau-vaudec. MM. Dormeuil, Victor, Numa. — Mmes Grévedon, Dormeuil, Dejazet, Adeline, Théodore, Lili.

l'Apothéose de Polichinelle. MM Dormeuil, Bernard-Léon, Gabriel, Armand, Numa, Breton, Georges. Mmes Dejazet, Rosalie, Lili-Bourgoin.

THÉATRE DES VARIÉTÉS.

Angéline.

Le Précepteur. — MM. Bosquier, Lepeintre Vernet, Tousez. — Mmes Pauline, Jenny-

Les Cuisinières. — MM. Brunet, Odry. Mmes Vautrin, Gontier, Flore, Aldegonde, Chalbos, Maria, Sophie.

THÉATRE DE LA GAITÉ.

Le Contrebandier. — Spectacle Gratis.

AMBIGU COMIQUE.

La première représentation de

Renard et Corbeau. — MM. Paul, Melcourt, Dubourjal, Derouvère. — Mme Palmyre, Constance. — *L'Auberge.* — *La Lettre Anonyme.*

THÉATRE DE LA PORTE St-MARTIN.

Les Sergens. — *Le Cuisinier.* — *Werther*

THÉATRE DE M. COMTE,

Physicien du Roi, passage des Panoramas.

Les Petits Maraudeurs. — *Mistenflûte.* — *Le Solitaire.* — *La Petite Valérie.*

THÉATRE D'ÉLÈVES (barr Rochechouard.)

Honorine. — *Valérie.* — *Encore une Folie.*

THÉATRE MONT-PARNASSE.

Au bénéfice de Mlle Phédora.

La Rosière de Verneuil. — *Le Petit Dragon.* — *Blaise et Babet.*

JARDIN MARBEUF.

Demain deuxième grande fête extraordinaire, course à pied, lutte, concert, illumination, etc. On trouve des billets de souscription chez les concierges des Mairies, dans les principaux cafés et rue de Rivoli, n. 50.

DIORAMA,

Boul St.-Martin, derrière le Château d'eau Tous les jours, depuis 10 heures du matin jusqu'à 5 du soir. — Prix de place : Intérieur de la cathédrale de Chartres. Vue du port de Brest. — Prix de place : balcon, 3 fr., Amphithéâtre, 2 fr. 40 c.

SALON D'EXPOSITION.

A page from the newspaper Le Corsaire announcing Joséphine's rôle in Le Nozze di Figaro. *(13 Sept. 1823)*

Suddenly, however, on 21 August, *Le Corsaire* was again in raptures about Joséphine's Carolina. 'Electrified by double and triple salvos of applause, she had succeeded in equalling Mme. Mainvielle and, sometimes, in surpassing her.' The public were exhorted to besiege the doors of the *Italiens* as they would for Pasta (who incidentally had measles at the time). If anyone found it hard to believe that there had been such a transformation in Joséphine, let him remember that such things can indeed happen and that Racine wrote *Andromaque* after *Alexandre le Grand*.

At the end of July, Joséphine was singing in the *Nozze di Figaro* with Cinti, Buffardin and Levasseur. Mlle. Bigottini was the Susanna. *Le Corsaire* wrote most scathingly about this revival. On the first night the house had been well filled. Then the audience progressively fell off. The critic laid much of the blame for this on Mlle. Demeri. She had failed to fulfil the early hopes and it was almost impossible to understand why, with such a fine though still unpolished voice, she had not profited from her lessons from an artist capable of turning her talents to advantage without impairing their richness. The critic had left after the first two acts, from sheer boredom.

Then on 25 September 1823, confounding all the wiseacres, the Italian Opera gave what proved to be a sell-out performance of *Don Giovanni*. Joséphine appeared for the first time in the great rôle of Donna Anna. The 'rare beauty of her voice' won her many rounds of applause. This was an occasion when she sang with her *maestro* Manuel Garcia I (as the Don). He, it was said, had recovered all his powers and had never sung or acted better. The unfortunate Mlle. Mori, as Donna Elvira, had fully satisfied the connoisseurs, but the public had perversely denied to her the *bravos* which they offered to Mlle. Demeri.

Galignani's Messenger, stressing that Donna Anna was a most difficult character, commended Mlle. Demeri for singing the part uncommonly well. ('Uncommonly' was one of this journal's favourite words.) Garcia 'had done all that was necessary', but was not in appearance or manner what the critic considered the famous libertine should be. Garcia was too boisterous and lacked the gentlemanly ease which the character required (the writer, one assumes, was English). As for Mlle. Mori, although she had not given the audience satisfaction at first, she had been frequently applauded later on. Mlle. Cinti, as Zerlina, had been pleasing. Joséphine had had to be ready to be either Donna Anna or Zerlina, the choice lying with Cinti. Graziani had been all life and spirit as Mazetto, 'only a little too boisterous'.

Don Giovanni was given again in December, demonstrating that though the *dilettanti* might have a passion for Rossini, they could also adore Mozart. 'XXX' stated simply that the rôle of Donna Anna was one which particularly suited 'the beautiful voice of Mlle. Demeri'. The *Journal de Paris* agreed. Donna Anna gave Joséphine the scope to display her voice in all its brilliance. All she needed was a more assured, classical method of singing.

The crisis at the *Opéra Italien*, however, had deepened. Garcia was leaving and it was too much to hope that Madame Pasta alone could hold the loyalty of the public. Furthermore, the *Théâtre Louvois* suffered from not having its own independent administration. It was not likely to be able to survive if it remained under the control of the *Académie Royale*, especially if this led to rivalries and dissension 'as had happened several times before'. Already on 13 September, *Le Corsaire* was forecasting that the *Opéra Italien* was threatened with losing Mlle. Demeri. Her modest salary was leading her to listen to proposals from several foreign houses.

Théâtre Royal Italien. Grand Concert - Vocal et Instrumental. Joséphine sings as Aménaïde in Tancredi.

(By courtesy of the Bibliothèque de l' Opéra, Paris.)

THÉÂTRE ROYAL ITALIEN.

SALLE LOUVOIS.

Le Dimanche 25 Janvier 1824,

GRAND CONCERT

VOCAL ET INSTRUMENTAL,

DONNÉ PAR M. LAFONT,

Premier Violon de la Chambre du Roi et Premier Violon accompagnateur de S. A. R. Madame la Duchesse de Berry.

PROGRAMME.

PREMIÈRE PARTIE.

Symphonie d'HAYDN.

Duo chanté par M. PELLEGRINI et Mlle CINTI.

Concerto de Violon, composé et exécuté par M. LAFONT.

DEUXIÈME PARTIE.

Grande Marche militaire variée pour deux Pianos, avec accompagnement d'Orchestre, composée par J. P. PIXIS, exécuté par lui et M. HERTE aîné
Cavatine de Rossini, chantée par Mlle CINTI.
Nouvelle Fantaisie et Variations sur des Motifs des Opéras de Rossini, Otello , La Cenerentola , etc., composées et exécutées par M. LAFONT.
Le Solo de Harpe sera exécuté par M. LABARRE.

Le Concert sera suivi du premier acte de TANCREDI, Opéra séria de Rossini :

Argirio-Bordogni, *Ocbassano*-Levasseur, *Ruggero*-Deville, *Tancredi*-Pasta, *Aménaïde*-Demeri, *Isaura*-Rossi.

PRIX DES PLACES : Premières loges , Secondes en face et Balcon des Premières. 10 francs ; Secondes et Rez-de-chaussée , 8 fr., Stalles 12 fr., Orchestre, Première Galerie et Balcon des Secondes, 7 fr. 50 c., Troisièmes Loges, Deuxième Galerie et Balcon des Trois 6 fr., Parterre et Troisième Galerie, 5 fr. 60 c. Amphithéâtre des Troisièmes, 2 fr. *Les Bureaux s'ouvriront à sept heures — On commencera à huit heures.*

On trouvera des billets de toutes places au bureau de la location, rue Grange-Batelière, Hôtel-Choiseul, jusqu'à 4 heures, et chez M. Lafont, le jour du Concert,

C. BALLARD Imprimeur du Roi, rue J. J. Rousseau, n. 8.

In addition to appearing in opera, Joséphine duly took her part in concerts for charity, e.g. in an evening of music, drama and ballet at the *Second Théâtre Français* (the *Odéon*) on 21 December 1823 for the benefit of a most unfortunate lady, Mlle. Petit, who, in a robbery, had lost both her savings and 'the very instruments of her profession'. Her past and her future were in ruins. Pasta had put herself out to participate and took the title rôle in the first act of *Tancredi*. As was to be expected, her *Di tanti Palpiti* brought the house down, but the 'dazzling voice' of Mlle. Demeri also evoked several rounds of applause. This first act of *Tancredi*, with Pasta and Joséphine, was a feature, too, of a grand vocal and instrumental concert in the *salle* at the *Théâtre Italien* on Sunday 25 January 1824 given by the violinist Lafont.

In November 1823, Rossini and his wife arrived in Paris on their way to London and decided to stay for a few weeks. Some of the composer's admirers arranged a festive banquet in his honour, on 16 November, at the restaurant *Veau-qui-tette*. Rossini was placed at table between Pasta and the famous actress Mlle. Mars. Mlle. de Méric was present and was seated close to Rossini.

Rossini already had thoughts of settling in Paris, the city which regarded itself as the capital of the civilised world, and M. de Lauriston, Minister of the *Maison du Roi*, had made overtures to him. At the time, Rossini declined mainly, it seems, because he was unwilling to deprive Paër of any of his advantages as Director of the artists of the *Théâtre Italien*, on which his livelihood depended. Regrettably, Paër was to abuse this position to injure the reputation of Rossini and of his works. Paër was deeply jealous of Rossini as composer, singer and accompanist and he had the support of much of the musical establishment and the press in his campaign against the 'foreign fad' of *rossinisme*. Later, critics such as Castel-Blaze came to be influential supporters of Rossini, but at this date, the end of 1823, the ranks of the *Rossinistes* were still thin. Nonetheless they were full of enthusiasm, and the attendance at the banquet had shown that Rossini had made some very important converts: Lesueur, de Boieldieu, Hérold and Auber among them. Mlle de Méric had openly demonstrated her sympathy for Rossini.

Galignani's Messenger gave Rossini a particularly warm welcome to Paris:' . . . in consequence of the arrival of Rossini, three of his pieces were played successively: *Il Barbiere di Siviglia*, *La Gazza Ladra* and *Tancrède*, and in a manner that must have been pleasing to the composer, as well as to the public. We can only say that there seemed to be a sort of emulation in the orchestra and the singers, and we confess that we should not be sorry if Rossini made a long stay. We wish, however, to be properly understood, – we are far from having the smallest reproach to make against Mesdames Pasta, Demeri, Cinti and Rossi, and Messrs. Pellegrini, Zuchelli and Bordogni; we merely mean to convey that the idea of Rossini being present produced an effect on all.'

It seems to have been a recurring feature of Joséphine's career, especially in Paris, that she went up and down very sharply in the estimation of the critics.

At the beginning of November 1823, *Le Corsaire* was declaring that she had in no way fulfilled the expectations aroused by her *débuts*. It was only as Carolina that she had been a success and she must wish that the *Matrimonio Segreto* was repeated as often as *Don Giovanni*. Although even Mlle. Demeri's beautiful voice had not sufficed to bring out all the expression required by the arias of Donna Anna, the young singer now seemed imperturbable and had taken a brilliant revenge as Carolina. Even so, she had been somewhat distrait and had unpardonably omitted two sections of the great aria in the second act. She seemed unable to comprehend the pathos of the part: 'So much coldness makes one doubtful about the singer's sensibility; and without that prime quality there is no song'.

Be that as it may, when *Tancredi* was repeated on 15 November, the house was full and Mlle. Demeri, wonderfully inspired, sang as she had never sung before, equalling Pasta in the delicious duet in the second act (*Le Corsaire*).

On 18 December a performance of Paër's *Agnese* was apparently given for the benefit of Mlle. Bigottini. On this one occasion, according to *Le Corsaire*, Joséphine had consented to take the minor part of Vespina.

As *Galignani's Messenger* put it, it was a good omen that the theatre had begun 1824 with Mozart's charming opera *Le Nozze di Figaro*. Levasseur had re-appeared as Almaviva after a long absence due to illness. His voice was unimpaired, though in acting he had suggested a gloomy chief of the Middle Ages rather than a civilised and voluptuous nobleman of modern times. Pellegrini, as Figaro, was excellent as always, though a little lacking in his usual vivacious bustle and comic verve. Mademoiselle Demeri, as the Countess, had been in good voice, but had committed musical sacrilege by adding ornamentation to Mozart's airs. *Le Corsaire* was more worried by Joséphine's acting. She had seemed so oblivious to what was going on around her between Susanna and Figaro that her performance lost all *vraisemblance*. Mlle. Cinti had played the part of Susanna with her usual piquant malice.

In *Don Giovanni*, which followed, Garcia had been successfully succeeded by Zuchelli, who received well-deserved praise for singing *Finch' han dal vino* and *Là ci darem la mano* in B flat, as written by Mozart, and not in C as Garcia had sung them. Joséphine had again played Donna Anna.

Now, the critic in the *Journal de Paris* felt it his duty to give her some stern advice. Nature had endowed her with wonderful resources, but she seemed bent on spoiling them. At one moment she would give her voice all the brilliance and range of which it was capable. Then, with no transition and quite unnecessarily, she would let it fade away and become inaudible. No singing master in Paris could be so stupid as to have advised her to behave in such a way. If she continued to neglect her talent, she would soon lose the favour she had won at her *début*. Once the public became convinced that she was not going to fulfil the hopes which she had raised, she would be shipped back to the provinces and perhaps never be recalled. The critic trusted that Mlle. Demeri would not make such a dire prediction come true.

Galignani's Messenger, influenced perhaps by the French critics, wrote in much the same vein. 'When writing of Mademoiselle Demeri, it is necessary to use both the white and black pencil, for this lady, for whom nature has done so much, seems determined to do little for herself. At times, she evinces capabilities of voice of the first description, and in the next moment appears removed to an interminable distance from good singing. If this eternal floating between extremes were to continue, a singer of unpretending but equable mediocrity would be preferable'. *Le Corsaire*, less indulgent, said that Joséphine was calmly destroying the reputation her *début* had won.

Happily, by the end of January, the critic at the *Journal* had been comforted by the assurance that Joséphine had decided 'to follow assiduously the advice of a master well known for the excellence of his methods'. She was to be congratulated on taking this brave resolution, but it was certainly high time.

The *reprise* of *Don Giovanni* had prompted 'XXX' in the *Journal des Débats* to warn that 'the decadence of the Louvois Theatre was bound very soon to lead to its demise'. There were simply not enough first-rank performers. The tenor who had taken Garcia's place had a good voice, but lacked the art to control it. Mlle. Mori, who had never claimed to be in the top class but who was valuable as *seconda donna*, had been dismissed. Zuchelli, as a bass, might have seemed more suited than Garcia to the rôle of Don Juan, but he lacked Garcia's verve and brio. The rôle of Donna Elvira had proved to be beyond the powers of Mlle. Amigo. There seemed to be a mania for engaging French *artistes* who all too often failed in their attempts to pronounce Italian properly and to sing the operas in the way they were sung in Rome or Venice.

As for Joséphine, she was undeniably out of place at the *Louvois*. Her voice was strong and sonorous. It had a wide compass, with a tone which was pleasing though lacking in agility. All she needed was more practice and study, to improve her voice control. If her talents could be allowed full scope, her deficiencies might pass unnoticed. Then, Mlle. Demeri might well take on the mantle of Branchu and become a major ornament of the *Académie de Musique*. However, she very rightly loathed the wretched style which was in vogue in Paris for the production of operas. The authorities seemed determined to persist with this style, the result being that 'our old opera will for ever be the laughing-stock of Europe'.

One has the strong impression that 'XXX' must have known Joséphine personally. No offers, he wrote, could lead her astray or make her change her attitude. Excellent musician that she was, she was determined 'to sing like an Italian or condemn herself to silence'. The *Administration* ought to have advised her to cross the Alps, where she would discover that there were fine theatres in Turin and Milan ready to welcome anyone who had the ability to do justice to such arias as *Il mio tesoro* and *Quest'alme reggere non sà*.

In fact, *Le Corsaire* had already announced on 9 February that Mlle. Demeri would shortly be leaving for Milan. At *La Scala*, would she find better judges than those at the *Louvois*? Would she find there a better mentor than Bordogni? Was it not rather to be feared that she would return from Italy with various bad habits – namely those which were so easily contracted on a stage where acting was of so little account? Mlle. Demeri certainly possessed an admirable voice and *Le Corsaire* had only criticised its waywardness. The paper had impressed on her that she should take a master and practise hard. Well, she had followed the advice; a master had been found and she was hard at work. This, alas, had to be just the moment when she decided to leave Paris. When she had gone, the rôles of the three ladies in the *Matrimonio Segreto* would be filled by Mlles. Goria, Amigo and Buffardin. That would be the time when people would recall the days when this great masterpiece had been entrusted to Mlles. Cinti, Demeri and Mori. What had come over the Administration of the *Opéra*?

The musical dispute in Paris was described in the *Harmonicon* in March 1824 as an argument between the abettors of Mozart and Rossini. The professionals sided with Mozart. The *dilettanti*, *literati* and editors of journals were for Rossini. The latter party had an immense advantage because of the influence of the press.

In the early months of 1824 a Grand Concert was poorly attended despite the announcement that Pasta would be singing. The *Journal de Paris* complained that Joséphine had sung the great aria *Son regina, son guerriera* very feebly, lacking the charm which Catalani had lent to it. In the course of this aria, where the singer keeps repeating *Son regina* (I am Queen) a wit in the audience whispered: 'That is what we shall see, when you appear shortly at the *Opéra* as Antigone.' Then again, the appearance of Joséphine in the audience at a performance of *La Vestale* was regarded as strong evidence that she was preparing herself to take the part of Julia in that opera. She had been seen to follow all Julia's actions very closely.

However, it was not to be in Paris that Joséphine first appeared in *La Vestale*.

Sunday concerts were in vogue. In January, Joséphine had sung with Pasta in part of *Tancredi*. Then she joined Levasseur, Nourrit and M. and Mme. Dabadie at a concert given by a Monsieur Herz on Sunday 14 March 1824 in the salons of Monsieur Pape, at the *Cour des Fontaines*. In its review, the *Journal de Paris* gallantly admitted that Mlle. Deméri, 'to whom they had sometimes given stern advice - though solely in the interests of art,' had been loudly applauded for a great aria which she had sung most ably. According to the *Journal des Débats* (XXX), the Mozart aria sung by Joséphine had been superb; though the orchestra had not given the singer as much scope as she needed to produce the greatest effect. (The *Journal de Paris* remarked that there was a growing custom in Paris of giving subscription concerts in private houses, an idea imported from England).

Théâtre Royal Italien – Playbill for Don Giovanni in which Joséphine played Donna Anna.
(By courtesy of Bibliothèque de l' Opéra, Paris.)

THÉÂTRE ROYAL ITALIEN.
SALLE LOUVOIS.

Aujourd'hui Samedi 24 Avril 1824,

D. GIOVANNI,

(*D. JUAN*),

Opéra semi-séria en deux actes, musique de *Mozart.*

ACTEURS : Mrs Bordogni, Pellegrini, Zuchelli, Graziani, Profeti; Mmes Cinti, Demeri, Mori.

Les Bureaux s'ouvriront à 7 heures. —— On commencera à 8 heures précises.

S'adresser, pour la location des loges, au bureau de location de l'Académie Royale de Musique, rue Grange-Batelière, Hôtel-Choiseul

C. BALLARD, Imprimeur du Roi, rue J.-J. Rousseau, n. 8.

The performance of *Don Giovanni* on 24 April, caused the critic in *Galignani's Messenger* to hope that he would never again witness at the *Opera Buffa* such a sleep-producing scene. An evil spell seemed to have hung over the whole *dramatis personae*. Mlle. Demeri had never sung so badly. Mlle. Mori had been unwell and had begged for indulgence. Even Zuchelli, Pellegrini and Cinti had lacked their usual spirit and as for Bordogni, he was on most occasions a man of wood but seemed in this instance to be transformed by the general torpor into petrified wood.

A benefit concert at the *Salle Favart* (the *Opéra Comique*) at the end of May 1824 had not attracted a large audience owing, it was said, to the heat and the high prices. Joséphine had sung, with Levasseur, Mlle. Cinti and others to well-deserved acclaim.

Towards the end of September, at the *Louvois*, Joséphine was first heard in the part of Juliet. This was in Zingarelli's *Giulietta e Romeo*, opposite Pasta, who had returned from London to take the hero's part.

Stendhal, in his *Life of Rossini*, devotes a page to Joséphine's performance. He begins on a critical note, complaining that Mlle. Demeri had almost entirely spoilt the effect of her duet with Mme. Pasta by singing too much like a schoolgirl repeating her lesson. This had deprived the moments of passion of their tragic impact. However, 'this schoolgirl possesses a magnificent voice. What a pity that she cannot afford to go and spend two years at Naples'. He urged the French Government to make funds available for her to go to Italy 'on condition that she sing once a week at the *San Carlo* Theatre or at *La Scala* in Milan'.

Stendhal maintained that Joséphine's voice was so amazing (*étonnante*) and so beautiful that even if she did not sing any better than she had in Paris on 28 September, surely M. Féron, the impresario at *La Scala* (i.e., surely Joseph Glossop, widely known as the husband of Madame Féron), would offer her 10,000 francs a year to sing just one aria in each new opera. All the same, she would need the courage to practise her scales four hours a day and he feared that she was perhaps 'too pretty to condemn herself to such a painful apprenticeship. There was no other way, though, to become a Catalani and earn two millions'. Stendhal considered that in Zingarelli's opera Joséphine had sung better in her own aria than in her duet with Pasta. Much later he was to express the opinion that she was a true Wagnerian soprano born half a century too soon.

After the performance of *Roméo et Juliette* (as the opera was styled in French) on 9 October 1824, the critic 'M' on the *Journal de Paris* said that even the long-suffering public at the *Louvois* could not contain its boredom. This, of all operas, had been worn threadbare. For the past two years, there had been a constant round of just three operas: *Roméo*, *Tancredi* and *Otello*. The point had been reached when even the presence of Pasta attracted no more than eight spectators to the dress-circle.

THÉÂTRE ROYAL ITALIEN.

SALLE LOUVOIS.

Aujourd'hui Mardi 30 Novembre 1824,

ROMEO E GIULIETTA,

(*ROMÉO ET JULIETTE*),

Opéra-séria en 3 actes, musique de *Zingarelli*

ACTEURS : Messieurs Bordogni, Levasseur; Mmes Pasta, Demeri, Rossi.

Les Bureaux s'ouvriront à 7 heures. --- On commencera à 8 heures précises.

S'adresser pour la location des loges, au bureau de location de l'Académie Royale de Musique, rue Grange Batelière, Hôtel-Choiseul.

C. BALLARD, Imprimeur du Roi, rue J.-J. Rousseau, n. 8.

The critic 'XXX', writing in the *Journal des Débats* of 28 October, mentioned a report that the Louvois was threatened with losing some of its French *cantatrices*. Indeed it was not to be long before Stendhal's wish that Joséphine should go to Italy was fulfilled.

On 1 December 1824, the *Journal des Débats* reported as follows:

> 'Italy is taking Mlle. Demeri from us. This young singer has just ended her engagement at the *Louvois*. Let us hope that she will return, having profited from the examples and lessons which she will find in the classic land of song. Mlle. Demeri takes with her the regrets and the esteem of her fellow-artists. It is well known that she has always held out against the proposals which she has received from the *Académie Royale*. This persistent refusal is a tribute to her taste and it preserves for the art of music a voice which the howls of our antiquated practice of intoning would in short order have either degraded or destroyed' (. . . *que les hurlements de notre vieille psalmodie auroient dégradée ou détruite en peu de temps*).

Théâtre Royal Italien.
Playbill for Romeo e Giulietta *with Pasta as Romeo and Joséphine as Juliet. (November 1824).*
(By courtesy of Bibliothèque de l' Opéra, Paris.)

The Paris correspondent of the *Allgemeine Musikalische Zeitung*, writing in January 1825, attempts to analyse why Joséphine's early success in Paris was not sustained. The article is critical but also sympathetic. At first she had been a sensation. Making her *début* as Amenaïde in *Tancredi*, she had displayed a great range of voice covering two-and-a-half octaves, from A to a thrice-accented E. In a smaller auditorium she could even encompass three octaves, from G to a thrice-accented G. 'The timbre of her voice is so fresh and penetrating that even in ensembles such as the finale of *Tancredi* her softest notes can be clearly heard above the rest in the furthest recesses of the hall'. Unfortunately, though, her singing entirely lacked style (*Spiel*) and technique (*Gesangmethode*). The extraordinary applause which she had received at first must therefore be ascribed to her voice alone and, perhaps, to the coincidence that she had appeared at a moment when the theatre in Paris was so denuded of *prime donne* that the *Administration* had more than once been constrained to discontinue performances altogether. Such interruptions in their evening entertainment had incensed the *habitués* and so nothing could have been more welcome to them than this 'gigantic voice'. Mlle. de Méric had been applauded for her voice, applauded for staying with the theatre and applauded also to give her encouragement, in the hope that with time and good guidance style and technique would develop. So far, alas, they had not done so. Ultimately, even the most beautiful voice palls when it is not continually being infused anew with spirit (*Geist*) and feeling. Like everything else, one becomes inured to it. That is what had happened in this case. The applause had ceased and finally, as Joséphine's voice lost some of its range, there had begun to be some hissing when she struck a wrong note. True, towards the end of her time in Paris, - but only then - she had made a recovery and proved herself better than ever before. Yet that was just when Paris lost her.

The AMZ drew this conclusion:

> 'The rich tones of Mlle. Demeri's voice are not suited to Italianate variations and that is why she has given more pleasure in German pieces. We have heard her sing most beautifully in Beethoven's *Christus* and in Mozart's *Requiem*. Therefore, since she can also sing in German, she would certainly enjoy great success on the stage in Germany. Despite all that has been said above, her singing, even beside Pasta, has often made a deep impression - and that is no small achievement.'

The *Almanach Royal* lists Joséphine for one year only, 1824, describing her as *seconda prima donna*, supplementary to the *prime donne.* By November 1824 it was being reported that Mlle. Demeri's engagement at the *Théâtre Royal Italien* had not been renewed, but Joséphine was still listed as Donna Anna there as late as February 1825. *Le Corsaire* maintained that the great popularity which *Don Giovanni* and *Il Matrimonio Segreto* had been enjoying had been due entirely to Mlle. Demeri and Mlle Mori, both of whom were about to leave the *Louvois*. In the *Journal de Paris* it was suggested that the young lady endowed with the amazing voice would be leaving for one of the premier theatres in Venice. No record has been traced of her having gone to Venice at this date, but she certainly went to Milan.

However, Joséphine did not go directly from Paris to Italy. She returned for a spell to her native Strasbourg, where her father and mother were still living. While there, she appeared once again on the concert stage, the AMZ *Referent* in Strasbourg remarking that 'Dem. Bonnaud was known in Paris as Demeri'. From her experience at the *Théâtre des Italiens*, the AMZ wrote, her voice had gained in power, but not in purity, and she was unfortunately persisting in ornamenting simple folk-songs with unsuitable *coloratura*. Her most successful piece had been a scene from the *Barber* which was new to the Strasbourg audience because it had not been included in the French score prepared by Castil-Blaze.

In a concert for the poor on 7 April 1825, Joséphine had sung *Lasciar di Morte* by Generali and the famous cavatina from *Tancredi*, *Di tanti palpiti*. The *Referent* had recognised that in this she had been guided by the example of Pasta, with whom she had sung in Paris.

Had *La Scala* been the foreign Opera House which made her the most attractive offer? Certainly the offer from the *Scala* must have emanated from Joseph Glossop, who was the impresario in charge of the Royal Theatres in Milan from 1 August 1824 until the Spring Season of 1826. If Joséphine had not met Glossop anywhere before, she must have come into contact with him in Milan in 1825 at the latest.

Joseph Gapper Glossop was to play a central role in her life.

3 *Joseph Glossop*

LONDON 1793-1822

ACCORDING to family tradition, Joseph Gapper Glossop was brilliantly clever and attractive; but he was definitely regarded as a black sheep.

He came from a Derbyshire family which traced its ancestry back to a Richard de Glossoppe, recorded as having lived in the small town of Glossop in 1200.

Joseph's father, Francis Glossop (1743-1835) moved from Derbyshire to London and in due course became a wealthy merchant and property owner in Soho and a Justice of the Peace. He had a house in Old Compton Street. This is in the Parish of St. Ann's, Westminster, and it was at St. Ann's that on 21 September 1776 Francis married as his third wife Anne Gapper, from Henstridge in Somerset.

Joseph seems to have been the last of seven or eight children, most of whom were duly baptised at St. Ann's. Joseph himself was born on 27 January 1793 and baptised on 24 February.

His father seems to have destined him, like two of his brothers, for the Church. Joseph declined to take holy orders.

In 1817, he had set up in business as a wax-chandler or 'spermaceti refiner' as some of the Directories say, but he soon 'closed his accounts and embarked on theatrical speculations'. While his brother Francis carried on in the wax business, Joseph prevailed on his father to help him to build and run the Royal Coburg Theatre, the seed-bed for the future Old Vic. This theatre opened officially, with melodrama and ballet, on Whit Monday, 11 May 1819, 'under the immediate Patronage of His Royal Highness Prince Leopold of Saxe-Coburg', widower of the Prince Regent's unfortunate daughter, Princess Charlotte.

For a while, despite being on the unfashionable South Bank, the Royal Coburg flourished and continued to enjoy royal support, with visits by the Duke and Duchess of Kent, the parents of the future Queen Victoria, and, in 1821, by Queen Caroline. However, it soon found itself in trouble with the law and Glossop began what was to prove a lifetime of litigation. At this period, the so-called Patent

Theatres, Drury Lane and Covent Garden, had monopoly rights over classical plays. Glossop had offended them, Drury Lane in particular, in two respects. He had put on a version of *King Richard the Third* and he had taken the liberty of engaging the actor Junius Brutus Booth on whom the Patent Theatres had a lien. Glossop was duly convicted and fined £50. He appealed (June 1821) but lost. Nevertheless, when disputes with the Patent Theatres were finally abandoned, it was judged to have been 'a drawn battle in which the Coburg had the advantage'. Glossop's advantage, such as it was, will have been due, in part at least, to his having taken his stand as a champion of all the so-called minor theatres in London. The Patent Theatres had the letter of the law on their side, but Glossop had a case and he was showman enough to give it full publicity in long letters to the *Theatrical Inquisitor*.

He took the high moral ground. It was monstrous, he claimed, that the minor theatres should be prevented from giving the public good plays. 'It would be an outrage on the intellectual character of the nation, an injury to public order and christian morality were you [i.e. the Patent Theatres] to force us back to ribaldry, nonsense, scrolls [sic] and orchestral tinklings.' It was in the national interest that the common people should be entertained with plays which were 'honest recreations'. . . . . 'The public-house broils that nightly disturbed our streets, and the excessive indulgence in drinking, attended with such fatal results, are now nearly done away with owing to that amusement and improvement afforded by the Minor Theatres.' Finally, Glossop pointed out that Paris, with less than half the population of London, had four times as many theatres.

Meanwhile, away from the theatre, Glossop had obtained what was for him a prestigious appointment at Court. From March 1821, for about a year, he enjoyed the position of Clerk of the Cheque to the King's Band of Gentlemen Pensioners (known today as the Gentlemen at Arms). This was a post of considerable responsibility, involving the general organisation of the Gentlemen Pensioners and their duties. No record has been found to explain how Glossop secured this appointment. His financial embarrassments are sufficient to account for his losing it. He apparently then became 'a noted Queenite', i.e. a supporter of Queen Caroline against George IV. Later, in Italy, he was to make much of having been attached to the Court of the King of England.

By the end of 1822 Joseph Glossop could no longer face his creditors. When he appeared eleven years later before the Bankruptcy Court, it was recorded that his accounts 'were of a very peculiar character'. The Commissioner then observed that Glossop had become embarrassed to a large amount [in 1822], had absconded from his creditors and gone abroad, where he again engaged in theatrical speculations. On 6 November 1822 an application had been made for a warrant to take up Glossop for forgery and Glossop had left for the Continent shortly afterwards. (In fact, after 1822, he disappears from the Directories in London).

However, before Glossop is pursued on his Continental escapades, it is important to go back to 1812, to the first of his matrimonial alliances.

It is on record that on 13 October 1812, at the Church of St. Mary-le-Bone, Middlesex, Joseph Glossop of St. Ann, Westminster, bachelor, married Elizabeth Feron, spinster.

The marriage was by licence (London Marriage Licence of 9 October 1812). In the sworn statement, each party was declared to be 'aged twenty-one and upwards'. However, since Joseph was born in January 1793, he was not yet twenty in October 1812.

As an acknowledged minor, he would have been obliged to produce evidence of his father's consent. The conclusion is that Joseph was lying about his age and that he feared that parental approval would not be forthcoming. It was natural enough that the marriage should be in the parish where the bride had been residing, rather than in the Glossop parish of St. Ann's, but it is significant that neither of the two witnesses came from the Glossop family. These were Amelia and C. Cobham, Cobham being a violinist to whom Elizabeth Féron was an articled pupil. It was unlikely that Francis Glossop would have wished a son of his to marry a mere singer and it seems fair to regard this marriage by licence as at least partially clandestine. To have a marriage by licence was fashionable at the time, but the avoidance of banns could also be the aim.

Both as the wife of Glossop and by virtue of her own operatic career, Elizabeth Féron has a part to play in this story. The date of her birth has yet to be established. *Wemyss' Chronology of the American Stage, from 1752 to 1852* states that 'Madame Fearon (Mrs. Glossop), surnamed the English Catalani, [was] born in London, 1793'. If this is true, she would not have been of full age at the date of her marriage to Glossop. Joseph Ireland gives 1797 as the birth date, agreeing that she was born in London. Féron's death certificate (May 1853) gives her age then as 55, which would support a birth date in 1797/8. It looks very much as though Elizabeth may have been only fifteen or sixteen when she married.

According to her grandson A. W. A'Beckett, she was the daughter of Comte de Féron, a French *émigré* from the Revolution whose father had been guillotined in Paris. This Count 'had entered the British Army as a surgeon, knowing something of medicine. He was in the 13th Light Dragoons, [but] changed his regiment so as never to fight his countrymen on the Calais side of the English Channel. His daughter, who subsequently became Mrs. Joseph Glossop, had a most lovely voice, and was a born musician.' She certainly became a singer of international repute.

The Army Lists state that a veterinary surgeon, John Feron, was with the 13th Regiment of Light Dragoons from October 1799 (the date from which his rank was calculated). This name appears regularly in the Lists from 1806 to 1824 inclusive. In August 1805 the officer was in the 12th or Prince of Wales' Regiment and in 1810 he was in the 15th or King's Regiment. By 1814 he was on 'English half-pay'. This may be the Feron to whom A'Beckett refers.

Joseph and his wife proceeded to have a family. The Registers at St. Ann's record the births of three daughters between 1813 and 1817: Frances Ann (born 9 September 1813), Mary Ann (born 29 April 1815) and Louise (born 27 May 1817). In all three instances, Joseph is described as a wax chandler, resident in Compton Street (presumably what is now Old Compton Street, Soho). Much later, there was to be a son, Augustus, born on 12 June 1825 at Portici, Naples. This son was to become known as Augustus Glossop Harris, the impresario. Augustus, in turn, became the father of Sir Augustus Harris (1852-96), lessee of the Drury Lane Theatre and the Royal Opera House, Covent Garden and Sheriff of the City of London.

JOSEPH GLOSSOP ABROAD (1822-1825)

When Glossop appeared in the Bankruptcy Court in London, in March 1833, he was called upon to give an account of his travels, so that the Court could decide whether he was entitled to benefit from the Statute of Limitations. This meant that he had to establish whether he had been in England 'during the last six years'.

He admitted that he had. He had left England, he said, in the middle of November 1822. He had travelled through Italy, Spain, Portugal and France and had returned to England 'about March 1827'.

However, he had then remained in England for only fourteen days, being obliged to make a hasty retreat to the Continent. His petitioning creditor, hearing of his embarkation from Calais for England, had instantly come over in another packet and issued a writ against him . This individual had declared: 'There is Glossop, going over to England; I'll follow and put him in Dover gaol.'

Glossop did not necessarily tell the whole truth in his 1833 statement, but there seems no reason to doubt the general accuracy of what he said. He stated that he had not been in England in 1823. In 1824 he was in Naples as Director of the Theatre there. He had also had the management of the theatre at Milan 'which he occasionally visited'. In 1825, he said, his time had been divided between Milan, Naples and Venice.

A Cruikshank cartoon illustrating Winston's ejection of Glossop's servant from Drury Lane and Glossop's subsequent assault upon Winston. (May 1821). From the Drury Lane Journal 1819-1827 by James Winston.

(Published by The Society for Theatre Research.)

Very little has so far come to light about what Glossop may have been doing in Spain and Portugal, but he was indeed in Milan in June 1823, because that was when he submitted his application for a contract as impresario at the *Teatro alla Scala*.

Among the voluminous documents preserved in the *Archivio Storico Civico e Biblioteca Trivulziana* in Milan is a letter in flowery Italian in which Joseph describes himself as a *cavaliere* attached to the Royal Court in Britain and as an officer in the 'Royal Guards'. He claimed to have accompanied George IV on his famous trip to Scotland (14-29 August 1822), but this so far lacks confirmation. Glossop believed himself to be well qualified, he maintained, to be awarded the contract for 'the first among the theatres of Europe': 'he had founded and managed one of the best theatres in London, at his own expense, for seven consecutive years, to the satisfaction of the public and to the great admiration of visitors from abroad . . . .'

In detail, Glossop's proposal was that he should take over at *La Scala* from 1 July 1824 until 20 March 1830, at a salary of *Lire* 240,000 per annum. At the same time, he did not hesitate to seek several modifications in the normal contract terms. He said that he would need to recruit a 'double company' of *primari cantanti* to

47

ensure that the public were given their due ration of new operas (serious, semi-serious and comic) as well as of works which had already won general acclaim.

At that period, Lombardy was under Austrian control and approval from Vienna was required for the appointment of a new *impresa* at the Imperial and Royal Theatres in Milan (*La Scala* and *La Canobbiana*). Indeed, a submission had to be made to the Emperor himself, and at one stage Glossop declared his intention of going in person to Vienna to press his case. There had been much hesitation in Milan about engaging the Englishman, but the police managed to satisfy themselves that Glossop was a *persona solida* who could be relied upon to fulfil his commitments. In June 1823 the banker brothers Marietti had certified that they knew *il Signor Glossop, cavaliere inglese*, personally and that they were prepared to stand surety for him. Glossop always made as much as he could about being a *cavaliere*. Meyerbeer, for instance, is recorded as referring to *il cavaliere Giuseppe Glossop*.

The Director of the Imperial and Royal Theatres in Milan declared that he had interviewed Glossop, who had made an excellent impression, 'inspiring confidence and good faith'. The Director informed Count di Strassoldi, President of the Government of Lombardy, that Glossop was the husband of the celebrated singer Ferron [sic], then in Naples, and had arrived in Milan under his wife's name on a passport issued by the British Ambassador in Naples. All in all, however, it seems likely that it was for the want of a better candidate that Glossop was given the Milan appointment. This was in December 1823.

Meanwhile, the impresario had been active in Naples. In November 1823, he applied to take over from Barbaja the management of the two theatres there, the *San Carlo* and the *Fondo*, from Passion Sunday 1824 to Passion Sunday 1830. Glossop described himself as a squire (*scudiero*) of the King of England, being an officer of the Royal Horse Guards (*ufficiale delle reali Guardie d'onore a cavallo*). He stated, accurately, that he was the son of Francis Glossop, still living.

Barbaja duly petitioned (on the ground of ill health) to be relieved of his own contract and to hand over to Glossop. The terms of Barbaja's contract were to remain substantially in force, though Glossop characteristically proposed various fairly important changes of detail concerning such matters as the number and regularity of performances.

Royal approval was given to the new contract with Glossop on 6 December 1823. Significantly, King Ferdinand reserved the right to cancel it at pleasure, on condition of giving notice to the impresario by the end of the preceding August. Furthermore, the possibility of Barbaja resuming charge was explicitly envisaged.

The ink was hardly dry on his contract before Glossop was seeking leave of absence and approval for the appointment of a procurator to stand in for him in Naples.

In May 1824, the *Harmonicon* noted that Barbaja had quitted the direction of Grand Opera at Naples and that his successor was Mr. Glossop. 'The Englishman is at the same time contractor for the Theatre of Milan, and wishes to add to it those of Rome and Venice. The English, who hold so great a share of the commerce, strive nevertheless to place themselves at the head of all the arts of Europe! The trade in female singers they take up instead of their traffic in slaves'.

It was overambitious of Glossop to attempt to manage two major opera houses at the same time. He became too heavily dependent on agents, and this contributed to his downfall.

San Carlo Theatre, Naples.
(From postcard by courtesy of Signor Gaspare Nello Vetro.)

In Naples, in April 1824, Glossop had announced an ambitious programme of operas and ballets to be performed at *San Carlo* and the *Fondo*. On 30 May, the name day of the King, *San Carlo* opened with *Semiramide*. In order to do justice to the work, Glossop had obtained royal assent to lease Madame Fodor-Mainvielle and Luigi Lablache from Barbaja, to whom they were contracted. Afterwards, Glossop was told that the performance had given the King satisfaction, but Ferdinand had been displeased that the advance notices had not made it clear that it was at his own express request that *Semiramide* had been the opera chosen.

San Carlo Theatre, Naples.
(From postcard by courtesy of Signor Gaspare Nello Vetro.)

Throughout the Summer, Glossop was responsible not only for the operas and bxallets at the two Naples theatres, but for Illuminations (grand or small) in honour of royal occasions. The Duchess of Parma was fêted with Grand Illuminations and the name day of Princess Amalia, Duchess of Orleans, was similarly marked.

At *San Carlo*, *Semiramide* had been followed, to quote the *Harmonicon*, by the 'old' Rossini operas *Zelmira* (actually produced as recently as 1822) and *Tancredi* (1813), and by Morlacchi's *Tebaldo ed Isolina*. These were not a success, due, it was said, to the singers. Mayr's *Ginevra di Scozia* had a somewhat better reception, but the King and Court had quickly become disenchanted with Glossop's management.

Certainly Glossop had a problem in recruiting first-class performers. In his defence, he claimed that 'he had undertaken a long and painful voyage, for the purpose of engaging the most distinguished artists, but that the number of these was at present so scarce, and the period so short, that he was unfortunately unable to answer the general expectations in the manner he had anticipated; but that by using every effort, and at considerable sacrifices, he hoped shortly to be able fully to correspond to the promises he had made'. This was an admission of failure and in June 1824 Glossop had had to issue an apology for being unable to give the performances which had been promised for *San Carlo*.

However, difficulties over singers and staging were only one aspect of Glossop's troubles in Naples. He believed himself to be the victim of cabals. The authorities, for their part, were worried about his caution money. In mid-April 1824 he had obtained the King's permission to go to London to raise funds for his *cauzione*. In mid-May, when the money had still not materialised, it must have become clear to the King and his advisers that Glossop was not the man of means he represented himself to be, but a man who had to ask to be bailed out by his family. It is not known whether or not he did go to England in 1824.

In Naples, Glossop was not well served by his agents. One of these was said to have been discovered to be fraudulent. This added a serious complication to a running legal dispute which Glossop had with Barbaja, mainly over the valuation of theatrical effects originally belonging to Barbaja. This litigation continued into 1826.

At the beginning of August 1824, the King of Naples had allowed Glossop to go to Milan to be present at the opening of the theatre there, leaving Luigi Drouet, a native of Amsterdam, as his legal representative in Naples. Perhaps Ferdinand was glad to have the Englishmen out of the way at this juncture, because in the middle of the month, and in strict accordance with the contract, he decreed that as from Passion Sunday 1825 Glossop's contract should be annulled and that Barbaja should resume charge of the Royal Theatres until Passion Sunday 1830. As a result, Glossop was effectively impresario in Naples for one year only.

As for the intrigues which there may have been against him, the *Harmonicon* believed that cabals were indeed involved. Rosselli in 'The Opera Industry in Italy from Cimarosa to Verdi', says that Barbaja liked to make himself indispensable, 'he detested any possible rivals for the Naples opera *impresa* and did his best to thwart them; he made short work of Glossop, that hopeful black sheep of an English gentry family'.

In Milan, things had started for Glossop well enough. The Season at *La Scala* had opened on 16 August 1824. According to the Theatre Counsellor (*Consigliere*) Renati, the performances had fulfilled the requirements of the contract and had pleased the public by the quality of the artists and the décor.

As the *Harmonicon* saw it, Glossop had given Milan 'splendour' as far as singers, dancers, decorations and dresses were concerned, but 'poverty' as regards the music – nothing but the old operas by Rossini or one still more out of date by Pacini. It was the great evil of the time that singers were allowed absolute power over the repertoire and would only show off their own hobby-horses.

Then the *Harmonicon* correspondent in Milan made a remark of great interest about Glossop and his feeling for music. Having the pleasure, he wrote, of being personally acquainted with the impresario, he knew him to be 'a zealous votary of Mozart'. Glossop, he believed, 'had the intention to bring out all the operas of Mozart, from the first he composed to his *Idomeneo*'. It was to be hoped that 'no intrigues behind the curtain' would prevent him from carrying this laudable intention into effect . . . .'

Most probably, Glossop was ahead of his time in musical taste. However that may be, his career as impresario in Milan was to end even more quickly and abruptly than in Naples.

Glossop lacked the administrative skill and business sense to take advantage of his dual rôle in Naples and Milan. As the *Harmonicon* pointed out (Milan, November 1824), by undertaking the direction of the two royal theatres in Milan and the principal theatres in Naples, Glossop was 'certainly playing a high card, and how he will finish time must show; certainly the moment for his speculation is not a very propitious one, from the scarcity of good composers and singers of excellence. It must also not be forgotten, that there are no good ballet-masters at present in Italy; the celebrated Vignano is no more, the still surviving Gioja is old, and all the others are good for little or nothing. From these causes, and from the nature of the music of the present day in general, it is not difficult to account for the apathy that prevails, at least in this place, for theatricals of all kinds'.

The *Harmonicon* had seen the theatre in Naples under Glossop going on 'very indifferently' and forecast that his first season in Milan would end in a deficit. 'It might be well for this director if he possessed a little more firmness of character, and did not suffer himself to be led by the singers . . . .'

By October 1824 Glossop was already in trouble with the theatre authorities in Milan.

In June, while in Naples, Glossop had formally appointed a Milanese, Antonio Fontana, as his legal representative (*procuratore speciale*) in Milan, with authority to act for him in all matters connected with the theatres there.

On this basis, Glossop had received permission, in October, to make what he no doubt correctly described as a necessary trip to Naples. However, his delay in returning to Milan alarmed Director Renati who had reason to fear that the arrangements for the forthcoming Carnival Season would not be completed in time.

Fontana hurriedly gave assurances that *La Vestale* was in preparation, to be followed by *Don Giovanni*, with a new libretto by the poet Romani, and by a grand ballet called *Tipo Sahib* by Signor Taglioni. Leading singers, he maintained, had already been engaged and Glossop was expected back 'any day'.

Fontana told the authorities that the Marietti brothers had received a private letter from Glossop from Naples dated 16 November stating that he would be leaving that very day for Milan. This meant that he should have arrived by 25 November, the day before Fontana had submitted his report. So he must have been held up by something unexpected – 'perhaps because he was accompanied by his wife and young daughter [sic]'. The wife was of course Elizabeth Féron. The baby must have been the boy Augustus, then only a few months old.

Renati was far from satisfied. On 27 November he reported to the Governor that Glossop had failed to return, as promised, by the middle of the month. Fontana's assurances were ambiguous and it was decided to invoke Article 37 of Glossop's contract and seek compensation from him. Effects not required for the Carnival would be put under sequestration, together with the rents for boxes etc. in the two theatres which had been assigned to Glossop.

When Glossop finally got back, he was persuaded that he must offer his resignation and seek the annulment of the contract. Yet even this proved troublesome. The annulment required approval from Vienna and there is an undated petition to the Emperor (addressed as *Sacra Cesarea e Maestà*) in which Glossop submitted that he had more than fulfilled the terms of his contract. For the first time, he claimed, the usual 'monotony' at the theatre had been relieved by a repertory of fine operas and ballets. These had given universal pleasure. He had flattered himself that all his efforts would have given satisfaction to the Governor – but, alas, *combinazioni* had produced the opposite effect. Finally, having submitted his resignation, he had assumed that it would be accepted without demur. This had not happened, so 'he prostrated himself at the feet of His Majesty, relying on His acclaimed justice and clemency, and imploring that he might be released from his contract'.

Whatever response may have been vouchsafed to this *cri de coeur*, Glossop duly bowed out, to be succeeded, as in Naples, by Barbaja. Also as in Naples, Glossop became involved in litigation in Milan which lasted for several years.

Interesting sidelights on Joseph's life and character are provided by James Winston in his Drury Lane Journal 1819-1827. Winston must be regarded as a somewhat hostile witness in that he represented Drury Lane in that theatre's legal disputes with the Coburg. However, he does not seem to be unfair in his comments.

According to Winston, in February 1821 Drury Lane had attempted to secure an injunction against Glossop for putting on a play called *Thérèse*, or *The Orphan of Geneva*, on the ground that it was the work of J. H. Payne on which they had a lien. However, this failed when it was established that the Coburg version was not Payne's, though it had been taken from the same French source.

In March 1821, Winston noted in his Diary that Glossop was believed to be angling for a knighthood. According to Winston, Glossop had gone so far as to pay the dramatist Moncrieff to write a pamphlet about the Band of Gentlemen Pensioners to be presented to the King on Glossop's behalf. However, this had led to a dispute with Moncrieff about the payment: 'Glossop took Moncrieff to Bath a short time back. He went away, unknown to Moncrieff, and left the bill unpaid. Moncrieff got away leaving all his clothes behind.'

If Glossop had left the King's service under some cloud and had been frustrated in the hope of a knighthood, it is understandable that he might have felt a grudge against the King and thus have become a supporter of Queen Caroline. Be that as it may, his hostility towards the King appears to have been the root cause of the affray on 10 May when Glossop physically assaulted Winston.

On 9 May, George IV attended a command performance at Drury Lane. A servant of Glossop's was in the audience. Winston claimed to have suspected that this man had been sent in by Glossop with the object of creating a disturbance. Winston therefore ejected the man. Glossop had witnessed this treatment of his servant and on the following day he lay in wait for Winston in Russell Street and struck him. The Bow Street magistrate, Sir Richard Birnie, had hoped to be able to hush the matter up, but the news spread quickly and even became the subject of a cartoon by Cruikshank. Finally, in the King's Bench, Winston was awarded £150 damages, which he donated to the Drury Lane Fund.

Glossop's proclivity to resort to physical violence is also evident from his attitude towards Robert Elliston, the lessee of Drury Lane. Winston records that in November 1821 Elliston had engaged Glossop's wife Elizabeth Féron to perform at Drury Lane. Glossop, at that time, declared that he did not approve of his wife acting and he secured an injunction which prevented her from fulfilling the engagement. This episode made bad blood between Glossop and Elliston and it was rumoured that Glossop planned to challenge Elliston to a duel in Paris. If Elliston would not fight, then Glossop would shoot him. (In all fairness, it must be noted that Elliston, who was frequently drunk, had been heard to threaten to shoot Glossop). There certainly seems to be little doubt that Glossop was nervous and highly strung. By his own admission, in Winston's hearing, he was physically sick, with vomiting, when anything went wrong 'in the management'.

Meanwhile, whether her husband approved or not, Elizabeth Féron had been pursuing a career of her own.

Elizabeth Féron

A pen-picture of Elizabeth Féron is provided by Cox in his *Musical Recollections of the last Half-Century.*

Elizabeth Féron.
(By courtesy of the Harvard Theatre Collection and the Civici Musei, Milan.)

As he recalled, her voice was 'brilliant in its tone, very extensive in its upward compass, and of great volume.' However, her tutor Cobham seemed to have drawn his ideas of vocal art chiefly from violin-playing and to have laid excessive emphasis on execution. Worse still, he had abused his pupil's talents by overworking her. She was 'taken round the country, announced with the cognomen of the English Catalani, and exhibited wherever a few guineas were to be earned.' This course of training had not been likely to confer any great celebrity on Miss [sic] Glossop and 'she quitted England for Italy, where she remained for a considerable time, enjoying good instruction and the advantage of singing in the first theatres, her husband having been joint proprietor with Signor Barbaja of those of Milan and Naples.'

Elizabeth Féron (or Ferron as she was sometimes known) went first, it seems, to Paris. She made her *début* there at the Italian Theatre on 20 January 1818 in Catalani's rôle as Mariette in Pucitta's opera *La Caccia di Enrico IV* (Henry IV's Hunt). *Galignani's Messenger* was surprised at her daring, but gave her unqualified praise for her style of execution: her voice was uncommonly sweet and powerful and her chromatic runs were admirable.

The *Journal de Paris* described Féron as a youngish English-woman, 'much too small for the stage', who pronounced Italian as though she would be more at home with German. However, she merited praise both as a singer and an actress: she always sang in tune and could reach very high notes without losing sweetness. Féron was given star treatment and seems to have been considered to be already well known to the sophisticated audience at the Italian Theatre. According to the *Journal des Débats*, she had been much applauded in *La Caccia*, 'despite Pucitta's music' and 'a formidable comparison' (presumably with Catalani). *La Caccia* had quite a long run.

On 17 February, Féron performed in the curious musical *farse Il Fanatico per la Musica* which was to become one of her hobby-horses. One report mentions both Mme. Féron and a Mlle. Féron as having sung together in this work in Paris, a reference, perhaps to one of Elizabeth's sisters. Later, Elizabeth played Faustina in Cimarosa's *I Nemici Generosi*, which was repeated several times. (On 10 February, it was when he was returning from the Italian Opera, that the Duke of Wellington had been the object of an assassination attempt). In March, Féron took part with Catalani and Cinti in a Sacred Concert at the Italian Opera and she was one of many well-known singers who founded the so-called *Concert d' Amateurs*, a group which performed in the *Salle de la Rue de Grenelle St. Honoré*.

Féron increased her reputation in Paris as the months passed. She seems to have stayed at the Italian Theatre until the end of the Season in the middle of May and may well have taken part earlier that month in the successful performance of Pucitta's *La Principessa in Campagna*. On the Continent, Féron was often accompanied by Pucitta, who had become her new teacher, and she was frequently applauded when singing his airs.

A series of concerts which Féron then gave in Marseilles had little success, but in 1819 she had better fortune in Berlin. There she was compared, mainly to her advantage, be it said, with Catalani. One English critic even called her second to no Italian but Pasta. According to the AMZ, she also sang in 1819 in several other German cities and in Vienna and Strasbourg, where it is possible that she was heard by Joséphine.

In the main, though, as Cox says, Féron's performances were to be in Italy, where in due course she was joined by her husband. She took major parts. In April 1820, she had the title rôle in *La Principessa in Campagna* at *La Scala*, with Filippo Galli. On 22 April, she played Ninetta in *La Gazza Ladra*, which ran to 41 performances. This was followed by leading parts in Carafa's *I Due Figaro* and in Generali's *Adelina*. The scenery in these operas was by the famous Sanquirico.

The Spring of 1821 found La Ferron billed with Pasta and Crivelli as a principal singer at *La Fenice* in Venice. There she received a chilly reception and she had no better success in the Summer in Bologna, in Mercadante's *Maria Stuarda*, an opera which was itself dismissed as a wretched copy of Rossini.

The town of Sinigaglia (Senigallia) on the Adriatic coast held an important fair each summer and in 1821 Féron was the *prima donna* there, singing in Rossini's *Edoardo e Cristina*. She was paid 500 scudi and given accommodation for herself and her family, plus a benefit evening. This suggests that her daughters were with her.

After Carnival appearances with Pasta and Tacchinardi in Turin in 1822, Feron obtained a two-year contract from Barbaja in his capacity as Director of the Court Theatres in Naples and Vienna. As a reigning star, she received 517.50 *ducati* a month, whereas a *seconda donna* got only 60.

Later in 1822, Elizabeth was with her husband in London. Winston says that in mid-March, after Glossop had returned from a trip to Paris, he and his wife had gone off into the country. In the light of subsequent events, there is significance in determining when Elizabeth and Joseph were known to be together.

On 29 June 1823 she was at *San Carlo* in the *première* of Donizetti's *opera seria Alfredo il Grande*, but was out of voice. Donizetti, writing in the previous April, had said that he had heard Féron singing badly in *La Donna del Lago* but, 'Heaven be praised, I am writing a cantata and an opera for her.' The opera, *Alfredo*, which 'indulged historical licence to unheard-of limits', was given only two performances. Elizabeth then appeared in *La Medea*, considered to be Mayr's masterpiece. She sustained the part of the heroine with great energy, admirably supported by Signor Nozzari. Their powers in the celebrated duet *Cedi al destin* had been crowned with universal applause (*Harmonicon*).

In the Autumn of 1823, the *Théâtre Italien* in Paris were in correspondence with their talent scout Turina in Naples about the possibility of recruiting Féron. Turina was told to proceed with caution, remembering that Féron was no longer young, a remark which suggests the earlier alleged birthdate of 1793. Furthermore, it was feared that the excessive demands being made by Pasta would encourage Féron's husband to be unduly grasping: Turina was urged not to let Féron and Mainvielle get together in a way that would embarrass the *Administration*. The fears proved well founded. Glossop made ever-increasing claims on behalf of his wife and these led to the abandonment of the negotiations to bring Féron to Paris in 1824 (Letter of 27 November 1823 to Turina). All the same, the *Administration* said that they wanted to keep in touch with Glossop, without commitment, as he had suggested that he might have an offer to make for April 1825.

By Christmas 1824 Feron was back at *La Scala*, where she sang the major rôle in Spontini's *La Vestale*. On Twelfth Night 1825 she took part in *Il Trionfo della Musica*. This is described as being by various *maestri*. According to the AMZ, the music was based on the old work by Mayr, *Gli Originali*, dressed up with a more fashionable title. Actually, very little of Mayr had been retained. Glossop asserted to the AMZ critic that two of the pieces in the work had been composed by his wife. She certainly liked it because it gave scope for the 'variations' for which she was always well known. These were very popular with some audiences, but were much frowned upon by others.

While Glossop was the impresario at *La Scala*, the *Harmonicon* had said that Féron was his wife but that she had no regular engagement. All the same, she was given some important parts. As Giulia in *La Vestale*, she had not been in the best voice owing to indisposition, but 'her style of singing is chaste, and without any superfluous ornaments, which in the performance of Giulia is an instance of self-denial, entitled to our warmest praise'. Perhaps, in this production at least, Glossop had imposed some discipline.

In *Semiramide* (29 December 1824), the name-part had been entrusted to Favelli, but when Favelli had been fairly hissed off the stage for singing so miserably out of tune, Elizabeth Féron, 'in her usual obliging manner' had devoted a week to studying the part and been able to take Favelli's place.

Still in Milan, Elizabeth sang in a short run of *Don Giovanni* in February 1825 and in April she succeeded a Mlle. Sicard as Amaltèa in Rossini's *Mosè in Egitto*', which ran to twenty-seven performances.

In 1825, Donizetti was under contract to serve as musical director of the *Teatro Carolino* in Palermo and he arrived in the Sicilian capital on 6 April 1825. In preparation for the production of his new opera *Alahor di Granata*, he had planned to engage three *prime donne*, Elizabeth Féron, Caterina Liparini and Marietta Gioja-Tamburini.

However, Feron's pregnancy and the birth of Augustus on 12 June kept her in Naples and this caused the *première* of *Alahor* to be delayed. She reached Palermo on 28 June, but *Alahor* does not appear to have been produced until 6 January 1826. It was given a favourable reception, but not repeated many times. On 26 January 1826, Elizabeth sailed for Naples, on the packet *Arturo*, accompanied by her baby and four servants.

Between 1824 and 1827, in addition to what has been described above, Féron is reported to have performed with some success in several Italian cities such as Modena, Sinigaglia, Verona and Lugo. She certainly returned to Sinigaglia for the fair there in 1826, when she performed in Meyerbeer's *Crociato in Egitto*. She apparently also sang in Vienna, under Barbaja, in 1824. She undoubtedly enjoyed the status of *prima donna* and was so generally well known in Italy that Glossop could be described there as 'the husband of La Ferron'. This again, in view of later events, is important.

Elizabeth remained in Italy until what was to be the fateful year, 1827. Throughout that Summer, she was at *La Scala*. She played Isabella in what was officially described as an excellent production of Rossini's *L'Inganno Felice*; in a wretched (*cattivo*) *première* of Frasi's *La Selva d'Hermannstadt* and in her favourite *Trionfo della Musica*.

In August 1827, while Féron was probably still in Milan, the event occurred in another part of Italy which was to bring about a radical change in her life and in that of Joseph Glossop and Joséphine de Méric. So it is that the story returns to the *début* of Joséphine de Méric on the Italian stage.

CHAPTER 5
Joséphine's first performance in Italy

IN 1825, *La Scala* had been undergoing restoration and in the Autumn Season the opera performances were given at the *Teatro alla Canobbiana*. Thus it was at *La Canobbiana* that Joséphine made her *début* in Italy.

A Dance Festival in the Teatro della Canobbiana, Milan (1825).
(By courtesy of the Museo Teatrale alla Scala, Milan.)

The Season opened on 16 August with the opera *semi-seria Elisa e Claudio* by Saverio Mercadante (1795-1870). Mercadante was a Southern Italian who wrote over fifty operas and enjoyed much popularity in his day. *Elisa e Claudio* is a romantic story of love and intrigue. It offers scope for *bel canto* and had been written for the great bass, Luigi Lablache. The opera was well received in Milan and ran to twelve performances. (It was successfully revived in 1988 at the Wexford Festival in Ireland).

The *Gazzetta di Milano* described La Demery as a young lady who had come to Milan from the French stage. She was endowed with a fine soprano voice, strong rather than flexible (*agile*), and was the only outstanding singer in the opera. The Milan reporter for the *AMZ* spoke of 'a certain Giuseppina Demeri' having a fine wide-ranging voice but not knowing how to use it. The *Harmonicon* said that Signora Demeri had arrived at a most lucky moment because Signora Colombella [sic] [?Coreldi] had been taken ill on the very day of Joséphine's arrival and had remained so ever since. Joséphine's graceful demeanour was praised.

Giacomo Cordella's *Gli Avventurieri*, which followed, was one of the operas which had been written for Joséphine. She sang at the *première*, which was given at *La Canobbiana* on 6 September 1825. It is described as a *melo-dramma giocoso* and proved a popular favourite, running to twenty-three performances, an exceptionally high number. The *Gazzetta* rated the composer as a poor fourth after Mercadante, Pacini and Carafa and the *Harmonicon* thought that only the friends of the author had received it with applause, 'the other part of the audience remaining silent, for fear that expressions of disapprobation might be punished by another infliction [sic] of *Cenerentolas.*' However, the *Gazzetta* considered that the rôle of Virginia, a girl both affectionate and lively, was well suited to the appearance and acting of the young Demeri. She had succeeded, in her high notes, in combining agility with strength.

Eleven performances of *Il Matrimonio Segreto*, officially described as good, were followed by twelve of *Le Nozze di Figaro*. The *Figaro* production was rated as only mediocre and had a generally cool reception, but Joséphine was applauded for her grace in the part of the affectionate but shrewd Countess. The *Harmonicon* credited Joséphine with a charming voice, only complaining that she was 'deficient in science'. The task of the singers was not made easier by the practice of having the orchestra on the stage, with 'as many as three trombones actively at work'. During this Autumn of 1825, Joséphine was often indisposed, with the result that the part of the Countess had to be taken by the *seconda donna*, 'who made sad work of it' (*Harmonicon*).

Vaccai's *Giulietta e Romeo*, also written for Joséphine, was given its *première* at the *Canobbiana* before the company returned to *La Scala*. The review in the *Gazzetta* gives a pleasing picture of Joséphine's appearance and also of the readiness to oblige which was a praiseworthy characteristic of her whole career. However, the paper thought that the singers had not been well suited to their rôles.

Joséphine, in particular, though a singer of great merit who had a charming presence and who was born to play brilliant parts, would need to transform her two bright eyes and her cheerful countenance into features furrowed with grief if she were to portray successfully the deeply passionate Juliet for whom Romeo was ready to sacrifice his life. All the same, she had received her customary applause from an audience who had appreciated the way she had replaced Coreldi.

Joséphine de Méric
(By Courtesy of the Musée Carnavalet, Paris).

This new opera was a popular success, running to eighteen performances, but the *Harmonicon* complained that Vaccai had felt 'compelled to sacrifice to the taste of the day and the influence of the singers' making no pretension to much novelty of ideas or to anything very exquisite in his instrumentation. Nevertheless, the opera was distinguished by great beauty and richness of melody. Romeo had been played with great feeling by Adele Cesari.

Joséphine's *début* at *La Scala* itself was in December 1825, when she took the part of Amalia in G.Pacini's *Il Barone di Dolsheim*. Pacini's music may have been but a pale imitation of Rossini, but it was much to the taste of the Milan audiences and the opera was given twenty performances. Joséphine, however, came in for some harsh criticism. According to the *Harmonicon*, she had sung wretchedly out of tune and had even taken the liberty of performing what should have been a quick and animated movement in slow time. With the memory of Camporesi still fresh, the public had had the good judgment to show their disapproval of 'this all-too-prevalent practice' in the most decided manner. However, shortly after the first representation of *Il Barone*, Joséphine fell seriously ill, so it seems highly probable that indisposition had adversely affected her normally very accurate pitch.

The Milan section of the *Harmonicon* of September 1826 contained a curious paragraph about Joséphine's surname. This ran as follows: 'We cannot, by-the-bye, help remarking the confusion that frequently arises from the custom, now so frequent among singers, of Italianizing their names. In the instance before us, sometimes in an opera libretto we find Mademoiselle De Mery, at others it is Signora Demery, and then on the opera bills Signora Demeri. Upon enquiry, it turns out that the lady is an honest Strasburger, and has no reason to be ashamed of the homely German patronymic of Demerick'. This, it must be said, is almost the only occasion when the name has been seen with a final k.

CHAPTER 6 *Joséphine and Joseph Glossop*

IN 1833 Glossop had told the Bankruptcy Court that in 1825 his time had been divided between Milan, Naples and Venice. In March 1826, he said, he had proceeded by way of Florence and Paris to England. By then he had lost his fortune and wanted to see his father and obtain something from him. He had spent three weeks in England, not concealing himself but also not going among his creditors. His father was his largest creditor and he had tried to make an arrangement with him and others.

There is some difficulty in following Glossop's movements, but he did not remain in England. In September 1826, he was in Turin. Surprisingly enough, he was acting there as a King's Messenger. This is the first evidence traced that he had added the carriage of diplomatic mail to his operations, but from what he explained it seems likely that he had already acted in this capacity in Spain.

On 1 November, Glossop told the Court, he had left Turin with a despatch from the British Ambassador there [actually the British Minister to the Sardinian Court, Augustus John Foster] to Lord Granville, the British Ambassador in Paris. Unfortunately, when he arrived at the frontiers, the Inspector of Police had invited him to supper and during that time his carriage had been rifled and the despatch carried off. He had hastened to Paris, only to find that the despatch had been delivered to Lord Granville two hours before. What was still missing, though, was 'an autograph letter of the King of Spain.' Glossop said that he believed that this had been the object of the thieves, 'because it was well known that he was in possession of it'. Glossop maintained that it had been discovered 'that a correspondence was carried on between the King of Spain and Charles X [of France] for the purpose of preventing the army of observation from being withdrawn'. Historians of the period will know whether there is any truth in this allegation.

Glossop might have heard Joséphine sing in Paris and they must have met when she was in Milan. However, it is in 1826 that there is the first clear indication of a connexion between the two. According to his own account, Glossop was in Turin from September to 1 November of that year. In Meyerbeer's *Briefwechsel und Tagebücher, Band II, 1825-1836*, there is a long letter which

Extract from: Giacomo Meyerbeer, Briefwechsel und Tagebücher. Ed. Heinz Becker. Band 2 (1825 - 1836). The text of the letter written by Joséphine to Meyerbeer

(Reprinted by courtesy of Walter de Gruyter & co).

Joséphine wrote to the composer from Turin on 30 October. This concludes with the postscript: 'Mr. Glossop a l'honneur se [sic] vous presenter ses hommages. Il sera sous peu à Paris'. As an impresario, Glossop was already well known to Meyerbeer.

This letter is of particular interest as one of very few letters written by Joséphine which has survived.

Monsieur le Baron!

Ja'i reçu la poste passée la lettre que vous m'avez fait l'honneur de m'écrire, Je ne puis vous exprimer combien je suis charmée de la flattaise préférence que vous voulez bien m'accorder en me proposant de composer un Opéra pour moi, certainement se serait le plus grand bonheur qui pourrait m'arriver et une Epoque bien mémorable dans ma carrière musicale, mais il faut croire que je n'en suis pas encore digne, puisque par une fatalité que je déplorerai toujours, je suis déjà engagée à Gênes pour le printems prochain. Je ne crois pas que Monsieur le Directeur de l'Odéon quand même j'eusse été libre, eut pu m'offrir la somme que je gagne actuellement en Italie, et qui est de trente à trente cinq mille francs par an. Je le remercie beaucoup d'avoir pensé à moi, je me souviendrai longtems de la manière offensante avec laquelle on m'a traitée quand j'étais sous la férule de l'administration du Théâtre Royal Italien, mais à quelque chose malheur est bon, parceque j'ai trouvé en revanche en Italie, amour du public, protection, et occasion de m'instruire dans mon art, Madame Pasta même, qui est passée dernièrement ici, a donc été négligée au point qu'on n'a pas renouvelé son Engagement, qu'on se tire d'affaire actuellement qu'on a perdu au moins pour 6 mois, le seul talent féminin qui soutenait encore le Théâtre Italien déclinant, on m'a préféré dans le tems une Demoiselle Amigo et compagnie, vous pourrez juger de leur talent étant sur les lieux, avec le moins d'amour propre possible, je ne puis m'empêcher de me mettre audessus de ces gens - là, je fusse restée il y a deux ans à Paris pour 12 à 15000 francs par an, avec ma voix de Clarinette comme on me reprochait, que par parenthèse je n'ai pas encore perdue, quoiquelle offuscat terriblement les oreilles des gens qui protegeaient tous les artistes féminins auxquels je fesais ombrage; je vais l'automne dans un an à Lucques, où la Duchesse m'a fait engager exprès pour chanter dans votre "Crociato", je brûle de m'y faire entendre, et j'ose croire que le rôle étant très haut, ma voix d'Instrument ne fera pas un mauvais effet dans les morceaux d'ensemble, Pour le Carnaval de 1827 à 1828 je suis engagée à Rome, je compte aussi y donner "le Crociato". Je crois que j'irai à Gênes pour l'ouverture de son Théâtre, et après à Lisbonne, je n'ai pas encore rien conclu, et je suis libre par consequent pour ce tems là, j'espère que quelques nouvelles musicales ne feront pas déplaisir à une personne aussi distinguée que vous dans ce bel art, Barbaja a donné votre Opéra "le Crociato" à Naples. Concevez-vous la combinaison malheureuse qu'on a faite des Artistes! Signor Winter a fait la partie du Ténor, avec des moyens physiques capables de ne se faire entendre qu'au 3me banc de la platea, pour executer le Rôle magnifique si merveilleusement chanté par la Bassi à Milan, on a fait le choix de Mme Lorenzani, Contralto Deciso, la partie del Basso, a été chantée par un débutant, fesant le métier de Basso Cantante, non pas par talent mais à force de protections, la seule personne à qui son Rôle convenait, était la Lalande, mais cela ne suffit pas, voilà pourquoi on n'a pas pas pu gouter cet Opéra à Naples, vous vous rappellerez sans doute que quand Mr Glossop était entrepreneur à Naples, quoiquil ait eu des talents gigantesques comme celui de Nozzari, celui de la Tosi, et Biondini bon dans le "Crociato", comme le Rôle de Mme Bassi ne convenait pas à La Liparini, Il a renoncé à donner cet Opéra quoique le Vestiario et les scènes fussent déjà faites. On donnera ce Carnaval prochain au Théâtre Reggio d'ici "le Crociato", on a eu du moins le bon esprit d'engager la Bassi, les autres personnes sont la Mélas, et Mari, Cavara pour Basse, voilà les nouvelles que je sais, peut être que vous en êtes déjà informé, pardonnez-moi mon verbiage et ayez la Complaisance de faire connaître mes intentions à Mr le Directeur de l'odeon. Recevez l'assurance de la haute Considération
avec laquelle j'ai l'honneur d'être
votre servante et admiratrice
Joséphine de Méric

P.S. Mr Glossop a l'honneur se vous presenter ses hommages. Il sera sous peu à Paris
Turin le 30 Octobre 1826

Meyerbeer had proposed that he should write an opera for Joséphine, to be performed in Paris at the *Odéon*. Joséphine was naturally delighted and highly flattered. However, she explained that to her eternal regret she was obliged to decline the honour because she was already engaged to sing in Genoa in the forthcoming Spring Season. Also, she very much doubted whether, even if she had been free, the *Odéon* would have paid her as much as she was already receiving in Italy, namely 30-35,000 francs per annum. She commented that she would long remember the offensive way she had been treated when she was under the 'rod' of the *Administration* of the *Théâtre Royal Italien*. But there had been compensations. In Italy she had found love from the public, protection [by Glossop] and the opportunity of progressing in her art.

Joséphine then launched into a diatribe against the Italian Opera in Paris in which a note of *Schadenfreude* can perhaps be detected. The Administration, she pointed out, had not even renewed the contract of Madame Pasta (who had just been in Turin). Thus 'the declining Italian theatre' in Paris had lost, for six months at least, the only feminine talent which had been keeping it afloat. Joséphine recalled that there had been a time when the *Administration* had actually gone as far as preferring '*une Demoiselle Amigo et compagnie*' to herself. Meyerbeer, being in Paris, would know how little talent the Italian Opera there could boast. In all modesty, she felt bound to put herself above people like that. Then there was the question of money. If she had stayed on in Paris, she would still have been getting only 12-15,000 francs a year.

At this point Joséphine refers to the characteristic feature of her own voice: '*ma voix de Clarinette*'. This, which she said she had not lost, had oh-so-terribly shocked the ears of those in Paris who were busy protecting the female artists who feared her as a rival.

Joséphine went on to emphasise to Meyerbeer that her '*voix d'Instrument*' would seem particularly well suited to the very high rôle in his opera *Crociato* which she was burning to sing when she went to Lucca in the following Autumn. The Duchess [Marie-Louise of Parma] had expressly engaged her to sing in *Crociato*, and Joséphine ventured to believe that her special tone of voice would be heard to good effect in the ensembles of that opera.

After mentioning some of her own future engagements, Joséphine said that Meyerbeer might like to hear some general opera news. Barbaja had put *Crociato* on in Naples, but it had been miserably miscast. The tenor, Winter, could not be heard. Most of the singers had only been engaged because of their protectors. The only one who had adequately fitted her part had been La Lalande [Henriette Méric-Lalande]. That, alas, had not sufficed and so *Crociato* had 'failed to please' in Naples.

This gave Joséphine her opening to mention Glossop and to put him in a favourable light. When he had been the impresario in Naples, she wrote, he had had 'gigantic talents' at his disposal such as Nozzari, Tosi and Biondini. It was only because the rôle previously taken by Madame Bassi did not suit La Liparini that Glossop had had to abandon the project of staging Meyerbeer's opera and that had been at the very last minute when the costumes and scenery had all been got ready. The good news, finally, was that *Crociato* was to be given at the *Teatro Reggio* in Turin at Carnival 1827 and that the theatre there had had the good sense to engage Madame Bassi.

Joséphine herself seems to have had some success in Turin. She and Cerioli were the *prime donne* at the *Teatro Carignano*. The season had opened with *Figaro* and the *Harmonicon* reported as follows: 'After the *Figaro* came *La Gazza Ladra*, which pleased much. The principal character was excellently sustained by Signora Demery, who is known here by the name of De Méric, and obtained great and merited applause. One of the journals observes that she has *una pronunzia, un canto, ed una voce veramente italiana.*' [pronunciation, singing and a voice which are truly Italian] High praise indeed.

To return to Glossop, at the end of 1826 he appears to have gone to England. He had returned to Paris, he stated, on 4 January 1827 to make an engagement for Madame Taglioni.

Meanwhile, Joséphine was in Trieste for the Carnival. Trieste, at the time, was a flourishing free city in the Austrian Empire. The Season at the *Teatro Grande* there had opened on 28 December 1826 with *Gli Avventurieri*, in which Joséphine was the heroine, Virginia. This was followed by Rossini's *L'Italiana in Algeri* (from 9 January 1827) with Joséphine in the contralto part of the Italian girl, Isabella.

On 30 January, the three-act version of Rossini's *Mosè in Egitto*, with the libretto by Andrea Tottola, found Joséphine singing the part of Elcia, the Hebrew woman secretly married to Pharaoh's heir, Osiride. *Mosè* continued in the repertory until 3 March 1827.

At this juncture there was an important development in Paris. Joséphine was offered a contract as *premier sujet* at the *Académie Royale de Musique*. She was in Trieste at the time, 17 February 1827, and was represented in Paris by 'Monsieur le chevalier' Glossop. Under the contract, which she accepted, she undertook to sing twice a week at the *Opéra Français*, with the option of performing once a week at the *Théâtre Royal Italien*. On her arrival in Paris, which was to be on 1 December 1827, or 1 March 1828 at the latest, she was to sing 'rôles from the old repertoire'. Her emoluments would amount in total to some Fcs 25,000, less 5 % for the pension fund. She had apparently been receiving better money in Italy, but perhaps she was feeling the lure again of the cultural capital of the world and believed that with all her experience in Italy she was now going to be able to take Paris by storm.

However, the move to Paris was not to take place until the end of the year. In the meantime, there were the 1827 opera seasons in Italy. Above all, though, there was to be a momentous change in Joséphine's personal life.

In February the arrangement with the *Académie* was duly concluded. In mid-March, Joséphine was in Milan where she and David sang in a Grand Concert at *La Scala* given by Mlle. Aline Bertrand which was described as one of the most brilliant given in Milan for a long time (*Journal de Paris*).

Then, as forecast in her letter to Meyerbeer, Joséphine proceeded to Genoa to take leading soprano rôles in the Spring Season at the *Teatro Sant'Agostino* there. With the *buffo* singers Giovanni Bottari and Angelo Ranfagna, she sang as *prima attrice* in *Il Barone di Dolsheim*, which proved successful, and in *Gianni di Parigi*, which did not. In May, Joséphine sang in *Matilde di Shabran* at the *Teatro del Falcone*. She seems to have missed several performances through illness.

However, it was not in either Milan or Genoa that the great change in Joséphine's life came about. This was in Livorno (Leghorn).

On 2 August 1827, in Livorno, a marriage was celebrated between Joséphine de Méric and Joseph Glossop.

Documentary evidence of this was first discovered in the Archives of the *Opéra* in Paris, by Mr. Brian Meringo. It has been confirmed both by the Guildhall Library in London and by the *Archivio di Stato* in Livorno.

There were two ceremonies. First, an Anglican wedding in the British Chapel in Leghorn conducted by the British Chaplain in the Grand Duchy of Tuscany. Then the civil registration at the *Cancellaria* in the town.

Clearly, this marriage raises a serious question: was it, on Glossop's part, bigamous? Was he still legally married to Elizabeth Féron, who had borne her son Augustus only two years before? No evidence has come to light of any legal separation or divorce. Glossop family tradition has it that Joseph was a bigamist.

Yet he, Féron and Joséphine were all well-known public figures in Italy at the time. Glossop was unquestionably known as the husband of the famous singer La Ferron. So it strains credulity to believe that an unlawful marriage could have been so openly performed.

The two registrations agree in describing Glossop as a bachelor and that must be how he represented himself. The bride was named as Marie Joséphine Bonnaud de Méric, of Strasbourg, a spinster.

Marriages solemnized in Leghorn in the grand Duchy of Tuscany in the year 1827

Gapper Glossop — Bachelor of London; and Marie Josephine Bonnaud de Méric of Strasburg in France.

were married in this Chapel, with consent of Parents, this second day of August, in the year of One Thousand Eight Hundred and twenty seven

By me Charles Neat, British Chaplain.

This marriage was solemnized between
In the presence of ⎨ Eugene de Méric
Wm Macbean .

Gapper Glossop
Marie Josephine de Méric

I hereby certify the above to be a true extract from our Register of Marriages, solemnized in the British Chapel at Leghorn. —

Charles Neat
British Chaplain

Je soussigné certifie avoir signé l'original de la présente copie d'acte de Mariage sur les register du prêtre anglican qui a marié les sieurs . I.G. Glossop et I. De Méric a Livourne —

E De Méric
frère de Joséphine de Méric

Certificate of the Marriage of Joseph Glossop and Joséphine de Méric at the British Chapel in Leghorn, 2 August 1827.
(By courtesy of the Archives de l' Opéra, Paris.)

A curious feature of the Anglican registration is that it states, with underlining, that the marriage took place 'with consent of parents'. This was as though the parties were minors, which they were certainly not. Glossop was later accused in his father's will of having forged documents and there must be the possibility that he forged his father's signature to satisfy the British Chaplain.

Joséphine may have acted in good faith, though she cannot be supposed to have been unaware of Glossop's marriage to Féron. Her brother Eugène de Méric signed as one of the two witnesses, thus implying the approval of her family.

The civil registration goes into some detail. Glossop's age is given as 33 and Joséphine's as 26, which is roughly correct. Glossop is described, no doubt in his own words, as *possidente*, or a gentleman of independent means. Joséphine is *benestante*, that is of good standing or well-to-do. It is noted that she is a Protestant. Her father having been a Roman Catholic, the inference is that her Federlen mother brought her up as a Protestant.

The mystery is such that one is driven to what may be wild speculations. Had there been, for instance, a public rift between Joseph and Elizabeth Féron which was accepted in operatic circles as a break-up of their marriage? Is it possible that Augustus was not in fact Joseph's son and that Joseph had repudiated his wife for adultery? Was Joseph just tired of Elizabeth and prepared to lie in his teeth to get married to someone else? Is there indeed some legal document of divorce which has yet to be found? Could it be that Joséphine had become pregnant and that the marriage was arranged by a general collusion? It seems likely that we may never know.

As for Féron, she left Italy and returned to England

JOSEPHINE IN ITALY AS MADAME GLOSSOP

By this time it would have been no part of Glossop's plans that a wife of his should abandon a lucrative career, and Joséphine was soon at the *Teatro del Giglio* in Lucca for the 1827 Autumn Season to which she had been looking forward with such enthusiasm.

The Season duly opened on 15 August with Joséphine as *prima donna* in *Il Crociato in Egitto*. The Duchess had come over from the Bagni di Lucca to honour the occasion with her presence. According to contemporary records, the singers had all acquitted themselves well and after the first few evenings *Il Crociato* had 'pleased'. The final performance on 16 September had been given to a full house.

The local Analysis of the Opera Company accorded Joséphine pride of place as a skilful soprano, but regretted that she had been obliged to miss several performances and had not been able to complete the Season.

There had been a report that she had arrived in Lucca pregnant. It was commonplace to attribute the indisposition of female singers to this cause, but the report does give some credence to the supposition that Joséphine might have already been in that condition when she married Glossop. Be that as it may, no record has been traced of the birth of any child before Joséphine's daughter Emilie was born, in Paris, in 1830. On the other hand, especially considering the many journeys on bad roads, she might well have suffered miscarriages.

From Lucca, Glossop and his new consort started on their way to Paris. Joséphine's health continued to give cause for concern. The situation is explained in a letter which Glossop sent from Marseilles on 9 October 1827 to Monsieur Lubbert, who was then Director of the *Académie Royale de Musique*. Lubbert had not unnaturally been worried because Joséphine had not yet arrived to take up the appointment which she had accepted in the Spring.

Glossop wrote that he wanted his wife to rest. She had been singing for nine Seasons in succession and he had just persuaded the impresario in Lucca not to induce her to perform in Livorno. He and his wife were passing through Marseilles on their way to Paris, but they were travelling by easy stages and he had promised his wife to take her to Strasbourg because he thought that she was feeling a little homesick. From Strasbourg they would go on to Paris before the weather got too cold. They expected to arrive at the end of November.

In this letter, Glossop maintains that he had recently received a very flattering offer for 'Madame' from Count Boronowski [Director of the St. Petersburg opera], who had proposed a three-year contract at 42,000 francs a year 'including accommodation and firewood'. Of course this had had to be declined because Joséphine was bound by her contract in Paris. It is not known whether Joseph was telling the truth. He would not have been above putting up a statement like this as a bargaining counter.

There are some further points of interest in Glossop's letter. He asks Lubbert to convey *hommages* from his wife and himself to the Vicomte de la Rochefoucauld (aide-de-camp to the French King, responsible for the *Département des Beaux-Arts*, the official who had signed the February Agreement with Joséphine) and also to Rossini and his wife. Glossop, in his capacity as an impresario, strongly advised Lubbert to engage the male singer Bottari (with whom Joséphine had sung in Genoa). Finally, Glossop asked for mail to be addressed to Poste Restante, Avignon, where he and Joséphine would be spending three weeks with an English family. This family has not been traced. The letter was signed 'Votre serviteur et ami, J.G.Glossop'.

Presumably the journey proceeded as planned. It is not known what happened in Avignon or Strasbourg. In Strasbourg, Joséphine will have been able to see her father and mother and introduce Glossop to them.

She arrived in Paris in time to present herself at the Opéra in December 1827.

Joséphine de Méric – Anonymous portrait.
(By courtesy of the Musée Carnavalet, Paris.

The contract with the Opéra in Paris, 1827-1831

JOSÉPHINE had been sent a welcoming letter from Rossini. Writing from Paris on 27 November 1827, he had expressed himself (in French) as follows:

> Paris, le 22 novembre 1827 - J'ai reçu, Madame, votre aimable lettre, et m'empresse de vous assurer qu'on vous attend ici avec la plus vive impatience. Soyez certaine que le temple qu'on vous y élève ne peut qu'ajouter un nouvel éclat à votre gloire musicale.
>
> J'ai fait part de votre lettre, Madame, au directeur de L' Académie royale, qui prétend vous avoir écrit, et désirerait, ainsi que vos nombreux admirateurs, être fixé sur votre prochain retour.
>
> Arrivez donc le plutôt possible, Madame, et croyez que le moment ne saurait être plus favorable à vos brillans débuts.
>
> Ma femme vous remercie de votre aimable et bon souvenir. Présentez mes civilités à Madame votre mère. et, je vous le répète, arrivez le plutôt possible.

"I have received your kind letter, Madame, and hasten to assure you that your arrival here is awaited with the most lively impatience. You may be certain that the temple which will be raised in your honour here can only add new lustre to your musical glory.

I have passed on your letter to the Director of the *Académie Royale*, who says that he has written to you. He, together with your numerous admirers, hopes that he will soon hear definitely that you will be returning shortly.

So please, Madame, come back as quickly as you can. Believe me, there could not be a more auspicious moment for you to make brilliant *débuts*.

My wife thanks you for your kind remembrances. Please give my regards to your Mother and, I repeat, come just as soon as you can."

If, as reported, this letter was addressed to Joséphine in Milan, she may well not have received it, since by the end of November she was already in France. However, it was possibly sent to her in Strasbourg, where her parents were living. In any event, the letter is evidence of an affectionate relationship between Rossini and the de Méric family and emphasises, albeit with some Italian hyperbole, that Rossini was an admirer of Joséphine's talents.

Unfortunately, despite the good omens, the return to the city of Joséphine's *début* was to prove sadly disappointing. Essentially, it would seem, Joséphine's classical Italianate style of singing was at odds with the prevailing demands of the *Opéra* in Paris. Almost at once, there were disputes with the Administration and in these Glossop played a part. Already in February 1828 he was writing to the Director of the *Opéra* asking him to make good an alleged underpayment to his wife. This letter was written from 42 rue d'Artois, Paris. Glossop drew a distinction between payments to Joséphine and to himself, so he was probably receiving commission as her agent. On 16 April, Joséphine wrote a note authorising the cashier to pay her salary to Glossop.

Joséphine's operatic test came when she appeared on 26 December 1827 as Anaï in the four-act French version of Rossini's 1818 opera *Mosè in Egitto* known as *Moïse*. This work of many titles had been first produced in its French guise at the *Opéra* in Paris on 26 March 1827, with Nourrit. (In London, later, it was to surface as *Pietro l'Eremita* and as *Zora*). The libretto was by Balocchi and Etienne de Jouy. The playbill had announced that *Moïse* was being presented '*pour les débuts de Mlle. Démeri.*'

The work, described as an oratorio, was also being given a command performance. The Regent of Portugal, Dom Miguel, had expressed a wish, after an absence of three years, to revisit the *Académie de Musique* before leaving Paris for Lisbon. The royal presence may have added to Joséphine's inevitable trepidation; but had Dom Miguel perhaps remembered hearing her as Aménaïde? May he perhaps too have played a part in the decision to invite her to the opera in Lisbon the following year?

Moïse was widely acclaimed as the success which had turned the tide of the fortunes of the *Opéra*, but the reviews of Joséphine's performance were uniformly unfavourable. As was unavoidable, she suffered by comparison with Cinti, whom she had replaced. Furthermore, Rossini had conceived the rôle of Anaï for Isabelle Colbran and 'it called for extreme agility, combined with richly dramatic powers of expression' (Nigel Jamieson in *The Times*, reviewing a performance of *Moïse* in Bologna in April 1991).

Certainly no such outcome had been foreseen. *Le Figaro* had hailed Joséphine's return to the opera stage in Paris as a *coup de maître* on the part of the Director of the *Académie Royale,* one which was likely to have a salutary effect on Mlle. Cinti. With all her pretensions, what she needed was a rival to stimulate her jealousy, 'that passion never mute in the heart of a woman.'

Mlle. Cinti in Moïse in costume which would also have been worn by Joséphine.

From La Petite Galérie Dramatique ou Receuil de différents Costumes d' Acteurs des Théâtres de la Capitale *(Martinet).*

(By courtesy of the Bibliothéque de l' Opéra.)

On 25 November 1827, *Le Figaro* had given reasons why it expected great things from Joséphine's return. Noting that she was a pupil of Paër, the paper recalled 'her brilliant *débuts* at the *Théâtre Italien.*' The young singer was gifted with an extraordinary voice. There had never been one more resonant, more sustained [*rempli*] or with greater range.

In the same vein, the *Gazette de France* (19 December) waxed lyrical about the pleasure which opera-lovers could expect from the return of Mlle. Demeri. They were far from forgetting the young lady who, arriving from Strasbourg with nothing but a voice and zeal, had made her *début* in Paris in one of the most brilliant and difficult of rôles, that of Aménaïde in *Tancredi*. Then, it had not been alone the rare beauty and range of her voice which had aroused so much admiration. Joséphine had shown that she was endowed with a live intelligence and great delicacy of feeling, qualities which were nowhere appreciated more highly than in France. Three years' experience in Italy must surely have brought her natural aptitudes to maturity. She could indeed not be making her second *début* under more favourable auspices.

Mlle. Cinti in Le Siège de Corinthe *in costume which would also have been worn by Joséphine.*
From La Petite Galérie Dramatique ou Receuil de différents Costumes d'Acteurs des Théâtres de la Capitale *(Martinet).*
(By courtesy of the Bibliothèque de l' Opéra.)

All the same, this euphoria was accompanied with some reservations. As *Le Figaro* recalled, unluckily one of her earliest performances in Paris had been in the 'terrible rôle of Donna Anna', rightly regarded as the most difficult part ever written for the stage. After a mere ten months of study, this had inevitably been beyond her powers. She had had flashes of perfection, but her lack of technique had all too soon become apparent. Oddly, *Le Figaro*, referring to Joséphine as Mlle. Démeri, remarked that she was born in Strasbourg 'despite the Italian ending of her name'.

At first, the adverse criticism was muted and every allowance was made. The *Nouveau Journal de Paris* reported that a new recruit had made her *début* in *Moïse*. Earlier, the paper recalled, Mlle. Démeri had been a success at the *Théâtre Louvois*. Unfortunately, her performance in *Moïse* had not given as much satisfaction as was to have been expected from the flattering recollections of the young singer which remained in the minds of the *dilettanti*. Perhaps she had been intimidated by appearing for the first time on the much larger stage. Perhaps, despite her French origin, Joséphine found that *Moïse* in French seemed to be in a foreign language. She had sung her arias feebly and it was only in the ensembles that her voice, which had always been a little harsh, had found the bite and firmness which were its distinguishing features. However, it would be unfair to pass judgment after a single performance.

In 1827/28 the *Théâtre Royal Italien* (*et Anglais*) was at the *Salle Favart* and the *Académie Royale* was at the Rue Le Peletier. In 1827, Laurent replaced Lubbert at the *Théâtre Italien* and Lubbert succeeded Dubois as Director of the *Académie*. Lubbert, it was thought, might introduce many improvements at the *Académie*, but rumour had it that he was so obsessed with the popularity in Paris of Rossini's operas (in French) that he would have them performed to the exclusion of everything else and that the ability of singers to produce good *roulades* would be the key to their success (*Le Corsaire*). So it indeed proved.

The *Revue Musicale* said that Mlle. Démery had seemingly been engaged in place of Mlle. Cinti, whose unexpected departure had embarrassed the *Opéra*. Cinti had just married Damoreau, one of the leading actors in Brussels. However, the paper claimed, it was well known that Joséphine's very heavy vocalisation did not fit her for parts which had been written for Mlle. Cinti. 'An evil genius seemed to be hovering over our theatres.' All the same, *Le Corsaire* looked forward to seeing Joséphine replacing Cinti in all her rôles.

In reviewing *Moïse*, the *Revue* devoted two paragraphs to Joséphine. They were not laudatory. If the Administration had hoped that she would replace Cinti, they must have been cruelly disappointed.

'Madame Démeri . . . possesses a beautiful voice; or, more accurately, she has some beautiful sounds, but these sounds lack liaison with one another. M. Paër, who had taken pains to train her vocalisation, had found her organ so heavy and inflexible that he was forced to abandon hope of making a singer of her. The proof that he was not mistaken in his judgment is that she has just spent two or three years unsuccessfully [sic] in Italy. There is no help for it; Mme. Démeri sings as she will always sing.

'She might have been of use to the *Opéra* fifteen or twenty years ago. Then, her main failing, namely her inability to vocalise runs and *fioriture*, would not have been noticed, because the music in the old repertory did not allow of any of this kind of ornamentation. Antigone, the Iphigenias, Alceste and even Hypermnestre and Armide might well have suited her. In such parts her splendid sounds would have worked wonders and might have earned her a great reputation. So it had been a mistake to have obliged her to sing the rôle of Anaï in *Moïse*, for which she is quite unsuited. There could have been no illusions about this because the rehearsals had demonstrated her incapacity. In this *début*, so baleful for her future, Mme. Démeri found herself forced to slow the *tempi* down in order to have time to reach the end of the runs. This led to weakness in the ensembles throughout the performance. Particularly distressing were her duet with Adolphe Nourrit in the first act, the finale of the third and the beautiful aria in the last act. That is not all. The efforts which she needed to make to sing this music upset her pitch, formerly so true. Taken together, all these faults produced a deplorable effect. The customary courtesy of the *Opéra* public saved Mme. Démeri from any fierce expression of displeasure; but the silence, broken only by a few involuntary cries, must have made her realise that she has mistaken her vocation and has nothing to hope for along the path on which she has so maladroitly been launched.'

Harsh words indeed.

Le Corsaire (27 December 1827) adopted a kinder tone. The outcome of Mlle. Demeri's *début*, it wrote, depended on the opera in which it took place. If this had been Gluck's *Oedipe*, she would probably have received well-merited applause in the rôle of Antigone. But Anaï, with all her groans and tears, drowned in a thousand *roulades*, could not be worthily interpreted by a singer whose voice was lacking in half-tones. *Le Corsaire* said that although her voice had shown to some advantage in the ensembles, she had not been able to repeat her former success at the *Louvois*. The young singer was perhaps overawed, but at times she had almost brought Nourrit down with her.

Then, in a column devoted to Joséphine, *Moïse and the Administration of the Académie Royale de Musique*, the paper explained that the Administration had made Joséphine learn the part of Anaï in great haste in order to discover whether she was capable of replacing Mlle. Cinti in the new school of opera, i.e. in all the intricacies of the *roulades*. They were not concerned to know how she would perform in the works of Sacchini, Piccini or Gluck. They were not even bothered about whether she could act: Cinti never was and never could be an actress. Cinti had been at the *Opéra* for her *roulades* and all the Administration wanted was someone who could sing *roulades* as she did. Joséphine's voice was deeply sonorous and capable of outbursts of great beauty: but could she lend herself to the 'incongruities' of the music of the fashionable new school?

Le Corsaire was prepared to suspend judgment. Let her be given time to recover from the strains inseparable from any *début*. Ever since her arrival in Paris she had been bombarded with advice and forced to abandon all she had ever learnt in order to follow Rossini alone. Every piece she was expected to sing had been retouched and adapted to her voice, then retouched again. The poor woman had been driven from pillar to post, fearful of the unfamiliar audience and of comparison with Cinti. Her anxiety had been all too visible. On several occasions her fellow-artists had needed to raise her faltering courage.

On 7 January 1828, *Le Figaro* reported that Joséphine was ill. This illness had caused the postponement of the production of *Masaniello*. If she were to suffer the same fate as Mme. Mainvielle-Fodor and lose 'that magnificent voice which we came to know four years ago' what would the Administration do? Madame Dabadie was too old to take all the *prima donna* parts and her health was precarious. There would be nothing left but to pay Cinti's debts and make peace with her.

On 18 January, according to the same paper, Mme. Démeri was still sick 'and had broken her engagement'. Still, negotiations with Cinti hung fire. As *prime donne* at the rue Pelletier, only Mmes. Dabadie and Jawurek remained. Neither would draw in the crowds. Meanwhile, Sontag was enjoying triumphs on the rival stage. It was to be hoped that M. Lubbert would succeed in engaging Mme. Malibran-Garcia 'who was born in Paris, speaks our language like a Frenchwoman, is at the same time a great tragic actress and a delightful singer' – altogether preferable to Cinti.

Also in January, the *Revue Musicale* reported that following her unfortunate experience in *Moïse*, Joséphine had asked to try again, this time in Rossini's *Le Siège de Corinthe*, agreeing to forfeit her engagement if she was not successful. With foreboding, the *Revue* feared that the proverb 'Not everyone can get to Corinth' would be proved only too true in this instance. (*Le Siège* is a French version of the *Maometto II* of 1820.)

Taking up the theme after the opera had been performed on 1 February 1828 with Joséphine as Palmyra, the *Revue* went into some detail, as follows:

Stage setting for Le Siège de Corinthe at the Opéra, Paris (1828).

(By courtesy of the Bibliothèque de l' Opéra, Paris.)

'Mme Démery did not consider that the judgment pronounced on her by the public and the critics should be accepted without appeal. Renouncing the rôle which she had played without success in *Moïse*, . . . she had hoped to be more fortunate in *Le Siège de Corinthe* and wanted to give that opera a trial. She thought that by omitting runs which could embarrass her, by reducing the *tempi* and by taking only the skeleton of the rôle, she would be more of a success. In this she was wrong. The very runs which she cannot achieve; the *fioriture* which for her are insurmountable obstacles; the rapid switches which she avoids – these are precisely what constitute the attraction of the music which she is striving in vain to sing. In fact, what she leaves out is the specific character of the music itself. One is tempted to believe that Mme. Démery was aiming at no more than a negative success; but in the theatre there is no middle way, one must either please or displease. Woe betide the performer who crosses the stage unnoticed: for such a person nothing can be done. Mme. Démery did not even achieve what she seemed to desire. There is something so painful in the efforts which she makes when she sings that the public cannot but suffer.

'I will refrain from analysing the effect which she produced in the various sections of the part. What could I say that is not already known in advance: some beautiful sounds, but in isolation. For the rest, no vocalisation nor phrasing at all. Finally, a total incapacity to sing Rossini's music, which is the only music now being sung at the Opéra.'

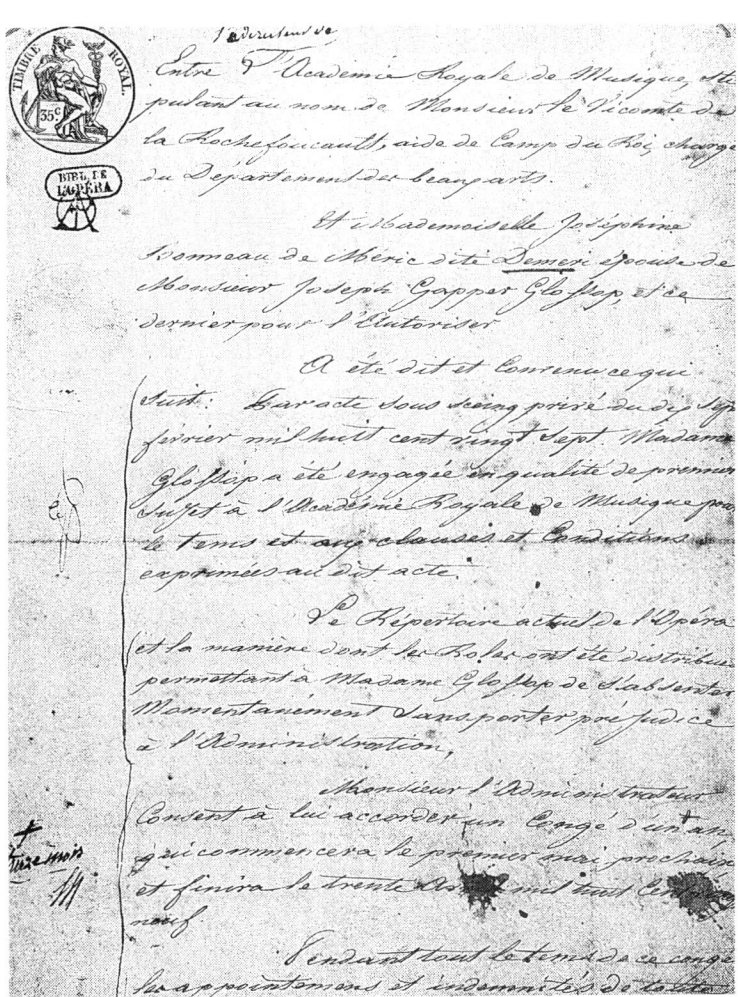

Joséphine, as Madame Glossop, granted leave of absence (1828).
(By courtesy of the Bibliothèque de l' Opéra.)

The critic on the *Revue Musicale* was none other than Fétis, Professor of Composition at the *Ecole Royale de Musique*. Drawing his distinction between 'beautiful sounds' and a 'beautiful voice', and stating that the latter required liaison between the various parts, he concluded that Joséphine had beautiful sounds but not a beautiful voice. According to Fétis, she suffered from a larynx which moved heavily in vocalisation and had a convulsive movement of the lower jaw which produced '*une intonation incertaine*'.

Almost alone, *Le Corsaire* spoke up for Joséphine. Despite certain prejudiced *dilettanti*, Mlle. Demeri had received some lively applause. Her voice did not possess all the flexibility of Cinti's; but 'we do not fear to maintain that it is more true and more resonant than any other on the stage in our time. Though she has some difficulty in interpreting Rossini's fiery and sometimes extravagant music, there is reason to hope that diligent study will soon place her among our very first *cantatrices*. Meanwhile she can render great service to the Administration, embarrassed by the disloyal flight of Mlle. Cinti and the pregnancy of Mme. Dabadie.' *Le Figaro* felt obliged to say that Mlle. Démeri had disappointingly not benefited, in her *méthode*, from her four years away. However, all the singers had suffered from the orchestra playing too loud.

The Administration, feeling that there was no alternative, had swallowed its pride and at great sacrifice had recalled that wayward nightingale, Madame Cinti-Damoreau. She returned to Paris in February 1828. With her support, it was hoped that it would at last be possible to put on Auber's *La Muette de Portici*.

Académie Royale de Musique – La Muette de Portici. Playbill for the return of Joséphine in April, 1831.
(By courtesy of Bibliothèque de l' Opéra, Paris.)

ACADEMIE ROYALE DE MUSIQUE.

Les Bureaux s'ouvriront à 7 heures. --- On commencera à 8 heures précises.
Aujourd'hui Vendredi 22 Avril 1831,

LA MUETTE
DE PORTICI,

Opéra en 5 actes, paroles de Mrs *Scribe* et *Germain Delavigne*, musique de M. *Auber*, divertissemens de M. *Aumer*, décorations de M. *Cicéri*, mise en scène de M. *Solomé*.

Mme DEMERIC–GLOSSOP fera sa rentrée par le rôle d'*Elvire*.

ACTEURS : Messieurs Dabadie, Prévost, Alexis, Ferdinand-Prévôt, Massol, Lafont, Pouilley; Mmes Noblet, Demeric-Glossop, Lorotte.

DANSE : Messieurs Albert, Ferdinand, Coulon, Barrez, Leblond, Capelle, Simon, Daumont; Mmes Julia, Elie, Buron, Alexis, Fourcisi, Leroux, Perceval, Louisa, Roland.

Dimanche 24 Avril, *pour le Départ de M. PAGANINI*, dernière représentation extraordinaire.

En attendant la 4e Représentation d'*EURIANTE*, Opéra en 3 actes.

Joséphine, meanwhile, had been giving some concert performances. She sang at the *Salle des Menus Plaisirs* on the same bill as an Italian prodigy on the violin. Then she was in the rue Chantereine, singing some arias before a select audience. On these occasions, according to the critic in *Revue Musicale*, she had had the good sense to choose music which suited her abilities and had given much more pleasure than in *Moïse* and the *Siège*. 'The duet from *La Vestale*, which she sang with Nourrit, proved that I was not mistaken when I said that the old repertoire would have suited this lady's voice much better than the new'. All the same, the critics in general considered that Joséphine's voice was not well adapted for singing in the relatively confined space of the concert room. *La Dilettante* (30 March 1828) complained that the duet from *La Vestale* was very hackneyed and needed to be sung in a much less dragging and dull way than it had been performed by Mlle. Demeri and Nourrit if it was to produce any effect. On the other hand, *Le Figaro* considered that the vocal honours at the concert were due to Mlle. Démeri. She had been more assured in the concert room than on the vast stage at the *Opéra*. Indeed 'she had rediscovered the talents of which a long illness had deprived her. She had had some fine moments in the duet from *Semiramide* and many of the judgments about her future career had been over-hasty.'

Clearly, Joséphine's failures in opera and the qualified success of her efforts in the concert rooms had caused much comment.

In the *Nouveau Journal de Paris*, *La Dilettante* expressed surprise that the Administration should have recalled her from Italy. They might easily have discovered, he maintained, that in Milan, Venice [sic] and the other towns where she had sung, she had not made any lasting mark and that her singing had not progressed in any way. *Habitués* would recall Joséphine as she had been in her initial *début* (1823). Then, her voice had been well-rounded, pure, wide-ranging and sonorous, though admittedly lacking in tone and sometimes in mellowness and even in daring. Despite imperfections, as Aménaïde in *Tancredi* she had succeeded in imparting strength and brilliance to certain of the passages. Then in the *Matrimonio Segreto* she had found the part which did her the greatest honour, one in which she had been far superior to Mlle. Sontag.

Now, though, she had become in some ways only a shadow of her former self. She had not improved in technique and 'that beautiful voice had lost all its freshness'. Her intonation had become stiff and laborious, uncertain and dragging. To hear her, one would think that she had perverted her talents 'by reciting in that French way of intoning which we Frenchmen complacently describe as music', an exercise which, over three or four years, makes a bad habit incurable. One can only suppose that instead of enriching her voice with the accents of the finest Italian compositions she had, on the contrary, persisted in singing in works of the hard, angular and jerky style of singing which is typical of *La Vestale*, making tiresome concessions to the prejudices and habits of 'a nation which, with unbelievable obstinacy, has always set its face against the charms of true melody'.

Mlle. Demeri, the critic went on, had failed completely in *Moïse* and had been hardly more happy or inspired in *Le Siège de Corinthe*. It was really distressing to see a young person fall in this way at the beginning of her singing career and 'I have not the courage to say how painfully I was affected by those two performances. I feel much more inclined to pity Mlle. Demeri than to offer her purposeless criticisms, since now the evil is beyond remedy'.

While it is plain that on her return Joséphine failed to satisfy the demands of her audiences, there is some ambiguity about the various explanations. Essentially, it would seem, despite her experience in Italy, she had reverted to a French style of singing which the French themselves had abandoned in the mania for Rossini.

The *Gazette de France* found it almost impossible to explain why *la jeune Alsacienne* seemed to have undergone such a complete metamorphosis. When she appeared in *Moïse*, she had perhaps been suffering from travel fatigue and had been overwhelmed by the solemnity of the occasion, the more so as *Moïse* was the chef d'oeuvre of the French lyric stage. After two months' rest, when she sang in *Le Siège de Corinthe*, there had certainly been an improvement, but she was still not *la petite Strasbourgeoise* who had rocketed from her native town with her superb voice, her youth and all her hopes. It was most strage that coming from Italy, the land of the roulades, it was in that very field that she was deficient. If only she had been given a rôle such as Iphigénie en Tauride.

There is almost certainly more to this sad story of Joséphine's return to Paris than meets the eye. In 1825 she had left Paris with hard feelings about the *Opéra* Administration and about what she regarded as the favouritism shown to certain singers. This cannot have been forgotten. Her provincial origins were unquestionably a disadvantage. Coming from remote half-German Strasbourg, she was certainly no Parisienne, nor did she have the cachet of being an actual foreigner, such as, of course, an Italian. She may well have had difficulty in switching from Italian to French. For whatever reasons, this was a time when she was not in good health and that alone could account for much.

Then there was Glossop. Her attachment to this rake of an Englishman will not have done anything to raise her standing in the French capital. Furthermore, this must have been the period when the personal strains in the relationship which were so soon to lead to their breakdown had begun to show themselves. In early 1828 high hopes had been dashed and Joséphine must have been in a mood which cannot but have affected her performance.

The outcome was that as early as April 1828 Madame de Méric Glossop was given a year's leave of absence, with permission to sing wherever she liked, in France or abroad, with the one exception of Paris.

This agreement, in which Joséphine is described as the wife of Joseph Gapper Glossop, states that the current repertoire at the *Opéra* and the manner in which the rôles had been distributed allow Madame Glossop to absent herself for a time without harm to the Administration. The leave would run from 1 May 1828 to 30 April 1829. During that period, Joséphine would cease to benefit from the financial terms of the Agreement of 17 February 1827, though in other respects it would be deemed to remain in force. She would however receive an indemnity of Fcs. 5,000, payable on 30 April 1828. The document is signed Joséphine Glossop née Deméric and countersigned (*apprové* [sic]) J. Glossop. A codicil stipulated that Madame Glossop would of course be allowed the necessary time to return.

This might have been the moment for Glossop to make an approach to the Opera in St. Petersburg, to see whether the lucrative offer allegedly made in April 1827 could be repeated, but no evidence has been found of any such move.

Six months earlier, Joséphine had already been thinking of a season in Lisbon and that is where she went, as *prima donna*, on 5 May 1828. She left with the *Nouveau Journal* wishing her more success than she had enjoyed in Italy and France. As a postscript to Joséphine's short season in Paris, it must be recorded that her presence had been almost entirely ignored by the *Journal des Débats*, an indifference which is a sad commentary on the impact which she had made - or failed to make.

LISBON 1828

As Josefa Glossop de Mery, Joséphine made her *début* in Lisbon at the *Real Teatro de São Carlo* on 19 June 1828 in the opera *Il Posto Abbandonato* (*Revue Musicale*).

This was one of the periods of high drama in the history of Portugal. Dom Miguel (1802-1866), third son of King John VI, had plotted in 1824 to overthrow the constitutional form of government granted by his father. The plot had failed and Dom Miguel had been banished. In 1826, John VI died and the throne devolved on Miguel's elder brother Pedro, Emperor of Brazil. Pedro, however, renounced his claim in favour of his daughter Maria, with Miguel as

Regent. The Regency decree had been promulgated in July 1827, but Dom Miguel was then in Vienna and he did not reach Lisbon till 22 February 1828. Then, he proceeded to dissolve parliament and convoke the traditional Cortes, which he packed with his own supporters. This subservient body offered Dom Miguel the crown which he took for himself on 4 July 1828.

As for *Il Posto Abbandonato*, the opera was well named. The auditorium had been almost empty. Most of the distinguished inhabitants of the capital had not ventured out for fear of being insulted by the populace. Frequent bursts of political feeling disturbed every opera performance and it was difficult to distinguish this from applause directed towards the artists.

Just a fortnight after Dom Miguel's coup, on 18 July, Joséphine appeared as Adele in Mercadante's *Adele e Emerico*, with the contralto Judith Schiroli as Captain Emerico Palmer.

Saverio Mercadante himself (1795-1870) was Director of the Royal Theatre in Lisbon at the time and Joséphine went on to sing the title rôle in his 'specially composed' tragic drama *Gabriella di Vergy* (8 August). Then on 29 September she once again took a title rôle, this time in an heroic drama called *Hypermnestra* which Mercadante had composed 'to celebrate that most auspicious occasion, the name day of His Majesty King Dom Miguel I.'

Unfortunately, Miguel's autocratic rule was far from auspicious for the musical life of Lisbon. The political tension caused by his usurpation and tyranny led to the virtual closure of the Opera between 1828 and 1833.

However, Joséphine had at least been given a benefit performance on 24 November, when she sang in Act I of *Elisa e Claudio* and in the last act of *Gabriella di Vergy*. *The Revue Musicale* records that on 8 December she sang in *Tancredi* with Mlle. Annette Calvi. The *Revue* said that Mme. Demeri had always given pleasure to the opera-lovers in Lisbon and the *Harmonicon* reported that the two favourite singers there at the time were Mlle. Demeri - now Madame Glossop - and the tenor Magnani.

This period was also one of crisis in the administration of the Royal Theatre. Mercadante was at daggers drawn with the leading singer Constancia Pietralia. She claimed to have been insulted by him and she had left the company in the early part of 1828 after publicly announcing in the *Gazeta de Lisboa* why she was declining to renew her contract. The impresario, Marrara, had engaged Joséphine, but his own contract had expired in September and it was only after some acrimony that Joséphine's contract was transferred to the new impresario, Madame Bruni.

The Portuguese Government closed the theatre on 18 December and the singers left for Madrid, Barcelona and Italy (*Revue Musicale*).

Joséphine, however, went to Cadiz, where she sang in the world première of Mercadante's *La Rappresaglia*.

The postscript to Joséphine's tour in Lisbon is that the Archives of the Paris *Opéra* record that in June 1831 a merchant in Lisbon had applied to have Fcs. 15,963.80 of Joséphine's fees blocked, claiming that she owed him that sum.

PARIS AGAIN (1829-1831)

Joséphine's twelve-month leave of absence having expired at the end of May 1829, she returned to Paris. Somewhat unaccountably, the authorities at the *Opéra* had apparently not expected her to come back. They did not go out of their way to smooth her path. She was once again called upon to appear in *Le Siège de Corinthe* and according to the Administration she was as unsuccessful as before. Nevertheless, she seems to have remained with the *Opéra* for eight months after her return, until the end of 1829, though this may have included the four months' holiday with pay to which she was entitled.

During the Summer of 1829, the Administration were pressing Glossop to come to a definitive agreement with them about Joséphine. They wanted her either to agree to sing rôles in their new repertoire or to accept an arrangement whereby she would retire from the *Opéra* altogether. The Glossops resisted this and the outcome was that Joséphine was once again given a year's leave of absence, this time with the higher indemnity of Fcs. 6,000. Thus, she found herself with leave of absence till the end of 1830.

(In 1829, the subsidy allotted to the *Théâtre Italien* had been reduced, but the Director, Monsieur Laurent, had been authorised to take his company to London during the Summer Season. London being a financial Mecca, this gave the singers much encouragement and led to the appearance in London of Malibran, Sontag, Donzelli and others. Joséphine, however, did not go to London until 1832.)

Much remains to be discovered about the lives of both Glossop and Joséphine in 1830.

From the Court hearing in 1831, it seems that Joséphine had had an agreement to sing in Madrid in 1830. If this is so, she presumably went there from Cadiz before returning to Paris. She and Glossop must presumably have been together at the beginning of 1830 because their daughter Emilie was born in October of that year.

In mid-October, *Le Corsaire* had announced the return of 'Madame Glossop de Méric' who had had such a brilliant début 'ten years earlier'. The paper pointed out that she had had a contract with the *Académie Royale de Musique* for a long time and was not alone in complaining about the 'absurd system' whereby the Administration engaged famous artists and then, once they had made their *début*, forced them to 'rest'. Mme de Glossop [sic] had been joined in complaint about this by Mme Baptiste-Quiney, who in a whole year had only been given a chance to sing twice.

In Paris, Madame Glossop served a writ on Monsieur Lubbert for two months' arrears of fees (November and December 1830). The defendant somewhat testily complained that she had come back 'extremely promptly' as soon as her leave had expired. Be that as it may, when the case was heard before the *Tribunal de Commerce* the result was a complete success for Joséphine, who duly received Fcs. 4,166 from the Administration of the *Opéra*.

1831 proved to be a critical year for Joséphine, both for her family and her career.

Above all, she now had her young baby, but her marriage must have already been running into trouble. On 3 May her father died, in his home town of Strasbourg, the declarant being Joséphine's youngest brother, Eugène Victor, who took over from his father at the school. He was described as being a Catholic. The eldest of her brothers, Hector Alexandre, was married on 25 May in Dôle, Jura, to Marie Louise Prévost.

Joséphine was in Paris in February 1831, when she sang at a concert in the *Salle Taitbout* in aid of Belgian refugees.

On the opera stage, at the end of April, Joséphine made one final attempt to retrieve her fortunes in Paris. Alas, without success. Her rentrée was in Auber's *La Muette de Portici*. The opera itself, based on the insurrection in Naples in 1647, involves mass scenes of rioting and an eruption of Vesuvius. It was hailed as a masterpiece and was indeed the first, in date, of the grandiose operas characteristic of the French theatre in the middle of the nineteenth century. With its libretto by Scribe and Delavigne, it had received its première at the *Opéra* in February 1828, featuring Cinti and Nourrit. It was revived at the Ravenna Festival in 1991.

Le Figaro of 23 April 1831 reviewed Joséphine's performance in *La Muette de Portici* on the previous evening in the most dismissive terms.

The critic began by calling to mind that his ears had taken six months to recover from a cruel sound with which they had been struck by Madame Glossop one evening, years before, at the *Théâtre Italien*. By now, surely, all that would have changed. Alas, no. There was not the slightest sign of any improvement. She still had her splendid voice, but there were times when she produced with it the most risky, yelping, uncertain and piercing notes - like those which Paganini drew from the highest string of his violin 'only far less accurate'.

As the Spanish Princess Elvira in *La Muette de Portici*, Joséphine had sung the cavatina 'as she sings everything'. She had been given the encouragement of rounds of applause. Yet she could not be said to have had a success, not in a theatre which called for genuine talent such as was being displayed by Mme Damoreau and Mme Dorus. 'If she does not manage to master the voice which is mastering her and abjure the bizarre taste which delights in the most unmelodious shrieking, she will be completely abandoned by the public'.

Joséphine's performance did not satisfy either the public or the Administration, which by the Summer of 1831 had come under the direction of the reforming Monsieur Véron. This change had followed the July Revolution of 1830 and the accession of Louis Philippe. When Véron took up the reins at the *Opéra*, he had claimed the right, on his own personal authority, to break an agreement which had been in force for four consecutive years. On this basis, he discontinued payments to Joséphine and this not surprisingly led to a second case brought by Madame Démeri Glossop before the *Tribunal de Commerce*.

This was in October 1831. Maître Victor Augier appeared for Joséphine. He argued that she should be paid Fcs. 8,333.33 in respect of the four preceding months, without prejudice to future emoluments. He maintained, with some eloquence, that his client had earned a brilliant reputation at the Italian Opera in Paris, after which she had sung in the theatre in Milan. Admittedly, when she returned to Paris, her *début* had been unfortunate, but this was because the part of Anaï in *Moïse* did not suit her voice. Instead of being given the means of recovering from this, her first reverse, she had been subjected to endless vexations. Madame Démeri-Glossop, said Maître Augier, embodied the methods of the great masters. She enjoyed the esteem of men such as Paër and Rossini. Distinguished composers had written no fewer than eight operas for her, in Italy, Spain and Portugal. She was not successful at the *Académie Royale de Musique* simply beause she was not given parts which suited her abilities. Instead, the Administration had preferred to give her leaves of absence, with greater or lesser indemnities.

The case was complicated by the administrative changes at the *Académie* which had followed the July Revolution. Responsibility had been transferred from the *Département des Beaux-Arts*, which had been under the control of the *Maison du Roi*, to the Ministry of Public Works. Maître Augier argued that the change had been on the clear understanding that the new Director (M. Véron) would honour the undertakings which had been duly entered into by his predecessors. The Agreement with Madame Démeri-Glossop, he maintained, had been approved by the persons who were entitled, at the time, to represent the *Académie* and to engage her. The Agreement was therefore valid. In any event, the advocate claimed, the Royal Household had not been released from their obligations. The Agreement had been signed by the Vicomte de la Rochefoucauld, aide-de-camp to the King, responsible for the *Département des Beaux-Arts*, and by Monsieur Duplantis in his capacity as Administrator of the *Opéra*. On these grounds alone, the *Liste Civile* must be in debt to the singer.

The case for Monsieur Véron was presented by Maître de Vatimesnil. He took the line that the February 1827 Agreement was null and void because it had not been signed by Monsieur Lauriston, then Minister of the Royal Household. He alone, and not the Vicomte de Larochefoucauld, had been entitled to commit the *Liste Civile*. Furthermore, according to the defence, the Agreement was invalid because under the regulations of the *Opéra* a *premier sujet* was not entitled to more than Fcs. 10,000 in fixed fees, and Madame Glossop had been granted Fcs. 25,000. This was an irregularity which made it impossible to allow the contract with the singer to continue any longer. M. Véron was indeed duty bound to terminate an arrangement which was invalid in two capital respects.

Maître Vatimesnil then proceeded to argue that even if the Agreement were valid in every way, the fact remained that Madame Démeri was simply not able to fulfil the obligations imposed on her. As a singer, she might have a talent for Italian songs, but she had none for French ones. Her failures in *Moïse* and the *Siège de Corinthe* had led to her being granted successive leaves of absence because the Administration could see no way of making use of her. She herself had declared that she could not sing in new operas and did not want any rôles except those of the type of *La Vestale* [Gasparo Spontini's opera with libretto by the French lyric poet de Jouy which had been a triumph when first produced in Paris in 1807]. But the *Opéra* could not rely for its repertoire on out-of-date works. Mme. Démeri, under the terms of the contract, had to sing twice a week. The *Opéra* gave only three performances a week, so they would be obliged each week to put on two old works. Such a situation was totally unacceptable. Thus on all counts the plaintiff's claims should be rejected.

The Tribunal retired for more than an hour and then pronounced a judgment which went a long way towards vindicating Joséphine's case. It was decided that she was entitled to regard her Agreement with the *Opéra* as valid and definitive. If it were otherwise, her confidence would have been betrayed.

Further, the Tribunal declared that under his covenants with the Ministry of Public Works, M. Véron had most certainly undertaken to comply with the Agreements previously concluded.

On the other hand, Madame Glossop's performances had not fulfilled the expectations of the Administration or indeed of the artist herself. By seeking and obtaining two successive leaves of absence, she had recognised that she could not be usefully employed on the *Opéra* stage. From correspondence subsequent to the expiry of the leaves of absence it had become apparent that she was not disposed to play all the parts assigned to her and hence could not fulfil her contract.

Accordingly, the Tribunal pronounced that the Agreement was annulled as from 1 October 1831, but M. Véron was to pay Madame Glossop the Fcs. 8,333.33 due to her for the four months June-September inclusive. He was also sentenced to pay the costs. (Véron may indeed have lost this case, but in all fairness it must be noted that in the informed opinion of M. Fétis of the *Revue Musicale*, he was the most active and intelligent man who had ever presided over the Paris *Opéra*).

Thus ended what is known as the Affaire Glossop. It had been a strange business and one which seems to be somewhat out of character with the rest of Joséphine's life. True, she was always alert to her financial interests, but at this period she was under the influence of Glossop. He acted as her agent. It was he, no doubt, who had arranged for her to be given the exceptionally high salary which was to become the source of so much dispute. It is more than probable that Glossop relied on his wife for money. Paid leaves of absence would also be very convenient when pregnancies were to be expected. Glossop, as we know, had already had experience of litigation and he was likely to be in a position to judge whether a case by Joséphine against the *Opéra* stood a good chance of succeeding.

The stark truth is that between 1827 and 1831, in Paris, Joséphine was a failure.

This may have been due in some degree to personal hostility and to the jealousy aroused by her high fees. The atmosphere at the *Opéra* seems never to have been congenial to her. However, if her performances had pleased the audiences, the Administration would have been under pressure to retain her in the casts. As it was, they were happy to see her go. She was felt to be *passée* and that, in Paris, was unforgivable.

As Ernest Legouvé put it, by the 1830s the Romantic Movement had thrown a dark shadow over the literary and musical lions of the First Empire such as Jouy and Spontini. Malibran had appeared, to supplant with her spontaneity and effervescence the classical dignity and nobility of Pasta. Yet could it be that Joséphine was ahead of her time? Stendhal, so far from regarding her as old-fashioned, declared that she was a true Wagnerian born half a century too early.

From comments made at various stages in her career, it is clear that Joséphine's voice had a distinctive, instrument-like quality which either charmed or repelled. In Paris, the early gasps of surprise and delight had given way to bored distaste. In Italy, she had achieved much success and there was more to come.

On Joséphine's voice, a revealing but undated document in the *Opéra* Library signed 'Jacques Meyerbeer' states that following Joséphine's performance in *La Muette de Portici*, Véron had asked Meyerbeer to give her an audition to see whether she should be asked to take the part of Alice in Meyerbeer's opera *Robert le Diable*. The composer had replied that he was not in favour of the suggestion because the character of the rôle did not seem to him 'to suit the individuality of the talent of Madame Glossop'. However before long, in London, Meyerbeer was to find himself coaching her for the very part of Alice.

The break with the *Opéra* in October 1831, which was final, forced Joséphine to seek her fortune elsewhere.

Members of the *Opéra* company had already blazed a trail in London and it was there that Joséphine was to spend the following two years. In London, she was to show no hesitation in accepting new rôles, and she indeed soon gained the reputation of being a willing horse and a most amenable member of whatever operatic company she joined.

The document signed by Jacques Meyerbeer, 1831.
(By courtesy of the Bibliœthèque de l' Opéra.)

92

Le Corsaire (24 April 1831) paid a somewhat melancholy farewell tribute to Joséphine in Paris. There were voices, it wrote, for which certain parts were altogether unsuited. Lablache could never sing Lindoro nor Bordogni Mustapha. Mme Glossop should never have tried to sing the part of Elvira in *La Muette de Portici*. The Administration had been at fault in condemning a voice like Joséphine's to a year or more of rest. That had jeopardised her reputation because her voice needed for its development a great auditorium with an orchestra to give it support and guidance. If a man accustomed to playing real tennis in a wide open court were confined to a small garden, he would hit the ball right across a dozen neighbouring walls.

On 22 April, Mme Glossop's admirable, resonant voice had started well, but very soon the singer had betrayed signs of surprise that her intonation was proving false and that she had misjudged her voice's carrying power. Yet, whenever she got everything right, her voice vibrated in the most magnificent way and one was left regretting that her great abilities were not being harnessed for some grandly dramatic rôle. With a good mentor, from the early days at the *Théâtre Italien*, she might have become another Catalani. *Habitués* of the *Bouffes* would recall her first appearance in *L'Italiana in Algeri* and the rounds of applause which greeted her first *cavatina*.

We are tempted, *Le Corsaire* went on, to ask Mme Glossop what she hopes to achieve at the *Opéra*. There had been a time when Rossini and Auber wrote music to suit the voices of the male and female singers there. Then, Mme Glossop had been away. The current régime of *roulades* would never suit her. Let her persist in cultivating 'one of the richest voices which we have ever heard. The public might well return to Gluck as it had formerly returned to Racine's *Athalie*.' However, by 6 May, the part of Elvira had been entrusted to a Mlle. Jawureck and Joséphine's operatic career in Paris was at an end. She had sung just twice in *La Muette* (the statutory minimum) and probably no more than four times during the whole period from 1827 to 1831.

By this time, too, the finances of the Glossop *ménage* were in a parlous state. A series of creditors had made claims against any monies to be paid by the *Opéra* to Joséphine and she had been obliged to submit to deductions from her fees. These, however, had been substantial. The Personnel Registers of the *Académie de Musique* record that in each of the years 1828 and 1829 Joséphine was paid a total of Fcs. 16,000 (*traitement* Fcs. 10,000 plus *gratification annuelle* of Fcs. 6,200). In addition there were the so-called *feux*, the fees payable in respect of each actual performance. For Joséphine the *feu* was Fcs. 50 and she had a guarantee of at least eight *feux* per month. She never sang more than twice in any month so her *feux* regularly amounted to Fcs. 400 for every month in which she was engaged. In

1828, for January to April, the *feux* were Fcs. 1,600, less deductions of Fcs. 40 per month. In 1829, similarly, she received Fcs. 2,400, for May to October, subject however to only one deduction of Fcs. 40. In 1830, Joséphine's *feux* amounted to only Fcs. 800, but in 1831 she was given Fcs. 2,000 (for January to May).

When Glossop married Joséphine, Elizabeth Féron had left Italy and returned to England. Before we follow the next stage in Joséphine's life, which proved also to be in England, it will be in place to give an account of the brief spell which Féron had in London in 1827-1828.

CHAPTER 8

Elizabeth Féron in England, 1827-1828

FERON'S re-appearance on the London stage had excited some high expectations, but these were to be somewhat disappointed. She was found to be 'of no school' and to have failed to bring her Italian experience to bear on her English performances. Her voice was described by one critic as having a wide range without being very agreeable.

From an article in the *Chronicle* of 8 November 1827, it appears that Madame Fearon Glossop [sic] made overtures to both Covent Garden and Drury Lane. Drury Lane engaged her 'at a salary reported to be so large in amount as to stagger belief' (*The Quarterly Musical Magazine and Review*). This was said to be no less than £40 a night. The same magazine expressed the opinion that Madame Fearon was one of a vocal corps of females at Drury Lane 'almost unequalled'. Others were the two Misses Paton, Mrs. Bedford and Miss Grant.

The Post reported on 4 December that there had been a distinguished company to witness the return of Mme. Féron to the English boards and *The Times* records that she gave a series of performances at Drury Lane lasting until April 1828.

The opera in which Elizabeth signalled her return to London was a pastiche of Storace's *Pirates* called *Isidore de Merida, or The Devil's Creek* (29 November 1827). The music was by various hands including not only Stephen Storace but Mercadante and Braham. The scene is set in Malta and Féron played the comic part of a lively waiting-woman. According to *The Times*, she was the principal attraction of the evening. Some years ago, the critic wrote, 'this lady appeared at Covent Garden Theatre, and she has since acquired considerable fame at the Royal Theatre of San Carlos at Naples. Her reception must have been exceedingly gratifying to her feelings. She possesses very considerable powers of voice, but her tones are sharp and wiry; they want that fulness and richness, in the absence of which it is vain, in serious songs, to hope for deep expression. She made nothing of Storace's exquisitely pathetic air of *Lullaby*; but in several compositions of a livelier character she exhibited great brilliancy of execution. Indeed, her object seemed to be rather to surprise by a display of science than to charm by a development of feeling. She was loudly encored in one of her airs, and also in a humorous duet with Mr. Harley, which her acting, not less than her singing served to embellish. Her last effort was a Neapolitan melody, with most difficult variations, which she executed with uncommon spirit. Her execution on her upper notes was remarkably clear and brilliant. The Neapolitan melody, after all, though it was encored, "plays round the head, but comes not near the heart." Mrs. Feron's acting throughout was full of vivacity. Her manner reminded us of that of the late Madame Storace, whom she considerably resembles in stature and bulk. Mr. Braham was in good voice . . . .'

In fairness to Madame Féron, it is to be noted that in *La Belle Assemblée* of January 1828, the critic said that she showed at times an undercurrent of melody and feeling which rescued her from the charge of being merely a scientific singer.

After the opera had been repeated, in an abridged form, *The Times* forecast that much of the music would become popular. The opera ran to eighteen performances and both Braham and Féron were 'greatly applauded and encored'.

Drury Lane, meanwhile, had also put on *The Cabinet* and *The Turkish Lovers*, in both of which Braham and Féron appeared. On 30 January, the Anniversary of the Death of King Charles the Martyr, the annual concert in 1828 included a selection of classical vocal pieces 'tastefully arranged by Mr. Bishop on the lines of the Lent Oratorios'. Pasta was the great attraction. She and Féron elicited great applause in the letter duet from *The Marriage of Figaro*, and Pasta also obliged with *Di tanti palpiti*. Unfortunately, Féron's rendering of a *rondeau* by Donizetti had been a total failure (*Revue Musicale*).

In March and April, Féron performed at Drury Lane as Mandane in Thomas Arne's *Artaxerxes*, in *The Castle of Andalusia* and in *The Prize*. She also took part in several concerts, e.g. one at the Guildhall on 13 February 1828 in aid of refugees from Italy and Spain and one at the King's Theatre in April.

The critics had not quite known what to make of the 'new' Elizabeth Féron. *The Quarterly Musical Magazine and Review* was impressed by her versatility. 'She flies with incalculable rapidity and precision of intonation through the most difficult passages, and sings two octaves of semitones, ascending or descending with the utmost apparent ease and certainty.' Furthermore, she possessed 'a flexibility and compass which have been very rarely attained and perhaps never exceeded.' She could sing soft or pour forth a swelling body of tone. Yet 'the intermediate quantity upon which the artist must rely for general use is not at her command. Her *mezzo forte* is infirm and tremulous . . . .' The critic concluded that over-exertion of her voice in her early career was to blame and that she did well, in her predicament, to cultivate and display to the utmost her facility of execution and her adaptation of ornament. As an actress she was of the first class, 'though she fails to move the affections in the degree which characterises the great singer'. This was penned, be it remembered, during the height of the Romantic Movement.

Meanwhile a great tragedy had befallen Féron and her family.

Theatre Royal, Drury Lane;
To-morrow, THURSDAY March 27, 1828,
His Majesty's Servants will perform the Opera of

ARTAXERXES;

Artaxerxes	Miss I. PATON;
Arbaces,	Miss LOVE,
Artabanes	Mr. BRAHAM;
Remines,	Mr. VARNOLD;
Mandane....[*first time*]....	Madame FERON;
Semira,	Miss A. TREE.

In Act 2.—The celebrated Composition,
"MILD AS THE MOONBEAMS,"
By Mr. BRAHAM, Miss A. TREE, Miss I. PATON, Miss LOVE, and Madame FERON;

After which (*Second Time at this Theatre*) the Farce of

Too Late for Dinner

Mr. Pincroft, Mr. W. BENNETT, Frederick Popple on, Mr. MUDE;
Nicholas Twili,............Mr. LISTON,
Frank Poppleton........Mr. JONES;
Rafter, Mr. SHERWIN. Monsieur Fumet, Mr. GATTIE,
Tailor, Mr. HONNOR; Gardener, Mr. FENTON,
John, Mr. E. Vining, Marker, Mr. Darnley Gentleman, Mr. Eaton;
Mrs. Thompson, Mrs. C. JONES
Emily, Miss E. TREE, Eliza, Miss I. PATON;
Letty, Mrs. ORGER. Maid, Miss WESTON;

To which will be added, the Popular Grand Serious Pantomime of The

O B I;
Or Three-Finger'd Jack

Produced under the Direction of Mr. W. BARRYMORE.
The Scenery Painted by Messrs. STANFIELD, ANDREWS, and MARINARI;
Three-Finger'd Jack. Mr. BROWNE,
Captain Orford, Mr. HOWELL, Planter, Mr. DARNLEY, Overseer, Mr. VARNOLD;
Tuckey, Master WIELAND, Quashee, Mr. WEBSTER, Sam, Mr. BARNES,
Negro Robbers---Messrs. Hope, Brown, Brady, Smith;
Slaves---Messrs. Robinson, Walsh, Beale, East, Eaton, Henshaw, E. Vining, Jones, Tolkien, Green;
Mesdames Gliddon, Willmott, Willmott, Webster, Wills, Munro, Rummens, Anderson,
Benston, Campbell.
Quashee's Child, Miss LANE, Sam's Child, Master LANE,
Rosa,............Mrs. BARRYMORE.
Quashee's Wife, Miss A. TREE, Sam's Wife, Miss GOULD,
Obi Woman, Mr. BARTLETT,
Dancing Negros—Mesdames Valancy, Carty, Wells, Gear, Blackford, Purton.

O B I; or, Three-Finger'd Jack,
Was received, on its revival, with the strongest marks of Approbation, and will be repeated
To-morrow and *Saturday.*

Mrs. DUFF,
Having been received with the kindest approbation, due notice will be given of her next appearance.

On Friday, there will be no Performance.
On Saturday, The CASTLE of ANDALUSIA. Alphonso, Mr. Braham, Pedrillo, Mr. Harley;
Lorenza, Madame Feron. With The PRIZE. Lenitive, Mr. Harley, Label, Mr. J. Russell,
Caroline, Madame Feron. And O B I; or, THREE-FINGER'D JACK.
For the Benefit of Madame FERON.
[*Being the last Night of the Company's performing till the Holidays.*]
A new Afterpiece, with new SCENERY, DRESSES, &c. will be produced on *Easter Monday*; to be called,

MONKEYANA;
Or, The Dumb Savoyard.

The public had been informed that the New Royal Brunswick Theatre would open on Monday, 25 February 1828 in Goodman's Fields in Stepney, with a performance of *The Mermaid's Well* or *The Fatal Prophecy*. Fatal Prophecy indeed.

Three days later, at about 11.45 a.m. on Thursday 28 February, while a rehearsal was in progress, the roof, which was of iron, fell in and nothing was left of the splendid edifice but 'a mass of frightful ruins'.

There was a long list of dead and injured. The dead were found in a most horrible state of mutilation.

At the inquest which opened at the Court House in Wellclose Square on 1 March, it was established that eleven persons had been killed, including Miss Mary Ann Fearon, 'a sister of Elizabeth Fearon [sic] (Mrs. Glossop).' The girl was described as a 14- or 15-year-old dancer, living with her widowed mother at No. 41, Wellclose Square. According to the *Weekly Despatch*, Mary Ann was a fine young woman who had been engaged as leader of the ballet. She had been one of the first sufferers brought to the watch-house and 'her corpse presented a most frightful spectacle, her head being literally severed in two, and it was with some difficulty that her features could

The collapse of the New Brunswick Theatre.

(By courtesy of the Theatre Museum, The Victoria and Albert Museum.)

be recognised by her friends.' The body had been officially identified by Elizabeth Andrews, 'servant to Miss Fearon.'

It is clear from the newspaper reports that several members of the Féron family had only just managed to escape with their lives. Survivors who had been at the rehearsal spoke of Elizabeth's brother, the conductor of the orchestra, her mother and three sisters apart from Mary Ann.

At the Greater London Register Office there are records of the Inquisitions (Inquests) held on four of the victims of the Brunswick Theatre disaster, but that of Mary Ann Féron has not survived. The jurors declared their opinion that the proprietors were highly reprehensible in allowing the heavy weights, which caused the fall of the roof, to have been attached to it.

The Morning Post of 3 March 1828 contains such a vivid first-hand account of the catastrophe that it cries out to be reproduced, the more so as it throws light on religious attitudes at the time.

The Reverend Mr. Smith, a Cornishman, was one of the first on the scene. He had been sitting alone in the Mariners' Church when he was told of the crash of the theatre.

'I came over immediately, and conceiving it to be my duty to prove that I was humanely concerned for the bodies of my fellow-creatures, as well as religiously interested in the salvation of their immortal souls, I ran up Grace's Alley, and in a moment was in Well's-Street. The scene was tremendously awful. The whole of this immense pile of building was, in one minute, a heap of ruins. The neighbourhood was in the utmost alarm and terror, running they knew not where, for the fall was like the shock of an earthquake.'

The priest worked indefatigably himself and 'having been accustomed to command in the navy, in time of great danger' he supervised a score of sailors and others in the work of searching for survivors and taking the injured to hospital. However, the reverend gentleman could not banish the thought that the Theatre, now destroyed, 'would have been fatal to the morals of thousands in a neighbourhood too densely populated, and too mightily depraved not to attract attention by every thinking man in the metropolis.' He could not but reflect, 'when working about the ruins, and the dead bodies, that so extraordinary had been the haste to put up this Theatre, that even . . . the hallowed Sabbath had been forgotten, and the sound of labour heard . . . .' However, God had shown great mercy: 'Had the Almighty . . . permitted the roof to have continued until eight o'clock at night . . . perhaps one thousand immortal souls would suddenly have been launched, unprepared . . . for an eternal world'.

On the mundane level, the disaster had attracted such huge crowds that troops had to be called in to keep the peace. Pickpockets were quickly on the scene, too, and both the workmen and some of the unprincipled visitors took advantage of the confusion to carry away every small article of value that they were able to lay their hands on.

Elizabeth stayed only a short time in England. Her last appearance may well have been as Despina in an English version of *Così Fan Tutte* called *Tit for Tat* which was performed in the Summer of 1828 at the Lyceum Theatre in the Strand. No evidence has been found to explain why she left, but the events of 1827 and 1828 cannot but have had a very unsettling effect. No doubt money will have been an important factor. Even when she had been with Glossop she had followed her own career and now she also had to provide for her three-year-old son, Augustus. It seems most probable that she was not offered lucrative engagements in London.

Be that as it may, she betook herself with Augustus to America, where she and Madame Mangeon, said to be one of her sisters, played a seminal rôle in introducing Italian opera to audiences in the United States. This will be reviewed in a later chapter.

CHAPTER

9 *Joséphine in England: operas in 1832*

IT would be natural to suppose that Joséphine's English husband, with his long-standing theatrical connexions, would have played a major part in introducing her to the London stage. Possibly he had, but so far not a shred of evidence to that effect has come to light. On the contrary, from 1832 Joseph Glossop seems to have disappeared completely from Joséphine's life. She ceased to use the surname Glossop and it must have been in her interest to distance herself from a man who was not only suspected of bigamy but was well on the way towards appearing in the Bankruptcy Court. No doubt, too, she wanted to keep the money she earned for herself.

Joséphine made her *début* in England on 4 February 1832 at the opening of the season of Italian and German opera at the King's Theatre. With her linguistic abilities she was a member of both the Italian and German casts.

The King's Theatre had been under the management of the actor Pierre Laporte (1799-1841) since 1828, and he was to resume control from 1833-41, but for the 1832 Season the opera there was effectively under the direction of the enthusiastic but over-ambitious Monck Mason.

He had engaged an impressive list of singers. Apart from de Méric (from the *Académie Royale*, Paris), there were Grisi, Tosi, Schroeder-Devrient, Cinti-Damoreau, Baptiste and Grandolfi. The men included Donzelli, Tamburini, B. Winter, L. Mariani, V. Galli, Arnaud, Arrigotti, Adolphe Nourrit and Levasseur. The orchestra was under the direction of Spagnoletti.

The season had opened with high hopes. In the end, it proved somewhat disappointing, partly, it seems, because Monck Mason could not make full use of all the talent which he had assembled.

As for Joséphine, she was singled out by the *Spectator* in April as the most gifted of all the singers. Giving the lie to her detractors in Paris, she was to take no fewer than fourteen major parts in the operas in London between February and July 1832.

Her performances are fully documented in the publications of the period and the problem is one of selection.

Detailed reports on operas and concerts were a regular feature of the newspapers and magazines of the time and this reflected the important place which serious music held in society in the nineteenth century. Unlike today, however, almost no attention was paid to the private lives of the artists and even their personality and appearance often received only passing mention. The English press in 1832 was silent about Joséphine having a husband and a daughter. When Joséphine came to London, Emilie was a baby of only fifteen months and is known to have been with her mother.

For the 1832 season, the King's Theatre had been redecorated, with lavish use of the fashionable Adelaide green (so named after the consort of Willian IV) and opera-goers were promised 'a greater abundance of novelty and variety than they have of late been accustomed [to]'.

Unfortunately, the first work chosen, the *opera seria L'Esule di Roma* (The Exile from Rome) did not find much critical or popular favour. The *Observer* regretted that the season should have opened with a work by that 'milk-and-water composer' Donizetti, 'who was nearly unknown in this country but has obtained much applause in Italy, especially in Naples.'

The opera had had its *première* in Naples in 1828 and had not been heard in England before. The story is of love by the heroine, Argelia, for Septimus who had been banished by the Emperor Tiberius. Joséphine played the part of Argelia.

The critic of the *Spectator* attended the final rehearsal. After praising the band [orchestra], he had good words to say about Madame de Méric:

> 'The lady is a delightful singer; her organ clear and melodious, and of sufficient power; her style pure and well cultivated; and her intonation good. Such a singer, Laporte would have announced with a flourish of trumpets; but Mr. Mason has chosen to let the talents of all his performers speak for themselves, and thus to impose upon English critics and the English public the task of thinking and judging for themselves'.

As for Joséphine's appearance, the *Morning Advertiser* went so far as to say that her figure was petite, her demeanour ladylike and her countenance capable of considerable expression.

The *Morning Post* said:

> 'Of the new singers we are bound to speak first of the Lady, Madame de Méric. Her name, we believe, had been unheard in this country, and the Manager engaged her

upon the sole recommendation of her talents, without that of fame. He has done right, for she is an acquisition, and will be popular. Her voice is of the beautiful round, full Italian quality, which never fails to delight. Her intonation is generally true, and she possesses sufficient power and considerable compass. Her school is not of the most finished, nor has she much facility of execution; but the great beauty of the voice would cover greater imperfections than these'.

The *Times* made the point that Madame Méric [sic] was making her *début* on the English stage and was not to be confused with Madame Méric Lalande who had often been seen on it. The paper described her as a native of France who would seem, from her style of singing, and the method of managing her voice, 'which was till lately so peculiar to France, to have received her musical education in that country.' The critic went on:

'Her voice is a clear soprano, to which the higher notes are more easily accessible than the lower ones. She went up to D above the lines without any apparent effort or any diminution of tone; but power is not a remarkable quality of her voice, nor flexibility. Her style, however, is pure, and her execution very accurate'.

The critic on the *Morning Chronicle* was the least enthusiastic. He forecast, with regret, that Madame de Méric's *début* did not afford the promise of her long filling the place of first woman at the King's Theatre to the satisfaction of the public. Although her voice was a high soprano, clear, sound and strong in some of the notes, it was generally of 'a quality not pleasing'. Where she scored was in the ascent of her scale and the force and steadiness of her high notes. She had sung her cavatina '*Tardi, tardi*' in the last act with much spirit and animation, though she lacked 'those personal advantages which would be necessary to make a very effective actress'. Her execution was criticised for want of agility, especially in the divisions. However, after he had attended some further performances, the same critic found himself able to praise Joséphine's powers as an actress, declaring ' . . . we do not despair of her profiting by a better occasion [than the 'wearisome' *Esule di Roma*] for their development.' The *United Kingdom* described her person as 'highly interesting, rather petite, but commanding in style and grace.'

In general, the first impressions which Joséphine made on the London critics were favourable. Almost all went into some detail. The highbrow *Atlas* commented as follows:

'Madame De Méric appears to us an excellent musician, and a singer whose good sense and judgment are evident in all she executes. The tone of her voice, which is rich and full, is little fitted to excel in the ornamental style, and she does not take distances with the rapidity and unerring precision to which some late singers of German training have accustomed us. But this lady has the soul of a singer; in the feeling of her *appogiature*, the exactitude of her time, the delicacy of her style, and her general truth of intonation, the superficial accomplishments of the artist are forgotten. One surprising interval in a cadenza of Madame De Méric deserves to be recorded as a remarkably bold and successful attempt; this was a descent from the D above the staff to the C below it, a distance of two octaves and a note . . . '

Describing Joséphine as a middle-aged French lady who had acquired the Italian style of singing, the *Athenaeum* spoke of her having a *voce di testa*, of an agreeable quality, extending to the C and D in alt. Although she lacked flexibility, she had successfully indulged in staccato passages of intervals in thirds, sixths and octaves, at the close of an aria, which from their novelty and perfect execution had elicited much applause.

The *Harmonicon* remarked that Madame de Meric was better known in Paris as Mlle. Demeri (not, be it noted, as Madame Glossop). She had a clear voice, not deficient in power, sang well in tune, attempted few *roulades*, perpetrated no runs or half-notes and seemed to be, what French singers generally were, a good musician. 'In person, she is of middle size, and in action free from all blame.'

Finally, to sum up the first impressions in London, here is the *Observer* of 5 February:

'All the principal artists,' it wrote, 'were new to this country . . . and we will speak of them in the order of merit, beginning with the *prima donna* . . . . Madame de Meric . . . is a woman of a lady-like figure, expressive features, and easy deportment; her voice is clear and harmonious, but not of much power or extraordinary compass, and her style of singing is pure and chaste, and remarkably free from everything like tawdry ornament: she never astonishes, but always satisfies; and good musical judges would be more apt to praise her more highly than the public at large would think she deserves. The music she had to sing was not of difficult execution, and we doubt if her voice would be sufficiently flexible for some of the most popular music of Rossini. She failed but once, when she endeavoured to strain her voice to reach a note above her compass, for although she did stretch to it afterwards, it was with considerable effort, and gave more pain lest she should not succeed, than pleasure after she had succeeded. She gave but one shake, and that in the Anthem of *God save the King* to Italian words which followed the opera, where she made a sacrifice to the expectations of an English audience. She was much applauded throughout, and was encored in the finale of the opera, which, in words as well as music, is an imitation, we may almost call it, of the finale of *Cenerentola*'.

By 11 February, the audience had not been quite so numerous as on the first night, but, if anything, they had been better satisfied. The boxes had been well filled. Joséphine had improved on her first representation of Argelia and had received very general applause (*Observer*). The heroine's aria *Ogni tormento*, at the end of the second act, was picked out as the most charming *morceau* in the opera and Joséphine received an unanimous encore for the 'inexpressibly graceful and accurate manner' in which she had sung it. At one of the representations of *L' Esule*, according to the *Court Journal*, Luigi Lablache had played his original character 'and exhibited as much purity of taste and depth of expression, as he did of comic verve and spirit in *Figaro*.'

Unfortunately, Monck Mason had opened with an opera which was not a popular success. It had mostly played to poor houses and *The Times* declared acidly that its general merit was that of brevity. The *Athenaeum* dismissed it as a *pasticcio* by Donizetti, Costa and Pacini, preceded by a good but inappropriate Overture by Monck Mason. It should be consigned to the care of the Neapolitan Ambassador, to be sent home by the first bag, as unprofitable material.

However let the last word be with the *United Kingdom*. 'Despite what some of our learned brethren have asserted', the *United Kingdom* (12 Feb) declared:

'We think this opera a good one. It is not gaudy and glaring in *roulade*-melody and consequently may disappoint some of those whose taste lies that way; but, on the other hand, it is full of feeling and passion; its phrases have meaning always and the sense of the words is never forgotten for the silly sake of florid or meretricious ornament. In the choruses particularly (a sure department to detect a pretender to composition), Donizetti has shown himself a master . . . . In one word, the choruses alone of this opera are a treat both as to composition and performance . . . . The melodies . . . are not numerous or striking . . . but to make amends we have occasionally . . . bursts of imagination and beauty. Donizetti does not, like Rossini and his school, give the same melody to 3, 4, 5 or 6 persons, all singing (together or in turn) under different and conflicting emotions – witness the trio at the conclusion of the first act; how artfully are the opposing feelings of the three reduced into a simple and splendid effect! . . . .

'But to the singers now – and first and dearest to us hail Madame De Meric! Go on, persist in your pure style, and you will reform us altogether. In the Celtic languages the song of the Nightingale is called *Rose-Music*; of a verity, so is thine – there is a perfume and a freshness (to make a mixture of metaphors) in your voice, that enchants us beyond measure. Where did you come from? Why have we not had you *puffed* for the last 3 months? You know better – *C'est ça!*'

Finally, the *United Kingdom* expressed the view that Winter, Mariani and de Meric, between them, would do much to reform 'the love for frippery and unseasonable ornament'.

The revival, in an abridged form, of Saverio Mercadante's two-act opera *Elisa e Claudio*, which followed, was the next opera in which Joséphine appeared. It was greeted with some enthusiasm.

This was the opera in which Joséphine had made her *début* in Milan in 1825. Later she had sung in it under the composer's personal direction in Lisbon. At the King's Theatre, she duly took the name part of the heroine, supported by Curioni as Claudio.

Elisa e Claudio had been preceded by an unsuccessful revival of *Il Barbiere di Siviglia*. Reviewing this production, the *Morning Chronicle* had said that it could not conceive why Joséphine had not been employed as Rosina (instead of Signora Albertini).

The London Literary Gazette, which evidently had a poor opinion of Rossini, hailed *Elisa e Claudio* as a welcome and delightful relief.

'Never was weary ear more rejoiced than ours by Mercadante's pretty opera, admirably sung and well acted. Meric, the Elisa, more than fulfilled the expectations we had formed of her, both as an *actrice* and *cantatrice*. She gave the music with a simpleness and sweetness that reminded us strongly of Veluti [Giovanni Battista Velluti (1780-1861), the famous *castrato* who had sung in Meyerbeer's *Crociato* in London in 1825] especially in the air beginning *Vado, senti*; and in the finale *Figli, sposo*. The duet with the Marquess [Galli] was also extremely fine.'

The Times considered that *Elisa e Claudio* had never been so well represented in London before. Madame de Méric had sung with great taste and dramatic expression and had been called before the curtain, with Curioni, at the end of the performance.

The *Sunday Times*, while admiring Joséphine's graceful and pleasing performance, nevertheless judged that her powers fell short of what was to be expected of a *prima donna* in a theatre of such magnitude. The *Spectator* critic, on the other hand, said that Madame de Méric had given him no inconsiderable pleasure: she never ventured out of her depth and therefore never failed. The more the *Harmonicon* heard her, the better they were pleased with her, both as a singer and actress – but she was having to work in unfruitful soil, and with little or no assistance.

The *United Kingdom* (25 March) had been given to understand that Madame de Méric was particularly anxious to identify herself with the character of Elisa 'and it will not be her fault if she does not succeed. The passionate vehemence of a mother, bereft of her children, is well depicted by her clever acting; and in this, as well as in her other impersonations, her voice admirably supports her histrionic powers.' Could this imply that Joséphine had experienced the loss of a child?

Reviewers of *Elisa e Claudio* were generally agreed in praising Monck Mason's company as a whole. No single artist, perhaps, had shown superlative talent, but that had been amply compensated by the uniformity of excellence in the cast of the opera, a virtue which had rendered its revival 'one of the best things Mr. Monck Mason has done since the commencement of his career.' (*Morning Advertiser*).

The *Spectator* had no time for Mercadante or his opera and the *Harmonicon* wanted *Elisa e Claudio* to be consigned to eternal oblivion; but it has survived. To quote a twentieth-century opinion, *The Times* critic John Higgins praised this 'slight but beguiling . . . work' in which 'nothing is less than eminently singable' and which shows that Mercadante's great gift was that of blending voices.

THE CHOLERA

The early Spring of 1832 had been marked by an epidemic of cholera in London. This was sufficiently severe for William IV to declare a National Fast. Reports appeared daily in the press giving the numbers of cases in the capital and the numbers of the dead. The cholera did not lead to the closing of the theatres and several even remained open during Lent, though this was regarded as a lapse from traditional practice. A singer brought over from Paris, Leontine Fay, demanded 'a considerable accession to her proposed salary' in consequence of the cholera outbreak and the *Sunday Times* thought the plea was so ingenious that they could almost pardon the cupidity which had dictated it.

Although the epidemic had not closed the theatres, it must have led to less full houses.

The next two operas at the King's Theatre were characterised by high seriousness. The first, on 10 March, was *Pietro l'Eremita* (Peter the Hermit), one of the versions of Rossini's *azione tragica-sacra Mosè in Egitto* (Moses in Egypt) which had been produced first in Naples, at the San Carlo, in 1818. In England, where there was a ban on theatrical representations of Biblical themes, the story of Pharaoh's persecution of Moses and the children of Israel had been converted into an account of the adventures of the French monk Peter (1050-1115), who had preached the first crusade and led it as far as Asia Minor. In that guise, the opera had been performed at His Majesty's in London in April 1822, but had not been revived for several seasons.

As has been seen, the French *oratoire* version entitled *Moïse*, produced at the *Opéra* in March 1827, had been the occasion of the great setback in Joséphine's career in Paris. She did not have an altogether smooth passage in London either.

The principal female rôle in the *Pietro* version is that of Agia, a noble crusader's daughter who is secretly married to Orosman, son of the Sultan of Egypt. The part of the Sultana, Fatima, is secondary and the bills had announced that Madame de Méric had 'kindly condescended' to play it. Such 'condescension' aroused the ire of the critics. The *Morning Advertiser* admitted that the rôle of Fatima did not afford much scope for individual display or solo singing, but pointed out that the numerous concerted pieces in which Fatima bore a prominent part made it imperative that only a good musician should be entrusted with them. 'Madame Meric is an accomplished artiste, and sang her music admirably; but remembering that Ronzi de Begnis [1800-1853] and Caradori [1800-1865] have likewise played Fatima, we are rather insensible to her kind condescension'.

Joséphine was similarly castigated by *The Times*. The *Morning Post* sprang to her defence, declaring that the announcement must surely have been 'a gratuitous piece of impertinence on the part of the printer.' All the same, the paper felt constrained to add that nothing had been heard of any 'kind consent' when Ronzi de Begnis, 'a singer with whom Madame de Meric is not to be named' had taken the part of Fatima.

As for the singing itself, *The Times* critic much preferred the style and voice of Caradori. Joséphine had sung with skill and spirit and, generally speaking, her tones had been good, but the shrillness of one or two of them in alt had been ear-startling.

Against this, the *Morning Post* wrote: 'The music of the part, and an introduced song, gave Madame de Méric a most favourable opportunity of displaying the beautiful quality of her voice, and thereby gaining a considerable advance in the popularity which we foretold for her upon her first appeareance.' The introduced song had been deservedly encored (*Observer*).

The *prima donna* given the part of the heroine in many of the performances was Signora Puzzi.

Puzzi had received applause, but the *Spectator* compared her with Joséphine much to the latter's advantage. Puzzi, the paper wrote, despite all the deficiences in both her voice and acting, had probably been applauded by 'the fashionables whose evening parties she is accustomed to visit . . . but we, being unaccustomed to measure a singer's capabilities by the quantum of noise which they produce, must award the palm to Madame de Méric, to whom the inferior character of Fatima was allotted. We have, before, alluded to the delightful precision of this lady's intonation; and she gave an extraordinary instance of the accuracy of her ear on Saturday night [10 March]. In the first scene, with Winter and Mariani, while they were wandering, most distressingly, from the pitch, she maintained it, in their despite, with her accustomed correctness.'

Within a week, there had been a redistribution of parts, with Joséphine promoted to the rôle of Agia and with Signora Albertini as Fatima. Despite the short notice, Joséphine 'had acquitted herself with great credit . . . and was much applauded throughout.' (*Morning Post*). The *Literary Gazette* declared that 'Méric improves nightly, and as we become accustomed to her bell-like voice, we are more and more pleased.'

For the opera as a whole, however, it seems that the employment of Joséphine in the principal part was offset by the weakness of Albertini as the second woman. The *Observer*, while agreeing that Madame de Méric unquestionably sang better than Signora Puzzi, still wished to see the part of Agia better sustained.

The *Court Journal* wrote that on 17 March the house had been well attended and the Duke of Gloucester had been noticed among the company. The opera had gone off with much spirit and Madame Meric and Signor Winter had been warmly applauded.

Joséphine was not in the cast of the March production of *Robert the Devil*. For this, the management was said to have purchased a peal of bells expressly to ring a triple Bob Major (*Sunday Times*).

Joséphine appeared next (24 March) in Spontini's three-act opera *La Vestale*, an heroic story of conflict between love and duty which is of interest chiefly for the opportunities which it offers to dramatic sopranos such as Callas. If we are to believe the testimony at the Tribunal in Paris in 1831, it was a work after Joséphine's own heart.

At the King's Theatre, where the opera had been set to Italian words, the cast was:

> Licinius (the Roman General) Signor Winter,
> Cinna (Chief of the Legion) Signor Calveri,
> The Pontiff Signor Giubilei,
> Chief Vestal Madame Battiste,
> Julia (a young Vestal) Madame de Méric.

Unfortunately, though the *Revue Musicale* claimed that the beautiful music had given great pleasure, *La Vestale* was not the type of work to appeal greatly to the English audiences of 1832. Both the *Morning Advertiser* and the *Harmonicon* thought that the indifferent success which it had achieved in 1826, when first produced in London, with Caradori and Curioni, should have dissuaded the manager from reviving it. The *Harmonicon* roundly declared that it would never succeed 'on an Italian stage.' It was essentially French music, suited to the French language, adapted to the national taste and unsuited to any other. Besides which, 'much of its effect depends on scenery, decorations, and, more than these, on a spacious stage, grand processions, and such accessories as the King's Theatre does not afford'.

The Times thought it was very long, very dull and very noisy. 'Of all the works belonging to the late and now obsolete school of the French *Académie Royale*, it would have been difficult to choose one less likely to gain favour here than *La Vestale*. All the same,' the critic went on, 'the leading lady singers had been well suited to their parts. Madame Battiste, a portly-looking matron, made an admirable Chief Vestal and the part of Julia sat most naturally on Madame Méric, the management of whose voice, and the style of whose singing reminded us strongly of the school to which she belongs. We could almost fancy that we were listening to a performance in the very *Académie* itself.'

From the diversity of critical reactions, it is apparent that there was indeed something special about Joséphine's voice. Some could not respond to it. The *Morning Chronicle* said that Madame de Méric had displayed her usual judgment and taste in the management of an indifferent organ, the defects of which no musical skill could entirely overcome. Yet the *Morning Post* considered that like all her previous performances this had been exceedingly pleasing and interesting, both histrionically and vocally. 'The emotions arising from the force of love conflicting with the remembrance of her vestal vows were portrayed with a degree of pathos and energy the effect of which we have rarely seen surpassed; while the pure and silvery quality of her voice afforded, as usual, great satisfaction to the audience. The duet with Winter in the second act was executed in most perfect style by both sides.' The *Observer* said that the way Joséphine had sustained the part of Julia had been excellent.

The *United Kingdom* predicted that De Meric's reputation as a *prima donna* would suffer no diminution from her appearance in this country; she was a talented woman, and deserved to the full the encouragement she had received.

The voice of Madame Battiste evoked less comment in the English press than her figure. Ungallantly, the *Morning Advertiser* wrote that she had 'arrived at that age which we shall not even venture to guess at; she is both *grosse* and *grasse*, and is as conspicuous amongst the stage ladies for her corporeal dimensions as Lablache was amongst his fellow artists.'

La Vestale had been sadly accident-prone. The *première* was delayed because a Royal Drawing Room had been deferred and because Signor Winter had fallen ill. When it did take place, there was an incident which was reported in the *Literary Gazette* under its headline 'Unrehearsed Stage Effects'. On the first night, the flash of lightning which should have ignited the vestal's veil on the altar, thus rekindling the flame and saving the vestal from her condemnation to death, had only knocked the veil off the altar on to the stage. However, that was as nothing compared with the disaster which struck when *La Vestale* was performed at the Wexford Festival in Ireland in 1979. The story needs to be read in the deathless prose of Bernard Levin in his 'Conducted Tour.' To put it briefly, the Wexford stage was raked and had become very slippery. As the hero entered, he fell flat on his back. Having struggled to his feet, he slid down almost into the orchestra pit. The next character to appear, his confidant, slid down and joined him. In the end, all the singers, realising that the only secure place was the small pillar holding the sacred flame, either clung to it or to each other. The audience were convulsed.

Finally a sudden indisposition on the part of Madame de Méric obliged Mr Mason to cancel the March 27 performance of *La Vestale* and substitute *Pietro l'Eremita*, with Madame Puzzi as Agia. Joséphine's illness was also given as the reason why she had failed to appear at the Third Concert of the Philharmonic Society on 26 March. The Directors announced that they had only been apprised of the indisposition that same morning. Mrs. H. R. Bishop had kindly consented to sing the pieces allotted to Mme. de Méric in the evening's Concert. A couple of days later, the *Morning Post* threw doubt on the genuineness of the illness, saying that the apology for Meric would have satisfied the audience if there had not been a rumour that she was 100 miles from London when she ought to have been at the rehearsal.

Donizetti's *opera buffa Olivo e Pasquale*, dating from 1827, was produced for the first time in England on 31 March. Joséphine took the part of the heroine, Isabella, 'with considerable success' (*Morning Chronicle*).

The opera itself was not generally thought to be very attractive or to possess 'superior claims to admiration'. However, it was credited with containing some pleasing and pretty music. *The Times* considered that the recitative was the best part of the musical element, but complained that the libretto as a whole had been translated disgracefully.

The *United Kingdom* noted with satisfaction that Mr Monck Mason was at last being rewarded with crowded houses. 'The press, with the solitary exception of the *United Kingdom*, has been loud and unceasing in its denouncement and abuse of Mr. Mason's management; there is scarcely one paper, daily or weekly, in which he has not been baited, badgered, and assailed. We saw small honour . . . in holding battle with a man engaged in a contest . . . of such fearful odds'.

As for *Olivio e Pasquale*, the *United Kingdom* (8 April) described it as animated and bustling and, judging from the plaudits, more in accord with English taste than the operas which had preceded it. 'Madame De Meric brightens all the characters she assumes . . . her acting was chaste, vivacious and well sustained. The music assigned to the heroine she executed with that precision and effect, for which her "bell-tone staccato voice", as it has been happily designated, is so well calculated.'

One critic noticed in Joséphine's performance in the early part of the opera a little of the langour of her late illness. This suggests that the indisposition had not been feigned. After she had rallied, she had sung her duet with Curioni *A te m'affido, O caro* with taste and judgment and had merited the unanimous encore which it received. According to the *Observer*, that was the only encore of the evening.

The *Literary Gazette* also had praise for Joséphine's solo finale *Se palpitai d'affanno*, declaring that de Méric had taken 'another step in that gradual and certain rise which her qualities and talents have so justly been effecting in popular favour.' The *Observer* agreed. She had sung the finale deliciously and 'improves on us every time we hear her.'

The Times said that the string of three arias which the composer had appended to the final act had been given by Joséphine with all the neatness of the staccato style at her command. In the opinion of the *Morning Post*, she had given the part of Isabella with all the charms of her pure and silvery voice and had sung very sweetly throughout. Yet the *Athenaeum* castigated 'her everlasting staccato passages.' These displays, the critic complained, were becoming the burden of her song, but 'attempting what instruments can do much better than voice is a bad substitute for sentiment and expression.'

As for Joséphine's acting, the *Morning Post* described it as lively and spirited, but felt that it seemed to want something of the archness which the author designed to be mingled in the simplicity of the character.

Somewhat exceptionally, the costumes in this opera elicited comment. *The Times* spoke of a want of propriety too glaring to be passed over. The *Sunday Times* pointed to the absurdity of a Lisbon merchant (Curioni) appearing in the uniform of a lancer.

The next opera at the King's Theatre in which Joséphine featured was Vaccai's *Giulietta e Romeo* (10 April), with Joséphine as Giulietta and Madame Grandolfi as the hero.

Vaccai had written the work for Joséphine and she had played the part of the heroine when the opera had its successful run in Milan in 1826. She had also sung as Juliet in Zingarelli's *Giulietta e Romeo* in Paris in 1824. Then, Stendhal had criticised her acting as lacking in tragic impact. Now, in London, the critics were almost at one in praising both her singing and acting. In this 'extremely arduous part', both were all that could be wished and deserved the highest commendation (*The Literary Gazette* and the *Athenaeum*).

There was also general agreement that 'the fair Méric' rose more and more in public esteem in every character in which she appeared. The *Morning Chronicle* had never heard her to greater advantage: her two duets, with Curioni and Mariani, had been the best performances in the opera and those most favourably received. *The Times* spoke of her usual correctness and purity of taste and the *Sunday Times* said that she seemed to act and sing her best.

It was left to the *Harmonicon* to complain that Joséphine was not exactly the Juliet to which it was accustomed. She lacked youth [at 31], gentleness and tenderness. Her voice was too hard for the part and her singing was deficient in the right kind of passion. So perhaps some of Stendhal's criticism still applied.

As a whole, the opera did not prove a great success, though the *Sunday Times* described the music as pretty and more than usually expressive and judged that the small amount of recitative was likely to make it popular.

According to the irreverent critic in the *Atlas*, Vaccai's opera had raised laughs at what were supposed to be the most tragic moments.

The composer himself had presided at the piano and was given a call after the performance: a thin man, with a sallow, intelligent countenance (*Sunday Times*).

The singer to receive the heaviest brickbats was the hapless Madame Grandolfi. Her engagement, said the *Spectator*, passed comprehension. In the opinion of the *Atlas*, she looked more like a methodist parson than one suffering the extremity of love – and anyway she could not sing. At the climax of the drama she had poisoned herself with a lozenge instead of a phial – a most absurd effect.

The *United Kingdom* thundered against *The Times* for having dismissed with a few disparaging words a major operatic event: the *première* in England of *Giulietta e Romeo* and the London *début* of Madame Grandolfi. In the opinion of that paper's critic, Vaccai was to be congratulated. The music of the opera was generally good, and in many passages strikingly beautiful. The duet between the lovers was lovely and a general encore had reflected the delighted feeling of the audience. As for Madame Grandolfi, printed notices had been distributed announcing her severe indisposition and it was positively malevolent of *The Times*, with its great reputation, to have said, in such circumstances, that 'what little voice the lady possessed might be said to be a contralto', which, 'besides being exceedingly feeble was disagreeable in tone.'

The *United Kingdom* added: 'we cannot but bestow our praise bountifully on the talented De Meric; the soul, the energy, the passion, with which she sang and acted, amply merit it. Her meeting with Romeo, we consider as fine an histrionic effort as can be seen.'

Fortunately, Madame de Méric did not participate in what the *Spectator* described as the outstanding novelty of the production: a quartet in which each singer had his or her peculiar pitch, and all differed from that of the band. All the same, the *Atlas* took Joséphine to task for treating the music as 'a sort of holiday singing . . . she went about paying little attention, as it appeared, to the composer's notes, and showing off her powerful and beautiful voice as she found opportunity.' Since she was singing in the presence of the composer, one may be permitted to surmise that she was taking advantage of the opportunities for *bel canto* which he had knowingly provided.

On 3 May 1832, Luigi Lablache, the famous bass, took his farewell benefit for the season as Don Giovanni and Don Geronimo.

In *Don Giovanni*, Joséphine was given the part of Donna Anna. This proved a notable success. 'We have never seen the part of Donna Anna better performed, we might perhaps say so well as by Madame Meric,' wrote the *Morning Post*. The *Athenaeum* had indeed heard the music of Donna Anna executed by a more agreeable voice, 'but rarely so well expressed.' The paper considered that Madame de Méric had completely established her claim to the rank of *prima donna*.

As Carolina, in the *Matrimonio Segreto*, Cimarosa's popular work with which Joséphine had been familiar from her earliest days in Paris and Milan, she had sung 'very sweetly . . . her silvery tones and graceful style did adequate justice to the exquisite music of the Opera, and her singing in the opening duet and in the trio *Le facio un inchino* was not surpassed by the best efforts of Sontag' (*Morning Post*). Several of the boxes had been graced by the presence of Ladies in Court dresses. De Meric, said the *United Kingdom*, was delightful as Carolina.

This production of the *Matrimonio Segreto* is notable as one of the few occasions when Joséphine sang with Luigi Lablache, the father of her daughter's future husband.

German Operas at the King's Theatre – Der Freyshutz, (May 1832).

(By courtesy of the Theatre Museum, The Victoria and Albert Museum.)

The performance of Weber's *Der Freischütz* which took place on 9 May was a landmark in London's operatic history. True, versions of the opera had been given before, e.g. at the Lyceum Theatre (the English Opera House) in 1824, but this was the first time that it had been sung with the original German text (subject to only a few slight deviations). A German company had been expressly engaged and the enterprise was under the royal patronage of Queen Adelaide. The 'Leader of the Band' was Signor Spagnoletti.

Joséphine alone, in the part of the heroine Agathe, was recruited from Mason's regular cast at the King's Theatre.

The occasion provided the music critics with a field-day for drawing comparisons between Italian and German opera, mostly to the advantage of the latter.

As *The Times* pointed out, this was the first time that the English public had had a real opportunity of judging the musical and dramatic merits of the work.

The Spectator, waxing lyrical, declared that the very words 'German Opera' marked an important era in Britain's musical history: 'Upon the fallen grandeur of the Italian Opera, will be erected the proud trophies of Mozart, Weber and Spohr. We class these names together, for the operas of Mozart, although chiefly written in the Italian language, are of pure German growth, and by the present race of Italian singers they are unapproachable. Of all Mr Mason's Italian company, de Méric is the only one who possesses any knowledge of them. The rest have been trained in a different school, if school it can be called, in which Pacini and Donizetti are held up as models'.

Looking forward to the promised productions of *Fidelio* and *Die Zauberflöte* (as distinct from *Il Flauto Magico*), *The Times* said that if those operas were brought out with as much care as the *Freyschütz* had been 'they will at least afford the public some indemnification for the shameful disappointments and failures which have attended the Italian opera during the present season.'

Der Freischütz received a warm welcome from *The Atlas*, which believed that Italian opera had lost its way and become just a vehicle for the individual performers to display their virtuosity. The pleasure the paper's critic had derived from the opera as a whole 'was as great as we ever received from dramatic music – MOZART alone excepted.'

The Atlas was almost alone in finding fault with Joséphine's performance. Haitzinger, the tenor, and Pellegrini, the bass, had left nothing to desire; but 'we wish it were possible to speak in the same terms of the Agathe of Mme. De Méric – but the truth is, that the part is somewhat beyond the powers of her voice – excellent as she is in some characters on the Italian stage. But there are required for the heroine of the *Freischütze*, much more flexibility, softness and delicacy of tone, than this lady can command; it is a tolerably good performance on the whole, well conceived and agreeably acted; but the music certainly falls short of perfection. The best part of Mme. De Méric's execution is the *bravura* of the grand *scena* of the second act. This lady injures the simplicity of the *cavatina* in the last act, by altering the close . . . .' In a second review, *The Atlas* accused Joséphine of lacking a *sotto voce* – a defect which had been greatly felt in the moonlight scene.

The *Literary Gazette* recalled that it had already spoken in terms of praise of Joséphine, 'but we are bound to confess that we had not thought so highly of her as is richly deserved by her execution of the music of the *Freyschütz*. Her singing throughout was marked with great taste . . . .'

The *Sunday Times* believed that Mme de Méric's Agathe was likely to add considerably to her reputation:

> 'The music of this part, which has been so often attempted, but from its difficulties, is so seldom attended with success, found in this lady a representative worthy of Weber. Her entire performance was characterized by her usual spirit and ability, and were we to particularize, we should select the grand scene in the second act as her happiest effort during the evening.'

As a summing-up, the *Harmonicon* reported that Joséphine was a very good Agathe and 'if she did but soften her voice occasionally, she would leave little to be wished.'

The fact that Joséphine was heard for the first time in London singing in German led to some curious comments.

Strasbourg, her native city, was French at the time, but it was a border town in which much German was spoken, so it was to be expected that she would be fluent in both French and German. However, *The Times* considered that because she was not a native of Germany she deserved special praise for the way in which she delivered her part in the dialogue, 'though we could occasionally detect something like un-German [sic] in her pronunciation.'

The *Morning Chronicle* saw Madame de Méric as 'three ladies at once – viz. a German by birth [wrong], an Italian by education [partially right] and a French-woman by marriage [utterly wrong].' The last statement strongly suggests that Joseph Glossop must have been keeping well away from operatic circles at the time. The *Chronicle* thought that Joséphine seemed more at home in the original language of *Der Freyschütz* than in her 'adopted tongue' meaning, presumably, Italian.

This German *première* of *Der Freischütz* had been conducted by the French composer and violinist Hippolyte Chélard (1789-1861), whose opera *Macbeth* was shortly to be produced at the King's Theatre. Ignaz Moscheles (1794-1870), the German-Bohemian pianist, composer and teacher, was in Meyerbeer's box and, according to his wife, 'everything went well; the public called for the singers repeatedly and cheered them enthusiastically.' *The Times* had not seen the pit so full since the days, or rather nights, of Paganini.

The décor came in for some comment. *The Times*, which had reported so unfavourably on the costumes for *Olivo e Pasquale*, liked the realism shown in the *Freischütz* production. 'The libretto contains minute instructions for dressing the characters, and the simple *haustragen* [everyday wear] in which Madame de Méric and Mlle. Schneider appeared . . . was infinitely more becoming and appropriate than the white satin and blonde [silk lace], in which we have been accustomed to see the characters dressed.'

Despite what Frau Moscheles said, there had been an unrehearsed stage effect in which Joséphine had been the victim. As recorded in the *Literary Gazette*, difficulties with the window-curtains had revealed her in a tussle with the scene-shifter. He had been discovered 'firmly planted in the lady's balcony, his paper-cap in bold relief against the moon, to the no small mirth of the audience.'

In Paris, in 1831, Meyerbeer's opera *Robert le Diable*, which was the next work to be performed at the King's Theatre, had had an unprecedented triumph, but it never achieved great popularity in England. For one thing, it is extremely long. Then the legendary story, by Scribe, involving the son of a mortal and a devil, a midnight orgy with ghostly nuns and a magic branch which enables the hero (Robert, Duke of Normandy) to gain access to his beloved (Isabella, Princess of Sicily), is far-fetched for even the most dedicated of Romantics. On the practical side, the opera calls for such elaborate scenic effects that it is difficult and expensive to mount. Where it has succeeded, the success has been due mainly to Meyerbeer's music.

A version had been staged at Drury Lane in February 1832, but the first performance with the full score was given at the King's Theatre on 11 June. Both of these are said to have been in English (Kobbé), but there is convincing evidence that the language at the King's Theatre was French.

Joséphine apart, the cast was the same as in Paris, with Cinti-Damoreau in the rôle of Isabella, which she had created, Nourrit (Robert) and Levasseur (Bertram, the devil-father). In Paris, the second soprano rôle, that of Alice, Robert's virtuous foster-sister who finally saves him from the devil's clutches, had been taken by Julie Dorus-Gras (1805-1896). In London, this part fell to Joséphine.

The composer himself had been in London for the rehearsals and there are letters dated 22 April and 17 May 1832, written to his wife in Baden-Baden, which throw light on Meyerbeer's attitude to Joséphine and prove that baby Emilie was with her mother in London at the time.

Meyerbeer was finding much about which to complain. As so often in London, there had been inadequate preparation for the opera. As late as the end of April, it had still not even been decided whether it should be sung in Italian or French. Giulia Grisi (1811-1869) had declined to take the part of Alice and all that was left was 'die jämmerliche Glosshop-Demeri'. The German adjective can perhaps best be translated as 'wretched', but its significance in the context is somewhat obscure. Probably Meyerbeer still considered that the character of the part did not suit the individuality of the talent of Madame de Méric. Perhaps, too, there was some resentment because Joséphine had not accepted his offer in 1826 to write an opera for her. On the other hand, it could well be that she herself was in a wretched frame of mind. She had just broken, in disagreeable circumstances, with the Opéra in Paris and was now to sing in a secondary rôle with the triumphant stars from the French company. On the personal side, her relations with Joseph Glossop had foundered. Meyerbeer's letter is the last example which has been traced where Joséphine is referred to as Glossop and this is probably a recollection by the composer of the Paris days.

By the middle of May, Meyerbeer seemed satisfied that the rehearsals, with Monck Mason, were going reasonably well. He told his wife that he went to see 'die Demerie' every day to din into her the rôle of Alice and added that she had with her a little girl who was just the same age as 'our own little angel', Bianca. Bianca had been born on 15 July 1830. Emilie reminded him so much of Bianca and he had become so fond of her that he could not let a day pass without seeing her.

On the whole, the critics praised the music of Robert le Diable. The Times said it deserved the highest commendation for lofty genius and bold originality of character. The Athenaeum considered that notwithstanding the high expectation raised, the success had been complete. The Literary Gazette rated the music of Robert above that of the Crociato. Almost alone, The Atlas was critical, while admitting that 'sometimes, in the multitude of his trials, the composer hits the mark, as in the romance of Alice in the first act, Va, mon enfant, which is new and beautiful.'

Joséphine received some good notices. De Méric had acquitted herself to perfection and it was impossible by verbal description to do justice to the cloister scene (*Literary Gazette*). As Alice, Madame de Méric had sung most enchantingly (*The Times*). The trio in the second act had exhibited the extraordinary compass of Nourrit, Levasseur and Madame de Méric (*Athenaeum*).

THEATRE ROYAL, DRURY LANE.

For the Benefit of Mr. HARLEY,

AND LAST APPEARANCE THIS SEASON OF

Mr. BRAHAM and Madame DE MERIC.

This Evening, MONDAY, MAY 21, 1832.

Their Majesties' Servants will act (by permission of S J. Arnold, Esq) the Opera of

THE DEVIL'S BRIDGE.

Count Belino, - Mr. BRAHAM,
Marcelli, Mr. HARLEY, Florian Mr. TEMPLETON,
Baron Toraldi, Mr. H. WALLACK, Pietro, Mr. J. RUSSELL,
Paolo, Mr. YARNOLD, Fabricio, Mr. YOUNGE, Julio, Miss MARSHALL,
Countess Rosalvina, Miss HYLAND.

Who was so favourably received in the Characters of Rosetta and Polly.

Claudine, Miss PEARSON, who will introduce the new Song,
'The Heart's first love.'—Composed expressly for her by Mr. H. R. BISHOP.)
Lauretta, Mrs. HUMBY.

Between the Acts of the Opera,

MADAME DE MERIC,

Who has kindly offered her assistance, will introduce

Two Favourite ITALIAN AIRS.

After which, [by Special Desire] an Original Domestic Drama, entitled,

THE RENT DAY.

Grantley, Mr. BRINDAL, Old Crumbs, Mr. YOUNGE
Martin Heywood, Mr. WALLACK, Toby Heywood, Mr. COOPER,
Silver Jack, Mr H. WALLACK, Hyssop, Mr. BEDFORD, Bullfrog, Mr. HARLEY,
Beanstalk, Mr. HUGHES, Stephen, Mr. SALTER, Burly, Mr. HATTON,
First Farmer, Mr. Fenton, Second Farmer, Mr. C. Jones, Sailor, Mr. Eaton,
Rachel Heywood, Miss PHILLIPS, Polly Briggs, Mrs. HUMBY.

In the course of the Evening, the following

NOVEL ENTERTAINMENTS,

Mr. BRAHAM:

His celebrated Scena, from OBERON,—'Oh 'tis a glorious sight!' 'Though Love is warm awhile,'
'Behold in his soft expressive face,' The celebrated Picture Song,
'The jolly young Waterman,' 'Then farewell, my trim-built Wherry,'
'John Anderson, my Jo,' and 'The Bay of Biscay!'

Mr. HARLEY

Will introduce a Comic Song, called 'The Parliament Man, or a peep at the Members!'

Mr. PARRY, Jun.

(For this Night only) will sing, the Ballad of 'Norah the Bride of Kildare!' Accompanied by himself on the HARP.

Miss HYLAND will introduce,

'Arise to matin call,' 'Oh, leave me to my sorrow,' and 'Robin Adair.' with Variations.

Mr. TEMPLETON,

New Song 'When rosy daylight hies,'—(De Pinna.) And (by desire) 'There lives a young Lassie.'
'Rest, weary Traveller.'—Mr BRAHAM and Mr. TEMPLETON.

'The Little Sailor Boy,' with a Hornpipe in Character, by Miss SMITH.

Zingarell's Song of 'Sweetly o'er my senses stealing,' by Miss FORBES, her First Appearance in Public.

The whole to conclude with (by particular desire) DIBDIN's Ballad Opera, called The

WATERMAN.

Tom Tug, ... Mr. BRAHAM,
Bundle, Mr. HUGHES, Robin (the Maccaroni Gardener) Mr. HARLEY.
In which he will sing the Comic Song of "CHERRIES and PLUMS."
Mrs. Bundle, Mrs. C. JONES. Wilhelmina, Miss PEARSON, in which she will introduce
The Ballad of "LA ROSE D'AMOUR."

To-morrow, The Comedy of **The Honey Moon. And Charles the Twelfth.**
Wednesday, Lord Byron's Tragedy of **WERNER. And other Entertainments.**
Thursday....The Comedy of **The School for SCANDAL.** And **X. Y. Z.**
Friday,....**JOHN OF PARIS. A ROLAND FOR AN OLIVER.**
And a Variety of Entertainments.
In which Madame VESTRIS, Mr. DOWTON, Mr. F. VINING, Mr. J. REEVE,
Monsieur ALBERT, and Mademoiselle HEBERLE, (the celebrated Danseuse of the
King's Theatre) will appear. For the Benefit of Mr. BUCKE.
The Last Night of the Company's performing this season.

Theatre Royal, Drury Lane. At a benefit performance Joséphine sings in the interval between dramas, (May 1832).

(By courtesy of the Theatre Museum, The Victoria and Albert Museum.)

The *Morning Chronicle* singled out for praise Joséphine's song in the third act *Quand je quittai la Normandie* and her part in the trio *Ses yeux sont baissés vers la terre*. However, another critic regarded the trio as a total failure when compared with the manner in which it had been sung by Mrs. Wood, Mr. Wood and Mr.H. Phillips. Madame de Méric, for all her versatile abilities, was not to be compared with Mrs. Wood. J. J. M., in *Fraser's Magazine*, felt that Joséphine, as Alice, had been only 'sufficiently good not to spoil the 'ensemble' and had appeared to less advantage in this part than in any character he had seen before. Curiously, he described her as Swiss and as pronouncing French badly. The *Harmonicon*, on the other hand, considered that she was 'entitled to a high degree of praise'.

By the time of the *première*, Meyerbeer had left London. His correspondent in London, Maurice Schlesinger, wrote to assure him that *Robert* had been a great success and that the four principal singers had all been given curtain calls. All the same, the orchestra and the conductor (Culeau) had not been good.

Whether or not *Robert le Diable* was an artistic success, it had an exceptionally short run. After only three performances, Nourrit and Levasseur's leave from the *Opéra* expired and Madame Cinti demanded more money than the management were prepared to pay. The result was that on 19 June the opera had to be reduced to the first, third and fifth acts only.

Things had gone wrong on the first night. Owing to the difficulties which the elaborate scenic preparations had caused, it was nearly nine o'clock before the curtain could be raised and Monck Mason had been compelled to come forward to quell the impatience of the audience. The opera did not end till forty minutes past midnight.

Yet there was some reward. As *The Times* wrote: 'The utmost attention has been paid to the getting-up of the opera. No expense has been spared to bring it out with brilliant effect. The scenery, by Messrs. Grieve, is magnificent'. "A Conventual Cloister" by moonlight, is a very noble scene; but it is eclipsed by that with which the opera terminates – "A View of the Interior of the Cathedral at Palermo", which is one of the most beautiful and elaborately painted scenes that was ever exhibited in a theatre. The house rang with acclamations at the falling of the curtain.' Unfortunately the composer was not there to enjoy the acclaim. Meyerbeer had left for Berlin, because he considered it his duty to his native city and to his King to direct the final rehearsals of his opera himself.

Chélard's opera *Macbeth*, which was staged on 4 July, is loosely based on Shakespeare. It had been produced at the *Opéra* in Paris in 1827. The libretto was by Rouget de Lisle. In London, the composer himself conducted the German company in what proved to be a very brief run indeed. According to the *Athenaeum*, *Macbeth* had been thinly attended on its 'second and last representation'.

The opera was rightly regarded as un-Shakespearean. It fell to Joséphine to play one of the two parts which do not exist in the original. To quote *The Atlas*:

> 'As there are no love passages in the original story, and as no opera can be supported upon the expression of fierce passions alone (for then there would be no room for melody), two new personages are introduced, Moina (Madame De Meric), a daughter of Duncan, and Douglas (Haitzinger) his kinsman [and heir to the throne], betrothed to her. These two personages are created for the express purpose of loving one another and infusing a little sweetness into the music; they are a characterless, insipid couple; and as the audience have not the slightest interest in them, their *amour* is only an impertinence . . . . As a whole, then, the work is a failure, though a splendid one . . . .'

Despite their minor parts, Joséphine and Haitzinger were singled out by the critics for commendation. Their songs and duets had been pleasing and expressive (*Athenaeum*). Madame de Méric's *scena* had contained pleasing and brilliant passages (*Spectator*). The *Morning Post* went further:

> 'The sweet tones and exquisite taste of Mme. de Méric never fail to delight her hearers; and the scenes in which she was engaged were the most pleasing in the opera. Her duet with Haitzinger in the second act is a beautiful composition, to which the singers did full justice; and at the commencement of the third act she has one of the most difficult concertos, if we may so call it, we have ever heard; the mere committing to memory of such a piece, not to mention the style of its execution, reflects the highest credit upon her.'

This *cavatina* had been warmly applauded (*Sunday Times*). It is in A major and *The Times* commented: . . . 'from its peculiar style, we should imagine had been composed expressly for her [Joséphine]. It had a delightful obligato accompaniment for the violoncello, ably performed by Linley.'

The 1880 edition of Grove's Dictionary says that in *Macbeth* Joséphine had distinguished herself by singing a most cramped and difficult song with astonishing truth and precision, a feat which added much to the estimation in which she was held.

On 11 July, under the title *Don Juan*, the German company staged a performance in German of Mozart's *Don Giovanni*, as a benefit for Madame Schroeder-Devrient. This was less successful than might have been expected. *The Times* condemned the production, as a whole, as being well below standard. *The Atlas* critic recalled with disappointment that he had heard the opera played with far more spirit and enthusiasm, and certainly with more intelligence and feeling for the music, by the Italian singers and by the English chorus.

Joséphine was Donna Elvira. Schroeder-Devrient, as Donna Anna, 'rather eclipsed her' (Grove's Dictionary). Interestingly, the *Morning Chronicle* remarked that Donna Elvira had usually been given to second or third-rate singers, but Madame de Méric had not considered it unworthy of her high abilities. This had given an importance to the character which it had not previously possessed on the British stage. *The Times* said that Joséphine's rendering deserved much praise.

This German production was notable, it seems, for having been the first to introduce *Non più andrai*, from *The Marriage of Figaro*, into the Don's supper scene (*Morning Advertiser*). *The Atlas* gave Joséphine credit for inserting in its proper place the song *Mich verlasst der Undankbare*.

As ill luck would have it, at the end of the performance *Don Juan* was seen in agony 'not at being in the clutches of the infernals, but at finding that the trap-door would not descend . . . . He was excessively ill-dressed' (*The Times*).

A benefit performance of *Don Juan* for Joséphine was given in mid-July and the *Morning Post* had hoped 'that her multifarious and indefatigable exertions to please during the past, her first season here, will be acknowledged by the public as they deserve.' Unfortunately, 'the excellent entertainments at the King's Theatre for the benefit of Donzelli and Madame de Méric had been given to empty benches.' According to the *Athenaeum*, 'The truth is that these benefits come too frequently, and are generally farmed by the manager at a certain sum, the *Beneficiare* being indifferent to the further result. In lieu of a faithful representation of an entire Italian opera, the subscription performances now consist of an unsatisfactory hodge-podge, compounded of acts from three different operas.'

Thus, on 14 July, the audience at the King's Theatre had been given an Act from *Gli Arabi nelle Gallie* and a few scenes from *Tancredi*. It was nearly ten years since Joséphine had made her Paris *début* in *Tancredi*. Now, according to the *Morning Chronicle*, her rendering of the part of Amenaïde had been 'in a manner that evinced more knowledge of how it should be sung, than a capability of executing her conceptions.'

In ponderous prose, the *Morning Chronicle* complained that Joséphine's organ 'is sadly inflexible, and this defect, which no skill can overcome or scientific acquirement palliate, impeding the natural flow and smooth current of vocalization, renders it incapable of executing with due facility the light and graceful music of Amenaïde.' More generously, the *Athenaeum* said that Joséphine had evidently been much fatigued from her too frequent exertions in Italian, French and German operas, and had not sung in *Tancredi* with her accustomed success.

As Ninetta in Rossini's *La Gazza Ladra* (The Thievish Magpie) (21 July), Joséphine acquitted herself more than respectably and proved that she was a very clever woman of extraordinary versatility. She had been a treasure to Mr. Monck Mason 'in his distress.' (*Observer*).

To her misfortune, though, she had had to compete with the memories of a greater star in the part. As the *Morning Chronicle* explained:

> 'If the exquisite portraiture of Madame Malibran's rustic maid . . . did not occur to our recollection, we should, perhaps, be inclined to render to Madame de Méric's representation of it a more extensive share of praise. Still it is scarcely fair to measure her performance by the standard of Malibran; few possess the physical and mental powers of that gifted woman, and rare indeed are the intervals at which such endowments are presented to us. Madame de Méric's performance embraced many excellencies, and it is only justice to her to notice the very commendable emulative spirit she displayed throughout it, and which will render her, if not a first rate actress and singer, a very valuable acquisition, as she has proved herself to be during the present management.'

The *Sunday Times* rated this production as being, in parts, worthy of the best days of the opera.

> 'We cannot speak in too high terms of the Ninetta of Madame de Méric; for a time she may be out of fashion, to make room for others of greater pretensions, but far less merit. Now that she has gone through the ordeal of rivalship, and has proved herself superior to other aspirants for the rank of *prima donna*, she begins again to

be duly appreciated. Although there is a sameness which characterizes her performances in either French, German or Italian, she always evinces sound judgment and an erudite study; and if there be nothing wonderful to astonish - nothing to render the senses captive - she is always effective and pleasing.'

THE 1832 OPERA SEASON IN RETROSPECT

It was generally agreed that Monck Mason had over-reached himself and that the 1832 Season at the King's Theatre had not been a success. In the opinion of *The Atlas*, both the German and Italian singers had outstayed their welcome and had finally played to 'ghosts of audiences'.

The *Spectator* was disappointed that Monck Mason had failed to fulfil the hopes which he had raised. With the solitary exception of Madame de Méric, the paper complained, his company consisted of singers who, to speak of them in the most favourable terms, were of mediocre talent. 'He has confessed the fact, by their speedy and abrupt dismissal. Where are Albertini, La Contessa Lasize, Puzzi, and the portly lady whose name we have forgotten? And where will be Grandolfi a month hence?'

Fétis, in the *Revue Musicale* in Paris, reported that 1832 had not been a good season for Italian opera in London. Mason had assembled a host of Italian singers, to whom he had to offer high salaries; but then he had not been able to make full use of them. Finally, Mason had been attacked by the singers for non-payment of salaries totalling £21,000.

Almost alone, J. J. M. in *Fraser's Magazine* came to Monck Mason's defence. Mason, he said, had had to contend with many peculiar disadvantages - some positive, others negative.

'Of these, it will be perhaps sufficient to recite two: he is a gentleman; he is not a foreigner. Both are heavy disadvantages, but the first is much the greater . . . . I do not hesitate to say, that, within my memory, we never yet had a better company, or so good a *corps de ballet*, in the earlier period of the season, under any preceding management. We had Madame De Meric, Winter and Mariani, from the first; and who will venture to deny that they are superior in their several positions to Mdlle. Blasis, Curioni and De Angeli, who were wont for months to enact the principal characters under the auspices of the much-lauded M. Laporte . . . ?'

J. J. M. admitted that in the latter part of the season, after Easter, Tosi and Donzelli had arrived, to put De Meric and Winter somewhat in the shade. Nevertheless, he was at pains to stress his view that Joséphine was 'a blameless singer in almost all she attempts (I say almost all, because in singing the ornate music of the modern Italian school she is sometimes betrayed into attempts at *roulades* and *fioritures* which she cannot accomplish, or can accomplish only with pain to herself, and therefore to the audience), and an actress, who, if she never have any inspirations, yet never misconceives or misinterprets her character – and who, although by no means entitled to the rank of *prima donna*, is one of the most useful *seconde donne* in the world.' If Joséphine ever read this criticism, it must have been balm indeed to be hailed later, in Italy, as *prima donna assoluta*.

The 1880 edition of Grove's Dictionary, over the initials J.M., gives an assessment of Joséphine's performances in London in 1832, describing her as very successful in an unsuccessful season and remarking that she performed in Italian, German and English, and could have done so equally well in Spanish had it been required. The article is in error, however, in stating that she did not appear in England again, because she played an important part in the following season too.

As for the relative failure of the season as a whole, it is to be remembered that 1832 was the year of the Reform Bill. In the *Harmonicon*, Dilettante explained:

'Music is suffering like everything else at the present moment [this was the end of April], from the agitated state of the public mind. A dilettante must listen to politics, or hear nothing; he must talk of reform or remain silent. The Opera is deserted – no wonder, however, for what are the operas given, and who the performers? But neither indifferent performers, nor bad operas, are the sole cause of the empty boxes and benches at the King's Theatre; the taste for amusement is superseded by a stronger element. Besides which, they who have money keep it, and those who have none – by far the greater number – cannot indulge in entertainments that are only given on condition of prompt payment. Concerts are badly attended; there is scarcely any music at the theatres. Harmony is almost mute!'

Concerts and provincial tour in 1832

LONDON CONCERTS

VOCAL and orchestral concerts, public and private, were a major feature of the musical scene in London at the time. Pride of place was held by the Philharmonic Society, with whom Joséphine sang once in 1832 and twice in 1833.

On 28 April 1832, the Society's rehearsal was attended by the critic of the *Spectator*, together with a galaxy of musicians. On that occasion, the critic wrote, 'were seated, side by side, Cramer, Field, Moscheles and Mendelssohn, and near them stood Meyerbeer. Such an assemblage of musical talent is seldom compressed into a similar space.'

The critic had noticed Joséphine's sensitivity to the music of Mozart. He castigated the vocal section of the concert as a failure, except for Madame de Méric's song *Non più di fiori,* Vitellia's great aria in the *Clemenza di Tito* from which alone he had derived real pleasure. 'It was impossible to forget the impression which Malibran made in it, and against this impression de Méric had to contend: but she evinced a correct knowledge of the duty which a singer of Mozart's songs has to perform; the rhythm was not violated by injudicious *ad libitums,* nor the band, and especially the accompanying instrument, perplexed by vain attempts to follow the singer's caprice. The unity and symmetry of the composition was perfectly preserved; and, therefore, the effect was most satisfactory.' The accompanying instrument was the *corno di bassetto.* The *Harmonicon* also singled out Joséphine's rendering of the aria from *Tito.* Though she had strained her voice in the high notes, 'she was sparing of those abominable ornaments, as they are miscalled, by which music of this high order is so much disfigured by ultra-modern singers, and gave Mozart's text with a purity rare in *prime donne,* or those who, at least, claim the honours of that station.' Joséphine had also sung in a trio and quartet from *Idomeneo,* a somewhat rare offering at the period.

When it came to the Concert itself, *The Atlas* was pleased with the choice of music, but considered the performers to have been incompetent. 'M. Begrez never, by any chance, sings in tune. Miss

Bruce is an English lady of riper age than musical talent. With Madame De Méric, an Italian or German, the voices and styles of the three performers being as many leagues distant as their places of birth, the consequence may be imagined.' Always hard to please, *The Atlas* thought that Joséphine appeared to greater advantage on the stage than on the concert platform. There seemed to have been a lack of softness, flexibility and delicacy in her rendering of *Non più di fiori*. However, some allowance should perhaps be made for the surroundings, the Concert having been given in the 'temporary and unsatisfactory rooms' at the King's Theatre.

Things could be very different at a private concert. At one of Miss Bruce's *Soirées Musicales*, to quote the *Literary Gazette*, 'a very elegant and fashionable company' were present and 'the occasion went off with much *éclat*; the audience enjoying all the comfortable advantages of a well-furnished mansion, where there are no such bars [i.e obstacles] as thorough [sic] draughts, slamming of doors, loud talkings etc. to the full enjoyment of music.' Miss Bruce had sung with great taste and had been particularly successful with *Dove sono*. 'It is quite unncessary to employ a word of praise on the never-failing excellencies of Nicholson, Meric or Donzelli who combined their powers on this occasion. A nearer view of Madame de Méric only superadds the attraction of beauty to that of harmony.'

On Friday 27 April 1832, a Grand Miscellaneous Concert of Vocal and Instrumental Music was given at the King's Theatre for the benefit of the theatre's New Musical Fund. This had been established

Front of the King's Theatre, Haymarket.

(From the Author's Collection.)

way back in 1786 for the relief of decayed musicians, their widows and orphans. Joséphine was among the 'eminent vocal performers' who had kindly promised their gratuitous assistance. She was encored with de Begnis for a duet which they sang together. Happily, the House had been crowded for this event.

1832 had marked the fifth season of a group known as the City Amateurs. Their performance on 23 February had much displeased *The Atlas*, which evidently saw itself as a custodian of the island race. 'The concert [had been] much too abundant in the music of modern Italian opera.' On the concert stage it was much better to have British singers. Madame de Méric, Mariani, Winter and Calveri had all sung at the top of their voices and made a prodigious noise. 'We believe this exertion, which is remarkable [noticeable] in all the foreign singers who appear here, is intended to gratify; but it has its cause in a contempt for the taste of the audience – for the impression abroad is that the English care for nothing but loud singing – and they do give it us with a vengeance . . . . Madame De Méric sang her aria from *L'Esule* [*di Roma*], with the *obligato corno Inglese*.' The *Sunday Times*, referring to her as Madame le Mere, said that in the song from *L'Esule di Roma* she did not produce the same effect as they had noticed on the stage, but 'she recovered all her best qualities in a beautiful aria from Pacini: *Salvo al fin*.'

Joséphine sang at two concerts given by the Società Armonica; at Madame Cellini's annual concert at Willis' rooms; at a concert given by M. and Madame Stockhausen at the King's Concert Room and at M. Bochsa's concert, in June, when she sang a German *scena* from *Der Freischütz*.

A highlight had been Mr. E. Taylor's concert at the Albion in Aldersgate Street on 26 April. There, according to the *Spectator*, the chief attraction had been a selection from *Die Zauberflöte*. 'It was committed to singers both able and willing to do justice to its unrivalled beauties – Madame de Meric, Miss Cramer, Miss Masson and Messrs. Horncastle and E. Taylor. Such a composition, performed as it was on Thursday, was a sumptious musical treat. Madame de Meric is evidently more at home in the operas of Mozart than in those flimsy compilations in which she has hitherto been employed at the King's Theatre. She appeared to enjoy her task, and to go through it not so much with a desire to exhibit her own powers, as to render them subservient to the general effect of every piece in which she was engaged.' The audience had been an appreciative one too – not just 'the Tuesday and Saturday regulars' who went to the opera as a matter of fashionable routine, simply to talk and be seen.

At Mr. Kiallmark's concert on 12 June, there had been a numerous and fashionable audience, but the *Spectator* had expected 'something better from Madame de Méric than such poor stuff as the air of Pacini's which she sang.'

Madame de Méric, 'from the King's Theatre,' made several appearances in 1832 at concerts at the Theatre Royal, Drury Lane. These took place at various dates between 11 April and 22 September. Joséphine sang arias from *Figaro*, *Elisa e Claudio*, *Tancredi* and the *Freischütz* and, on two occasions, Rossini's *Di piacer mi balza il cor*. When Cinti-Damoreau made her *début* at Drury Lane on 1 June, she and Joséphine sang the *Sull'aria* duet from *Figaro*.

An opera called *The Devil's Bridge* was billed to be performed at Drury Lane on 21 May. Joséphine was not in the cast, but she had 'kindly offered her assistance' by singing two favourite Italian airs between the acts.

Following the close of the opera season in London, Joséphine was to have taken part in the Music Meeting at Gloucester. That event was all but cancelled owing to the fear of cholera. However, 'the engagements had been too far concluded' (*Harmonicon*). Madame Caradori was to have been one of the leading female artistes, but she pulled out for what were considered to be reasons which she must have known about beforehand – and Joséphine agreed to fill the gap. Then she in turn was 'prevented by sudden indisposition' and her songs were divided between Mrs. Knyvett and Miss Shirreff. The songs were an *Agnus Dei* (Mozart), the aria *Ah parlate* (Cimarosa), a *scena* from *Der Freischütz* and, with Tamburini, the duet *Io di tutto* (Mosca).

PROVINCIAL TOUR IN 1832

In the Autumn of 1832, although she did not go to Gloucester, Joséphine embarked on a provincial tour. The complete itinerary has probably not yet been traced, but it is known that she performed in Cheltenham, Manchester and Edinburgh.

CHELTENHAM

An advertisement in the local paper in August 1832 proudly announced that 'There is no Watering Place, nor indeed any Town of fashionable resort in Great Britain, or on the Continent of Europe, that has arrived at that state of perfection which Cheltenham has attained; and such was the opinion of the Grand Duchess of Russia, during her residence here. Her Grace the Duchess of St. Alban's has evidently the same way of thinking; and indeed no person who has pretensions to good taste can form a different opinion.'

Appropriately, then, the Nobility and Gentry were notified that a Grand Concert of Vocal and Instrumental Music would take place in the Assembly Rooms on Friday, 7 September, 1832, commencing at Eight precisely.

Madame de Méric headed the list of performers. With her were to be Signor De Begnis, his pupil Miss Waters and Signori Arigotti and Giubilei, both, like Joséphine, from the King's Theatre.

In the advertised programme, Joséphine's solos were to be *Di piacer mi balza il cor* and the grand *scena* from *Der Freischütz, Wie nahte mir der Schlummer*, in German. She was to take part in the quintet from *Il Turco in Italia, Oh guardate che accidente* and to sing with De Begnis the duet *Io di tutto mi contento*, by Mosca.

Assembly Rooms, Cheltenham.
by G. Rowe.
(By courtesy of the Cheltenham Art Gallery and Museum.)

A special feature of the programme was that Signor Emiliani, 'the modern Paganini', would give a solo violin performance of an *Imitation of Paganini's Difficulty*. De Begnis, the organiser of the tour, would introduce a grand *scena* and aria of his own, *Il Fanatico per la Musica*, representing a composer superintending a rehearsal of his new overture.

The concert was evidently a success. The audience had been splendid and numerous 'including, we believe, all the nobility at present in Cheltenham.' The performances were repeated on the following Monday and there was satisfaction that the Assembly Rooms had proved admirably suited to concerts 'on an extensive and first-rate scale.'

Joséphine was described as having an exquisitely brilliant voice. She had been rapturously encored in most of her songs.

Signor De Begnis announced in the *Guardian* of 15 September 1832 that he would be presenting several Grand Operas and Divertissement Ballets at the Theatre Royal, Manchester, opening with Paër's *Agnese*, or *Father and Daughter* on Monday 17 September. De Begnis explained that he had been obliged to make a slight alteration in the prices because of the highly talented company which he had engaged and also because he intended to produce 'the splendid opera *Don Giovanni* by the immortal Mozart in a style never before equalled.'

Madame de Méric, *prima donna* of the King's Theatre, was billed for the name part in *Agnese*, a now-forgotten work by her former *maestro*. De Begnis was her father, the Count, and Donzelli her lover, Ernesto.

The opera was repeated on 20 September, but the house was only 'respectably' attended on both occasions. The *Guardian* considered that *Agnese* contained much sterling music, but was on the whole 'of too sombre a cast to be generally pleasing.' It had been exceedingly well got up, 'though it might be wished that there were less need of the prompter.' (The under-rehearsed works of the period often called forth this complaint).

Madame de Méric had sustained her part with great ability. Her voice was one of pure tone and considerable power. Donzelli possessed decidedly the best tenor voice ever heard in Manchester and the reconciliation duet between the two lovers had been a transcendent effort which evoked a most enthusiastic encore. As the maniac father, De Begnis had acted well, 'but his voice is not what it was, and we could not admire his singing.' The length of the opera had obliged the manager to give a mere apology for a ballet.

Il Barbiere di Siviglia, the greatest possible contrast to *Agnese*, was given on Saturday 22 September, with Joséphine as Rosina. The *Guardian* liked her in this part even better than as Agnese and Donzelli's splendid voice had been heard to great advantage as Almaviva.

For *Don Giovanni*, on 25, 27 and 29 September, the strength of the orchestra had been increased and the audience had been given one of the richest treats ever enjoyed out of the metropolis. The soul-piercing tones of Madame de Méric (Donna Anna), when she discovered the body of her murdered father, 'were certainly equal in pathos to anything we ever heard.' De Begnis, as Leporello, seemed to have regained the power of his voice. Unfortunately, Signor Arigotti did not play Don Ottavio with much spirit 'and there were scenes in which De Méric suffered from the want of better support in his voice.' Miss Phillips, from the Theatre Royal, Drury Lane, as

Donna Elvira, fell below the standard set by both Joséphine and Miss Waters (Susanna). The orchestra had been very effective, but was regrettably not always heard to advantage owing to noises in the gallery.

As if the whole of *Don Giovanni* were not enough, the opera was billed to be followed by the Overture to *Guillaume Tell*; by Joséphine, in character, singing the grand *scena* from the *Freischütz* and by De Begnis with his *Fanatico per la Musica*.

EDINBURGH

De Begnis opened in Edinburgh on Tuesday 27 November 1832, with *Don Giovanni*. The *Evening Courant* praised the company as being 'decidedly superior to any that has appeared in this city.' They had been rewarded by an overflowing house.

Donzelli, as the libertine hero, received the most enthusiastic notice. Joséphine (Donna Anna) was described as having a grand and powerful voice 'which, if it has any fault, is that it is somewhat deficient in sweetness; it seems more suited to express lofty emotion than feelings of tenderness. Her best song was *Non mi dir*, to which she gave its true character and expression.'

The *Courant* recorded on 15 December that the Italian Company continued to attract crowded houses. Both *Il Barbiere* and *Le Nozze di Figaro* had been successes. In the latter, Joséphine had interpreted the part of Susanna with freedom and vivacity.

The novelty, for Edinburgh, was provided on 11 December with the first full performance in the city of Rossini's serious opera *Otello*. Along with *Mosè* and *Semiramide*, it showed that Rossini's excellence was not confined, as many imagined, to the lighter kind of musical composition. Of all operas, the *Courant* said, it was perhaps the one best suited for the display of Donzelli's magnificent voice.

No less, the part of Desdemona was well adapted to 'the talented De Meric.' Her great powers of voice were fully equal to the very trying scenes of the latter part of the opera, 'while she gave the more tender parts with feeling and judgment. She displayed with grace, pathos and dignity the gentleness of Desdemona's character. Her acting was spirited and natural; and to the pathetic passages her plaintive voice gave the true and characteristic expression . . . . The passage *Se il padre m'abbandona*, with the plaintive responses of the chorus, is very striking, and was executed in the most touching manner by Madame de Meric. In the third act, she also sung the *Romanza* with great feeling, and shewed her good taste in preserving its beautiful simplicity unhurt by too much ornament, of which, we confess, we were afraid. We are sorry it should have lost anything from the want of its proper harp accompaniment.'

CHAPTER
11

London again: operas in 1833

DESPITE the financial disappointments of the previous year, Joséphine returned to London for the 1833 Season. The *Morning Advertiser* reported that ever since her *début* at the King's Theatre in 1832, she had continued a great public favourite, 'and we are sorry to be informed that as far as her engagement at that theatre under the last management is considered, the good opinion of the public is the only advantage she derived . . . .'

Laporte had now taken over at the King's Theatre from Monck Mason and the current quip was that Laporte [the door] was much better than Ma[i]son [the house].

Joséphine had been engaged by Laporte, but he had granted her permission to appear first at Drury Lane in an English version of *Don Giovanni*, billed as *Don Juan*. Drury Lane, under Alfred Bunn, was in rivalry with the King's Theatre, and the *Harmonicon* had heralded the new season at Drury Lane as having 'the strongest operatic company that ever congregated in an English theatre.' Malibran was Bunn's great prize. All the same, it was Madame de Méric who was greeted by the *Morning Advertiser* as 'the great star' who was to appear in the first opera of the season at the Lane.

The opera was staged on 5 February. In 1832, Joséphine had played Donna Elvira. Now she was Donna Anna and the occasion was billed as her first appearance in an English character (meaning, presumably, singing in English).

The first night had been marred by a near riot, caused by the decision of Bunn to close off part of the pit. With order restored, the production had proceeded with a modicum of success. The opera was given in an almost complete form, 'as arranged by Mr. Bishop with the most scrupulous fidelity to the original score.' (*Morning Post*). The only part omitted had been the solo and chorus following the fiery catastrophe, 'it being perhaps concluded that the frizzling of the worthy hero of the piece needed neither note nor comment even from Mozart himself.' There was some splendid scenery, by Stanfield, and the English words went smoothly with the music (*Literary Gazette*).

THEATRE ROYAL, DRURY LANE.

Mr. BRAHAM

Has the honor of announcing to the Nobility, Gentry, and the Public generally, that his

B E N E F I T

TAKES PLACE

On WEDNESDAY NEXT, April 24th, 1833,

On which occasion, in addition to the established Talent of the Company,

Madame DE MERIC

will, by Permission of Monsieur Laporte, perform her popular Character of

DONNA ANNA, in the celebrated Opera of DON JUAN.

The Performance will commence with MOZART'S Opera of

DON JUAN.

With the Whole of the Music.

Don Juan, - - Mr. BRAHAM,
Don Octavio, Mr. TEMPLETON. Don Pedro, Mr. BEDFORD.
Masetto, Mr. SEGUIN.
Leporello, - - Mr. MARTYN.
Donna Anna, - - Madame DE MERIC,
Donna Elvira, Miss BETTS,
Zerlina, - - - Mrs. WOOD.

NEW SCENERY.—A STREET IN SEVILLE, WITH THE COMMANDANT'S HOUSE
EXTENSIVE VIEW IN THE ENVIRONS OF SEVILLE.
GARDENS OF DON JUANS PALACE, DECORATED FOR A FETE CHAMPETRE.
THE CEMETRY AND CATHEDRAL AT SEVILLE.
With the EQUESTRIAN STATUE of DON PEDRO.

GRAND BANQUETING HALL:
And Descent of Don Juan to Pandemonium.

In the course of the Evening, a MUSICAL MELANGE, entitled The

Festival of Apollo.

In which will be introduced the following Songs, &c.

Here's a Health to the King! God bless him!
By Mr. BRAHAM.
"BID ME DISCOURSE," by Miss BETTS.
"THE BANKS OF ALLAN WATER,"
By Mrs. WOOD.
A FAVORITE SONG, by Mr. WOOD.
Bruce's Address to his Army!
By Mr. BRAHAM.
"The Lass with the bonny blue een," by Mr. TEMPLETON.
The popular Song of "Manhood," by Mr. SEGUIN.
"The DEATH of ABERCROMBIE,"
By Mr. BRAHAM.

The Evening's Performance to conclude with the Musical Farce of The

QUAKER.

Steady, - - Mr. BRAHAM,
(His First Appearance in that Character on this Stage)—In which he will sing
"When the Lads of the Village."

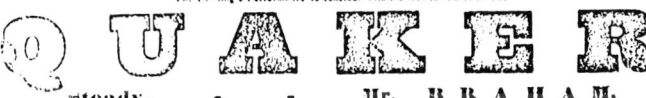

Boxes 7s. Pit 3s. 6d. Lower Gallery 2s. Upper Gallery 1s.
Doors open at Half-past Six; Performances commence at Seven o'Clock.

Theatre Royal, Drury Lane – Don Juan. Joséphine tops the bill as Donna Anna, 1833.

(By courtesy of the Theatre Museum, The Victoria and Albert Museum.)

135

All the singers were praised for adhering faithfully to the text, though Braham (the Don) and Templeton (Don Ottavio) had proved disappointing. As Leporello, H.Phillips had 'realised every expectation', but it was Joséphine who received the highest commendation. She had given great *éclat* to the general effect of the opera . . . by the purity and excellence of her voice' (*The Times*).

Cox, whose judgment was much respected, said that she made an excellent Donna Anna, and the *New Monthly Magazine* praised her in these terms: 'Madame de Méric, whose voice seems capable of every modulation, and is excellent in them all, exerted herself to the uttermost, and did not, when we heard her, suffer a note of the divine music to lose its expression. Her enunciation of our gutteral English is admirable, and her conception of the character of Donna Anna was perfection.'

At the first performance, the *Morning Advertiser* had been impressed by Joséphine's 'great spirit', and by the power and flexibility of her voice, marred only by 'the hard tones in the upper register.' After a later performance, the paper roundly declared that Madame de Méric was unquestionably one of the cleverest singers of the time, as had been demonstrated by her ability to sing as perfectly in English as in Italian and French.

The *Athenaeum* considered that, taking both singing and acting into account, no character in *Don Juan* had been represented to perfection, with the exception of Donna Anna by Madame de Meric:

> 'This lady's performance was an opera in itself. The sweetness of her voice, the purity of her style, the correctness of her execution, the lady-like grace of her demeanour, and the calm yet earnest excellence of her acting, left nothing to be wished. Owing to a disturbance in the house, she was not acknowledged as she deserved to be upon her first *entrée*; but ample amends were made afterwards. Evincing a proper contempt for everything but a genuine delivery of the music, as written by the great master, she proceeded steadily in her task, making her slow but certain way, like plain honesty through a crowd of liars and sycophants, until . . . she eventually stood honoured and alone. In saying this, we have no wish to detract from the merits of the other performers, but simply to pay the greatest homage where the greatest is due . . . . Upon the whole, although we have doubtless seen this opera much better performed on the Italian stage, it by no means follows that Drury Lane is not entitled to its full share of credit for the best English version yet produced.'

Madame de Méric, *The Atlas* wrote, 'is particularly well fitted for the part of Donna Anna; she evidently knows the music well, and in the declamatory and impassioned style is a most valuable performer. The difficulties of a foreign language were not felt by the auditor.' The *Revue Musicale* considered that the honours of the evening had gone to Miss Paton (Zerlina), Mlle. de Mery [sic] (Donna Anna) and the male singers Phillips and Séguin. Braham's Don had plumbed the depths of absurdity.

Don Juan was performed some twenty-one times, which was unusual for the period. It had been regarded as a triumphant success 'in the estimation of a brilliant audience' and 'one of the most crowded houses ever witnessed'.

The review in the *Harmonicon* may be quoted, if only for its curiosity value, as a summing-up by a knowledgeable music critic of the day:

> 'Never was foreign music produced with more success on our national stage than in the present instance, and the vast trouble and expense bestowed in getting it up have been amply repaid by the most unequivocal sign of public approbation – large receipts.
>
> 'The dialogue seems to have been taken from the English version made in 1817, and is adapted for the present purpose by Mr. Beazley. It departs in no way from that translation, except in a few merely verbal alterations. The music is said in the advertisements to include all that was originally written by Mozart; but this is not exactly correct, for the manager has, and very wisely, omitted the last scene, which, splendid as is the concluding chorus, is injurious to the effect of the opera as a whole. But the pieces published in the appendix to the German editions of the music have now all been introduced, and embodied in the opera, an alteration certainly well meant, but by no means to be approved, for they add to the length of the drama and diminish its interest. It is worth while, in the case of so important a work – the glory of the lyric stage – to have this matter properly understood.
>
> 'Mad. de Méric makes an excellent Donna Anna, and with Mesdames Camporese and Ronzi de Begnis fresh in the memory, we yet were perfectly satisfied with the new representation of the character . . . .'

It must be recorded that on a couple of occasions the rôle of Donna Anna was taken by a Miss Duff, who apparently 'squalled'. The playbill had graphically promised the spectacle of the 'Descent of Don Juan to Pandemonium'.

At the King's Theatre, the Opera Season had opened 'with much éclat' on Saturday 16 February with *Cenerentola*.

In that opera, Joséphine yielded pride of place to Madame Boccabadati, from Paris and Naples. A coal-heaver, reading the playbill which advertised this lady's strange name, nicknamed her Shocking-bad-hatty, a reference, no doubt, to the one-act Aristophanic Anecdote called *What a Shocking Bad Hat* which had been on the boards at the Coburg Theatre in 1831.

The King's Theatre.

THIS PRESENT EVENING,

Will be performed ROSSINI'S Opera Semi Seria, in Two Acts, entitled

La Donna del Lago

THE PRINCIPAL CHARACTERS BY

Madame **DE MERIC**,

AND

Mademoiselle **SCHIASETTI**,

From the Theatres Royal, Italien, Paris, & that of Dresden,---(her First Appearance in this Country.)

Signor **DONZELLI**,

Signior G. **GALLI**,

Signor **ARRIGOTTI**, and Signor **V. GALLI**

After which, will be repeated the NEW GRAND BALLET, in Three Acts, founded on the Romantic Story of

FAUST.

In Which will be introduced THE PRINCIPAL SCENES of the Opera Ballet produced at Paris, under the name of

LA TENTATION!

Composed by Monsieur DESHAYES.   The Music by Monsieur ADOLPHE ADAM.
The Scenery by the Messieurs GRIEVE.   The Dresses by Mr. HEAD and Mrs. JACOB.
The Properties by Mr. KELLY.   The Machinery by Monsieur PUGIN.

PRINCIPAL CHARACTERS BY

Mademoiselle **CHAVIGNY**,   Mademoiselle **ADELE**,
Madame **PROCHE GIUBILEI**,   Madame **COPERE**

AND

Mademoiselle **PAULINE LEROUX**.

Monsieur **ALBERT**,   Monsieur **COULON**,

Monsieur **THEODORE**,

Monsieur **ALBERT**, Fils,

Monsieur **GUERPONT**,   Monsieur **MICHAUD**,
Monsieur **GOURIET**,   Monsieur **O'BRYAN**,

The King's Theatre – La Donna del Lago with Joséphine as Elena.
(By courtesy of the Theatre Museum, The Victoria and Albert Museum.)

Cenerentola was followed by Rossini's *Donna del Lago*, based on Sir Walter Scott's *Lady of the Lake*. This opera was very popular in the early part of the nineteenth century, but then suffered a period of neglect.

Joséphine took the part of the heroine, Elena. The critics gave her a mixed reception. The *Literary Gazette* considered that their 'favourite De Meric' had been below rather than above mediocrity and criticised her 'unbending German style of singing' as being ill adapted to the graceful music of Elena. The *Morning Post* said that her well-known talents were a sufficient guarantee that she would acquit herself well, but felt that her style was not of that easy, flowing character which had made the part so celebrated in the hands of Ronzi De Begnis and Sontag.

The *Morning Chronicle* said that Joséphine had both acted and sung delightfully, from the opening *cavatina*, *Oh mattutini albori* – the melody so frequently repeated – to the splendid air at the close of the opera. It was regrettable that the singer representing Uberto had sung about his ecstasy 'with an air of imperturbable gravity' which was in ludicrous contrast with the sentiment and harmonised ill with the sweet sounds echoed by his fair partner in the song. The paper described the chorus as lamentable.

The *Sunday Times* was critical of the production as a whole. The opera had been unjustifiably cut:

> 'The first act was gone through rather respectably, considering that we are now in the early part of the season, when it is not the fashion to produce more than one or two persons whose vocal talents rise much above mediocrity. The second was that selected for the operations of the pruning knife, and some of the best compositions of the opera were lopped off with as little sangfroid as if they were not of the slightest consequence, and provided only that the name of the opera and its general character were preserved, no more could be desired . . . Madame de Meric was not in good voice. She laboured under the effects of a cold, which rendered her exertions unavailing.'

The breeches part of Malcolm, later to be taken by Joséphine's daughter Emilie, fell to Mlle. Schiasetti, who was making her first appearance in London.

Rossini's *Matilde di Shabran*, a two-act *opera buffa*, was presented on 2 March. Its first performance had been conducted by Paganini in Rome in 1821. According to *The Times*, the opera was revived in London for the purpose of putting forward Madame Boccabadati in the character of the heroine, because her representation of the part on the Continent had been regarded as one of her most attractive efforts. At short notice, Joséphine took the minor rôle of the Contessa. The *Literary Gazette* praised her for always being ready to oblige and the *Morning Post* said that she had given the part an importance which it had not possessed before. Much credit was due to her for taking it.

In this opera, the two principal ladies are rivals for the favours of the supposedly obdurate warrior, Corradino, played on this occasion by Donzelli. *The Times* judged the work to be a second-rate affair, but a very large audience had been highly pleased with the whole performance.

At the end of March, Joséphine took over from Mlle. Schiasetti as Suzanna in *Le Nozze di Figaro*. Both she and Donzelli were much applauded. *Figaro* had originally been billed for 19 March. The *première* had been postponed and this occasioned an outburst from the *Sunday Times*: 'Some of the irregularities which were the order of the day last season have lately come into full play here. The *Nozze di Figaro* was advertised . . . but suddenly, without any reason assigned, that everlasting makeshift – that refuge of the destitute – that threadbare worn out *Cenerentola* was given instead.' And it had been appallingly sung.

At about this time, Joséphine must have had some kind of dispute with Laporte, who seems frequently to have been at odds with his singers. On 8 April, the *Morning Chronicle* reported that the difference between Madame de Méric and Laporte was at an end 'in the consequence of which she does not appear, as announced, as Alice at Drury Lane tomorrow'. In the event, it was Miss Betts who played Alice when *Robert le Diable* opened the season at Drury Lane. The *Morning Post* was unimpressed by the opera, declaring that it required a Nourrit, a Cinti, a Levasseur, and a Dorus or a Méric to prevent its being tedious.

THE INFLUENZA EPIDEMIC

The Spring of 1833 was marked in London by an exceptionally severe epidemic of influenza. This was described by a correspondent to the *Morning Post* (16 April):

> 'In the whole course of thirty years' experience, I recollect no visitation of what the French call *La Grippe* equal in extent to the present. In almost every family at the west end of the town the disease has spread through the whole establishment. In one commercial concern near Hanover-square there are thirty-two in bed; and in another at Charing Cross forty persons; at Devonshire House nearly the whole of the household; at Northumberland House also many. Go where you may it is the same. Since Saturday morning no patients are received at St. George's Hospital.'

UNDER THE ESPECIAL PATRONAGE

OF

His Majesty!

DRURY LANE
THEATRICAL FUND,

Established for the Relief of Indigent Persons belonging to their Majesties' Company of Comedians, and their Widows and Children,

BY THE GREAT MASTER OF HIS ART, THE LATE **DAVID GARRICK.** IT IS MOST RESPECTFULLY ANNOUNCED THAT THE

Sixteenth Anniversary Dinner

In aid of this Institution, will take place at the

FREEMASONS' HALL,

To-morrow, WEDNESDAY March 20, 1833.

President,
HIS ROYAL HIGHNESS THE DUKE OF SUSSEX.

Vice Presidents,

His Grace the Duke of ST. ALBANS,
His Grace the Duke of BEDFORD, K.G.
His Grace the Duke of DEVONSHIRE, K.G., L.Ch.
His Grace the Duke of GRAFTON,
His Grace the Duke of RUTLAND,
His Grace the Duke of SUTHERLAND,
Most Noble the Marquis of LANSDOWNE,
Most Noble the Marquis of LONDONDERRY,
Most Noble the Marquis of WESTMINSTER,
Most Noble the Marquis of CLANRICARDE,
Most Noble the Marquis of WORCESTER,
Rt. Hon. the Earl of ESSEX,
Rt. Hon. the Earl of CHESTERFIELD,
Rt. Hon. the Earl of ABERDEEN,
Rt. Hon. the Earl HOWE,
Rt. Hon. the Earl of WILTON,
Rt. Hon. the Earl of AMHERST,
Rt. Hon. the Earl of COVENTRY,
Rt. Hon. the Earl of MUNSTER,
Rt. Hon. the Earl of FIFE,
Rt. Hon. the Earl of LONSDALE,
Rt. Hon. the Earl of MEXBOROUGH,
Rt. Hon. the Earl of ERROL,
Rt. Hon. the Earl of GLENGALL,
Rt. Hon. the Earl of GROSVENOR,
Rt. Hon. the Earl of BELFAST,
Rt. Hon. Viscount PALMERSTON,
Rt. Hon. Viscount GODERICH,
Rt. Hon. Viscount VALLETORT,
Rt. Hon. Viscount MORPETH,
Rt. Hon. Viscount ALLEN,
Rt. Hon. Viscount RANELAGH,
Rt. Hon. Lord DUNDAS,
Rt. Hon. Lord CARRINGTON,
Rt. Hon. Lord SALTOUN,
Rt. Hon. Lord SEGRAVE,
Rt. Hon. Lord DURHAM,
Rt. Hon. Lord AUCKLAND,
Rt. Hon. Lord VERNON,
Rt. Hon. Lord TULLAMORE,
Rt. Hon. Lord W. LENNOX,
Rt. Hon. Lord F. L. GOWER,
Rt. Hon. Sir R. PEEL, Bart. M.P.

Rt. Hon. Sir G. WARRENDER, Bart. M.P.
Rt. Hon. Sir JOHN CAM HOBHOUSE, Bart. M.P.
Rt. Hon. GEORGE PONSONBY,
Hon. GEORGE LAMB, M.P.
Hon. General PHIPPS, M.P.
Hon. C. B. PHIPPS,
Hon. ANDREW RAMSAY,
Sir GILBERT HEATHCOTE, Bart. M.P.
Sir T. H. FARQUHAR, Bart.
Sir HARRY GOODRICKE, Bart.
Sir RICHARD WILLIAM BULKELEY, Bart. M.P.
Sir GERARD NOEL, Bart. M.P.
Sir F. BURDETT, Bart, M.P.
Sir PHILIP SIDNEY, Bart.
Sir WYNDHAM CARMICHAEL ANSTRUTHER, Bart.
Sir T. B. LENNARD, Bart. M.P.
Sir W. CURTIS, Bart.
Sir GEORGE POCOCK, Bart.
Sir E. CODRINGTON, Admiral, Bart. M.P.
Sir W. BROWN FFOULKES, Bart. M.P.
Sir ANDREW BARNARD, Major General, K.C.B.
Sir RONALD FERGUSON, General, K.C.B., M.P.
Sir C. THORNTON, Colonel,
Sir JOHN SOANE, R.A.
BAINBRIDGE, E. T. Esq. M.P.
BARNETT, Charles James, Esq. M.P.
BARTON, Hugh, Jun. Esq.
BERENS, R. Esq.
BRIGSTOCK, W. P. Esq. M.P.
BOND, A. C. Esq.
BYNG, G. Esq. M.P.
BUNN, A. Esq.
CABBELL, B. Bond, Esq.
CALCRAFT, Granby, Esq.
CHANTRY, F. Esq. R.A.
COHEN, B. Esq.
COX, R. H. Esq.
CROMBIE, Lewis, Esq.
DAWKINS, John, Esq.
DANVERS, G. J. Butler, Esq.
DOTTIN, J. R. Esq.
DUNCOMBE, T. Esq.
DURRANT, J. R. Esq.
ELLIS, Charles, Esq.
EWING, J. Esq. M.P.
FANCOURT, Major, M.P.
FAIRLIE, John, Esq.
FLOWER, W. Esq.
FOLEY, E. Esq. M.P.

GORDON, R. Esq.
GORE, Montague, Esq. M.P.
GRANT, G. Esq.
GRIFFITH, Thomas, Esq.
GRIFFITHS, J. Esq.
GRONOW, Captain, M.P.
HARRISON, W. Esq.
HOPKINSON, Charles, Esq.
KNIGHT, H, Gally, Esq.
KAY, John, Esq.
LEIGH, Chandos, Esq.
LEVY, Samuel, Esq.
LINLEY, W. Esq.
LITTLEDALE, Joseph, Esq.
LOWDHAM, L. A. Esq.
MACKENNON, W. A. Esq.
MASH, T. B. Esq.
MEASURE, John, Esq.
METCALF, T. Esq.
MILLS, F. Esq.
MURRAY, John, Esq.
OAKLEY, B. Esq.
PARKINSON, Joseph, Esq.
PARLETT, J. Esq.
PHILIPPS, I. H. Esq.
PETTIWARD, Roger, Esq.
POLHILL, Captain,
PRICE, Stephen, Esq.
RAMSBOTTOM, J. Esq. M.P.
RAPHAEL, Alexander, Esq.
RAYMOND, J. Esq.
RICHARDSON, Edward, Esq.
ROBARTS, A. R. Esq. M.P.
ROBINS, G. H. Esq.
ROOLS, J. Esq.
ROSSITER, J. Esq.
SALOMONS, Philip Joseph, Esq.
SAVORY, T. F. Esq.
SMITH, G. Esq. M.P.
STANFIELD, Clarkson, Esq.
STEPHENS, S. Lyne, Esq.
STEWART, Robert, Esq.
SPOTTISWOOD, Andrew, Esq. M.P.
SUTTON, C. Manuers, Jun. Esq.
TYNTE, C. Kemeys, Esq. M.P.
YORKE, Captain, M.P.
WARWICK, W. T. Esq.
WILSON, R. Esq.
WILLIAMS, T. P. Esq. M.P.

List of Officials of the Drury Lane Theatrical Fund. (Charity Performance in which Joséphine took part, March 1833).

(By courtesy of the Theatre Museum, The Victoria and Albert Museum.)

Two days later it was stated at the Westminster Medical Society 'that so prevalent a disorder had not existed within the memory of the oldest medical practitioner'.

Somewhat surprisingly, the theatres mostly managed to remain open, but they were by no means unscathed. On Tuesday 16 April no opera could be performed.

Joséphine was one of the sufferers. She was apparently extremely ill. Her sickness prevented a performance of *Il Pirata* from being given. At the King's Theatre on 13 April there had been a 'seld-seen spectacle'. Madame de Méric, Mlle. [Nina] Sontag and Mlle. Taglioni had all been unable to appear. 'Where', the audience cried, 'is Madame de Méric?' Laporte came forward and said: 'I assure you that she is so ill that it is utterly impossible for her, with all her willingness, to appear before you' (*Morning Post*). Joséphine had recovered sufficiently to return to the stage on 18 April.

On Saturday 20 April, London was given two versions of *The Barber of Seville*, one at Drury Lane and the other (first act only) at the King's Theatre.

At the King's Theatre, Joséphine, as Rosina, sang with Donzelli and the famous Italian baritone Antonio Tamburini. Both Joséphine and Donzelli were out of voice and she was even out of tune, 'a rare defect in her' (*Morning Chronicle*). However, 'she does not profess to be able to sing the music of Rosina, and as she was only a substitute for a better, it is hardly fair to criticise her' (*Observer*).

On 21 April 1833, *The Atlas* had come out with a report that 'The Coburg promises, under a new government, to excite attention. Mr. Glossop, the old proprietor, has regained possession, and, in a spirit of good taste which augurs well and wisely, appointed Mr. Broad to the management'. The Coburg, renamed the Victoria in honour of the heiress presumptive, duly re-opened on Monday 1 July, but there seems to be no truth whatever in the rumour that Joseph Glossop had resumed charge.

As the heroine in the King's Theatre production towards the end of April of *La Gazza Ladra*, 'the ever-useful de Méric was satisfactory and effective' (*Morning Post*). *The Atlas* also praised her though adding that dramatically she could not bear comparison with Malibran, 'a lyric actress, who, we firmly believe, will never have a successor in the part'.

La Gazza Ladra proved to be very much to the taste of the critic on the *Sunday Times*. 'A change is at length effected. The ghosts have departed to the shades, and we are to be served for the remainder of the season by the longed-for realities of harmony. The veriest grumbler and railer against the "men and manners" of this house must have been content on Tuesday evening [23 April]. Every part (even the subordinate) of *La Gazza Ladra* was well performed. De

Méric found herself in good company, and laid aside the carelessness of manner and the airs which, good innocent lady, she had thought it right to assume of late. She is a pleasing – a useful – and at times, when in good voice, an effective singer; but she is one of those by no means *rarae aves*, in the theatrical population of any country, who choose not to exert themselves unless the house is well attended.'

Theatre Royal, Covent-Garden.

The Public is respectfully informed that

On WEDNESDAY NEXT
January 30, 1833,

Will be presented at this Theatre, a

Grand Performance
OF
Sacred Music

UNDER THE DIRECTION OF
Mr. ROPHINO LACY.

Singers already engaged:

Madame DE MERIC,
Miss INVERARITY, & Miss H. CAWSE
Signor DONZELLI, Signor GALLI,
Mr. WILSON, Mr. SEGUIN,
Mr. I. BENNETT, Mr. RANSFORD,
AND
Mr. H. PHILLIPS.

Among the Instrumental Performers will be the following——
Mr. LINDLEY,
Who will perform a NEW FANTASIA on the VIOLONCELLO
Mr. NICHOLSON,
Who will perform a NEW CONCERTO on the FLUTE,
Sig. DRAGONETTI, Mr. WILMAN,
&c. &c.

THE CHORUSES
will be under the Superintendence of Mr. G. STANSBURY, assisted by the Young Gentlemen of the *Chapel Royal, St. Paul's,* and *Westminster Abbey,* under the Direction of Mr. HAWES.

Theatre Royal, Covent Garden – Concert of Sacred Music.
30 January, 1833.
(By courtesy of the Theatre Museum, The Victoria and Albert Museum.)

Wednesday 1 May 1833 had been memorable for the first appearance in London of Malibran in *La Sonnambula*. This was at Drury Lane. The audience included 'nearly all the great musical talent in the metropolis'. The *Morning Chronicle* identified Paganini, Hummell, Madame Pasta, Mme. Cinti-Damoreau, Mme. de Méric, Mme. Schroeder-Devrient, Haitzinger, Mrs. Wood, Mme. Vestris, Miss Shirreff, Braham, Wilson and others. Mlle. Taglioni and a party occupied one of the private boxes. The paper's critic bore witness to the pleasure which Pasta seemed to receive from the performance.

Pasta had created the name part in Donizetti's *Anna Bolena* in Milan in 1830 and had been acclaimed when she appeared as the Queen in London in 1831, with Rubini and Lablache. Now, at the King's Theatre on 2 May, a full and exceptionally fashionable audience assembled 'to hail, with pleasure' Pasta's first appearance 'these two years'.

As described in *The Times*, Pasta was Queen and woman beautifully blended. In the final scene of madness, she had fairly established the character of being the Siddons of the opera. The *Literary Gazette* thought that her voice, if anything, had improved, having entirely lost the slight huskiness with which it had been affected, and her acting was perfect.

Both as actress and singer, Pasta's great triumphs were in the second act, wrote the *Morning Post*. 'Her interview with Jane Seymour [Joséphine], in which she discovers that the latter is the rival who has supplanted her in the affections of the King [Tamburini], considered merely as to dramatic effect, has never been surpassed on any stage; seldom, indeed equalled . . . . The opera was in all parts exceedingly well done. Madame de Meric has seldom appeared to so much advantage as in the part of Jane Seymour; the presence of Pasta seemed to excite her emulation, and in the scene above alluded to, which is her principal one, she acquitted herself in first-rate style.' *The Times* said that she had proved that she was no ordinary acquisition to the Italian opera. 'In the great scene with Ann Boleyn, where she entreats the pity and forgiveness of her mistress for an unintentional fault, she evinced very superior powers'. The *Literary Gazette* reported that Joséphine had been very enthusiastically received by the most crowded audience of the season and had acted up to Pasta in a manner that did her the highest credit.

The opera enjoyed a long run and most of the adverse criticism was directed against the libretto for being unnecessarily unhistorical.

The wide appeal of *Anna Bolena* may perhaps be judged from a complaint in *The Times* that Laporte had allowed unkempt 'couriers and others of that class' into the pit with their dirty shirts and muddy boots.

144

Anna Bolena was frequently to be performed in the following years, e.g. with Grisi and Tietjens, but then fell out of the repertory until it was revived by Visconti in Milan in 1957, with Callas.

Scenes from The Barber of Seville *and* Anna Bolena *at* The King's Theatre – Joséphine *as Rosina and Jane Seymour.*

(By courtesy of the Theatre Museum, The Victoria and Albert Museum.)

THE KING'S THEATRE

FOR THE BENEFIT OF MESDLLES

Teresa and Fanny Elsler.

THIS PRESENT EVENING

Will be Performed, compressed into One Act, ROSSINI's Opera Buffa, entitled

IL BARBIERE DI SIVIGLIA

Count Almaviva, the lover of Rosina   Signor DONZELLI.
Rosina, Ward of Doctor Bartolo   Madame DE MERIC
Doctor Bartolo Sig. DI ANGELI. – Baslo, a Music Master Sig. GIUBILEI
Figaro, the Barber   Signor TAMBURINI.
Betra, the Governante   Madame CASTELLI.
Fiorello, a Servant   Signor G. GALLI.

After which will be presented

A DIVERTISSEMENT,

IN WHICH WILL BE INTRODUCED

A Grand Pas de Deux by Monsieur Albert and Mademoiselle Taglioni.

After which will be presented a Scena from

Anna Bolena.

Henry III King of England   Signor TAMBURINI.
Anna Boleyn, his Queen   Madame PASTA.
Jane Seymour, her lady in waiting   Madame DE MERIC.
Lord Rochford, Anne's Brother   Signor DE ANGELI.
Lord Percy   Signor DONZELLI.
Smeaton, the Queen's Page and Minstrel   Mll. H. CAWSE.
Sir Harvey, the King's Officer   Signor GALLI.

To conclude with a New Ballet, entitled

LA FER ET CHEVALIER.

PRINCIPAL DANCERS

Madlle. Taglioni, Madlle Pauline Leroux,

Mesdlles. TERESA AND FANNY ELSLER,

Monsieur Albert, Monsieur Coulon & Monsieur Theodore Guerinot.

On 11 May, at the King's Theatre, a two-act opera seria on the Medea story called *Medea in Corinto* does not seem to have received much critical comment. The composer was the Bavarian Johann Mayr (1763-1845), who taught Donizetti. Pasta was in the title rôle, supported by Donzelli, Rubini, V.Galli and Madame de Méric. The *Morning Chronicle* judged that the whole opera had been at least as

145

well cast as at any theatre in Europe. *Lodoïska* (1800) and *Medea in Corinto* (1813) are generally regarded as Mayr's best operas. Mayr had been very popular in Italy until eclipsed by Rossini.

Joséphine was to have made her first appearance at the Theatre Royal, Covent Garden on Whitsun Eve 1833 in a performance of an oratorio called *The Israelites in Egypt* written by Michael Lacy (1795-1867), with music composed 'wholly by Handel and Rossini'. She was billed to take the part of Annai, one of the Israelites, a rôle which would no doubt have evoked unhappy memories. In the event, she pleaded indisposition and her place was taken at short notice by Miss Romer, who had a success.

On 6 June, at the King's Theatre, Joséphine played Rosina and Jane Seymour in scenes from *The Barber* and *Anna Bolena*, at a benefit for Teresa and Fanny Elsler.

Early in June, Joséphine was at Covent Garden in an ill-adapted version of *The Marriage of Figaro*. She played the Countess Almaviva. Billed as an extraordinary musical attraction, the opera had a strong female contingent, with Malibran as Susanna and Vestris as Cherubino. The *Guardian and Public Ledger* (17 June) wrote that Madame De Meric had been in very good voice. Also, her acting had been very good, 'but rather marred by her continental accent, which at times was not a little ridiculous.'

Pasta had created the rôle of the heroine in Bellini's *Norma* in Milan in 1832. On 20 June, in the first performance of the opera in England, she appeared at the King's Theatre with Joséphine as Adalgisa and Donzelli as the Roman warrior Pollione. The production was under Bellini's personal direction.

The auspices were bad. The critic Dilettante, who contributed a Diary in the *Harmonicon*, had declared that every reliable source in Italy agreed that music in that country was at its lowest ebb. 'Nothing new is brought forward but the vilest trash, and even Rossini is no longer the idol'. Bellini was a prime target. 'It seems that, after Easter, we are to have thrust down our throats – or rather crammed into our ears – Bellini's *Norma* and also *Beatrice Tenda*, both, it is said, the feeblest of modern weaknesses, the first especially, which all but Italians agree in admitting to be the veriest rubbish that ever disgraced the lyric stage. We are also to have *Montecchi e Capuletti* of the same composer, which I can, from my own knowledge, say, is as wretched stuff as any that our Italian theatre has produced during the last five or six years. I cannot say more.'

With puffs like that, it is not surprising that the opera was not very well received. There was some praise for the *mise-en-scène*, but *The Times* found *Norma* dull and the *Morning Advertiser* described the music as a series of plagiarisms from Rossini which produced a cold effect. The *Harmonicon* considered that, with a couple of exceptions, the music, while conforming to the rules of composition, possessed the most fatal of all faults - it was deplorably uninteresting. The overture and most of Act I produced intolerable din.

THE KING'S THEATRE

FOR THE BENEFIT OF

M. LAPORTE

This Present Evening, June 27, 1833

Will be Performed, a New Opera entitled

NORMA

Pollio, a Roman Proconsul Signor DONZELLI.
Flavius, his Friend Sig. GALLI.   Oroveso Arch Druid Sig. V. GALLI
Norma, Druidess, Daughter of Oroveso   Madame PASTA.
Adalgisa, a young Priestess of the Temple of Irminsul   Madame DE MERIC·
Clotide, Confidant of Norma.   Madame CASTELLI.

After the Opera, SIGNOR

PAGANINI,

Who has obligingly offered his services, will play some of his celebrated variations.

After which, the Third Act of Rossini's Opera Seria, intitled·

OTELLO

THE PRINCIPLE CHARACTERS BY

Signor DONZELLI, (For this Night only) And Madame Malibran.

To Conclude with the New Ballet of

La Sylphiad.

The Sylphiad   Mademoiselle TAGLIONI.
James Reuben, a Scotch Peasant   Monsieur ALBERT.
Anne Reuben, his Mother   Mademoiselle PAULINE LEROUX
Effie, a Peasant. Anne's Niece   Madlle F. ELSER.
Gurn, a Scotch Peasant   Monsieur GUERINOT.
Old Madge, a Scorceress -   Mademoiselle LEROUX

In Act I, a PAS DE DEUX, by

Madlle. Pauline Leroux & Mons. Daumont.

A PAS DE DEUX, by
Monsieur Theodore Guerinot & Madlle Fanny Elsler
In the Second Act will be introduced A GRAND PAS DE DEUX, by

Madlle. Taglioni & Monsieur Albert

Application for Boxes, Stalls, and Tickets to be made to Mr. SEGUIN, at the Box Office,
PIT 10s. 6d   GALLERY 5s.
Printed by T· BIRT, No. 39, Great St. Andrew Street, Seven Dials.

The King's Theatre – M. Laporte's Benefit, Joséphine in Norma *in the same bill as Paganini, Malibran, Taglioni and Fanny Elsler.*

(By courtesy of the Theatre Museum, The Victoria and Albert Museum.)

There was not even universal praise for Pasta. The loyal *Morning Chronicle* sprang to her defence, and after the performance on 29 June the *Morning Advertiser* said that she was in superb voice. However, on the first night her talents had evidently failed her. According to Cox, who seems to have been in error as to the date, Pasta's voice had all but gone. So defective, indeed was her intonation, that in the celebrated duet, *Deh! con te*, she had gradually gone down a whole tone. 'Expecting the whole thing to come to grief, I listened in agony for the result which might be expected on the instant of her having finished her line. When she had done so the band altogether ceased to play; but then Mdme. de Meric . . . manifested on the instant how clever and well-instructed a musician she was by taking up her line in such perfect tune that it could only be compared to the clearness of a bell'. The *Morning Post* said that Pasta's straying off key had put the orchestra off, but fortunately Joséphine's correct ear had brought them back to the correct road . . . and it was only Pasta's power as an actress that had saved her from disaster.

The *Morning Advertiser* referred to 'the chaste sweetness and perfect science of Du [sic] Meric'. *The Times* commended Joséphine and Donzelli for their duet, *Vieni in Roma! Ah! vieni o cara*. The *Observer* found fault with Joséphine's articulation and suggested, surprisingly enough, that being a Frenchwoman she was afraid to trust herself with the pronunciation of Italian. In Italy itself, it will be recalled, she had received praise for her command of the language.

Weinstock, in his *Vincenzo Bellini* (Weidenfeld and Nicolson 1971) says that on 11 May 1833 a German version of *Norma* was performed at the *Kärntnertor* Theatre in Vienna with the same cast as in London, but no other evidence has been found that Joséphine made any such break in her London season. According to the Viennese *Allgemeine Theaterzeitung* of 13 May, a German version was indeed given at the *Kärntnertor* on 11 May, but with Madame Ernst as Norma and Fräulein Löwe as Adalgisa.

There was a gala evening of opera and ballet at the King's Theatre on 4 July, when 'the most elegant dancer of the age, Taglioni' took her benefit. As *The Times* put it, Taglioni's own merits were sufficient to have filled the house, but to make assurance double sure she had secured the assistance of Pasta, Malibran, de Méric and Donzelli.

The opera, Rossini's *Tancredi*, was beautifully performed. Pasta gave the universally admired *Di tanti palpiti* with exquisite effect. Joséphine, *The Times* said, added very considerably to her rising fame. The *Morning Advertiser* praised the production as the best cast opera of the season, even though Joséphine was not as good as Cinti in the rôle of Aménaïde.

The opera was followed by excerpts from the ballets *La Bayardère* and *La Sylphide*. Taglioni 'displayed all that agility of foot, grace of motion, and picturesque elegance of gesture, which have deservedly placed her at the head of her profession'. As compared with opera, ballet at this period was 'a quite minor consideration with the public', if we are to believe the *Sunday Times*.

Joséphine took the part of Giulietta in the London *première* of Bellini's opera *I Capuleti e i Montecchi* on the Shakespearean theme of *Romeo and Juliet* which was given at the King's Theatre on 20 July 1833. The other principal rôles were taken by Pasta (Romeo), Donzelli (Tebaldo), and Vincenzo Galli (Capellio).

The opera was taken off after only a couple of performances. The *Athenaeum* dismissed it as a complete failure, regarding the music as trash unworthy of comment. In the opinion of the *Spectator*, the characteristic of Bellini was sheer dullness. The *Morning Advertiser* reported that the opera had been received with 'composed apathy – if it did not offend, it did not please' – and it was a pity that Joséphine and not Malibran had played Juliet. The *Harmonicon* rated the wretched work as inferior even to *Norma*: even Pasta's acting could not save it.

The revival of *I Capuleti e i Montecchi* at Covent Garden in 1984 gives a special interest to the reactions of those who witnessed the *première*. *The Times* wrote on 22 July 1833:

> 'It [the opera] is founded on the story of *Romeo and Juliet*, on which, we believe, not less than four or five different masters have exerted their abilities. Amongst these, Zingarelli, whose opera was brought out here a few years ago, stands most conspicuous. His work, which is distinguished by fancy and originality, was extremely successful, and for three successive seasons was frequently performed. We fear that Bellini's opera will not be so fortunate. It was but little admired on the Continent, and it was received by the great body of the audience, on Saturday evening, without any of that enthusiasm which nothing but first rate talent can command. Bellini, however well versed he may be in the theory of the art which he professes, is manifestly deficient in invention. We perceive very little that is novel in his compositions, whilst we often recognise imitations of other masters, and he is not infrequently a borrower from himself.
>
> '*I Capuleti* is, we think, a better opera than his *Norma*, which, though aided by the glorious powers of Madame Pasta, was speedily thrown aside. The first act of the new opera is decidedly the best. The finale is excellent. It is extremely spirited, and, throughout, enchains the attention. Had the whole opera been composed with equal felicity, it must have been triumphantly successful. [The principal singers] did ample justice to the composition. [The finale] was indeed admirably sung, and produced the only encore of the evening . . . . Madame

Pasta, as Romeo, sang with all her accustomed truth of expression, and acted with all her wonted commanding yet graceful dignity . . . .

'Madame de Méric was an efficient representative of Juliet, and sang with much taste and purity. Her opening soliloquy, *Eccomi in lieta vesta – eccomi adorna come vittima all ara* was delivered with much sensibility.'

The *Literary Gazette* claimed that Pasta had been hoarse and out of tune, but de Méric 'had warbled sweetly as the heroine'.

At the revival at Covent Garden in 1848, the final scene from Vaccai's version of the opera was used instead of Bellini's. This did not prevent the *Athenaeum* from declaring roundly that 'there never was an audience in England for *I Capuleti* and now [1850] we do not apprehend that there ever will be . . . .'

THE 1833 OPERA SEASON IN RETROSPECT

Opinions about the 1833 Opera Season differed markedly. The critic on the *Morning Chronicle* said: 'We never recollect a season when there was so much and such extraordinary musical and vocal talent assembled in the metropolis, and (with the exception of Malibran at Drury Lane) all at the King's Theatre.' Yet when the King's Theatre closed on 10 September, with Paër's *Agnese*, the *Harmonicon* complained that the season had been distinguished by the performance of thoroughly worn-out operas and of two new ones 'which proved less endurable than the hacks that preceded them'.

On the practical side, Laporte seems to have been no more successful than the hapless Monck Mason. According to the *Harmonicon*, nearly half the subscription nights passed with scarcely a tolerable performer on the stage. From Easter, twice as many performers were engaged as could be properly employed. As a result, performers had been sent off with bills at enormously long dates. The artists had become thoroughly discouraged and few had felt disposed to return to London another year.

For her part, Joséphine did not perform in London again.

150

Concerts and provincial tours in 1833

LONDON CONCERTS

BETWEEN the end of January and the end of July 1833, Joséphine sang in some two dozen concerts in London. Some were private ones, arranged by people of substance, often vocalists themselves. Several were for charity or as benefits. Twice she was engaged again with the Philharmonic Society of London.

Unfortunately, at the Society's second concert on 11 March, she arrived at the Hanover Square Rooms after her exertions as Donna Anna at Drury Lane. The rendering she then gave of *Per pietà*, from *Così fan tutte*, caused *The Atlas* to complain that she had scarcely sufficient voice left to do justice to the aria. The *Athenaeum* said bluntly that Madame de Méric had blundered in *Per pietà*, 'a difficult song for even a better singer.' The *Spectator*, on the other hand, declared that in most parts of the song she had left nothing to desire. At the following concert, this aria was entrusted to the *débutante* Clara Novello, then not quite fifteen, but Joséphine returned for the Society's fourth concert (15 April) when she sang *Tutto un concerto* from Weber's *Euryanthe*, an opera which was not to be produced in London until a couple of months later. She then joined Bishop and James Bennett in the trio *Qual canna al suol* from Ludwig Spohr's opera *Jessonda* (1823).

Joséphine had been expected in London at the very beginning of the year and had been prominently billed in a list of singers due to take part on 30 January (the anniversary of the execution of King Charles I) in a performance at Covent Garden of sacred music under the direction of Rophino Lacy. However, it is uncertain whether Joséphine appeared. The other ladies named were Miss Inverarity and Miss Cawse.

Madame de Méric was among the numerous 'distinguished professors' who had volunteered their services for the Sixteenth Anniversary Dinner of the Drury Lane Theatrical Fund, held at the Freemasons' Hall on Wednesday 20 March 1833. This Fund, enjoying the Especial Patronage of The King, had been established by David Garrick for 'the relief of indigent persons belonging to their Majesties' Company of Comedians, and their widows and children.'

The Fund's President, in 1833, was the Duke of Sussex. Tickets for the Dinner, including wine, were one guinea. The Hall was to open at five o'clock, with 'Dinner on table on the arrival of His Royal Highness.'

In the middle of April, Miss Mounsey, a pianist, gave a concert at which Joséphine was engaged to sing.

Notable among the *Soirées Musicales* of the season were those given by Miss Bruce at the residence of J. Taylor, Esq., at 30 George Street, Hanover Square. Joséphine was one of the performers engaged by Miss Bruce. There were three *soirées*, in May and June. They began at 9 o'clock and tickets cost half-a-guinea, but one guinea entitled the purchaser to attend all three.

The famous pianist Moscheles gave an afternoon concert in the Great Concert Room at the King's Theatre on 1 May at which Joséphine sang a Rossini duet with Miss Masson.

A concert in the same Room on 8 May, given by Messrs. Nicholson and Willman, was graced by Madame Pasta. Joséphine sang the *scena* and air *A celui que j'aimais* from *La Muette de Portici*.

The concert-promoters of the period were eager to secure Royal Patronage and were particularly gratified when they could boast that the patronage was 'immediate'. Thus when Mr. J. N. Hummel, *Maître de Chapelle* to the Grand Duke of Saxe-Weimar and Director of the German Opera at the King's Theatre, gave his one and only concert of the season there on 13 May, he announced that he had been accorded the immediate patronage and sanction of Queen Adelaide. Joséphine had obliged with an aria.

For her concert at the King's Theatre on 20 May, Madame Dulcken had secured the patronage of the Duchess of Kent, mother of the Princess Victoria. Most of the principal singers then in London, including Joséphine, took part. The Princess Augusta gave her immediate patronage to the evening concert in Hanover Square which the Misses Mills gave on 14 June. There, Joséphine sang in company with Pasta, Cinti-Damoureau, Clara and Cecilia Novello – and, of course, Miss H. Mills.

The *Literary Gazette* reported that Madame de Méric had sung *Non più di fiori* with great spirit at the annual concert given by Mr. R. Dressler and Mr. F. Pelzer, before a very numerous and delighted audience, on 15 May.

It was under the immediate patronage of the Duke of Sussex that Mr. Salamon gave his Evening Concert in Hanover Square on 30 May. Joséphine sang a duet with Donzelli from Paër's *Agnese* and took part with M. Correldi's two daughters in a *Trio à la Tyrolienne* which had been composed for the concert by Correldi himself. She also sang the *cavatina Dio di bontà* by Bellini.

The bass Giuseppe De Begnis, described as the leading *buffo* of his day, had engaged a galaxy of talent for a Concert of New Italian Music at the King's Theatre Room on 24 June. Joséphine took part in two *terzetti*: with Donzelli and Giubilei in *Tu sospiri e incerta stai*, from Pacini's *La Schiava in Bagdad*, and with Miss Bellchambers and Signor Salvi in *Le faccio un'inchino* from the *Matrimonio Segreto*. Unfortunately, both Madame Schroeder-Devrient and Herr Haitzinger had failed to appear, 'being indisposed', and Signor Arigotti had sung out of tune, but Pasta, Malibran and de Méric had all sung charmingly and 'the clear and powerful tones of the latter lady had imparted a beautiful effect to the finale of *Don Giovanni*.'

In 1833 there was a succession of concerts for worthy causes in many of which Joséphine participated. The leading musical artists were indeed expected to lend their 'gratuitous and powerful assistance'.

Madame de Méric headed the list of artists, mostly English, who took part in the Great Miscellaneous Concert on 19 April, in the King's Antient Concert Rooms in Hanover Square, in aid of the Choral Fund, instituted for the relief of distressed members, their widows and orphans. This was under Royal patronage. The concert was notable for performances by two infant prodigies: Master Henry Charles Litolff (a pupil of Moscheles) on the grand pianoforte, and Master Hughes, the Infant Harpist.

The Hanover Square Rooms.
(By courtesy of the British Museum.)

FRENCH PLAYS,

KING'S THEATRE, HAYMARKET.

M. MARS,

Late Editor of the *Furet de Londres*, Author of several Vaudevilles,
Begs respectfully to inform the
Nobility, Subscribers to the French Plays, and the Public, that

SEVERAL EMINENT PERFORMERS

and Amateurs having kindly offered their assistance, he will take

HIS BENEFIT

AT THE

KING'S CONCERT ROOM,

Which has been fitted up in the neatest manner, as an elegant and
complete Theatre,

On *FRIDAY, 5th JULY*, 1833.

The Performances will commence, at half-past Seven o'clock, with

Le Jeune Homme à marier;

Ou, LA HAINE D'UNE FEMME.

M. Philippon, vieux Précepteur, M. ARNAUD.
Léon, son Pupile, Mlle. FOURCISY. Ursulle, jeune Veuve, Mad. ST. ALPHONSE.
Juliette, } jeunes Filles à marier, { Mlle. AMELIE.
Malvina, }   { Mlle. ADELE.

In the Course of the Evening a

MÉLANGE OF MUSIC

BY

Mad. DE MERIC.

Mad. KYNTHERLAND.   Mad. SALMON HANTUTE.

Signor TAMBURINI.   AND   Signor DONZELLI.

Signor DE BEGNIS,

Who will sing a new RONDEAU written expressly for this occasion by M. MARS,
and composed by M. A. DONNADIEU.

Conductor,   M. PIO CIANCHETTINI.

The favourite Piece of M. JOVIAL; ou, L'HUISSIER CHANSONNIER, having
been received with unbounded Applause on its first representation, and numerous
Applications having been made for its Repetition, M. MARS has selected the piece
for his Night, in compliance with the Desire of his Patrons.

JOVIAL;

Ou, L'HUISSIER CHANSONNIER.

Vaudeville nouveau, en Deux Actes, de M. THÉAULON.

M. LAPORTE remplira le Rôle de *Jovial.*
St Léon, M. ARNAUD.   Vincent, Garçon Restaurateur, M. CLOUP.
Ducroisé, Tapissier, M. JULES.
Elise d'Albi, Madame St. ALPHONSE.   Cécile, son Amie, Mlle. AMELIE.
Justine, Femme de Chambre, Mademoiselle ADELE.

TO CONCLUDE WITH

Le Concert de Village.

Folie-Vaudeville in One Act, by **M. MARS,**
In which he will perform himself the Character of *Tintamarre.*

M. LAPORTE remplira le Rôle de *Clarinette.*
Lambert, Pâtissier-Traiteur, M. CLOUP.
Babet, Fille de Lambert, Mlle. LARCHER.   Gueraleau, Souffleur d'Orgues, M. SALABERT.

*Private Boxes, £3. 3s. & £2. 2s.; Public Boxes, 7s.
Stalls, 10s. 6d.; Pit, 3s. 6d.*

Private Boxes, Stalls, and Places may be secured and Tickets may be had on Application
to Mr. MARS, 19, Welbeck Street, Cavendish Square; of Mr. SEGUIN, at the Box-Office
of the Opera, from Ten till Five daily; of Mr. BUCKNALL, Bookseller, 2, King Street,
Covent Garden; at the Libraries, as usual;

And at the Theatre during the Performance.

By permission of the Dowager Marchioness of Salisbury, a Concert was given on 22 April at her residence, 20 Arlington Street, Piccadilly, in aid of the Royal Infirmary for Cataract and other Diseases of the Eye. The principal performers were Madame de Méric, Madame Puzzi, Donzelli and De Begnis.

It was the New Musical Fund for the Relief of Decayed Musicians, their widows and orphans, which benefit-ed from the concert on the stage at the King's Theatre on 3 May. This Fund had been set up in 1786 and the Patrons were Their Majesties and the Royal Dukes. Joséphine appeared with Cinti-Damoureau and Puzzi. Paganini gave a demonstration by playing on the fourth string of his violin only.

After taking part in a *Mélange of Music* in the King's Concert Room on 5 July and a concert in the Argyll Rooms for the young singer H. Russell on 8 July, Joséphine sang at a special concert on 10 July for the benefit of the most unfortunate Mr. Wood whose uninsured lodging-house had been completely destroyed by fire. Her aria was Bellini's *Deh non ferir*.

A Grand Morning Musical Meeting was held on 12 July in aid of the Royal Metropolitan Infirmary for Children. This was given in the 'splendid Picture Gallery of H.T.Hope, Esq., M.P., Duchess Street, Portland Place' under patronage which included the Duchess of Gloucester, the Duchess of Northumberland and the Duchesse de Dino. Pasta and de Méric appeared by permission of M. Laporte, while Malibran was released by Mr. Bunn. Donzelli, Tamburini and De Begnis were among the male vocalists and Moscheles and Herz executed a pianoforte duet, but the special attraction was no doubt Paganini. The reporter from *The Spectator* described the scene:

> 'The orchestra was arranged in one of the principal picture-galleries; which was of course crammed with the fashionable world. Arriving somewhat late in the day, we were well content to take our ease in the cool and classic retreat formed by the gallery of sculpture adjoining . . . . The choicest refreshments were provided in profusion for the whole company; an instance of hospitality quite unexampled and not to be expected on such occasions . . . We could see nothing of the musical performers; and only got a glimpse of Paganini's bow through the legs of a Greek warrior'.

For Joséphine, a busy July concluded with a concert in Willis's Rooms, a Grand Fancy Fair at the Vauxhall Gardens in aid of the Royal Dispensary for Diseases of the Ear, both on the 15th of the month, and a benefit performance for M. Théodore Guérinot which was given at Covent Garden on 22 July. At the latter, she joined Tamburini and Zuchelli in the trio from *La Gazza Ladra*.

Joséphine had offered her services in a Grand Gala for the Benefit of the Distressed Poles which was to have taken place in the Gardens on 8 July, but this had to be abandoned 'because of frequent and noisy disturbances'.

PROVINCIAL TOUR IN 1833

The London opera season was followed by concert tours in major provincial towns and *The Athenaeum* of 3 August 1833 states that Madame de Méric had left on a musical tour of the West of England. So far, no evidence of this has been traced and she does not appear to have been at the Worcester Festival in that year. On the other hand, she certainly took part in the Northampton and Norwich Musical Festivals which began on 10 and 17 September respectively. The published accounts of these provide a vivid picture of Joséphine's repertoire at the time and of the tastes of the provincial audiences.

NORTHAMPTON – 10 AND 11 SEPTEMBER 1833

As the *Allgemeine Musikalische Zeitung* remarks, music festivals were rare in Northampton. However, the paper explains, the organist at the main Church there, All Saints, a Mr. Korkell [sic], being anxious to encourage a taste for music in the provinces, had for several years put on concerts with the help of the choral society which he had nurtured. In Northampton, the clergy would not allow him to hold his concert in the Church, so he had been obliged to hire 'a not very large hall'. As performers, he had engaged Madame de Méric, the beautiful young Clara Novello and Messrs. Pearsall, Taylor and Hobbs. Mr. Hobbs, it transpired, was taking the place of Mr. A. W. Roche, who was to have been one of the principal vocalists. Roche had had to cancel his engagement because of a sudden domestic calamity: his sister and nephew had been drowned off the coast of Norfolk in a shipwreck. François Cramer was the leader of the orchestra, which was largely drawn from the King's Theatre and the Royal Academy of Music.

The *Northampton Mercury* gave the concerts full coverage. The hall was the Assembly Rooms at the George Hotel. Both the Rooms and the Hotel have since been demolished, but Northampton residents at the end of the twentieth century would be able to understand the directions that carriages 'to set down' should have their horses' heads towards the County Hall, while carriages 'to take up' should have their horses' heads towards Gold Street.

The concerts were supported by a noble array of patrons and stewards. These included the High Sheriff, the Duke of Grafton, the Marquis [sic] of Northampton, Earl Spencer, Earl Fitzwilliam and the Earl of Euston. There were three M.P.s, Althorp, Brudenell and Milton; also the Mayor of Northampton and Sir William Wake, Bart., scion of the family of Hereward the Wake. The list contained no fewer than ten Reverends, so the clergy were clearly not opposed to the enterprise, even if they did not feel able to offer Church premises for the performances.

The full name of the organist was Mr. Charles M'Korkell, a native of the town. He had had a large and powerful organ erected for the occasion, which he played himself. He also conducted, played the harp and performed on the pianoforte: 'one of the newly invented instruments by Erard'.

At these Northampton evening concerts, Joséphine sang the following pieces:

On 10 September

> Grand Scena from Der Freischütz (Weber)
> Sull'aria from Le Nozze di Figaro, with Clara Novello
> Duet Se un istante from Elisa e Claudio, with Mr. E Taylor
> The Di piacer aria (Rossini)
> Trio Vadasi via di quà (Martini) with Novello and Taylor

On the morning of 11 September, a Wednesday, there was a performance of sacred music at which Joséphine sang:

> With verdure clad from Haydn's Creation
> Recitative and air But thou didst not, from Handel's Messiah
> Gratias agimus (Guglielmi)

The proceeds from this event were for the erection of the proposed Lunatic Asylum.

At the second evening concert, Joséphine gave renderings of:

> Duet Ah perdona from La Clemenza di Tito, with Clara Novello
> Air Su Griselda, with violin obligato by Mr. Eliason
> Duet Crudel perchè (Mozart) with Taylor
> Deh non ferir (Bellini)

After this concert there was a Ball. 'The whole of the splendid Assembly Rooms' were thrown open, all 120 feet of them.

According to the *Harmonicon*, Joséphine had also sung in the trio *Tremate, empi, tremate* from *Fidelio*. This 'hackneyed piece' had been correctly performed, but needed the stage. 'In a concert room it ranked as a second-rate composition – whatever the through-thick-and-thin admirers of the author might say to the contrary'.

Artistically, the concerts seem to have been a great success. According to the *Mercury*, 'Madame de Méric's voice is of astonishing compass, and she possesses a perfect command over all its extensive capabilities. She won the "golden opinions" of her audience immediately. In the splendid *scena* from *Der Freischütz*, the orchestra itself joined warmly in the plaudits with which she was greeted at its conclusion. Miss Novello's voice is very different in its character from that of Madame de Méric, but in its simplicity and sweetness, is not a whit less delightful . . . Martini's laughing and laughter-exciting trio *Vadasi via di quà* . . . was encored.'

The *Mercury* reviewer had been impressed most by the sacred music and spoke of the 'fresh and natural beauty' of Joséphine's *With verdure clad.*

The *Northampton Herald* spoke of the brilliancy and flexibility of Joséphine's voice and the impassioned style of her delivery. 'Of the *scena* from *Der Freyschutz* . . . given by Madame de Meric, we feel at a loss to express ourselves, never was triumph of the sublime art more complete.'

The *Atlas* of 22 September commented on the Northampton concerts and referred to Joséphine in these terms:

> 'Madame de Méric was never in better voice, and in the Italian and German *scenas* outsang all competition; but in Handel's music she is not yet sufficiently drilled, and it is somewhat late in the day for her to acquire the purity of this style [she was 32 at the time]. Those only to whom the music is "native" can convey all the pleasure which it is capable of affording. It is in this unimpassioned but elevated style that Miss Clara Novello excels'.

Financially, the concerts had been a disappointment. There had been a loss amounting to £122. 7s. 3d. This was sad for the Asylum Fund and for Mr. M'Korkell, who had expected at least to cover his expenses. As the *Mercury* reflected, the serious extent of the deficiency was 'such as will check any thoughts of a similar attempt for the future'.

In the words of *The Spectator*, 'Norwich takes the lead [among the Musical Festivals] in magnitude of dimension, and of attraction of every kind, as it does in point of time'.

In 1833 it had been announced that at St. Andrew's Hall in Norwich there would be an orchestra of 360 performers, conducted by Sir George Smart. The principal musical offerings would be *The Last Judgment*, by Spohr; Haydn's *Creation*; Handel's *Israel in Egypt* and F. Schneider's *Deluge*. The main singers billed, apart from Joséphine, were Malibran, Miss H. Cawse, Miss Bruce, Master Howe, Donzelli, Horncastle, Hobbs, Phillips and E. Taylor.

The notices in the *Norwich Chronicle* were imbued with the euphoria which the city felt in maintaining its tradition of triennial Musical Festivals and in securing the services of so many singers and instrumentalists of international repute. Behind the scenes, though, there was a political rumpus. As the Festivals were supported by the local Tories, led by the Wodehouses, they were boycotted by the Whigs (the Cokes, Ansons and Keppels and the Member of Parliament for the County alone excepted). Such was the political bitterness in the year following the Reform Bill.

The first concert opened, appropriately enough, with *God save The King*. According to the *Chronicle*, Madame Malibran, Madame de Méric and Mr. Phillips 'imparted the peculiarity of their respective styles, each to a verse.' If only that *tour de force* could have been recorded for posterity! The trio from *Don Giovanni*, sung by Malibran, Joséphine and Donzelli, had been 'a specimen of perfect harmony and splendour of effect' and had met with great applause. Then in the quintet from *Fidelio*, *Now with joy each heart is bounding*, 'Madame de Méric absolutely filled the hall with the instrumental force and silvery clearness in the upper notes of her finely cultivated organ'. *Ma voix de clarinette* again.

At the second evening concert, Malibran and Joséphine sang the duet *Ah perdona*, which was encored.

Haydn's *Creation* was performed without cuts, and *The Spectator* considered that it was eminently suited to the talents of the principal singers, Malibran and de Méric. However, the reasons adduced were more than a little odd. The two ladies, the critic declared, 'who would have failed in *The Messiah*, were here on familiar ground; the school of Germany is De Méric's by birth and Malibran's by adoption'. No doubt it was the same critic who informed his readers that Joséphine's selection of songs at the evening concerts 'told us the style she loved, and the correct and faithful performance of her songs indicated her German training.'

At a time when German music was becomimg very fashionable,

this will certainly have been intended as praise. It was wide of the mark in that when Joséphine was born in Strasbourg, that city had been French for some 150 years. Her principal teachers had been French, Italian and Spanish . All the same, there is the comment in the *Concise Dictionary of Opera* by Rosenthal and Warrack that Paër 'managed to match his [Italian] style more successfully to German requirements than to French' and Joséphine had no doubt suffered from this when she tried to satisfy the demands of the *Opéra* in Paris. As for Malibran, the French musician Portmartin recorded that when he was dancing a waltz with her she had admitted that she did not do it very well: *C'est que, Dieu merci! je n'ai rien de germanique [tedesco]*'. (Thank goodness! There's nothing germanic about me).

When the critic sensed that Joséphine's choice of concert pieces indicated the style she loved, perhaps what he had detected was that she had a special affinity for Mozart. It is significant that an 'esteemed correspondent' who published a report on the 1833 Norwich Festival in the *Chronicle* drew attention to her rendering of *Jesu Domine*, from a *Litany* by Mozart, which, he said, had been sung with 'exquisite finish and a thorough knowledge of the Author'. The same writer also singled out Joséphine's *Parto ma tu ben mio* for praise.

In Haydn's *Creation*, the *Chronicle* said that Malibran had produced two gems in the first part, while in the second part Joséphine's song *On mighty pens* had been 'not less excellent'.

The third evening concert seems to have pleased the audience less than its predecessor, 'but the exceptions to this were very striking: Madame de Méric's Aria *Su Griselda*, with Blagrove's *obligato* accompaniment, and Cimarosa's Duet, sung by Malibran and Donzelli, made a deep impression'. On the final day, Friday, Joséphine's rendering of Cherubini's *Ave Maria* had been 'eloquently delivered'.

Strangely, in the notices about the Festival, it was Malibran who, in the midst of all the provincial eulogy, received one or two unkind cuts. In some of her *National Airs*, it was claimed, 'nothing but her exquisite tact could have secured her from touching at times on the confines of – we had almost been guilty of the profanation (when a lady's in the case) of saying – the vulgar'.

The Festival ended with a Fancy Ball. It was described as a glittering occasion, with nearly twelve hundred of 'the most distinguished persons of this and neighbouring counties present'. The names of Malibran and de Méric are not to be found in the *Chronicle's* long list of those attending, so it seems likely that they were not there. At the bottom of its list, the names of Horncastle and Hobbs appear: Horncastle in court dress and Hobbs, first in full dress and then in the costume of a Mameluke.

Most of the main singers went on from Norwich to Worcester, but the *Chronicle* announced that Madame de Méric had left for Munich. Her further career was to be on the Continent, but before she is followed there some further attention must be paid to the later years of Joseph Glossop.

13 *Glossop, 1833-1850*

IN March, April and June 1833, when Joséphine was taking leading parts in operas at the King's Theatre, Joseph Glossop found himself before the Bankruptcy Court in London. His creditors were demanding the repayment of loans and the settlement of debts for goods and services supplied at the Coburg Theatre 'upwards of six years ago'. As there was a question whether the Statute of Limitations might apply, Glossop was called upon to state if he had been in England 'during the last six years'. His reply provided much of the information about his travels and activities on the Continent which have already been described.

In Court, the Commissioner observed that Glossop's accounts were of a very peculiar character. After being engaged in business as a wax chandler, 'he closed his accounts and embarked on theatrical speculations. Having become embarrassed to a large amount, he absconded from his creditors and went abroad, where he again engaged in theatrical speculations, but finally became a picture-dealer by transmitting pictures to this country to a very limited extent, and thus brought himself within the bankruptcy laws . . . . He had resided abroad for 10 or 12 years, until he almost became a foreigner'.

Counsel for one of the creditors noted that the bankrupt was described in the fiat as 'formerly of Piccadilly, and of Manor House, Lambeth; afterwards of the Coburg Theatre; afterwards of Milan, Naples and Paris, and now of Brussels; wax chandler, oil merchant, dealer and chapman'.

In view of the unsatisfactory nature of Glossop's accounts, the Court was not prepared to allow him to 'pass his examination' and the case was adjourned for three or four months to give Glossop time 'to communicate with the countries abroad where he had been engaged and from whence he must either obtain copies of the accounts in which he was concerned or evidence that it was impossible to procure them'. Glossop stated that 'he really could not do it – he had no money.'

The examination was adjourned till the first Saturday in November 1833, but no record of a hearing on or about that date has been traced. However, Glossop was up before the same

Commissioner, Merivale, in April and May 1835. Then, he was described as being of the Victoria Theatre, Waterloo Road, printer. On 6 April, there was a very numerous meeting of creditors and 'the proceedings appeared to excite much interest.' Glossop's liabilities were stated to be about £5,000, but there were encumbrances on the theatre itself to the amount of £15,000. One colourful character who came forward as a creditor was the Red Indian Chippewa Chief, 'the celebrated rifle shot'.

On 13 May, Glossop appeared for the purpose of passing his last examination. The Court was 'literally crowded with creditors and parties interested in the case, among whom were observed some of our popular actors'. Unfortunately, these were not named.

At one point, Glossop angrily rejected a charge that he had wasted away his money on gambling. He declared on oath that he had never thrown a dice in his life. 'Upon this, a person stood up in the Court, and addressing Mr. Glossop said: "How came you, then, to ask me to accompany you to a gambling-house?" Mr. Glossop: "Because you had expressed a wish to see the inside of a gambling-house and I had a friend who could introduce us"'.

In the outcome, the Court allowed Glossop to pass his examination and that was presumably the end of the matter. There is no sign that any of the creditors got their money.

By 1833, Glossop seems to have passed out of Joséphine's life. Whatever their personal relations may have been at that time, Joséphine could not have welcomed, in London, a public association with a discredited speculator who was appearing before the Bankruptcy Court. Strange as it would be in the days of sensational journalism, no mention has been discovered in any of the reports on the opera in England that Joséphine was connected with Joseph Glossop. She was billed as Madame de Méric. No trace has been found of any connexion which either Joséphine or her daughter Emilie had with Glossop after they came to England in 1832.

Joseph's life after he parted from Joséphine is no longer an essential part of this narrative and very little has come to light about it. He died in Florence on 14 November 1850 and was buried in the foreign cemetery there.

Glossop had lived for the theatre and had been ruined by his obsession with it. To be blunt, with all his charm and sensibility, he was a confidence man and a singularly unsuccessful one. All the same, posterity can do him the justice of remembering him as a man of boundless enthusiasm who planted the seed which was to grow into the Old Vic. By his marriage to Elizabeth Féron, he became the father and grandfather of men who played key rôles in the development of opera and drama: Augustus Glossop Harris and Sir Augustus Harris. Albeit fleetingly, he had managed the two greatest opera houses in Italy. His daughter Emilie became a singer of international fame.

It is still an open question why Joseph's son Augustus chose to take the stage name Harris. If he wished to distance himself from the bankrupt who had been involved in so many unsuccessful theatrical speculations, that would explain avoidance of the name Glossop. But why Harris? No evidence has been discovered to solve this mystery. Just possibly, Augustus saw himself as following in the footsteps of the famous Thomas Harris (died 1820), who had for many years been the proprietor and manager of Covent Garden Theatre - a highly respected man. Or is it just possible that not Joseph Glossop but a man by the name of Harris was his natural father?

Gentlemen. [...] Yours &c. Francis Glossop.

Codicil to Will, showing Francis Glossop's distrust of his son Joseph.
(Original held at the Public Record Office (Prob 11/1843.)

Joséphine on the continent again

MILAN 1834

IT has not been discovered whether the *Norwich Chronicle* was right in saying that Joséphine went from Norwich to Munich. What is known is that she was engaged by the impresario in Milan, Visconti, to sing there in 1834. As Giuseppina De Méric, she was to be one of the three *prime donne*, the other two being Henriette Méric-Lalande and Marietta Brambilla.

Teatro alla Scala, Milan.
(By courtesy of the Teatro alla Scala.)

John Rosselli (*opus cit*) gives a list of the fees paid to the leading singers from which it appears that in the carnival season *La Scala* paid Lalande Fcs.32,000 against only Fcs.10,250 to Joséphine. In this list, Joséphine is somewhat surprisingly described as '*musico*', i.e. mezzo-soprano or contralto singing breeches parts; but this is perhaps just a recognition of the wide range of her voice.

The Carnival opened on 4 January with G. Pacini's *Ivanhoe*, in which Joséphine took the part of Rebecca. This opera folded after two evenings and, according to the *Gazzetta Privilegiata*, gave the singers little scope to display their talents.

On 17 January came the first of ten performances of *La Gazza Ladra*, with Joséphine as Ninetta and Brambilla in the breeches part of Pippo. This production was officially described as very good indeed (*buonissimo*).

The next opera in which Joséphine appeared, L. Ricci's *Un' Avventura di Scaramuccia* (8 March), received the supreme official accolade (*ottimo*). This was the first performance of the work which was to become Joséphine's great standby for the rest of her career. The *Gazzetta* considered that Joséphine was outstanding in comic works and that there was no other singer of the day who could match her in the part of Sandrina. The whole opera was a great success (11 performances) and both the *maestro* and the performers were given repeated curtain calls. Mariani, bass, had taken the name part of Scaramouche and Vincenzo Galli, *buffo comico*, was Tomaso.

Joséphine was not assigned a part in either *Norma* or *Otello*, in May, but by then Malibran had been engaged for the principal female rôles. However, these two great operas were given only three and two performances respectively, whereas Rossi's *La Casa Disabitata*, which opened the Autumn Season on 16 August with Joséphine as Sinforosa, ran to eleven performances. The AMZ had considered that Rossi's opera was best passed over in silence, but the Milanese audiences evidently thought otherwise.

These productions in Milan of *Scaramuccia* and *La Casa Disabitata* were world *premières*, so Joséphine created the rôles of both Sandrina and Sinforosa. *Scaramuccia* was repeated at *La Scala* in September 1834, with Joséphine again in the main female part, and ran to no fewer than twenty-six performances.

At the height of the Autumn Season, the four *prime donne* were Malibran, her half-sister Josepha Ruiz, Joséphine and Manzocchi. The AMZ considered that Joséphine and Manzocchi were splendid interpreters of *buffo* rôles and Joséphine was described as having a splendid voice.

BERLIN (1834)

Meanwhile, during the Summer break in Milan, Joséphine had been engaged as a guest artist in Berlin at the *Königsstädtische Theater*. Here, reports are available in both the AMZ and the *Berlinische Nachrichten* (BN). According to the AMZ, Theatre Director Cerf had made Joséphine a substantial offer to attract her to Berlin. The BN

166

extended a warm welcome to her as an artist from *La Scala* who arrived with the aura of international acclaim.

The season had opened with *Norma*, but Joséphine made her Berlin *début* as Ninetta in *Die diebische Elster (La Gazza Ladra)*. The *AMZ* did not regard the production as a notable success, but the *BN* praised Joséphine for having lived up to her high reputation, thanks to her wide-ranging, strong voice – used with particular effect in the high notes – and to her lively acting. However, the critic thought that these attributes were even more suited to tragic works and he therefore had high expectations from her in the serious operas which were to follow. (Was this balm to Sandrina?) Joséphine had been frequently applauded and was duly given a curtain call.

On 26 April, *Semiramide* was performed in Italian. The *BN* wondered why Madame de Méric had not chosen to make her *début* in this opera rather than in *Die diebische Elster*. In the tragic rôle she had proved herself to be one of the most outstanding singers to have appeared on the Berlin stage for several years. Her voice was rich in fine tones and the assurance which she had displayed in her *coloratura* bespoke an artist familiar with all the requirements of the stages of Milan and Naples. If there had to be a criticism, it was that at one moment her voice would be perfectly pure and then, almost unbelievably, would suffer a 'not imperceptible tremor'.

As an actress, she had shown more temperament than the 'cool' Germans were accustomed to expect from their tragédiennes, but her poses and gestures demonstrated how well fitted she was for tragic parts. Joséphine had been ably supported by Mlle. Hähnel, as Arsace.

It was in the title rôle in *Anna Bolena* on 14 May that Joséphine truly came into her own in Berlin. The *AMZ* spoke of a triumph and the *BN* could hardly believe that this was the same singer as had played Ninetta in *Die diebische Elster*. As the Queen, she had evinced two rare qualities: originality of conception and a correct interpretation of the demands of a tragic rôle. She had sung the music precisely as the composer had written it and the result was that several passages had sounded more impressive than at any previous performances. Joséphine's 'beautiful, bell-like high notes' were ideal for the part. However, as elsewhere, the now-famous *voix de clarinette* evoked some adverse reaction. It was objected that the 'too frequent raising of the pitch to high C, reliable and fine though it was, came close to being a mannerism'.

The *AMZ* granted that the voice had great mobility and sparkled in *coloratura*, but found it somewhat sharp and thin. But then, Madame de Méric was no longer young [at 33]. The *BN*, on the other hand, maintained its favourable stance and referred to the gales of applause which had greeted Joséphine both during and after her performance. The part of Jane Seymour, which Joséphine had played in London, was taken by Mme. Schodel. The production had apparently been 'in the latest Italian style'. This struck the *AMZ* reviewer as rather affected, 'if at times most effective'.

After her success in *Anna Bolena*, Joséphine tackled the part of Palmide in Meyerbeer's Italian opera *Il Crociato in Egitto*. In the opinion of the *BN*, there were very few singers capable of doing full justice to this demanding task, so that it was genuine praise to say that Madame de Méric had given satisfaction 'in all essentials'. She had won the unanimous approval of the audience and had shone particularly in the more rhetorical (*deklamatisch-musikalische*) sections. Her voice might not be consistently beautiful, but she had some fine notes and commanded a wide range of the soprano scale. She had valiantly maintained her powers throughout the unbroken three-hour-long opera; and though she had been at her best at the beginning, she was still remarkably successful by the end. The 'distinguished foreign singer' had received a well-merited ovation. No suggestion here, be it noted, that Joséphine was German.

The climax of the Berlin guest-appearance was the production of Bellini's *Capuleti e Montecchi*. The *BN* had been specially anxious to hear Joséphine as Giulietta because of the reputation which she had gained in this part outside Germany. She had not had time to master the text in German, so the opera had to be sung in the original Italian, which was, of course, an advantage from the musical point of view. The result went beyond all expectations. 'Madame De Méric sang with such genuine artistry and acted with such Mediterranean fire that the applause almost exceeded that of her earlier successes and also won the esteem of the many connoisseurs who were in the audience on this occasion'. Mlle. Hähnel had shown that she was unrivalled as Romeo.

It seems that Joséphine did not take advantage of the offer of a benefit performance in Berlin, but after twelve *Gastrollen* returned to Milan. Reports that 'Madame de Méric' sang in Munich in 1833 and/or 1834 seem to refer to Henriette Méric-Lalande, who was one of the principal guest artists there in 1833.

After her return to Milan in 1834, Joséphine pursued the rest of her operatic career in Italy. It was in Italy that she seems to have felt professionally most at home and where, in general, her talents were the most highly appreciated. All the same there had been an early prediction that she would do well in Germany and that had proved to be true in Berlin.

MANTUA – CARNIVAL 1834-35

In the 1834-35 Carnival in Mantua, Joséphine (as G. De Merich) took a leading part in what was described as a completely successful opera season. The impresario, Giacomo Morosi, produced *Anna Bolena* and Rossini's *L'Assedio di Corinto (Le Siège de Corinthe)*.

For Joséphine's private life, Mantua assumes significance as the first place where she was billed to sing with the tenor Timoleone Alexander who was henceforth to be her partner and to be generally viewed as her husband until his death some twenty years later. It will be in place here to give a brief account of his early career.

CHAPTER

15

Timoleone Alexander

THIS singer was an operatic tenor of some note in his day. He is said to have been born at the end of the eighteenth century, in the Duchy of Parma. It is recorded that he descended from a singer in the Delisle Company which went from France to Parma in the middle of the eighteenth century. He studied under maestro Finali. The above information about the date of his birth comes from reputable Italian sources, but it must be admitted that if consistent statements by Timoleone himself on, e.g. passports, are to be believed, he was born in Piacenza as late as 1811 or 1812, in which case he must have been something of a youthful prodigy. Perhaps the truth lies in some date between.

Timoleone is credited with having had at least four operas written for him. One of these was *Il Supposto Marito* by Vincenzo Fioravanti (1799-1877), a composer who enjoyed great popular success in Naples. Another was *Colombo*, by Luigi Ricci (1805-1859). Ricci is not now widely remembered, but he was highly successful during his lifetime and his best-known opera, *Crispino e la Comare*, was revived in Wexford in 1979.

The AMZ of January 1835 describes Timoleone in flattering terms: 'He not only has an agreeable voice and sings with grace, but is young and handsome, which is a capital advantage on our [presumably Italian] stage.' This suggests that it may not have been the tenor voice alone which commended him to Joséphine and provides support for a birth later than the eighteenth century.

The first time Timoleone appeared on the public stage seems to have been in the Summer of 1826, in Rossini's *Bianca e Falliero* at the *Teatro Filodrammatico* in Milan. With him was the English singer Marianne Lewis, and these two amateur *Dilettanten* were the outstanding performers (AMZ). In 1827, the year of Joséphine's marriage to Glossop, Timoleone sang in a sacred concert in Milan and as first tenor at the Summer Festival in Vicenza (*Revue Musicale*). This was at the *Teatro Eretenio* in Mercadante's *Caritea Regina di Spagna* and Rossini's *Bianca e Faliero*, with the famous soprano Violante Camporese.

Timoleone then moved to Genoa, for parts in *Tancredi* and Mercadante's *Dido Abandonnata* and to the *Teatro Nuovo* in Naples, where Ricci's *Colombo* was given its local *première*, with Timoleone as Zamoro. This 1828 season was an early peak in the singer's career. He also appeared in *Il Supposto Marito* and in *Gli Sposi Fuggitivi*, by Luigi Carlini, another opera said to have been written for him. The *Revue Musicale* reported that he had sung with success in *La Cenerentola*, which was put on in Naples in the Summer.

Colombo was one of the operas performed at the Grand Opening of the *Teatro Ducale* in Parma in the Spring of 1829. Timoleone again played Zamoro, while the name part was taken by the great *basso* Luigi Lablache. The heroine, Zilia, was played not by Joséphine, but by Henriette Méric-Lalande. In the Summer of 1829, Timoleone was in Piacenza for a production of *Cenerentola* which led to stormy scenes in which all the singers except Cipriani were booed.

In 1830, Timoleone had a Spring Season in Pavia, appearing in Rossini's *Conte Ory*, in which he had given proof of his ability to sing with expression.

Timoleone was the principal tenor in three operas which were produced in the *Teatro della Nobile Società* in Bergamo for Carnival 1833-34. These were *Anna Bolena*, *Mathilde di Shabran* and *La Sonnambula*.

From manuscript records held at the *Biblioteca Civica Angelo Mai* in Bergamo, it seems clear that *Anna Bolena* was the most successful of the three works. Donizetti being a native of the town, there was naturally a predisposition in his favour. At the *première* in Milan in 1830 there had been a prestigious cast with Pasta and Rubini. So the Bergamo audience, reputedly, after Parma, the most difficult to please in the whole of Italy, approached their provincial production with some apprehension. The first Act, indeed, was coldly received; but then, with Act II, the public burst out with unanimous and ever-increasing applause. Even the connoisseurs, 'who make life so difficult these days for impresarios', were satisfied. The chief laurels were reserved for the ladies: *prima donna assoluta* Antonietta Vial, a distinguished imitator of Pasta, in the name part, and Giuseppina Fontana as Jane Seymour. However, Signor Timoleone Alexander, as Percy, was highly praised, especially for his aria *Vivi tu te ne scongiuro* and for the trio which he sang with Vial and the bass, Antonio Colla. His voice was described as having great delicacy and as being able to express genuine emotion. It was a beautiful voice, with fair strength, and was a 'virile' rather than a 'contralto' tenor. However, Timoleone was not always able to bend it to his will and to sing like Rubini. He sang best in the lower tenor register.

Mathilde di Shabran proved to be an almost total failure, lasting for only two nights. This despite good performances by Vial and Timoleone. *Sonnambula* was a success, though taking second place to *Anna Bolena*. Timoleone had the honour on several occasions of sharing curtain calls with Vial.

It is recorded that in August 1833 Timoleone sang in Luigi Ricci's *Chiara di Rosemberg* at the Opera in Como.

In the Spring/Summer of 1835, Timoleone had the distinction of singing in two successful productions at *La Canobbiana* in Milan. The first was the *première* of *Leocadia*, by L. Rossi on 30 April. Then at the end of June he was in a new version of Rossini's *Mosè*.

Though his subsequent career was not always with Joséphine, from this point it will not be treated separately, but in its relation to Joséphine.

Side entrance of the Teatro della Nobile Società (or Teatro Sociale), Bergamo.
(By courtesy of Signor Ermanno Comuzio.)

172

Joséphine's later career

GENOA – SPRING 1835

JOSÉPHINE was the leading female singer in the Spring Season at the *Teatro Carlo Felice* in Genoa in 1835, singing in each of the five operas which were produced.

UN' AVVENTURA

DI SCARAMUCCIA

MELODRAMMA COMICO IN DUE ATTI
da rappresentarsi
NEL TEATRO COMUNALE
DI RAVENNA
NELLA PRIMAVERA DEL 1837.

Offerto a Sua Eccellenza Revma
MONSIGNOR
LUIGI DE' CONTI VANNICELLI CASONI

Canonico della Patriarcale Basilica Vaticana, Prelato domestico della Santità di Nostro Signore, Proto- notario, Referendario dell' una e dell' altra Segnatura, e della Città e Provincia di Ravenna

PRO-LEGATO APOSTOLICO

TIP. DI A. ROVERI E FIGLI

PERSONAGGI	ATTORI [7.]
SCARAMUCCIA, *Poeta e Di- rettore dei Comici ita- liani in Parigi*	Sig. Costantini Natale
LELIO, } *Comici*	,, Alexander Timoleone
DOMENICO, }	,, Tinti Giuseppe
SANDRINA, *fantesca di Sca- ramuccia*	,, Demery Giuseppina
TOMMASO, *contadino*. . . .	,, Cavalli Girolamo
IL CONTINO DI PONTIGNY .	,, Angiolini Dossi Giu- seppina.
IL VISCONTE DI S. VALLIER.	,, Mercuriali Giuseppe
ELENA, *contadina*	,, Branzanti Luigia.
Uno Staffiere.	,, N. N.

Cori - Cavalieri - Dame - Commedianti, e Comparse

BALLERINI
Signori
Olietti Teresa - Montallegro Giacomo - Ravaglia Rosa

La scena è nel palazzo di Borgogna, indi in casa di Scaramuccia per ultimo in un casino di campagna del Contino di Pontigny.
L'epoca del 16....
Musica del Maestro Sig. LUIGI RICCI.
Rammentatore
Sig. Gaetano Bughigni.
Le Scene sono nuove d'invenzione, ed esecuzione del Sig. Romolo Liverani di Faenza.
Macchinista
Sig. Giuseppe Gardella.
Attrezzista
Sig. Giuseppe Rubbi di Bologna.
Il Vestiario è di proprietà del Sig. Alessandro Lanari.

Scaramuccia, one of Joséphine's major successes. She sings here with Timoleone Alexander.
(By courtesy of the Comune di Ravenna.)

Scaramuccia (18 April) was followed by *Anna Bolena* and by *L'Elisir d'Amore*. The third Donizetti work, *Gli Esiliati in Siberia* (13 June) was a failure, but a new farce by Maurizio Sciorati, *Il Sarto e i Tabarri* (27 June) was well received.

A commentary by Raffaele Scalese and Carlo Crosa attributes the overall success of the season to the cast of distinguished singers. There was not a corner of the auditorium where '*la gentile, l'intelligente prima donna signora De Mery*' was not esteemed and applauded. The tenor Giovanni Basadona had also given great pleasure. The performances had been well attended and the last evening but one had been one of the most brilliant of the whole season. Sciorati, a talented pupil of Zingarelli, was praised for having composed music which was admirably suited to the *Tabarri*.

Timoleone Alexander was not among the singers with Joséphine in Genoa in the Spring of 1835.

A report, so far unconfirmed, speaks of Joséphine in Lisbon in September 1835, in *Il Posto Abbandonato*.

PALERMO (1835-36)

The opera season in the Sicilian capital in 1835-36 can literally be described as ill-starred.

First had come the shock news of the untimely death in Paris of the great Bellini, 'regenerator of Italian music, the pride of Sicily'. Then, in October 1835, the appearance of Halley's comet cast a baleful influence over the musical scene. By January, in Naples, the failure of St. Gennaro's blood to liquefy and the death of Queen Maria Christina had intensified the atmosphere of gloom. Furthermore, an outbreak of cholera in Southern Italy had led to the imposition of *cordons sanitaires* which delayed the arrival of many singers, including Joséphine, and upset the opera programme at the *Teatro Carolino*.

The Palermo theatre, 'graveyard of tenors', proved also to be one of the few Italian stages where Joséphine failed to win the favour of the audiences. Unfortunately, the opera in which she first appeared, despite being by Bellini, did not satisfy the Sicilians.

This opera was *I Puritani*, disguised for political reasons as *Arturo e Elvira* and deprived by the censors of some of its most telling passages. However, it was known to have been a great success in Paris and the coolness of its reception in Milan, Parma and Rome was attributed, at least in part, to the imperfect scores which had been used in those Italian cities. For this reason, the *Teatro Carolino* had taken the precaution of obtaining an authentic copy from the composer himself. This contained a closing *cabaletta* for Elvira which Bellini omitted from the so-called 'Malibran' version. All to little avail. The audience in Palermo felt that the opera had been tailored too much to suit French tastes and it did not please.

The principal parts were taken by Joséphine and Santi, neither of whom shone to advantage. It seems to have been Joséphine's acting rather than her singing which evoked the criticism. Both the *Giornale Officiale di Palermo* and *Il Vapore* praised her fine voice, 'matured by artistry' as the *Giornale* put it, but her Elvira struck the *Vapore* as cold in the extreme (*fredissima*) and lacking even a spark of the fire which had burned, in Paris, in 'Bellini's very own Elvira, the beauteous Grisi'. All in all, the Sicilians recognised that their cast could not hope to rival the way the *maestro's* music had been interpreted by such giants as Grisi, Rubini, Lablache and Tamburini.

Towards the end of the Carnival Season in Palermo, Joséphine took the part of Eleonora in Donizetti's *Torquato Tasso*. *Il Vapore* considered that she had sung her main aria '*benissimo*', giving full play to her delicious high notes. However, the aria itself was voted worthless and Joséphine had faced whistling as well as applause. Only Barroilhet's rendering of the name part, it seems, had saved the opera from fiasco.

Joséphine was never to sing in Sicily again, but before she left she had done what she could to give her audience in Palermo cause to regret her going. She had sung the cavatina '*di piacer mi balza il cor*' with every grace and skill, seeming to will the public to allow her to interpret it in her own way. The warm-hearted Sicilians had responded, bidding her farewell with their plaudits.

It is in connexion with her Palermo engagement in 1835-36 that the first reference to Joséphine as the wife of Timoleone Alexander has emerged. He too was in the cast at the *Teatro Carolino*. It remains to be discovered whether there was any formal dissolution of the Glossop marriage and also whether Joséphine went through any ceremony of marriage with Timoleone. Both seem somewhat unlikely.

MILAN AGAIN – SPRING AND SUMMER 1836

For the Spring Season in 1836, Joséphine was once again in Milan, this time at *La Canobbiana*.

She had been engaged, perhaps at short notice, to take the place of Tadolini as a *prima donna*. She was not in the cast of the opera which opened the season on 4 April, when the Hungarian

Gued took the female lead, but duly appeared on 26 April for the *première* of the now long-forgotten comic opera *Don Chisciotte*, by Mazzucato.

This is rated in the official records as a mediocre work, but it ran to fourteen performances. *Il Vapore*, in Palermo, somewhat gleefully reported that la Signora Demery had been the cause of its 'total failure', just as she had been of the *Puritani* at the *Carolino*. Beautiful though her voice undeniably was, she was just 'a statue'.

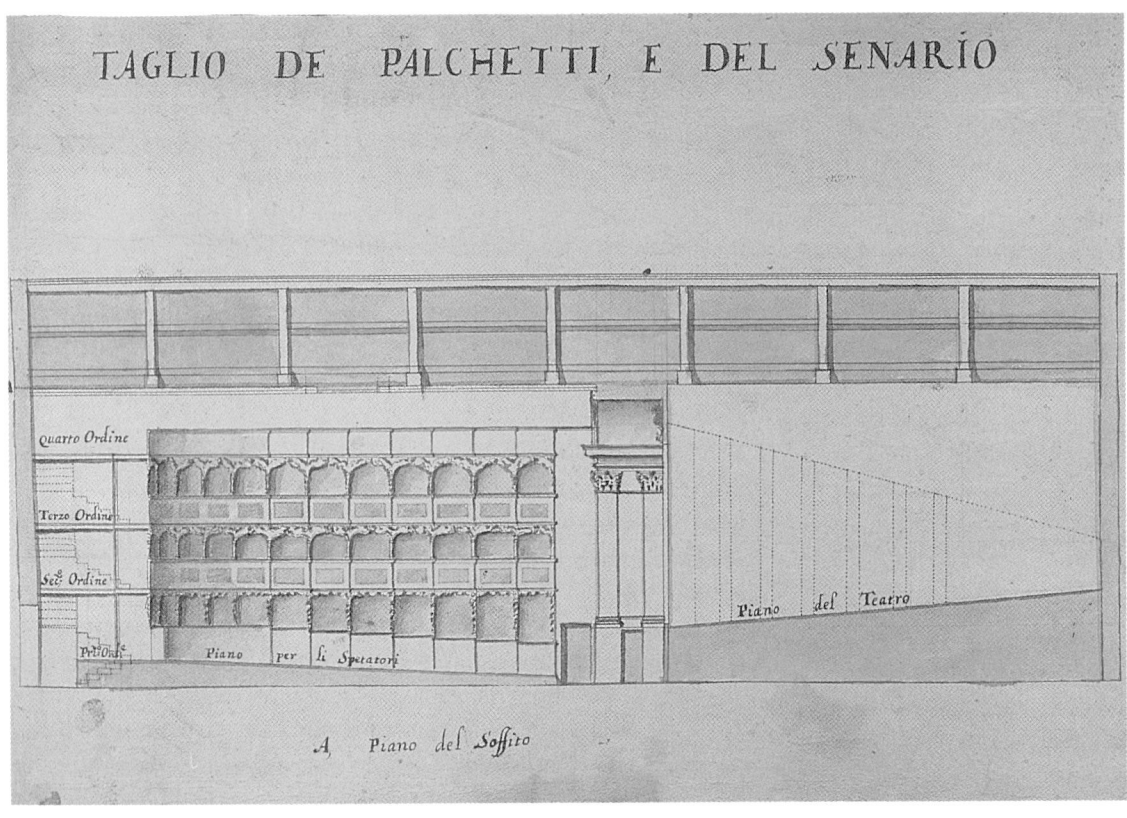

TAGLIO DE PALCHETTI, E DEL SENARIO

Be that as it may, Joséphine was fast acquiring a reputation for the successful performance of *buffo* parts. These were the staple fare at *La Canobbiana* at the time. *Don Chisciotte* was followed by *Elisa e Claudio* (*buffo*, mediocre, 15 performances); Fratelli Ricci's *Il Disertore per Amore* (*semi-seria*, excellent, 25 performances); Bazzoni's new farce *I tre Mariti*, which died after one showing; and, finally, on 17 July *Un' Avventura di Scaramuccia*. This proved a great success, but perhaps because the Season was about to close it ran for only eleven performances.

The Teatro Comunale, Ravenna. Cross-section showing the stage and sets.
(By courtesy of the Biblioteca Classense.)

176

Il Disertore may since have been forgotten, but her appearance in it must have been memorable for Joséphine. As a token of the gratification which her performance had afforded him, the Duke of Orleans, eldest son of King Louis Philippe, presented her with a splendid armlet richly decorated with jewels. This was conveyed to Joséphine by the French Consul in Milan.

RAVENNA – SPRING 1837

After performing at *La Canobbiana* in Milan in March 1837, in *Gabriella di Vergy*, Joséphine went to Ravenna.

The Spring Season in Ravenna in 1837 at the *Teatro Comunale* marks a high point in Joséphine's career in Italy. It may well also have been a time of great happiness in her personal life. She and Timoleone were together, performing in the same operas, and the extravagant praise which was heaped upon her suggest that she must have been singing and acting at her highest level.

Between April and June 1837, Joséphine sang in twenty-two performances of *Scaramuccia* and five of Ricci's opera *semi-seria Chiara di Rosenberg*. Timoleone took the tenor rôles.

On the evening of 30 May, two poems were devoted to the praise of Joséphine as *prima donna assoluta*. The Italian texts are printed here and translations are in Appendix B. The occasion was her benefit performance. Timoleone enjoyed a benefit on 10 June.

The performances in Ravenna were judged to be comparable with those at *La Scala (Teatri Arte e Letteratura di Bologna)*. Joséphine, 'the famous *buffa* artiste', and Natale Constantine, the *basso cantante* who played the part of Scaramuccia, were singled out for special commendation.

In addition to her operatic performances, Joséphine sang at a concert given in Ravenna by the *Accademia Vocale-Strumentale* on 8 June.

FINAL PERFORMANCES – 1837-1844

For the Summer Season of 1837 Joséphine was at the *Teatro Ducale (Regio)* in Parma, with Manfredi as the leading tenor. The operas were *Scaramuccia*, Coppola's *La Nina Pazza* and *La Sonnambula*.

A
GIUSEPPINA DEMERY
Che nella Primavera del 1837
RALLEGRAVA RAVENNA COL DOLCISSIMO SUO CANTO
ALCUNI AMMIRATORI
NELLA SERA DI SUA BENEFICIATA
OFFRIVANO

Quando Saturno col suo casto impero
    Fè d' oro i tempi, in lieta compagnia
    Con le muse albergò Filosofia,
    E ai cor discese in dolci note il vero.

L' oro in ferro si volse, e menzoniero
    Fu de' Poeti il labbro; oscura e ria
    La sacra vena, che già chiara uscia
    Rispose al piè del meduseo destriero.

E il ferro anche rinnova, e carmi inetti
    Ode l' ausonia scena; il volgo applaude,
    Fremente il senno antico in pochi petti.

O donna, o Euterpe nova, che puoi tanto
    Sol della voce, or qual sarìa tua laude
    Se giunto fosse il prisco verso al canto?

Poetic homage to Joséphine.
(By courtesy of the Comune di Ravenna.)

In the Autumn, at the *Nuovo Teatro* in Padua, Madame Demeric Alexander was at the top of the bill as *prima donna assoluta* in *Scaramuccia*. This was on 28 October and Timoleone was first tenor.

    Scaramuccia was followed by *L'Elisir d'Amore* and *La Sonnambula*. These lacked the required charm of novelty. *L'Elisir*, though only five years old, was described as 'rancido'; but both Joséphine and the *primo basso cantante* Giuseppe Scheggi distinguished themselves in it. The same could not be said of the tenor, Alexander: 'it was not enough to be the husband of la Demery' (*La Gazzetta Privilegiata di Venezia*, as quoted by Bruno Brunelli in his *I Teatri di Padova*).

A
GIUSEPPINA DE-MÉRIC
PRIMA DONNA ASSOLUTA
NEL TEATRO COMUNALE DI RAVENNA
QUESTO TRIBUTO DI LAUDE

Nella sera del 30.ᵐᵃᵍᵍⁱᵒ 1837.

DESTINATA A SUO BENEFICIO

SI OFFERIVA

Chi te non loderà, Donna, che tanto
    Per natura, e per arte in pregio sali?
    E chi in lodarti s' ergerà sull' ali,
    Sicchè raggiunga di tuo merto il vanto?

Per te sola si sente in prova quanto
    É dato di fruire a noi mortali,
    Per te, che in ogni cor cantando vali
    A tuo senno destar or gioja or pianto.

Non chiude petto uman cura si forte
    Che non sia vinta, se a tue dolci note
    L' alma per breve tempo apra le porte;

Per simil guisa dell' eteree ruote
    Al suon s' allegra la celeste corte,
    Quando Giove co' strali il mondo scuote:

Joséphine hailed in Ravenna as Prima Donna Assoluta, (1837).
(By courtesy of the Comune di Ravenna.)

RAVENNA
PRESSO ANTONIO ROVERI E FIGLI
Con Approv.

179

For her *soirée* in Padua, Joséphine had chosen Donizetti's short comic opera *Le Convenienze e le Inconvenienze Teatrali* . No doubt she could sing this with feeling, from long personal experience of stage life. Despite appalling weather, the theatre had been crowded and Joséphine was showered with flowers, garlands and poems. The only criticism came from some who thought that she had overdone her flourishes (*fioriture*).

Padua – Nuovo Teatro.
Joséphine as Prima Donna Assoluta and Timoleone Alexandre as First Tenor in Scaramuccia, (1837). (Joséphine billed with the surname Alexandre.) (PROT. No. 576 SEZ X/1 of 15 Feb 1993.)
(By courtesy of the Archivio di Stato, Padua.)

According to the AMZ, Joséphine and Timoleone sang together in Modena in mid-1838 in *La Nina Pazza*. By this time, in the opinion of the AMZ, Joséphine's talent in *buffo* parts militated against her giving a convincing portrayal of Nina in her madness. As for Timoleone, though he had a beautiful voice, complete with falsetto, he had seemed unable to sing the music of his rôle.

IN PADOVA
NEL
NUOVO TEATRO
PER LA PROSSIMA FIERA DAL SANTO 1858
Si Rappresenteranno due Drammi Serj e due Balli

PRIMO DRAMMA
IL GIURAMENTO
Parole di Gaetano Rossi.
Musica del Sig. M.º Saverio Mercadante

SECONDO DRAMMA
DA DESTINARSI.

ARTISTI DI CANTO

Prima Donna Assoluta per la prima Opera
M.ᴬ DEMERIC ALEXANDER.
Socia Onoraria dell' Accademia di Mantova

Prima Donna Assoluta per la seconda Opera
M.ᴬ EUGENIA GARCIA.
Cantante di Camera di S. M. la Duchessa di Parma

Prima Donna Contralto
sig. **CLEMENTINA TOMMASI.**

Primo Tenore Assoluto
sig. **GIO. BATTISTA GENERO.**

Primo Basso Assoluto
sig. **VINCENZO NEGRINI.**

Seconda Donna
sig. **FELICITA GRANDI.**

Secondo Basso
N. N.

Secondo Tenore
sig. **LORENZO LOMBARDI**

Rammentatore
sig. **GIOVANNI DA-PACE.**

Instruttore, e Direttore del Coro
sig. **GIOACHINO GRAZIANI.**

Coriste N. 10

Coristi N. 14

Statisti N. 50

Li Balli saranno composti, e diretti dal Coreografo Sig. Emanuele Viotti.

PRIMO BALLO STORICO SPETTACOLOSO
MARGHERITA DI SCOZIA.

SECONDO BALLO DI MEZZO CARATTERE
DA DESTINARSI.

ARTISTI DI BALLO

Primi Ballerini Danzanti Assoluti
sig. Conjugi PRIORA.
Primi Mimi Assoluti
sig. PAOLINA MONTI.
Prima Ballerina per le Parti
sig. RACHELE VIOTTI.
Ballerini per le Parti
sig. MARIA RIZZO.
Ballerino per le parti Giocose
sig. GIOVANNI FRANCOLINI.

sig. MICHELE D'AMORE.

sig. CARLO MARTINI.

sig. DAVIDE VENTURI.

sig. FRANCESCO MAZZIGNAN.

Padua – Nuovo Teatro, Joséphine in Mercadante's Il Giuramento, (1838). (PROT, No. 576 SEZ X/1 of 15 Feb. 1993.)
(By courtesy of the Archivio di Stato, Padua.)

Certainly Joséphine, though not Timoleone, was in Padua again in June 1838, for the Saint's Day Festival, when she was billed as *prima donna assoluta* in Mercadante's *Il Giuramento*. This, as the impresarios stressed, was a new opera for Padua, but it had a cool reception, ascribed, however, more to the music than to the singers. From the papers in the *Fondo Teatro Verdi*, it appears that Joséphine was also in the cast of the two following operas, Bellini's *Beatrice di Tenda* and Donizetti's *Lucia di Lammermoor*, but the *prima donna assoluta* in those works was Eugenia Garcia.

On the Padua playbill for the *Fiera del Santo* 1838, Madama Demeric Alexander is described as an honorary member of the Mantua Academy (*Socia Onoraria dell'Accademia di Mantova*). The Academy were not able to confirm this, but their records for the period are incomplete.

For the Carnival of 1839, Joséphine was again in Trieste, where she is recorded as having sung in *Scaramuccia* with the *buffo* Rovere. Adelaide Kemble was performing in Trieste at the same period.

In the Spring of 1839, Joséphine crossed the border into France as leading lady in an Italian opera company directed by Signor Grini for a three-month Season at the *Grand Théâtre* in Marseille. There had been fears that the Italian company would face a hostile reception, in retaliation for the unfriendly treatment which the French singer Nourrit was believed to have been given in Naples. However, these fears proved to be unfounded and on the first night the house was full and the audience well disposed. As time went on, though, public support fell off. Marseille prided itself on its musical good taste and it was felt that the Italian company was no better than mediocre and that their repertoire was of too low a standard.

The Season opened on 27 April with Donizetti's *Gemma di Vergy*, the story from Dumas of a wife repudiated and the husband murdered by a jealous slave. The public showed appreciation, but for the critic X.X in *Le Sémaphore* the work did not show the composer at his best. Joséphine played the wronged heroine. X.X described her voice as a light soprano (*sfogato*) marked by accuracy and strength. He noted that she was a distinguished artist who had held her own on the major stages in Italy, yet she seemed to lack power to touch the heart, and her breath control was not perfect.

Gemma was followed by Donizetti's *Il Furioso all'Isola di Sto. Domingo*, of which X.X also had a low opinion. Two of the performances were interrupted by a strange commotion. A wild-eyed man in the audience, who proved to be British, distracted everyone by beating time loudly with his fist on a balustrade and bawling out the tunes at the top of his voice. He had to be forcibly removed.

Mme Alexandre De Méric (1839), in Donizetti's Gemma di Vergy. *Portrait by Pissarello fils.*

(By courtesy of the Bibliothèque Nationale, Paris.)

The next opera was *Norma*, with Joséphine in the name part. She rose to the challenge of this difficult assignment. The critic in *Le Sémaphore* devoted a paragraph to her performance, offering her 'sincere praise' for the way in which she had tackled a rôle 'which had killed more than a score of singers before her, including Mme. Meric Lalande'. It was to her credit that she had sung the part in the original key without changing a single note, thus demonstrating the

183

nature and range of her voice. In the dramatic episodes she had acted with much energy and intelligence. All that could be criticised was a certain lack of flexibility. This had been apparent in the *allegro* of *Casta Diva*, but after the *andante* she had been loudly applauded.

Elisa e Claudio (16 May) was the first of Mercadante's operas to be performed in Marseille. Unfortunately, some absurdities in costume and *mise-en-scène* caused the work to be drowned with booing. However, Joséphine had excelled herself, as Elisa, both as singer and actress. This opera was of course very familiar to her and it received a better reception at a second abridged performance.

X.X rated both Bellini and Donizetti well below Rossini, but Donizetti clearly loomed large in Grini's repertoire and the next two operas were both by him: *Belisario* and *Torquato Tasso*. In *Belisario*, Joséphine played the part of Antonina, Belisario's disaster-causing wife. These two operas had no appeal. The theatre was empty to the point where the authorities were constrained to draft members of the armed forces in to fill the void. To his cost, Grini had failed to grasp that 'at Marseille the musical education of the public was too advanced, thanks to familiarity with numerous *chefs d'oeuvres*, to take seriously the paltry lucubrations of the feeble heirs of Rossini'. That, at least, was apparently the general attitude of the French public. They had become so indifferent that the Italian opera in their midst had even ceased to be a subject thought worth discussing. *Torquato Tasso*, long though it was, had indeed been well received when the company had put it on in Nice, but then Nice was not (at that time) in France and was 'notoriously a place full of consumptive Englishmen and failed speculators.' It was obvious to the Marseillais that *Torquato Tasso* was largely an amalgam of music from other works. Joséphine seems not to have had a part in this production and she had apparently not been with the company in Nice.

The public had become so disillusioned, it was said, that they had become suspicious of any opera whose composer's name ended with an i. Thus even Rossini's *Otello*, with Joséphine as Desdemona, and Bellini's *Sonnambula*, in which Joséphine played Amina, failed to attract full houses. However, patriotism ensured that the *Grand Théâtre* was crowded on 26 June 1839 for the special performance of *Sonnambula* devoted to raising funds for a monument to the unfortunate Adolphe Nourit, who had jumped to his death in Naples in March.

On 3 July, the Italian company staged Bellini's *La Straniera*. This was the first time that this opera had been seen in Marseille. The repeat on 5 July was a benefit for Joséphine, billed as Madame Demeric-Alexandre. Finally, on 9 July, after a well-attended performance of *Le Barbier de Séville*, Joséphine sang a cantata in honour of Nourrit, with words and music by a local Marseillais.

Marseille must have been determined that Nourrit should have the last word.

The AMZ records that Joséphine and Timoleone were together in Treviso in the early part of 1840. Confirmation from Treviso is lacking, but it seems clear that Joséphine sang in Donizetti's *Marina Faliero* in June for the Feast of St. Martin. This was a success and 'the well-known French lady Demeric' is described as having sung harmoniously with the even better-known tenor, Bonfigli. In May, Joséphine and Timoleone had been singing together in *Scaramuccia* and *L'Elisir d'Amore*.

The Summer of 1840 found Joséphine in Verona, having her usual success as Sandrina in *Scaramuccia*. This was at the *Teatro Filarmonico*, where *Scaramuccia* was all the rage, despite having already been produced four times before in Verona. *Teatri Arte e Letteratura* reported that la Demeric, for whom it had been written, had been loudly applauded throughout, as had the *basso comico*, Fontana. Joséphine also sang in *Prigione di Edimburgo*, by Federico Ricci.

In October 1840, for the festival opera season in Rovigo, 'Joséphine Démery Alexander' took the leading parts in two operas by Donizetti. These were *Roberto Devereux*, in which she played Queen Elizabeth, and *Gemma di Vergy*. The impresario was Nicola Orsini.

For the 1840-41 Carnival in Bologna at the *Gran Teatro Comunale*, Giuseppina Demeric Alexander played Susanna in a melodramatic *opera buffa* called *I due Figaro*, with music by Antonio Speranza and a libretto by the prolific Felice Romani. This opened on 26 December 1840 and was not a success. Donizetti's 'well-known' *Gemma di Vergy* fared much better (2 January 1841), with Joséphine giving 'a thoroughly good rendering' of the title-rôle. She then sang in *La Sonnambula* (19 January).

Later in 1841, Joséphine returned to Leghorn, the scene of her marriage to Joseph Glossop in 1827. Full details have not come to light, but according to the AMZ she performed at the *Teatro Carlo Ludovico* (later *San Marco*) in an opera by Nini called *Marescialla d'Ancre*, which was a resounding fiasco. The reviewer for the AMZ wished that the Season had opened with something else. Joséphine was given a benefit in Leghorn.

1842 was the year in which Joséphine was made an honorary member of the *Accademia di Santa Cecilia* in Rome. She was admitted on 16 April as *socio onorario esercente*, on the proposal of G. Zacchia and four Wardens, being described as *prima donna* at the *Teatro Metastasio*. It was at this theatre, on 29 March 1842, that she had appeared in Donizetti's *Olivo e Pasquale*, the opera which had received its London *première*, with Joséphine, in 1832. In Rome, she was extremely warmly welcomed, being given no less than four curtain calls. The critic writing for the *Tiberino*, as quoted in *Teatri Arte e Letterature*, remarked that she was new to Rome. Both her singing and acting had demonstrated beyond the slightest doubt that she was a true artist. She had performed the most demanding passages with remarkable precision, especially in the final *rondo* where her voice had displayed all the beauties of its extensive range.

In May, at the *Metastasio*, Joséphine sang in a new work by Maestro Simeoni called *Contradizzione e Puntiglio* (Contradictions and Obstinacy). She was the only singer who was considered to have studied her part adequately and was applauded accordingly.

While in Rome, Joséphine had also sung, with Bartolini, in Donizetti's called *Il Furioso*, which was a failure. An *opéra bouffe Don Desiderio*, the music for which had been composed in 1841 by Prince Poniatowski, was more successful. Joséphine supported the bass Gennaro Luzio who created the name part. This work was revived in Paris in 1858, when the critic in the *Revue et Gazette Musicale de Paris* recalled that it was Joséphine who had created one of the rôles.

Joséphine's operatic career in Italy continued throughout 1843. In April, in Padua, she won general acclaim as Sandrina in *Scaramuccia*, but the theatre had been poorly attended. Later in the year, playing the same rôle at the *Teatro Maurorer* in Trieste, *prima donna* Demeric had raised the roof (*machte Fanatismo* – AMZ). By then, she was thought to have sung the part a thousand times. Her success in it was still assured, but she was beginning to be past her best (*schon im Abnehmen*).

Towards the end of 1843, the well-known Demeric was still evoking *fanatismo* in *Scaramuccia*, this time in Belluno. An unconfirmed report speaks of Joséphine having been in Venice on 17 June 1843, at the *Teatro San Benedetto*, in *Lucia di Lammermoor*.

1844 seems to have been the last in Joséphine's career on the operatic stage. Local reports are lacking, but according to the usually reliable AMZ, she sang in *Gemma di Vergy* in Feltre early in the year and also appeared in Palmanuova.

By the time that *Scaramuccia* was given in Vicenza, at the *Teatro Eretenio*, the opera could no longer hold its own, even with the old and tried Demeric and the *buffo* Pozzesi. Then when Bellini's *Capuleti* was put on, only the singer Mala made *furore* – everything else was *orrore* (horror). A sad anti-climax. It had become time for Joséphine to return to her roots in her native Strasbourg.

CHAPTER 17
Back home in Strasbourg, with Timoleone and Emilie

Joséphine de Méric.
(By courtesy of the Comune di Milano.)

JOSÉPHINE had arrived back in Strasbourg by August 1844, when she placed an advertisement in the *Courrier du Bas-Rhin* to announce that she intended to reside for some time in her native city, at 90, Marché-aux-Vins. She would be giving lessons in voice production and in singing in French, German and Italian, either at her own home or at the residences of her pupils. No doubt Timoleone and

187

Emilie were with her. Timoleone was certainly in Strasbourg by 14 December 1844 when he sang, with Joséphine, in a major concert there. She chose a *cavatina* from *La Gazza Ladra* and they sang together the duet *Mira la Bianca Luna* from Rossini's *Soirées Musicales*. The family were in the Alsatian capital during 1845 and remained there for at least three years.

Joséphine's mother was still alive in 1845 and was most likely also in Strasbourg.

The AMZ notes that both Madame Alexander and Timoleone were teaching singing and giving concert performances. Emilie, by then an adolescent contralto, would often join them in concerts. She is referred to at this period as Dem[oiselle] Glossop de Méric.

Joséphine and Timoleone, described as Monsieur et Madame Méric-Alexandre, frequently sang at concerts in the *Salle de la Réunion des Arts* with Monsieur Schwaederle, a violinist of some distinction who 'received applause even when playing beside Liszt'. One of the earliest of such concerts was given on 19 April 1845. Concerts were also held in the Great Hall in the Château, where Joséphine was billed to sing on 27 April.

On 2 March 1846, Joséphine sang *casta diva*, from *Norma*, 'to universal and well-deserved applause'. She and Timoleone took part in a quartet from Rossini's *Bianca e Faliero* and Timoleone sang with Emilie in a duet by Gabussi, *La Calabrese*.

An influential organisation in Strasbourg devoted to the musical education of the young was the *Académie de Chant*, founded in about 1841. On 15 April 1846, Joséphine and Timoleone took a major part in one of this society's concerts, together with Schwaederle and others. The pair sang a duet by Rossini at a morning charity concert at the Château on Sunday 26 April.

On 28 November 1846, all three members of the family sang in a vocal and instrumental concert at the Strasbourg *Salle de la Réunion des Arts* organised by Monsieur Schwaederle. Emilie, 'whose splendid contralto voice is always heard with pleasure' (AMZ) sang Romeo's *cavatina* from *I Capuleti e i Montecchi*. Timoleone gave a rendering of a romantic song by Prince Belgioioso and the family combined for the trio from Vaccai's *Giovinetta Pellegrina*. Finally, Joséphine and Timoleone sang in the soprano and tenor duet from *I Puritani*. Clearly, Italian music continued to hold appeal for the audiences in Strasbourg in the latter years of the July Monarchy.

There was an occasion when a benefit concert was given for 'the young contralto Glossop-Demeric' at which Emilie sang a duet with her mother from Mercadante's *Giuramento* and the family joined in a trio from Rossini's *Ricciardo e Zoraïde*.

Then, as later, charity concerts were much in vogue. At one of these (19 December 1846), Emilie foreshadowed her performance in London by singing an aria from Rossini's *Donna del Lago*.

In an early description of Emilie's singing, the AMZ wrote that Nature had endowed her with a splendid 'metal-rich' voice with deep masculine strength. She was urged to confine herself to her inborn contralto and not to try to sing soprano, where her voice tended to become too strident (*schneidend*).

The Courrier du Bas-Rhin of 13 December 1846, reviewing the concert on 28 November referred to above, gave its verdict on Joséphine, Emilie and Timoleone. Joséphine's singing was distinguished by '*une méthode pure*' and, as a teacher, she had developed her daughter's talent. Mlle. Glossop had sung Romeo's initial aria with perfect precision. Timoleone possessed almost to perfection the Italian manner of singing, clearly enunciating every syllable and bringing out all the nuances of the music. The only regret was that he had chosen to sing such short pieces.

There had been another charity concert at the Château on 27 April 1847. This time, Emilie sang in a duet from *La Gazza Ladra*. She then joined her mother and Timoleone in a trio from Rossini's *Ricciardo e Zoraïde*. In all probability, Emilie performed in further concerts in Strasbourg in the course of 1847, but all that is certain is that she gave a farewell concert towards the end of November. Announcing this, she paid a graceful tribute to the people of Strasbourg 'who had always shown so much kindness to her and her family'.

The last time that Joséphine, Timoleone and Emilie sang together in Strasbourg seems to have been on 18 December 1847, at the *Réunion des Arts*, for the benefit of the poor of the *Société de St. Vincent de Paul*. Mother and daughter gave a rendering of a duet from Rossini's *Stabat Mater* and the three sang what appears to have been a local favourite, the trio from *Ricciardo e Zoraïde*.

The AMZ reported that Emilie, 'that highly-valued singer', left Strasbourg to continue her training in Paris. She will be followed there in the second part of this biography.

It is not easy to follow Joséphine's life after the end of her singing career. Her mother lived until 1857 or thereabouts and Joséphine may have been based in Strasbourg until then. She was billed to sing with Timoleone at a concert in the theatre foyer on 16 May 1848. This event was for the benefit of a Monsieur Valtier, a former army captain in Belgium, who was going to join the expeditionary force opposing the Austrians in Lombardy. Timoleone, perhaps, was an ardent Italian nationalist. It is known that in November 1853, Joséphine and Timoleone were with Emilie in St. Petersburg. This is clear from a letter which Luigi Lablache wrote from there to his wife on 8 November of that year. Timoleone, Lablache said, was gravely ill and the doctors had told him that it was serious.

Joséphine was with her daughter in Paris when Emilie married Lablache's son Nicola in September 1854, but by then Timoleone was dead. Registers in Strasbourg record that Joséphine and Emilie had returned to that city on 25 March 1856, but it is not known how long they may have stayed. In 1865 and 1866 Joséphine was living in Paris, first in the rue de la Madeleine and then in the rue Boissy d' Anglas. During at least part of those years she had the comfort that Emilie was also in Paris.

Joséphine's youngest brother, Jean-Jacques Victor de Méric, had settled in London as a surgeon. Victor, as he was known, made a will in March 1876 in which he empowered his widow, at her discretion, to give his sister, Joséphine Alexandre, widow, up to £10 a year.

This was never to become a burden because Joséphine died, in Bloomsbury, London, on 26 December 1877. She was buried in the cemetery at Kensal Green, the ownership of the grave being vested in 'Emilia de Méric', her daughter. The cause of death was given on the certificate as pneumonia and the informant was her grandson H. Lablack [sic]. Joséphine was described as the widow of 'Alexander de Meric', an operatic singer. Henri Lablache had been present at the death and gave as his residence 10 Woburn Place, which was where Joséphine died. Not far from Joséphine, at Kensal Green, lies the body of Settimio Alexandre, her son by Timoleone. The burials are duly recorded in the cemetery files, but if there was ever a monument to Joséphine it has not survived.

Joséphine's long life had been devoted to music and she had depended on music and her own talents for her living. She had been endowed with a fine voice with an exceptional bell-like quality. On occasion, both as singer and actress, she had risen to great heights. Being a true musician and a dedicated professional, she had rarely fallen below a high standard of competence. She had grace and charm and seldom if ever fell out with her colleagues. She sang with many of the greatest singers of her time and, except perhaps in Paris, did not fail them. She bequeathed to the lyric stage a daughter who was to hold her own among the stars of the second half of the century.

PART TWO *Emilie*

Emilie as Orsini in Lucrezia Borgia (signed portrait, 1852).

(By courtesy of the Museo Teatrale alla Scala, Milan.)

Emilie de Méric (Glossop): early life in Strasbourg and début in Paris

A letter from Meyerbeer provides an early reference to Joséphine's daughter, Emilie. The clear inference from Meyerbeer's correspondence with his wife is that Emilie was born in 1830. In fact, she was born on 6 October 1830, in Paris (2nd arrondissement).

As a two-year-old baby, Emilie was with her mother in London in 1832 and the presumption is that Joséphine took the child with her on operatic tours. Emilie is reported to have 'left Parma' at an early age and she will no doubt have been there with her mother in 1837.

It was from Joséphine that the young girl received much of her early vocal training. From 1835, for some ten years, Joséphine was in Italy where Emilie also had the benefit of tuition from Italian singing masters. According to the *Teatrale Ottocentesca*, by Ferrarini (Parma, 1978), she was given lessons by Rossini in Bologna (where Joséphine had spent the Carnival of 1840-41).

By 1845, when Joséphine was back in her home town of Strasbourg, it was evident that Emilie was embarking on a singing career. For further training and experience on the national stage she needed to go to Paris.

The Population Registers in Strasbourg record that she left Strasbourg for Paris on 25 October 1848, with her mother and Timoleone.

In Paris, Meyerbeer, notes in his diary entry for 7 November 1848 that he had received a visit that day from the singer Demerie [sic], who had sung Alice under his direction sixteen years earlier. Joséphine had brought Emilie to Meyerbeer for him to hear her sing and his verdict was that she had a marvellous contralto voice (*eine wunderschöne Altstimme*). The *Teatrale Ottocentesca* records that Emilie continued to receive tuition from Rossini in Paris. Somewhat unexpectedly, however, she does not appear to have been registered as a student at the *Conservatoire*. The archives there do indeed record the admission of a Mlle. de Méric in the first quarter of 1848, but this lady proves to have been not Emilie but a Mlle. Hélène de Méric de la Tournerie, no relation, who was also some nine months younger than Emilie.

Within a month, on Saturday 25 November 1848, Emilie made her Paris *début* in Donizetti's *Maria di Rohan*.

The Paris correspondent of the *Illustrated London News* had noted that at this performance two singers had made their *début*: Madame Ronconi and Mdlle. de Méric. 'The new contralto, Mdlle. Méric', he wrote, 'is a charming singer. She played Alboni's part of Gondi. It was her first appearance on any stage, and a more triumphant one has rarely been witnessed. She is about twenty [sic], and is handsome, with an easy and graceful deportment. Her voice is of extensive compass, combining the registers of mezzo soprano and contralto, rich and round in volume, sweet and sympathetic in quality. Her method is raw, but where nature has been so bountiful, art will soon follow to give finish and polish to the style. It is a long time since I have met with such a promising *début*'. A week later, the correspondent, who was well informed, had this to add:

'The great success of Mdlle. Meric, the young and handsome contralto, was recorded in my last letter. She made her *début*, and the next day awoke and found herself at once famous; for the directors of the Italian Operas in New York, Madrid, Naples, London etc. were besieging her with offers. The Royal Italian Opera [in London] has gained the victory in the field of temptation; and it is London, therefore, which will have the advantage of having, next season, one of the finest and most sympathetic organs I have ever listened to. Mlle. Meric, although born in Paris, and educated in Italy, has her English rights, for she is the daughter of Mr. Glossop, and is half-sister to Mrs. Gilbert A'Beckett, who has composed operas. Mdme Meric-Glossop is a vocalist who has gained glory in England, France, Italy and Germany; and her daughter has had the advantage of maternal tuition as well as a first-rate musical education'.

The half-sister, née Mary Anne Glossop, was known in her day as the composer of operas such as *Agnes Sorel* (1835) and *Little Red Riding Hood* (1842), for which her husband provided the libretti.

Le Menestrel, also, reminded its readers that Emilie's talent was hereditary. Her mother, Madame de Méric-Glossop, had possessed a strength of voice and a purity of tone which the older regulars at the *Opéra* had not forgotten. Mlle. de Méric, as Gondi, had shown herself to be a charming young lady. Her bearing was easy and she had a pure, expressive and particularly sympathetic contralto voice with a wide range. Her low notes had a velvety tone and a roundness which contrasted most pleasantly with the harsh and guttural rattle of so many contemporary singers. It was a pity that her voice was not more agile. However, perhaps some more schooling was all that was needed. She had impeccable taste and, in a word, was a worthy daughter of her mother. Her triumph had been complete.

Théâtre Royal Italien.

Engagement.

Entre les soussignés:

M. *Georges Romani*, Directeur-Entrepreneur du *Théâtre royal Italien*, demeurant à Paris, rue ~~~~, ~~~~, d'une part;

Et *Mademoiselle De = Merie* demeurant

d'autre part;

a été convenu et arrêté ce qui suit:

M. *Mademoiselle De = Merie* libre de tout engagement, ainsi qu' *elle* le déclare, s'engage, pour *la saison Théâtrale* à partir du *1er Février* 1849 jusqu'au *premier Mars 1849.*

à jouer, chanter et réciter l'opéra séria, semi-séria et buffa, en qualité de *Contralto*

————————————————— tant dans les opéras que dans les concerts, oratorios et cantales, sur ledit Théâtre, ou sur tout autre de la Capitale, et jusqu'à six lieues de distance de Paris.

Le présent engagement est en outre fait aux conditions suivantes de la part de M. *Mademoiselle De = Merie*

1° De se prêter à tout ce qui sera utile aux intérêts de l'entreprise, notamment de se trouver exactement, aux heures indiquées, aux assemblées ou représentations, ainsi qu'aux répétitions, à quelque heure que ce soit, même le soir après le spectacle, et de se conformer aux réglemens et usages du Théâtre royal Italien;

2° De se transporter en outre, d'après les ordres de l'Entrepreneur ou de son représentant, partout où l'exigera le service de la Cour, sans pouvoir prétendre autre chose, pour frais de déplacement, que les voitures qui lui seront fournies à cet effet, et une indemnité de dix francs par jour;

3° De ne pouvoir, pendant la durée de son engagement, faire usage de ses talens sur aucun théâtre, ni dans aucun concert public ~~~~~~~~~, soit gratuit, soit à billets payans, abonnemens ou souscriptions, sous peine, en cas d'infraction, d'une amende d'un mois d'appointemens;

4° De ne pouvoir refuser ou quitter aucun des rôles de son emploi, bien que ces rôles aient été joués antérieurement ou pendant son engagement, et par des artistes du même emploi ou d'un autre emploi; se soumettant en outre à jouer, chanter et réciter ces rôles tels que l'Entrepreneur les aura fait arranger, dans l'intérêt de son service, pour le bien de l'exécution et les convenances de la scène;

5° De ne pouvoir, en cas de maladie ou d'indisposition, se refuser à ce que ses rôles soient remplis par un autre artiste désigné par l'Entrepreneur, ni à reprendre ses rôles aussitôt le rétablissement de sa santé;

De ne pouvoir se refuser à céder les rôles de son répertoire pour les débuts des artistes nouvellement engagés; ~~s'obligeant en outre, en cas de maladie d'un artiste du même emploi que le sien, à le remplacer pour autant qu'on lui donne le temps nécessaire pour apprendre les rôles qu'il n'aurait pas eue à jouer~~;

6° De ne pouvoir se dispenser du service, pour cause de maladie, qu'en rapportant un certificat signé du médecin du théâtre, et constatant l'impossibilité absolue de concourir aux répétitions ou représentations, sous peine, dans le cas où ce certificat ne serait pas représenté, d'encourir la peine stipulée pour le cas de refus de service;

Ce certificat devra être renouvelé tous les trois jours, et même plus souvent si l'Entrepreneur l'exige;

7° De se soumettre, en cas de maladie qui se prolongerait au-delà de huit jours, à ce que ses appointemens soient suspendus jusqu'à la reprise régulière du service;

8° En cas de clôture du théâtre par ordre de l'autorité supérieure, ou par force majeure, incendie, grosses réparations, de ne pouvoir exiger ses appointemens pour tout le temps de la clôture;

9° De se contenter des costumes qui lui seront fournis par l'Entrepreneur, et qui seront propres, convenables, en bon état, et tels que le comporte l'importance des rôles, étant bien entendu qu'il n'en sera établi de neufs que suivant l'exigence des ouvrages et les besoins reconnus du service;

Emilie's contract with the Théâtre Royal Italien, 1849.

(By courtesy of the Archives de l' Opéra, Paris.)

195

De se fournir à ses frais du menu vestiaire, c'est-à-dire de l'habit de ville complet, de la coiffure, des gants et de la chaussure de tous ses rôles, sauf les souliers et gants de caractère, qui seront seuls fournis par l'Entrepreneur;

10° De ne pouvoir s'absenter de Paris, même pour un jour, sans le consentement par écrit de l'Entrepreneur, sous peine d'une amende de quinze jours d'appointemens pour chaque infraction;

11° De se tenir à la disposition de l'Entrepreneur les jours de représentation jusqu'à huit heures du soir) quand même *elle* ne jouerait pas dans la pièce annoncée, afin d'être prêt dans le cas d'un changement de spectacle, et de laisser à cet effet, dans le cas où *elle* s'absenterait de son domicile, l'indication de l'endroit où l'on pourrait *la* trouver, à toute heure de la journée, sous les peines portées en l'article suivant;

12° Dans le cas où, par sa mauvaise volonté, son absence du théâtre, ou toute autre cause de son fait, hors les cas d'empêchement par force majeure, il y aurait nécessité de changer le jour même une représentation annoncée, de supporter une amende égale à un mois de ses appointemens; et dans le cas où la même cause aurait entraîné la fermeture du théâtre, de rembourser le montant de la recette, fixé dès à-présent, à forfait, à la somme de six mille francs;

13° De payer une amende d'un mois de son traitement, si, après avoir refusé de jouer pour cause de maladie ou d'indisposition, *elle* était aperçu dans un spectacle ou tout autre lieu d'amusement, ou chantant dans un concert particulier;

14° De subir une amende d'un jour d'appointemens, faute d'arriver aux répétitions à l'heure indiquée;

15° De ne pouvoir, en cas de contestation avec M. *Romani*, se refuser à l'exécution du présent engagement, s'obligeant, dans ce cas, à continuer provisoirement son service, à toute réquisition de M. *Nixen*, jusqu'au jugement de la contestation, sous les peines portées aux articles qui précèdent;

16° Et enfin, en cas de rupture par son fait du présent engagement, de payer à M. *Nixen* une somme de *Mille Francs* — irrévocablement fixée à titre de dédit et de dommages-intérêts, et exigible du jour où le refus d'exécution serait constaté, en quelque part que le contrevenant se soit retiré.

Il est formellement convenu que dans le cas où Mad= *De = Merie* ne serait pas arrivé à Paris le jour fixé pour le commencement du présent engagement, et dans le cas où, pendant sa durée, *elle* quitterait Paris pendant plus de trois jours sans autorisation, M. *Romani* aura le droit de *la* considérer comme ayant rompu ledit engagement, et d'exiger le paiement du dédit ci-dessus stipulé.

Le dédit sera exigible en totalité, quel que soit le temps qui resterait encore à courir du présent engagement.

Sous foi de l'exécution pleine et entière des clauses et conditions ci-dessus, M. *Romani* s'engage à payer à Mademoiselle *De = Merie* 15 une somme de *trois cent francs* — payable en *six* portions égales, de *mois en mois*, à partir de *16 Février* — 1849 sans aucune retenue, si ce n'est celle des amendes encourues conformément aux articles qui précèdent.

Le paiement ne commencera toutefois que du jour où l'artiste se sera mis à la disposition de M. *Nixen*, en état de répéter et de débuter.

Dans le cas où M. *Nixen* céderait son entreprise, il aura le droit de mettre l'exécution du présent engagement à la charge de son cessionnaire, et dans ce cas, Mad= *De = Merie* devra accepter ledit cessionnaire pour débiteur à la place de M. *Nixen Romani*.

CLAUSES PARTICULIERES.

M. *Romani Nixen* fait élection de domicile au théâtre, et Mad=lle *De = Merie* à Paris, en sa demeure, rue auquel lieu *elle* consent la signification de tous actes et ajournemens, sans autres délais que ceux qui lui seraient donnés si ce domicile était son domicile réel. Ce domicile sera attributif de juridiction. En conséquence, toute contestation devra être jugée à Paris.

Les frais de timbre et d'enregistrement du présent, de même que l'amende et double droit, tomberont à la charge de celle des parties qui, par son fait, aura mis l'autre dans la nécessité de remplir cette formalité, et que le jugement condamnerait.

Mad=lle *De Merie* — quoique étranger, déclare connaître parfaitement la valeur des expressions contenues dans le présent engagement, et renonce à élever aucunes difficultés à ce sujet.	Mad=lle *De Merie* quantunque forestiere, dichiara conoscere perfettamente il valore delle espressioni contenute nella presente scrittura, e rinuncia alle difficoltà che potrebbe sollevare sopra questo oggetto.

Fait double et de bonne foi, à *Paris* — le *Janvier 1849* —

F. Romani

Emilia de Merie

Timoleone Alexandri

The critic in the *Revue* recalled having heard Emilie first at a *soirée musicale*. She had made a successful *début* and had a beautiful contralto voice. There was perhaps some affectation in her use of it, a fault common with contralto singers, who aimed at amazing their hearers by the strength of their deep vocal chords. All the same, she sang as a true musician, with her own style, and well deserved her place alongside Mesdames Bosio and Sara in the cast at the *Théâtre Italien*.

For its part, *Le Corsaire* welcomed the *débuts* of Madame Ronconi and Mlle. de Méric and praised both for the accuracy (*justesse*) of their singing, a most precious quality which was becoming more and more rare. Emilie showed every sign of both musical and dramatic promise. Her only fault, alas a grievous one, was the exaggerated rolling of the uvular 'r' (*grasseyement*).

Unfortunately for Emilie and the rest of the operatic company, the *Théâtre Italien* had scarcely opened before it was faced with closure. The new Director, Dupin, had failed to recruit a sufficient number of first-rate singers and was accused of offering only the 'stale old Italian music'. As the *Revue* put it, the whole raison d'être of the *Théâtre Italien* in Paris was that it should be excellent, offering better singing than could be heard anywhere else. There was no good new music coming out of Italy and everyone knew all the old scores by heart.

Dupin's enterprise had failed, both artistically and financially, and he resigned.

The closure was received in Paris with consternation. For decades, the *Théâtre Italien* had been a highly-valued cultural ornament of the capital, and the French themselves were prepared to admit that the Italian singers had given them instruction as well as pleasure. However, all was not lost. Ronconi was prevailed upon to undertake the onerous task of administering a revived theatre, supported by his wife, by Mesdames Alboni and Castellan and by Lablache.

Emilie was re-engaged under the new régime. Her new contract with the *Théâtre Royal Italien* came in January 1849. It was concluded between the *Directeur-Entrepreneur*, Georges Ronconi, and Mademoiselle De Méric (no mention of the surname Glossop). Emilie undertook to play, sing and recite opera seria, semi-seria and *buffa* as *primo contralto* for one month from 1 February to 1 March 1849. The contract is signed 'Emilia de Méric' and countersigned by Timoleone Alexander, probably because Emilie at the age of eighteen was regarded as a minor. She is described as a foreigner.

Emilie's nationality would seem to be in some doubt. On the assumption that Joséphine's marriage to Glossop in 1827 was valid, she would derive British nationality from her father. If that marriage were invalid, then she might be stateless unless the *lex loci* conferred on her the nationality of the country where she was born. Under French law, it would seem, birth in Paris would not suffice to confer French nationality.

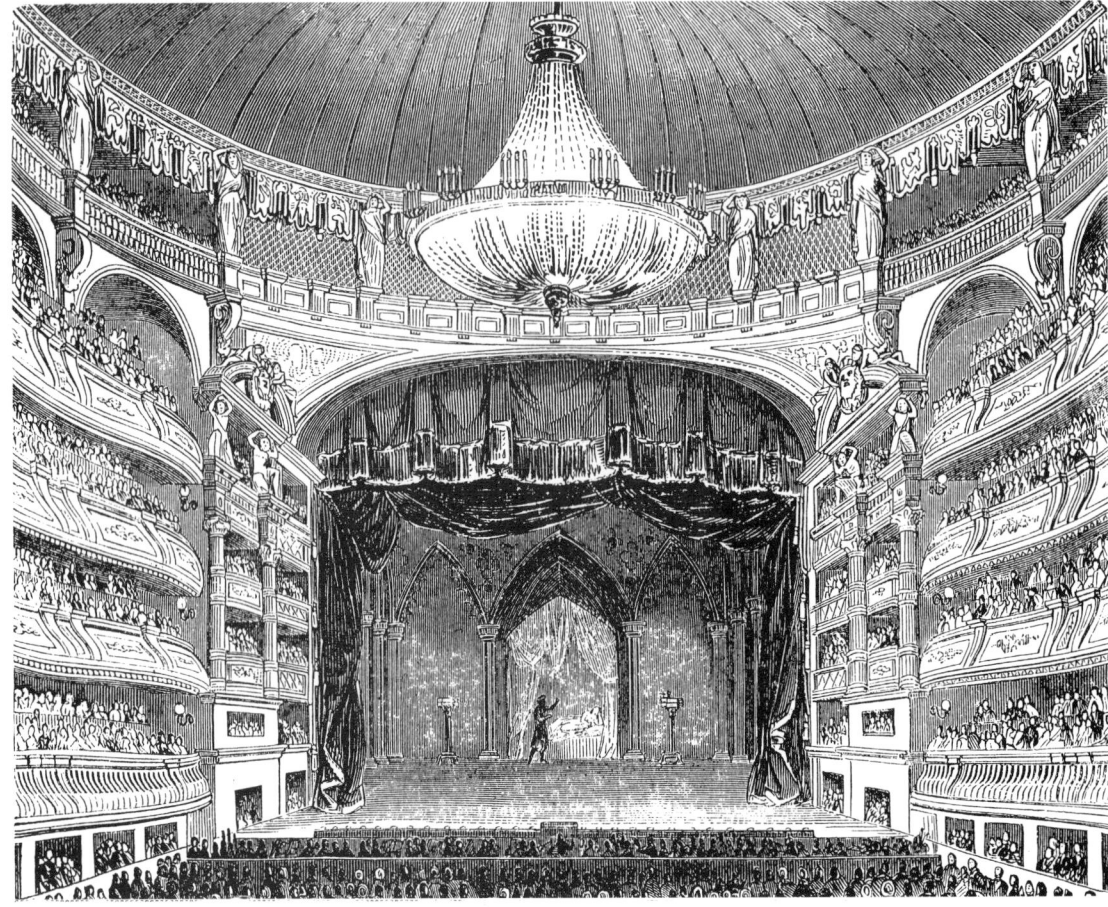

Théâtre Italien – The Salle Ventadour.
(By courtesy of the Archives de l' Opéra.)

By 16 January, the *Théâtre Italien* had already reopened, in the *Salle Ventadour*, with *La Cenerentola*. Emilie did not appear on that occasion, but on 20 February she took part in a successful performance of *La Gazza Ladra*. Alboni, who in 1848 had taken the contralto rôle of Pippo, appeared this time as Ninette, with the necessary transpositions into the lower register. Emilie had the daunting task of following her as Pippo. She did her best to rise to the challenge and *Le Menestrel* (E. Viel) declared that it adhered to all the encomiums which it had given to her before. Mlle. de Méric had been applauded both after Alboni and alongside her. Her voice was charming and practice would make it more nimble. 'But let her for God's sake rid herself of the abominably exaggerated rolling of the uvular 'r' which mars her singing'.

The *Revue* described the performance of the opera as brilliant and said that Emilie had supported Alboni perfectly in the duet in the second act – perhaps the first time that it had been sung by two contraltos. *L'Illustration*, too, did not hesitate to praise Emilie's contralto voice 'even beside Alboni's'. The prison duet had been accorded three rounds of applause, so anxious were the audience to hear it sung twice.

La France Musicale (O.P.R.A.), on the other hand, considered that Emilie was not up to the rôle of Pippo. She needed three years at the *Paris Conservatoire* or in Milan before she could take her place as an artist alongside Ronconi, Morelli and Alboni. One could never get used to 'the Provençal [sic] accent with which she clothed the language of Petrarch and Tasso'. This journal, it should be said, had previously forecast that Signor Ronconi's enterprise was doomed: above all, he was attempting the impossible by trying to manage without a major soprano or tenor. *La Gazza Ladra* had proved the point, with Alboni vainly trying to sing as a soprano. Two contralti singing together had resulted in a monotony of tone which was musically deplorable. The audience at the *Théâtre Italien* had been satisfied, but the general public did not look at such things too closely.

La Gazza Ladra was given four nights in succession, followed by a Sunday performance. In the opinion of the *Revue*, at least, Alboni's performance had added to her reputation as a dramatic artist and Emilie's beautiful voice had established itself more and more.

In Paris, Emilie had had a baptism of fire in the furnace of the professional theatre. It must have been a shock, after a spectacular *début*, to be faced with the imminent closure of the theatre where one had just appeared. Yet she had her compensations. If *Le Menestrel* is to be believed, she had shared in a great occasion: thanks to *Maria di Rohan* and the performances by Madame Ronconi and Mlle. de Méric, the *Théâtre Italien* under Dupin had been like a lamp which makes a mighty flare before it goes out, dying in a flash of brilliance. Emilie had had her month under Ronconi, with the chance to play opposite Alboni. Above all, she had been given the opening for her engagement by another major opera house, in London.

19 *Emilie's début in opera in London, 1849*

IN 1849, rivalry between the two Italian theatres in London had reached a high pitch. Faced with Jenny Lind and Alboni at Her Majesty's, the Royal Italian Opera at Covent Garden had engaged Mlle. de Méric, and on 17 February *The Times* referred to 'the great sensation' which she had produced at her recent *début* in Paris. 'She is only twenty years of age, and her contralto organ is described by those who have heard her to be of extraordinary compass and delicious quality, having that pure and sympathetic tone which at once touches the heart.' At the same time, the *Musical World* warned against indulging in too great expectations. The young contralto was almost a novice on the stage.

In March, *The Times* reported that Mademoiselle Méric, daughter of the Madame Méric well known in German and English opera some fifteen years earlier, would be taking the light contralto parts such as Orsini (*Lucrezia Borgia*) and Pippo (*La Gazza Ladra*) which Alboni's singing had made so unusually prominent. This was to prove more true of 1850 than of 1849.

In the event, Emilie made her London *début* on 10 April 1849 as the Savoyard boy Pierotto in Donizetti's *Linda di Chamounix*. On the same night, the Irish soprano Catherine Hayes (1825-1861) was first heard in London. She played the main part. Both singers were enthusiastically received. The house was crammed to the roof. The only question was whether the gentlemen in the audience were correctly dressed. At the opening of the season, *The Times* had complained about the informal clothes which men had been seen wearing at the opera. Its readers were informed that 'the costume for gentlemen consists of a dress coat, plain black or white neckcloth, and black or white trousers. The waistcoat may vary according to the fancy of the wearer'.

Early impressions of an artiste's talents have a special interest. After Emilie's second performance, *The Illustrated London News* said that, like Miss Hayes, she had met with a decided success.

> 'Mlle. Méric is very young and prepossessing, with one of the most magnificent voices we have ever heard. It is sweet, sonorous and powerful, with great tractability. The

first air of Pierotto, *Cari luoghi*, is sung behind the scenes
with a concertina accompaniment and no sooner were
the luscious tones of Mlle. Méric's voice heard, than a
burst of enthusiastic encouragement emanated from the
auditory; and on her coming on the stage she was
cordially received. The *ballatta Per sua madre* is by no
means an effective composition; but Mlle. Méric
confirmed the impression in her favour. Her great
triumph was in the duo with Miss Hayes in the second
Act, *Ah bel destin*, which received a double encore. The
deep pathos with which Méric sang in this air created the
greatest sensation. The two voices blended beautifully and
the cadenzas were executed with unerring precision by
both singers'.

The article concluded with the correct statement that Emilie was the
daughter of Madame Méric (not Méric de [sic] Lalande) who had
sung at the King's Theatre and Drury Lane some years earlier.
Incorrectly, the paper said that Emilie had been born in England.

Most of the reviews were similarly favourable. The *Literary Gazette*
said that the new contralto had fully realised their expectations. 'She
is a very clever and elegant singer; her voice is in perfect tune, and
possesses the rare *simpatico* quality, so charming to the ear'. The
Athenaeum spoke of her as a young lady of excellent promise, her
voice having that rare quality, a true, even, sweet and sufficient
contralto. It was a voice which recalled Mrs. Shaw when she was in
her prime. Mrs. Shaw, née Postans (1814-1876), sang at Covent
Garden and Drury Lane from 1842.

Adverse criticism of Emilie's voice was aimed at her lower notes.
These were described as somewhat hard, throaty and wanting in
mellowness. It was also stressed that, as she was so very young, her
voice had not yet been cultivated to the degree of which it was
capable. Nevertheless, her style of singing was always intelligent and
often reached a high point of expression. The *Musical World*
concluded that while Mlle. de Méric had acquitted herself exceedingly
well in the small part of Pierotto, she would have to be heard in
another part before confirmed opinions could be offered. The music
of Pierotto was merely pleasing and laid little tax on the vocal artist.

The only sour remarks came from *Fraser's Magazine* which
maintained that the double shakes exhibited by Miss Hayes and
Mlle. de Méric had produced a ludicrous effect. (Shakes, no doubt,
were going out of fashion).

As an actress, Emilie was still inexperienced, and despite her
animation she had not appeared entirely at her ease on the stage.
However, the *Musical World* said that she had shown considerable

sensitivity in her acting and the *Athenaeum* found nothing unfinished or gauche in her performance. The *Morning Post* praised Emilie's acting for its great simplicity and truthfulness.

As a last word on Emilie's *début* in England, *The Morning Chronicle* may be called in aid. Donizetti, the paper wrote, had illustrated Pierotto's simple fidelity with some of his tenderest strains. Emilie's voice, a pure contralto with a wide range into the upper register, contained a fine sentimental expression, which burst forth upon the audience in the second act, when Pierotto discovers Linda. *Or che v'ho ritrovato* had been full of affection and pathos and the acting of Mlle. de Méric claimed equal praise.

An engraving of *Linda di Chamounix* in the *Illustrated London News* shows Emilie with Catherine Hayes and the Italian baritone Tamburini.

A scene from Linda di Chamounix with Emile in the breeches part. Photograph by Graham Brandon.
(By courtesy of the Trustees of the Theatre Museum, Victoria and Albert Museum.)

One wonders whether any of Emilie's family witnessed her London *début*. Surely, it seems, her mother must have been there, but no evidence has been found. It was a year before her father, Joseph Glossop, died, but he had almost certainly been out of England since about 1835. Emilie's maternal uncle, the surgeon Victor de Méric FRCS, settled in London after studying under Ricord in Paris in 1847-1848, but may not have been in England as early as 1849. The highest probability is that Elisabeth Féron might have been in the Covent Garden audience to hear Glossop's daughter sing. Féron was performing at the Princess's Theatre in March 1849 as the Marchioness in a production of Donizetti's *La Vivandière* (*The Daughter of the Regiment.*) With her was her twenty-four-year-old son, Augustus, Emilie's half-brother.

Despite the excitement aroused by her arrival from Paris and the success of her *début*, Emilie was not given major rôles during the 1849 Season and was soon eclipsed by singers of greater experience and fame. Her arrival in London had been almost immediately followed by that of the contralto Mlle. Angri, an Ionian by birth, who became 'the ruling object of attraction' at Covent Garden. Furthermore, interest naturally centred on such established stars as Grisi and Persiani who, with Mario and Tamburini, had arrived from Paris early in April.

Both Emilie and Mlle. Corbari, for instance, found themselves 'consenting in the kindest manner' to sing in the chorus in several performances of Meyerbeer's *Le Prophète*. *Le Menestrel* pointed out that such acts of self-sacrifice proved that nothing had been neglected to ensure that the production of *Le Prophète* should be a complete success [which indeed it was], but Emilie had to content herself with a word of praise from the *Musical World* for having sung the contralto solo with admirable effect.

Emilie's youth and lowly status at the time is reflected in the salary which she was paid. According to the *Annual Register*, she received £500, as against £1,300 for Catherine Hayes and £2,500 each for Alboni and Grisi. However, she had made only a few appearances.

THE 1849 OPERA SEASON IN RETROSPECT

The Season as a whole was judged to have been a success. *The Times* said that the opera company had kept faith and redeemed every pledge in their prospectus. Four operas new to the theatre had duly been produced: *Masaniello, Roberto Il Diavolo, Il Matrimonio Segreto* and *Le Prophète*. There had been three artists new to the London Opera: Miss Catherine Hayes, Mlle. Angri and Mlle. de Méric. *Masaniello* had proved a new triumph for the conductor, Costa, and his orchestra and chorus. Donizetti's *Linda di Chamounix* was unfortunately a feeble opera, but thanks to the singers the performance had offered several attractions. 'The success of Miss Hayes, who being a compatriot, had naturally enlisted the sympathies of the public, was decided; and although she did not prove herself a cantatrice of the first rank, she produced a highly favourable impression. Mademoiselle de Méric's success was not less unequivocal. She was at once acknowledged as a contralto of promise, and her improvement during the season has been gradual and sure.' Presumably *The Times* had been impressed by changes for the better in Emilie's rendering of the part of Pierotto. From the comment about Miss Hayes, it seems that this paper, at least, did not regard Emilie as British.

The *Annual Register* declared that the lovers of opera had for two seasons enjoyed their luxury 'in the highest perfection'. Thanks to Mr. E. T. Delafield, the old theatre had been entirely reconstructed, new and gorgeous scenery had been provided and the most celebrated singers of the Italian stage had received engagements without stint. *Primos* and *Prima Donnas* had abounded. Alas, this had led to Delafield going bankrupt and being obliged to publish details of the salaries paid to the performers – 'the prices at which the public are supplied with operatic luxuries.'

Thus, even though she had not been given much scope to shine herself, Emilie had had the inestimable advantage, in this early stage in her career, of being in the company of a galaxy of brilliant stars. This gave her the experience which was above all what she needed. Perhaps, too, it saved her from aspiring too high too soon. As the *Musical World* had said, she had yet much to learn and must not be persuaded by indiscriminate praise to fancy herself already perfect. Cox put the matter like this: ' . . . the Royal Opera Season of 1849 commenced with the defection of Mdlle. Alboni, who transferred her services to Her Majesty's Theatre, apparently without any compunction whatever. Mdlle. Alboni was succeeded by Mdlle. Meric and afterwards by Mdlle. Angri, each of whom would have been considered competent for the position of contralto, had they not followed so great a favourite as that lady had made herself.'

For some strange reason, Cox, who had at first correctly stated that Mlle. de Méric was the daughter of Joséphine, subsequently changed his mind and added a footnote to say, erroneously, that she was the daughter of Mme. de Méric-Lalande. This has led to much confusion since.

The *Literary Gazette* summed up Emilie's performances by saying that although she had but seldom performed, 'yet what has been undertaken by her has always been well done, and in concerts she is a very agreeable singer'. This brings us to the 1849 concert scene.

Concerts and provincial tour, 1849

LONDON CONCERTS

IN 1849, concerts continued to be a prime feature of the London musical scene. On 7 May, for instance, the Italian Company gave a Grand Morning Concert at which the Hayes-de Méric duet *Ah bel destin* came in for a liberal share of the applause. The two young ladies also sang *Oh luce di quest'anima* from *Linda di Chamounix*. At similar concerts during the Summer, e.g. at Covent Garden on 30 May and 6 July, Emilie took a prominent part. She had sung the pretty air *Deh non voler* from *Anna Bolena* 'very expressively' and had given an exquisite rendering of a contralto air from the *Maria di Rohan* of her Paris *début*.

There had been some good singing at Sir Henry Bishop's Concert in July, with Mlle. de Méric meriting emphatic commendation (*The Athenaeum*). Bishop (1786-1855), composer and conductor, was a founder member of the London Philharmonic Society and the composer of *Home, Sweet Home*. In a concert at the splendid mansion of Lady Vassall Webster in Roehampton, 'little Mdlle. de Méric' sang 'in her contralto which would fain (if it could) eclipse the luscious richness of Alboni's' (*Musical World*).

For Emilie, a highpoint in the concert round will have been the Grand Evening Concert at the Theatre Royal, Drury Lane on 15 August given for the benefit of none other than her half-brother Augustus Glossop Harris. A long list of eminent artists gave their services, not least Grisi, Mario, Madame Viardot and Tagliafico. In its review of this concert, *The Athenaeum* paid this tribute to Emilie:

> 'Mdlle. de Méric, in spite of the "wanderings of the band", delivered *Voi che sapete* in a style so distinguished as to get her encore too [that is, following one for Miss Hayes' *Kathleen Mavourneen*]. It is long since we have been so favourably impressed by promise as in the case of this very young lady, who ought to become the greatest contralto of her day'.

Certainly Emilie became one of the leading contraltos of the second half of the nineteenth century; but in the Romantic period between about 1830 and 1850 the hero's part, formerly the domain of the contralto (or castrato) had been transferred to the tenor.

PROVINCIAL TOUR IN 1849

When the Royal Italian Opera season closed, many of the singers from both Covent Garden and Her Majesty's embarked on a short provincial tour.

Willert Beale, in his *Light of Other Days*, has given a vivid account, based on his experience as a bear-leader, of the daily routine which was followed by singers performing in English towns in the middle of the nineteenth century.

The company would travel by train and would always put up at the 'first hotels'. Dinner was at three o'clock, followed by a concert or an opera in the evening, and then supper. When Beale was in charge, he would sit at the head of the table with the conductor facing him and the singers sitting on his right and left. They all drank claret. However, 'it must be a vintage wine, for although each takes but a small quantity, we are very particular about the quality. We insist upon coffee immediately after dinner, and are not always pleased with the way in which it is made. It is not French, nor even Italian coffee, by any means.' Above all, though, it was the monotony of the English dinners which were found wearisome. The same bill of fare wherever they went: macaroni soup with never more than a few sticks of the pasta in each plate, boiled turbot with pink sauce, the inevitable saddles of mutton, boiled fowls, cabinet pudding and indigestible-looking apple-tart, relieved some times with Devonshire cream, to which Madame Alboni was very partial.

Happily, some hotel-keepers were willing to provide menus sent to them by Mr. Beale in advance. A Mr. Radley, of the Adelphi Hotel in Liverpool, was singled out for praise. In 1847, he had provided a dish of genuine Italian macaroni, which he called 'the Alboni', and this name was retained for many years.

Emilie seems not to have been with the Royal Italian Opera Company when it took part in the opening of the new Philharmonic Hall in Liverpool on 27 August 1849, but she was one of the principal vocal performers at the four-day Birmingham Musical Festival which started on Wednesday 5 September. This was the 26th Anniversary of a triennial event which had been established as far back as 1773, in aid of the Birmingham General Hospital. The Festival Concerts were given in the Birmingham Town Hall.

Exterior – Town Hall, Birmingham.
(By courtesy of Birmingham Central Library.)

In the centenary year, 1873, John Thackray Bunce published *A History of the Birmingham General Hospital and the Musical Festivals.* In this book, he makes some interesting observations about musical taste in the city. He writes:

> 'It is gratifying to observe that from the first the Festivals have been marked by the selection of music of the highest class. Notwithstanding that even at the remote period of which we are writing Birmingham was decidedly a musical town, it still must have been a bold experiment to have offered to the public a series of performances including the *Messiah* and other works then scarcely appreciated even by persons of cultivated taste, and certainly distasteful to many, if not most, of the amateurs who had acquired a relish for inferior and frivolous music, against the popularity of which Handel found it so difficult to contend.'

In 1849, the Festival was under the special patronage of The Queen, the Queen Dowager (Queen Adelaide), Prince Albert, the Duke of Cambridge and the Duchess of Kent, the Queen's mother. Apart from being comprehensively covered by the local press, it also received reviews in *The Times*.

The programme included such major works as Mendelssohn's *Elijah*, which had been composed for the 1846 Festival, *Athaliah*, the *Messiah* and part of *Israel in Egypt*.

The first Grand Miscellaneous Concert went on until midnight and was considered by *The Times* to have been overlong. After Beethoven's *Pastoral Symphony*, 'the appearance of Madame Sontag was looked forward to with eager and general expectation. This did not prevent, however, the clever Mlle. de Méric from obtaining much deserved applause in the quaint romance of Seyton from *Anna Bolena, Deh non voler*.' The local *Gazette* said that she had interpreted this with great taste, displaying a voice of considerable extent, power and sweetness.

The orchestra was conducted by Michael Costa. He had made his *début*, as a singer, at the Birmingham Festival in 1829. In one of Costa's own quartets, *Ecco quel fiero istante*, Emilie sang with Madame Castellan, Mario and Frédéric Lablache, the bass who was to become her brother-in-law. This had been much and deservedly applauded.

Although evidently suffering from nervousness, Emilie had given Cherubini's beautiful sacred number *O Salutaris Hostia* in a highly artistic manner. She had joined Mlle. Jetty de Treffz, Mario and Machior in Mozart's *Ave Verum*.

On the Thursday, the Hall had been crowded to suffocation with 2,433 people present. *The Times* wrote that 'A feature of general interest . . . was a grand chorus, interspersed with solos, *L'Invocazione all'Armonia*, the composition of His Royal Highness Prince Albert . . . . The music is highly creditable to the illustrious amateur. The chorus in C Major, which forms the burden of the *morceau*, is rhythmical and animated, and the solos are melodious and effectively written for voices . . . . The execution was admirable and the encore unanimous. Mme. Castellan, Mlle. de Méric, Mario and Lablache, sung the solo voice parts with great care and effect.'

Emilie had sung the duet *Lasciami*, from *Tancredi*, with Mme. Castellan. This had been very pleasing, though there had been an evident misunderstanding about the cadenza at the close (*Aris's Birmingham Gazette*).

On the Friday, a notice was circulated asking for no encores, so that the performance could be over by 11 o'clock. This had little effect, however. Mendelssohn's *First Walpurgis Nacht* did not come on till 11.30. Mozart's *Splendente te* had been very well executed, the solo parts having been sustained with great ability by Mlle. de Treffz, Mlle. de Méric, Mr. Sims Reeves and Herr Pischek. One of the gems of the evening had been the *Benedictus* from Mozart's *Requiem*, in which Emilie had sung with Mme. Castellan, Sims Reeves and F. Lablache.

Summing up, *The Times* concluded that the 1849 Festival might be counted among the most successful ever given at Birmingham. On the financial side, though, there had been some disappointment. In 1846, donations had constituted a very important part of the receipts, whereas in 1849 these had fallen considerably beneath the usual standard. On the other hand, the amount derived from the sale of tickets had far exceeded the average. Three reasons adduced for the drop in donations were the depreciation in railway property, doubts about the success of free trade and, finally, the cholera. Though Birmingham had escaped the last visitation, the epidemic discouraged people from venturing into large and populous towns.

Emilie did not go on to the Three Choirs Festival at Hereford, where Mme. Castellan was the only foreign artist engaged. Emilie went much further afield, to a new and glittering stage, St. Petersburg.

CHAPTER 21 — *The Italian Opera in St. Petersburg*

THE mid-nineteenth century was a period when opera played a major rôle in the life of polite society in St. Petersburg. In his *History of the Resident Italian Theatre in St. Petersburg* (St. Petersburg, 1895), Ivanov points out that opera and art were the only distractions and entertainment for the intellectual circles of the time. His work gives detailed accounts of the opera performances and the artists taking part.

There had been an Italian Court Theatre in the Russian capital since the early 1730s and it existed more or less without interruption until 1798, when the Czar Paul closed it down to save money. There was a brief and undistinguished rebirth in 1829 which lasted only a couple of years. Then in 1843 the Italian Court Theatre was placed on a new and durable foundation.

This was achieved following the intense enthusiasm generated by the tenor Rubini when he performed with the local Russian and German troupes in the Spring of 1843. When Rubini played Edgar in *Lucia*, virtually the whole audience were in tears. Until Rubini came, St. Petersburg society had had no conception of the glorious state of operatic art as it had developed in Western Europe. The Russians had never known anything like the passionate way he acted and sang. By midsummer he had been given a contract to return for the 1843/1844 Season, with a company mainly of his own choosing. Thus the Resident Italian Theatre of St. Petersburg was well and truly launched.

The new Season, at the Bolshoi (Grand) Theatre, opened in October 1843, with Rubini, Tamburini and Pauline Viardot-Garcia. All three had the gift of electrifying the audiences, but it proved to be Viardot, until then completely unknown in St. Petersburg, who took the public by storm.

The success of this first Season was repeated in the immediately following years. 'There was no salon', writes Yakhontov, 'where the conversation did not continually turn to the Italian opera.' The critic P. M. Zotov argued that the success of the productions was due entirely to the talent of the performers. The same operas had been heard before, but now everything seemed new and delightful. 'We had known all about the vocal difficulties, but had not experienced sounds which touched the heart . . . . With Rubini, there were moments when the audience forgot themselves, and from a surfeit of emotion, jumped up to applaud the famous singer. Even his fellow-performers submitted to his authority and once when Rubini and Viardot were called forward in *La Sonnambula* amidst shouts and applause, Viardot went down on her knees and kissed Rubini's hand.'

The Bolshoi (Grand) Theatre, St. Petersburg.
(By courtesy of The Architecture of the Leningrad Theatres by M.Z. Taranovskaya, 1988.)

The three Seasons from 1843 to 1846, when Viardot left, were considered by Yakhontov to have been the first golden era of St. Petersburg's Italian opera. The second Season, when Viardot, Rubini and Tamburini were again engaged, had been even more brilliant than the first. Then, the chief soprano had been Jeanne Anaïs Castellan, the creator of Bertha in *Le Prophète*. The contralto parts had been taken by Marietta Alboni, to whom 'one could listen for ever. Her strong, sweet notes penetrated right to the soul.'

The third Season, without Alboni, had not been considered to be quite up to the standard of the first two; and the fourth (1846/1847) had marked 'a significant step down from the third'. As regards the contraltos (or mezzo-sopranos), the public had thought Vietti a poor substitute for Alboni and they liked her replacement, Amelia Poppi-Mazheroni, even less. Furthermore, the novelty of having Italian singers was beginning to wear off. Contemporaries at this period speak of a cooling-off of public feeling towards the Italian theatre 'which would now be partly empty'. It was not that there was anything amiss about the repertoire, which included all the favourite operas of the time. So the fault must have lain with the singers. Donizetti's *Fille du Régiment* had been a failure at the Italian Opera, but 'became fashionable in the very same season, when performed by the Russian dramatic actors on the Alexandrinsky stage.'

By the fifth Season (1847/1848), the revolutionary movement throughout Europe was having its effect on taste in opera. The high drama in Verdi's works such as *Ernani* and *I Lombardi* was exerting an appeal which the operas of Rossini could no longer match.

In this and the following Season, the chief contralto was Angri. She starred in an opera called *Il Biricchino di Parigi* (The Rascal of Paris), by the Russian composer F. M. Tolstoy. Incidentally, Angri was so pleased with her part in this opera that she tried, unsuccessfully, to have *Il Biricchino* put on for her *début* in London.

This brings us to the seventh season (1849-50).

CHAPTER 22
Emilie's début in St. Petersburg

AS Elizabeth Forbes has recorded in her book *Mario and Grisi*, the tour which those two singers usually made in the provinces in Britain was curtailed in 1849 because Mario and Grisi had been lured to the Russian capital, St. Petersburg. Emilie, too, had been recruited to sing at the Italian Opera there: 'a brilliant engagement', wrote *La France Musicale*, which had resulted from her successes in Paris and London.

It was reported that the singers going to St. Petersburg would all travel together, taking the train as far as Warsaw, from where they would have no more than a four-day journey. At this period, it was only artists already engaged by the authorities who were permitted entry into Russia. Mlle. Ida Bertrand, for instance, got no further than Berlin.

The death of the Grand Duke Michael had led several journals to announce that the theatres at St. Petersburg would be closed for three months. However, the Prince was found to have expressed in his will the wish that they should remain open and on 13 October 1849 the Winter Season duly began, with a performance of *Semiramide*. The artists had reached the capital on 6 October.

For Emilie, the move to St. Petersburg marked a new and highly important turning-point in her career. She was to become a favourite with the Russian opera-goers and was engaged for every Season in St. Petersburg from 1849 to 1858. Throughout her twenties it was above all in Russia that her talents were to be displayed.

It was thus in the seventh season (1849-1850) that Emilie de Méric made her *début* in Russia. By then, there was a revival in the feelings of the St. Petersburg audiences towards the Italian Opera Company. Emilie was fortunate, too, in appearing with Mario and Grisi when they gave their first performances on the Russian stage. That exceptionally talented pair reminded the *habitués* of the great days of Rubini and Viardot. At the same time, the Company had the bass Tagliafico and the baritone Tamburini. With justice, the *Revue et Gazette Musicale de Paris* could declare that in that Season St. Petersburg had the finest singers in the world. The Italian Opera alternated at the Grand (Bolshoi) Theatre with the Russian Opera Company and was managed on a season-ticket system.

It is not known for certain how Emilie travelled to St. Petersburg. It is recorded that Tagliafico had arrived at Cronstadt from Luebeck on 24 September 1849, on board the *Nicholas I.* St. Petersburg was isolated by sea during the Winter and navigation at Cronstadt did not resume until the ice had melted, which was usually in May.

It was on 13 October 1849 (1 October Old Style) that Emilie made her *début.* playing Arsace in *Semiramide.* The house had been full, to hear the famous Giulia Grisi, and the opera ran to nine performances. However, while *Semiramide* had given great pleasure to the cognoscenti, it was not popular with the general public and many spectators had left after the first act, not liking the music.

Emilie received encouraging notices. The Russian musical chronicle *National Records of 1849* devotes a paragraph to the first impressions which her singing and acting had made in St. Petersburg. The young contralto, the critic wrote, was a welcome addition to the Company. As a whole, her voice was even and agreeable, without that rough transition from the lower to the higher register which had so marred the singing of Madame Angri. Owing to her youth, her voice was not yet fully formed, the lower A flat being somewhat weak, but her technique was excellent and showed great promise. At her age, she could not be expected to display great intensity of feeling, but she had a warmth and animation which were a sure sign of future success. In the difficult part of Arsace, she had given an excellent performance. There had not been any of the highlights for which Angri had evoked so much applause, but the part as a whole had been more even. In the duet with Grisi, de Méric had seemed to draw inspiration from the presence of that great singer.

The *Northern Bee* greeted Emilie's *début* in somewhat similar terms. Her voice was pure and polished, with a wide range. Her highest note had been in *qui volava sull'ali dell'amore* and her lowest in *vita e onore a lei servar*. She had sung the final phrase of the adagio *il sue core palpitai* with much feeling. Her duet with Tamburini had evoked well-deserved applause, but it was the duet with Grisi which had brought the house down. After that, the audience had been in raptures.

In this her first season in Russia, Emilie sang in *Lucrezia Borgia*, *Linda di Chamounix*, *Il Matrimonio Segreto* and *Les Huguenots*, camouflaged as *Les Guelphs et les Gibelins*. The last two were both being given their first performances in St. Petersburg.

In November, Emilie was given half a benefit from a performance of *Lucrezia*. Her regular salary was Fcs. 21,000. Tickets for the benefit evening had been sold out on the first day of sale.

The *Matinée Musicale* was a feature of the musical life of St. Petersburg at the time. In December 1849, at 2 o'clock in the afternoon, one of these concerts was given by Mr. A. Cecconi at the residence of Her Excellency Madame de Miatleff in the Rue de la Poste. Tickets cost three silver roubles. Mlle. de Méric sang a solo *cavatina* from *L'Italiana in Algeri* and a duet with Mlle. Corbari from Meyerbeer's *Le Prophète*. One of the other performers was Signor Ciabatta, who seems to have become a family friend. He was to be one of the witnesses at the wedding in London in 1865 of Emilie's niece Thérèse Lablache and the singer Johann Rokitansky.

The interior of the Bolshoi Theatre, St. Petersburg.

(By courtesy of The Architecture of the Leningrad Theatres, by M.Z. Taranovskaya, 1988.)

It was generally considered that the Company's talents had been displayed at their best in *Les Huguenots* (February 1850). Meyerbeer's opera, with an almost complete score, was performed ten times and the *mise-en-scène* was of a magnificence possible only at the Russian Court.

Contemporaries claimed that never before had the duet in Act IV been heard with such perfection in the balance between the vocal and dramatic elements. Ivanov, writing forty-five years later, says that Mlle. de Méric was so successful that 'to this day her name is remembered by old devotees'. Ivanov describes Emilie as being from Parma. She had indeed been there when a very young child, but no doubt it was assumed by Ivanov, as by many others, that she was the daughter of her stepfather, Timoleone Alexandre, who was from that city.

The Czar Nicholas was present at the final performance of the opera, when every main singer was given a sumptuous present from the Imperial bounty. Public enthusiasm had known no bounds, especially for Grisi and Mario. This had led to dangerous crowd surges at the box office.

Opera in London, 1850

MLLE. de Méric was re-engaged for the 1850 Season of the Royal Italian Opera at Covent Garden, under *régisseur* Augustus Harris. This proved more rewarding than her experience in 1849, though she continued to suffer from comparisons with Alboni (her voice) and Angri (her acting).

The prospectus for the Italian Opera's fourth London Season had informed the public that the principal contralti would be Mlle. de Méric, 'who at St. Petersburg had created such a furore', and Mlle. d'Okolski.

This was a period when Covent Garden was in direct competition with Her Majesty's Theatre, then under the ambitious direction of Lumley, who could boast that Mme. Sontag, Mme. Frezzolini and the great Luigi Lablache himself were members of his Company. The London correspondent of *La France Musicale* maintained that London, with its two Italian troupes, had enough talent to serve all the capitals of Europe at once. He pitied Paris for having lost all its best *Italiens*, with the sole exception of Mme. Persiani: but she, though she could still be a ravishing warbler, looked desolate, as in a golden cage, seemingly unable to live or sing now that she was separated from the artists with whom she had spent so many happy years.

Emilie was to have appeared in *Lucrezia Borgia*, with Tamburini, Mario and Grisi, on Tuesday 9 April 1850. However, she had been taken ill en route from St. Petersburg and her place that evening was entrusted to Mlle. d'Okolski. This substitution redounded to Emilie's advantage. The audience had greeted d'Okolski's rendering of the famous *Brindisi*, *Il segreto per esser felice*, in the profoundest silence, whereas this had unfailingly earned a triple encore for Alboni. *The Athenaeum* said that the less that was seen and heard of Mlle. d'Okolski the better.

By 13 April, Emilie was able to make her 1850 *début*, though she had only arrived in London the same morning. She faced a crowded house which included national figures such as the Duke and Duchess of Norfolk, the Dukes of Wellington and Devonshire and the Marquess and Marchioness of Salisbury.

The advertisement for Lucrezia
Borgia on 9 April 1850 (when in
fact Mlle. d'Okolski took Emilie's
place).

(By courtesy of The Theatre Museum, Victoria
and Albert Museum.)

ROYAL ITALIAN OPERA,

COVENT  GARDEN.

On TUESDAY NEXT, April 9th,

LUCREZIA BORGIA,

IN WHICH

Madlle. de MERIC,   Signor TAMBURINI,

Madame G R I S I,   AND   Signor M A R I O,

Will make their First Appearances this Season.

THE DOORS WILL BE OPENED AT HALF-PAST SEVEN, AND THE PERFORMANCES
COMMENCE AT EIGHT O'CLOCK PRECISELY.

*N.B.—In compliance with the wish of many Subscribers, the Entrance in the Piazza in
Covent Garden will for the future be opened every Evening.*

Tickets for the Boxes, Stalls, or the Pit, may be had (for the Night or Season), at the Box-
Office of the Theatre, which is open from 11 till 5; and of Messrs. CRAMER, BEALE, & Co.,
Regent Street; also of Mr. SAMS, St. James' Street; Mr. MITCHELL, Mr. ANDREWS,
Mr. HOOKHAM, and Mr. EBERS, Old Bond Street; Mr. ALLCROFT, Messrs. LEADER
and COCK, Messrs. C. and R. OLLIVIER, Mr. HAMMOND, and Mr. CHAPPELL, New
Bond Street; Messrs. BAILEY and MOON, and JULLIEN and Co., Regent Street; and of
Messrs. KEITH, PROWSE, and Co., Cheapside.

Correct Copies of the authorized editions of all the Operas may be had of Mr. BRETTELL,
Rupert Street; and of all Booksellers and Music Sellers,—Price 1s. 6d.

Subscribers for the Season will have the option of paying their Sub-
scriptions in advance, (as heretofore), or by Monthly instalments.

The Terms may be obtained at the Box-office of the Theatre, (corner of
Hart-st. and Bow-st.) which is open daily, from 11 till 5 o'clock.

R. S. FRANCIS, Printer, 25, Museum Street, Bloomsbury.

The *Morning Chronicle* said that in Mlle. de Méric's hand the *Brindisi*
had regained its wonted honour. The advantage of a competent
contralto had told very decidedly through the whole performance of
the opera. Emilie's voice might lack the rich mellowness and massive
breadth of Alboni's tones, but it was nevertheless an organ of
considerable power and flexibility, displaying a certainty of
intonation and facility of execution which made its possessor an
eminently *safe* singer.

The *Illustrated London News* considered that Emilie had sung and
acted excellently. She had 'a most lively organ, especially in the lower
notes, the sympathetic quality of which is very touching. Her method
is of a thorough musician . . . her Orsini is attractive in its saucy
vivacity. With experience she may occupy advantageously the ground
of her gifted predecessors in the contralto parts.'

From the review in *The Times*, it seems clear that Emilie was
already acquiring a sound reputation. 'The merits of this young
singer,' the critic wrote, 'whose voice retains all its strength and full
quality, are well known. She was honoured with a warm reception,

was much applauded in the first romance, and unanimously encored in the second couplet of the *Brindisi*.' However, the writer went on, though she had every qualification to make a thoroughly competent second contralto, she had yet to establish her ability in the more important parts that belonged to her register – Arsace, Malcolm and the like.

The *Musical World* found that Mlle. de Méric now had plenty of confidence and the *Morning Post* gave her this succinct eulogy: 'She possesses an excellent voice, sings with feeling, and is an admirable actress.'

Orsini was to be one of Emilie's key rôles. She can be seen in the costume of this part in a signed portrait, dated 1852, which is on display at *La Scala* in Milan. However, *La Scala* has no record of Emilie having performed there, so the picture, which is inscribed '*offert à La Scala*', was probably intended to be a kind of *carte de visite*, sent perhaps in the hope that it would lead to an engagement.

When *La Donna del Lago* was performed at the King's Theatre back in 1833, Emilie's mother had taken the soprano part of Elena. In the 1850 revival, at Covent Garden (on 25 April), Emilie made her first appearance in the breeches part of Malcolm Graeme. Grisi sang Elena and the two tenors, Mario and Tamberlik, performed together. The production kept the music originally written for the part of Roderick as a *tenore robusto*. This had frequently been transposed for a baritone, but Tamberlik was available to sing it in the correct key.

The critics were divided about Emilie's performance and her 'energetic manner of singing'. Inevitably, she had to face comparisons with the great Alboni. As one wrote: 'The two airs of Malcolm Graeme, *Elena, oh tu*' and *Ah si pera*, have been so associated with Alboni that it is an ungrateful task for any singer to attempt them after her'. In the event, the *Ah si pera* was omitted 'perhaps judiciously, since the triplet passages in the *cabaletta* demand a facility of execution which Mlle. de Méric has not yet given proof of possessing.'

The *Athenaeum* criticised Emilie's voice for being stiff. It required assiduous and unremitting practice. However, this would be repaid. She had already gained in style and confidence since the preceding year.

The *Morning Post* praised the young lady for her fresh and sonorous contralto, 'rich in quality, though not remarkably flexible'. Her florid passages had been somewhat laboured, but the *portamento* was good. She phrased correctly and possessed in an eminent degree the higher qualities of feeling and expression. 'The tedious recitative *Mura felici* . . . and the well-known aria *Elena, oh tu* were admirably sung.'

Interior of the Royal Italian Opera House, Covent Garden, as refurbished in 1847.

(By courtesy of The Royal Opera House Archives.)

Emilie had made a highly favourable impression on the critic of the *Illustrated London News*, who singled out the aria *Oh, quante lagrime* and the duet with Grisi *Vivere io non potrò*. The most enthusiastic notice of all appeared in the *Morning Advertiser*. 'Mdlle. de Méric was most effective [as Malcolm] and fully confirmed the favourable opinion entertained of her marked and rapid progress as a charming and accomplished contralto. In the great *scena Mura felici*, and especially in the exquisite air *Elena, oh tu*, she was heard to particular advantage; while in the fine duet with Grisi *Ciel qual destin terribile* she was exceedingly effective, even by the side of the great *prima donna* herself . . . . There were bouquets for Grisi and de Méric from one of the most crowded and brilliant houses of the season'.

The composer came in for some brickbats. The *Morning Chronicle* referred to the 'difficult and somewhat ungrateful music of Malcolm'. Nevertheless, the music had found 'a very efficient interpretation in Mdlle. de Méric, who sang it like a thorough artist, declaiming the recitatives with a sustained vigour which was highly effective, and giving her arias with the purest intonation, and a chaste and finished vocalization which bespoke the accomplished musician.' As the *Morning Post* acidly remarked, Emilie was not responsible for the composer's sins. She had acquitted herself admirably throughout and had rendered a somewhat dull and inexpressive air interesting by her clever performance. She was entitled to our thanks and commendation.

Meyerbeer's grand opera, *Les Huguenots* (2 May), proved to be highly popular. It was performed twelve times in 1850, more than any other opera during the season.

One reviewer was so delighted with the production that he declared that 'even in the palmy days of Grand Opera [with Falcon, Dorus-Gras, Nourrit, Levasseur and Duprez] it may be doubted whether the ensemble . . . approached that of Covent Garden at the present period.' The *Revue et Gazette Musicale de Paris* reported that Mme. Castellan, Mlle. de Méric and Formes had all three had a great success.

Emilie was in the part of the page, Urbano. True, 'she was still not comparable, as a singer, to Alboni.' But Alboni was after all 'one of the greatest contraltos in operatic history' (Rosenthal and Warrack). The *Athenaeum*, in its measured terms, wrote that Emilie had performed her vocal task (for the *rondo* in the garden scene was a task) with great spirit and a fair amount of executive power – and had acted her part excellently, being the very Page of historical fiction.

Emilie's rendering of the popular *aria d'intrata* had at once won the suffrages of the cognoscenti (*The Morning Post*). The singer had imbued it with considerable archness and 'a kind of coquettish mystery admirably appropriate to the situation'. The second air, *No, no, no*, which Meyerbeer had composed expressly for Alboni, was another matter. One critic maintained that it presented unusual difficulty and demanded more study than Mlle. de Méric had so far seemed able to bestow upon it. Against this, the *Morning Post* considered that she had acted it with a joyous, buoyant spirit, which was quite exhilarating, and had executed the somewhat difficult passages with considerable grace and certainty. All the same, the paper's critic delivered himself of the opinion that the air itself was entirely out of place. It suspended the action of the piece and it was extremely improbable that a page would sing or speak in so familiar a manner in the presence of the Queen. 'However, what are kings or queens, authors or artists, common sense or reason, compared with the whims of a pet singer? Alboni wanted the air, and she had it, and made a *hit* of it, and was encored, and so no more of dramatic propriety or scenic illusion.'

The *Morning Advertiser* said that Emilie had rendered the music 'with all its peculiarities' with the grace and finish of the perfect artiste and the *Morning Chronicle* praised the contralto's musician-like tact and steadiness. In a nutshell, the *Musical World* wrote that de Méric's Urbano had been admirably acted and cleverly sung.

Somewhat exceptionally, the stage costume for the opera came in for adverse comment. 'If we might presume to give a hint upon such a delicate matter as ladies' costumes', wrote the *Morning Chronicle*, 'we might remark that a change of *chaussure* would improve Mlle. de Méric's appearance, as well as harmonise to a greater degree with the drawing-room notions which we associate with a page.' More bluntly, the *Morning Post* said: 'We did not admire the costume she wore on this occasion. It may be chronologically correct, but it is certainly not becoming.'

On 29 June, a performance of *Les Huguenots* was given by the special desire of Queen Victoria, who for the third time in one week had honoured the theatre with her presence, again accompanied by the Prince of Prussia and Prince Albert. 'The opera had never gone off with more *éclat*' (*Morning Advertiser*). When the Queen entered the Royal Box in the second scene, during the duet between Madame Castellan and Mario, 'the outbreak of loyal feeling from every part was overwhelming. The band immediately obeyed the unanimous call for the National Anthem, and Mme. Castellan, Mlle. de Méric and Grisi sang the solos amidst bursts of cheering, every allusion being taken up with the greatest eagerness and spontaneity' (*Illustrated London News*).

ROYAL ITALIAN OPERA,
COVENT GARDEN
THEATRE.

The Nobility, Subscribers, and the Public generally, are respectfully informed that

THIS EVENING,

Thursday, May 16th, 1850,

Will be performed Meyerbeer's Grand Opera

LES HUGUENOTS.

Valentina,	Made GRISI,
Margarita di Valois,	Made CASTELLAN,
Dama d'onore,	Madlle COTTI,
Urbano,	Madlle de MERIC.

The Huguenot Soldier,	Sig. LAVIA
Il Conte di San Bris,	Sig. TAGLIAFICO,
Il Conte di Nevers,	M. MASSOL,
De Cosse, -	Sig. LUIGI MEI
De Retz,	Sig. POLONINI
Meru,	Sig. ROMMI
Maurevert,	Sig. SOLDI
Capitano della Guardia	Sig. TALAMO
Marcello	Herr FORMES
Raul di Nangis	Sig. MARIO.

Advertisement for Les Huguenots with Emilie as the Page.
(By courtesy of The Theatre Museum, Victoria and Albert Museum.)

223

On 15 June, Emilie took the part of the country lad, Pippo, in Rossini's two-act opera *La Gazza Ladra*, the story of the servant-girl condemned to death for stealing a spoon who is reprieved when the spoon is found in the nest of the 'thieving magpie'. Grisi sang the leading rôle as Ninetta.

Emilie's singing and acting received much praise. Her Pippo had been 'interesting, full of animated action, and very nicely sung, especially in the *Brindisi Tecchiamo* and in the duo *Ebben per mia memoria* with Grisi' (*Illustrated London News*). Her impersonation had been 'replete with naïveté and rustic manner, while her singing was that of a consummate artiste' (*Morning Advertiser*).

However, the *Musical World* had reservations. Mlle. de Méric had looked and acted Pippo excellently, 'but her singing was exaggerated, and wanted finish. She was very forcible in the duet in the prison with Grisi, which, nevertheless, escaped the usual encore.' Though she had acted with considerable spirit, Emilie 'did not make as much of the music as she might have done.'

La Gazza Ladra had not been put on in London for three years and in 1850 it only ran to a couple of performances.

Rossini's two-act opera *Semiramide*, taken from Voltaire's play *Sémiramis*, was produced on 23 July. It is a tragedy in which Semiramide, Queen of Babylon, and her lover Assur murder the King. She later falls in love with a young man, Arsace, who proves to be her own son. The Queen receives a mortal blow from Assur, which he intends for Arsace, who then kills Assur and becomes King.

In London, Grisi was in the name part. Emilie's performance, as Arsace, seems to have caused some disappointment, though *La France Musicale* found her charming in the part and full of promise. This was what the *Musical World* had to say:

> 'The exquisitely perfect vocalization of Mlle. Alboni and the dramatic fire of Mlle. Angri were still too fresh in the remembrance of the English public to allow of anything less than an artist of first-rate abilities appearing with success in the arduous part of Arsace. That Mlle. de Méric, in spite of her powerful voice and splendid demeanour, fell short of the mark on this occasion was not surprising. This young lady has decided talent, but her vocalization is crude and there is a want of style in her singing, which indicates either a deficiency of schooling or a perverse adherence to errors too easily contracted in early years. Mlle. de Méric has evident means of becoming a good artist, but she must learn and unlearn a great deal before she can hope to make a favourable impression in such a part as that of Arsace.'

Hard words for a twenty-year-old battling under the shadow of Alboni.

The *Illustrated London News* reacted in much the same way. After Alboni and Angri, Emilie's Arsace was tame and inefficient, but she had one of the finest contralto organs of the day and with its truly sympathetic quality she ought to have achieved a more decided success.

However, the *Morning Chronicle* wrote that Emilie had made a very creditable figure as Arsace. She had evidently laboured under considerable trepidation throughout the first scene, but this feeling had worn off as the opera proceeded. Eventually, in spite of the recollections of the great Alboni's performance, she had made a highly favourable impression on the audience. The house had been well attended.

So perhaps the public were better pleased than the critics. Be that as it may, it was to be some years before Emilie was to return to sing in London. She had won acclaim in St. Petersburg and it did not surprise *La France Musicale* that she was re-engaged there for the following Winter Season.

THE 1850 OPERA SEASON IN RETROSPECT

The 1850 Season at Covent Garden, which had opened on 14 March, closed on Saturday 31 August with an extra performance of *Les Huguenots*.

The early Summer in London had been suffocatingly hot, but public enthusiasm for music had been at such a high pitch that the two Italian theatres were not sufficient to satisfy the eagerness of the patrons and Morning Concerts were also the rage. Enjoying such strong support from the Queen, Covent Garden had increased its popularity and the *Musical World* considered that the fourth Season of the Royal Italian Opera had closed more prosperously and felicitously than any of its predecessors. This, furthermore, was despite the competition which music had to face from drama. In July, the great tragédienne Rachel was at the St. James's Theatre, taking the leading rôles in French classical plays.

Emilie, despite her youth and relative inexperience, would seem to have been fairly successful in all but the most taxing of the contralto assignments. Summing up, the *Morning Post* wrote: 'To Mdlle. de Méric, who undertook for the first time the arduous duties of principal contralto, we can speak in terms of encouragement. She possesses an excellent voice and a highly vivacious and energetic temperament, which cannot fail, when directed by more mature judgment, to lead their possessor to Fame's temple.' The *Musical*

World recalled that Mlle. de Méric, as Orsini, had been a decided advance on Mlle. d'Okolski. All the same, the performance had not been entirely satisfactory. Emilie's figure had pleased, but:

> 'We very much fear that this talented young artist is not seriously inclined to study, and that she does not make the best use of nature's kindnesses. With her voice and energy, Mlle. de Méric is capable of far greater things than she has yet accomplished. The fair artist displayed but small improvement on last year.'

On 29 March 1851, a review of the Royal Italian Opera's prospectus commented that the company would be the stronger for not including Mlle. de Méric. Though she was a promising singer, her 'insufficiency . . . to sustain the duties of the first contralto in a theatre like the Royal Italian Opera Company was frequently commented upon last season, and the substitution of Mlle. ANGRI in her place cannot but be a matter for general congratulation.'

Emilie had indeed proved to be too young to cope with all the demands of the major contralto rôles.

Concerts and provincial tour, 1850

LONDON CONCERTS

EMILIE had some success on the concert platform in London in 1850. On 10 May, in Rossini's *Stabat Mater*, her sterling qualities of voice and style had been heard to great advantage in the long cavatina *Fac me vere* (*Morning Chronicle*). The *Musical World* agreed. The *Illustrated London News* singled out for praise the quatuor *Quando corpus*, sung by Grisi, de Méric, Tamburini and Mario. Costa had conducted.

At the second Morning Concert on 24 May, Emilie's solo was the aria *Elena, oh tu* from *La Donna del Lago*. Her duets were with Mme. Castellan. One was *Dolce conforta al misera* from *Il Giuramento*.

On 10 June, a Grand Morning Concert was given at Covent Garden by Mrs. Anderson, *pianiste* to the Queen and musical instructress to the Princess Royal. Emilie was among the artistes from the Royal Italian Opera to take part and she sang with Mlle. Vera the duet *Ah bel destin* from *Linda di Chamounix*.

Almost all the leading singers who were in London at the time appeared at the *Matinée Musicale* which Signor Brizzi held at the New Beethoven Rooms in Queen Anne Street on 28 June. This was exclusively for vocal music. Emilie sang Rossini's *Pensa alla Patria* which, the *Musical World* said, had brought out her energetic manner of singing in advantageous prominence.

Italian patriotism, together with Rossini's music, was in vogue with liberal opinion at the time, following the attempts in 1849 to free Italy from foreign domination. The failure of these attempts had led to a flood of Italian refugees coming to London and musical events were organised in 1850 in aid of these exiles. One of these was a special Grand Morning Concert at Covent Garden on 12 July at which the great Madame Pasta had consented to sing. Emilie and Mlle. Vera were to contribute the duet *Perchè mi guardi*. Regrettably, wrote the *Morning Chronicle*, the British public as a whole did not appear to sympathise with the object of the concert, for the house was very thinly attended.

In July 1850, the *Illustrated London News* had announced that the cast of the Italian Opera Company at St. Petersburg for the Winter Season 1850-1851 would comprise Grisi, de Méric and Frezzolini, with Mario, Tamberlik, Tamburini, Napoleone Rossi, Coletti and Tagliafico. In the event, Grisi became pregnant and Mario went without her.

Meanwhile, there were performances to be given in England outside London and Emilie embarked on a short provincial tour.

The *Illustrated London News* reported that Mr. Beale had engaged, for the first week in September, Mlle. Parodi, Mlle. de Méric and Signor Coletti (with whom a tenor would be associated) to give Italian operas in Manchester, Liverpool etc. The horn-player Vivien would be included in the company. The tenor proved to be Gardoni.

Theatre Royal, Liverpool.
(By courtesy of The Theatre Museum, Victoria and Albert Museum.)

In Manchester, the offering was in fact a so-called 'miscellaneous dress concert' which was given in the Concert Hall on Monday 2 September. Other concerts followed during the week, all conducted by Mr. (later Sir) Charles Hallé, the celebrated founder of the Hallé Orchestra.

The pieces which Emilie sang in Manchester are a good example of her concert repertoire at the time. These were:

> *Cavatina Cruda sorte (L'Italiana in Algeri)*
> *Si dira* (Trio from Paër's *Agnese*) with Parodi and Coletti
> *Quante core* (duet from Rossini's *Demetrio e Polibio*) with
>   Parodi

Mi manca la voce (Quartet from *Mosè in Egitto*)
Oh patria – Tu che accende (Recitative and aria from
    Tancredi)
Dolce conforta (duet from *Il Giuramento*) with Parodi
Quartet from Biletto's *I Poveretti*
Di tanti palpiti (from *Tancredi*)
The *Brindisi* (from *Lucrezia Borgia*).

The *Manchester Courier* was pleased with the general style of
Mademoiselle de Méric. Her voice was not of the most telling quality,
but it was nicely managed.

This brief provincial tour was no more than an interlude before
Emilie's next major appearance, in St. Petersburg.

The Visa Registers at Boulogne provide evidence that Emilie
travelled from England with her mother and Timoleone Alexandre.
Timoleone had been given a passport by the Russian Embassy in
London on 10 September 1850, in which he was described as a
musician aged 38 (though 48 seems much more likely). The family,
Timoleone being recorded as Joséphine's husband and Emilie's
father, crossed the Channel from Folkestone to Boulogne, then
proceeded overland via Calais to Russia. Most of the other singers
went by sea. A favourite route was from one of the German ports,
e.g. Stettin, to Cronstadt, but Joséphine was probably a bad sailor.

St. Petersburg, 1850-1852

1850-1851 (THE EIGHTH SEASON)

THE Czar Nicholas I took the greatest personal interest in opera and did not stand on his dignity with the artistes. He himself, acting as Director of the *Théâtre Italien de St. Pétersbourg,* sent a trusted envoy to Paris in 1850 to recruit the most famous performers. This envoy offered Luigi Lablache every possible inducement to go to Russia, but Lablache could not be persuaded. First, he excused himself on the ground of his age and the severity of the Russian Winter. Then he confessed that he did not dare to risk facing an audience which had never seen him before. The envoy laughed this off, adding that in a Russian theatre no one would dare to hiss without His Majesty's authorisation and Lablache would be applauded by Imperial Decree. When Lablache remained adamant, he was assured that the Czar would be going to Paris in the following Spring to hear him. Subsequently, Lablache relented and was in the Russian capital for the 1852-1853 Season.

It was in this atmosphere that Emilie entered upon her second season in St. Petersburg. She was the only contralto, and her salary had risen to Fcs.25,000, once again with the addition of half a benefit. This year, it is not known how she travelled.

The absence of Grisi was much regretted, but Persiani was singing, Mario and Tamburini had returned and Tamberlik was making his early Russian appearances. Emilie sang in *Lucrezia Borgia, Linda di Chamounix, La Donna del Lago* and *Le Nozze di Figaro.* She was given her benefit in *La Donna del Lago.*

The Russian critics were much impressed by Emilie's youthfulness and one, at least, had no doubt that she would rise high in her profession. F.Koni described her voice as sonorous and strong, being especially pleasant in the lower register; she seemed to lack self-confidence rather than skill. Somewhat surprisingly, she was criticised for emphasising the singing to the detriment of the dramatic action, but that can perhaps be attributed to Russian love of vigorous histrionics.

The Russian publication *The Contemporary* stated in 1850 that in Rubini's time the Italian singers had brought to Russia the fashion of presenting artistes with bouquets of flowers and gifts of jewellery.

This had made fortunes for the leading florists and jewellers. It is recorded that on one occasion at least Emilie had been presented with a bracelet.

Alexandrinsky Theatre, St. Petersburg.

During the Winter, Emilie sang at various private concerts. She gave her rendering of the *cavatina* from *L'Italiana in Algeri* at a December concert given in the Hall of the Nobles (with tickets this time at only two silver roubles) and she sang at the concert given by her friend Ciabatta in January 1851.

This was a period when ballet had become a very important element in the programmes at *Le Grand Théâtre*. In the 1850-1851 Season, the famous dancer Carlotta Grisi had been engaged. Notably, she performed in *Le Diable à Quatre*, both as a benefit for herself and for the choreographer Petipa.

DEATH OF JOSEPH GLOSSOP

On 14 November 1850, while Emilie was in Russia, her father Joseph Glossop died in Florence. She appears to have lost all contact with him. From the statements made at her wedding four years later, it appears that she did not know when or where he had died. Equally, Elizabeth Féron and their son Augustus affirmed in 1846, when Augustus married, that she was a widow and that he had no father living. This was when Joseph still had four years to live. He had gone out of all their lives.

Details are lacking about Emilie's career in the Spring and Summer of 1851, but she was back in St. Petersburg for the 1851-1852 Season, as principal contralto among a galaxy of stars. Grisi had returned, with Persiani, Marrai and Medori. The baritone Ronconi (at Fcs.80,000 and a benefit) and the German bass Formes were making their Russian *débuts*. Tamburini, who enjoyed the Czar's special favour, was still there, albeit for his last season.

Emilie had been given an eulogy before the Season began. In the *Russian Artistic Bulletin* of September 1851, V.P. Vasil'ko-Petrov had remarked that when Mlle. de Méric arrived in St. Petersburg from London in 1849, the Russians had known so little about her that one of the critics had taken her for her mother (an indication that the fame of Joséphine had penetrated to the Russian capital). While Emilie was not to be compared with Alboni, 'Alboni was probably the only contralto in Europe who surpassed her.'

The opening of this, the ninth Italian Season, was marked by the first appearance in the *Journal de St. Pétersbourg* of *Feuilletons* with reviews of the performances. At first these were by the gifted critic B. Damcke. Later, the Russian Rostisleff took over. He too was very perceptive, though he tended to concentrate on the sopranos and tenors.

In an introductory article on 30 October/11 November 1851, Damcke declared that the Italian Company was one of extraordinary richness, including almost all the leading Italian singers of the day. This was of crucial importance because in so much of Italian opera, he said, it was the quality of the singing which was the 'question of life or death'. Italian audiences would forgive almost any shortcomings in the score or the orchestra provided that the *prima donna* and the *primo uomo* were given their chance to shine. The Russian critic Serov also described the make-up of the company as very rich.

Emilie seems not to have been in the first opera of the Season, *L'Elisir d'Amore*, in which the *débutant* tenor, Pozzolini, had been spectacularly successful, especially in *La furtiva lagrima*. In *Maria di Rohan*, which followed, she was praised in the *Journal de St. Pétersbourg* for singing, to perfection, the couplets in the first Act, which had 'singular echoes of Weber's *Oberon*', and the beautiful *cavatina* in Act II, which had been deservedly applauded.

Maria di Rohan, however, was most notable for the *début* in St. Petersburg of Mme. Medori, née Wilmot, a beautiful singer of French extraction whose young promise had first come to light in Brussels. After a striking success in *Maria*, she had a triumph as Elvira in *Ernani* which was 'almost without parallel in the whole course of the performances of the Italian Opera in St. Petersburg.'

In October, the company performed *Les Guelfes et les Gibelins*. Damcke could hardly find words to express his admiration for the production. Here was an opera which was in many respects the very opposite of *la musique italienne*. In such a work, it was not enough to be a great singer – the opera called for the singer to be also a good musician, 'a quality rarely found among the Italians, which was without doubt the reason for the lack of success in Italy of the operas of Meyerbeer's great period.' The excellent rendering of *Les Guelfes et les Gibelins* therefore proved the exceptional superiority of the Italian Company which St. Petersburg was fortunate to possess at the time. The chief honours naturally went to Mario, Grisi and Mlle. Marrai (as the Princess), but Mlle. de Méric had been found charming in her page's costume and was loudly applauded for her pretty *cavatina*.

Impressed as he might be by the grandiose splendours of Meyerbeer, Damcke also had a great love for the 'perfumed garden' of Rossini and he was more than happy to sit back and enjoy *La Gazza Ladra*, especially when it was interpreted by Grisi (Ninetta), Tamburini (Ninetta's father) and Ronconi (the *Podestà*). As always, Emilie had been a charming Pippo. 'In her one important piece, the duet with Ninetta, she had taken full advantage of her beautiful voice, with all its poise and noble tone, and of her fine diction and perfect vocalization.'

The *Northern Bee* spoke of Mlle. de Méric as one of the favourites with the Russian public. Her excellent talent also gave much musical enjoyment to the *dilettanti*. During this Season, the choice of a benefit opera for Emilie posed a problem. As the critic explained, contemporary composers did not write operas for contralti 'because that voice had become a rarity in Italy.' Mlle. de Méric had therefore been obliged to choose for herself a work from the older repertoire. She selected *La Donna del Lago*, in which the rôle of Malcolm had in the past enabled contralto-singers to make brilliant first appearances.

As reported, the opera had been well performed, with a full house for three evenings running. However, the verdict of the general public was that it was boring. Against this, the *cognoscenti* were delighted to hear an opera from an earlier age (*La Donna del Lago* had first appeared in 1819) and to compare the merits of the various singers they had known. For the *Northern Bee*, only Mme. Borgognio had surpassed de Méric as Malcolm.

In mid-December 1851, the *Gazette Musicale* in Berlin had reported a rumour from Paris that Grisi, Persiani, Rubini and Tamburini had all just expired. In fact, Grisi, Persiani and Tamburini were appearing in *La Sonnambula* in St. Petersburg, with Emilie also in the cast.

The composer Federico Ricci sent a letter from Warsaw on

2 December 1851, addressed to his friend Mariani, saying that he was planning to write a comic opera for Vienna in which Maray and Deméric would sing. He said that he was about to leave for St. Petersburg, where he would be seeing and hearing Emilie. Unfortunately, Ricci was to die on that journey.

For Emilie, the 1851-1852 Season in Russia ended with an appearance in *Le Nozze di Figaro*, followed by the world *première* of *Sardanapale*, an opera by the young French composer Giulio (Jules) Alary. This was a particularly remarkable event, because there existed an Imperial *ukase* forbidding the production in St. Petersburg of any opera which had not already been performed in France, England, Italy or Germany. For *Sardanapale*, the Czar had made an exception to the decree. Alary had written the work for the Imperial Theatre and for Mario and Grisi, who duly performed in it, with Formes, Ronconi and Emilie. The opera was given a spectacular production. In the fourth Act, for instance, the harem was replete with gardens, fountains, drunken slaves and the King garlanded with flowers. Mario, in the title rôle, had a drinking song which brought the house down and became the rage throughout St. Petersburg. Alary himself was present and received an ovation. Ronconi had been regarded as the lion of this Russian Season, but Formes, with his magnificent deep bass, achieved a signal triumph as Silva in *Ernani*.

Together with the other members of the Italian Company, Emilie once again took part in a number of major concerts during the Season. The Belgian Monsieur Vieuxtemps, the Court violinist, gave one at the Hall of the Nobles, costing three silver roubles, at which Emilie sang an air from *Le Nozze di Figaro*. There was a full house and an enthusiastic audience. Concerts in which the Italians took part were given at various theatres in the capital and at private houses.

From 1852, Emilie embarked on a programme which for several years took her to Vienna in the Spring and St. Petersburg in the Winter.

Vienna and St. Petersburg, 1852-1853

26

VIENNA

EMILIE was the principal contralto with the *Italiens* when they re-opened in Vienna, at the *Kaerntnertor Theater*, on 15 March 1852. The first opera was *Lucrezia Borgia*, in which Medori took the name part. This was Medori's Vienna *début* and it proved to be a triumph for her, in the presence of the Emperor and the Imperial Family. Emilie appeared also in *Linda* and *Maria di Rohan*, but these operas were less popular than *Lucrezia*, which was given eight times. On 9 June, she played the part of Lisetta in Federico Ricci's *Il Marito e l'Amante*. The impresario, Merelli, was considered to have assembled for *Fasching* (Carnival) 1852 the finest Italian Troupe which Vienna had seen for a long time. The Season closed on 15 June.

The Kärntnertor Theatre, 1763-1868.

(From 'Vienna' by Martin Hürliman, Thames and hudson, 1970.)

Meanwhile, for Emilie, there had been important events, in Paris and London, connected with her family and family-to-be.

On 18 March 1852, almost certainly in Paris, was born Joseph Glossop's grandson, Augustus Henry Glossop Harris. In his short life, Sir Augustus, as he became, was 'probably the greatest caterer of theatrical amusement England has ever seen' (*Illustrated London News*).

In London, the Register of the French Chapel records that on 22 May 1852 a requiem was held for the late Madame Benedict, widow of the composer, pianist and conductor, Julius Benedict. The choir included Luigi Lablache, with his son Frédéric (Emilie's brother-in-law to be), Frédéric's wife Fanny Wyndham, Clara Novello, Madame Castellan and some fifteen other principal artistes of the Italian theatre.

ST. PETERSBURG

When the tenth Italian Season opened in St. Petersburg on 1 October 1852, with a brilliant performance of *Ernani*, Luigi Lablache, with a vast amount of baggage including macaroni, was at last in the city. With him were, Emilie, Joséphine, his son Nicolas and his daughter Marie, both singers.

Emilie's first appearance in the Season was in *Maria di Rohan*, with Medori, Tamberlik and Ronconi. This opera was a great favourite with the public and there could hardly have been a better cast. Emilie usually gave much satisfaction in the small but charming part of Gondi, in which she had made her *début* in Paris, but on this occasion the audience failed to warm to her.

Lablache, taking no chances, made his first appearance before a Russian audience as Don Pasquale. Some indeed thought that age had had an effect on his voice, but the general view was that both his singing and acting were still beyond praise. Certainly the public responded to his talent. Ivanov records that he was greatly loved and given endless ovations. In both *Don Pasquale* and *La Cenerentola* he appeared with that other operatic giant, Ronconi. It is noteworthy that it was in *Cenerentola* (known in Russia as *Zamarashka*) that he seems to have performed for the first time with Emilie. It was this opera which was chosen for Emilie's benefit.

The other operas in which Emilie sang in this Season were *Lucrezia Borgia*, *Les Huguenots* and *Rigoletto*, which was given its Russian *première* in January 1853. She may also have been in the cast of *La Gazza Ladra*.

Les Huguenots (to give the opera its proper name), with Emilie as the page, was highly successful. All the same, it was being said that

Emilie, formerly so much loved, was losing much of her popularity. She was accused of attempting to force her mezzo-soprano voice to become *soprano acuto*. However, she had only to abjure such aberrations and revert to singing naturally and in good taste to be sure to regain the favour of the public (*Revue et Gazette Musicale*, echoing the *Journal de St. Pétersbourg*).

Rigoletto achieved a success more brilliant, it was claimed, than the Imperial Theatre had ever seen before. This was attributed mainly to Mario, Ronconi and Mlle. Maray, but Emilie played her part in the quartet with them which was encored every time it was sung.

No record has been traced of Nicolas Lablache singing in St. Petersburg, but early in March there had been a performance at Court of the *Figlia del Reggimento* for the *début* of Mlle. Marie Lablache, 'a beautiful young lady who delighted the Imperial Family.'

The 1852-1853 Season had certainly been a success. Only London, it was believed, had a comparable Italian Opera. At first, the unexpected absence of Grisi, 'through illness', had cast something of a shadow, but the other singers had been enthusiastically received. Then, late in the Season, Madame Viardot arrived. She scored a triumph in *Le Prophète*, 'sublime, moving and as great a tragic actress as a singer' (Damcke). Praise and presents were heaped upon her. During her benefit in *La Sonnambula* (21 February) she was given more than twenty curtain-calls. The Czar went on to the stage to congratulate her. He gave her his arm to escort her to the Imperial Box, where she was presented to the Czarina and the Grand Duchesses. Needless to say, the Czar gave Viardot a magnificent present.

Some idea of the scale of the Imperial generosity and of the relative importance of the artists on a given occasion may be derived from the list of the gifts which the singers received after the performance of the *Figlia del Reggimento* mentioned above. With the value in brackets, these were:

Marie Lablache, a diamond brooch (Fcs.3,000)
Luigi Lablache, a solitaire ring (Fcs.2,000)
Mario, a ring (Fcs.2,000)
Emilie de Méric, a brooch (Fcs.1,500)
Tagliafico, a ring (Fcs.750)

This Season saw the farewell concert for Henri Vieuxtemps, who had been Court violinist for six years. All the Italian Company took part and the hall was so full an hour before the concert was due to begin that the artists themselves had to fight their way in.

In the New Year 1853, the 'charming singer Mlle. Dobré' gave a concert in which Emilie took part. This provides evidence that Joséphine was with her daughter in St. Petersburg at the time. The two sang with Lablache, Ronconi, Tamberlik and Madame Tagliafico in the sextet from *La Cenerentola*.

On 1 February 1853 an afternoon concert was devoted to the works of Michael Balfe, who was present himself and conducted from the piano. Emilie sang the romantic air *La Speranza*.

The star of the St. Petersburg Concerts in 1852-1853, however, was considered to have been Luigi's daughter, Marie Lablache (*Le Menestrel*). A portrait of her had been on show in the studio of the famous artist Monsieur Pérignon. In the *Journal de St. Pétersbourg*, Charles de Saint-Julien describes the picture as a masterpiece: with the calm, pure head of a dreaming Southern Muse and the elegant pose of one of the Graces of Antiquity. Where can that portrait be today?

Luigi Lablache and Emilie were engaged for the following Season. So was Mario; but neither he nor Grisi were to be seen in St. Petersburg again.

Vienna, Trieste and St. Petersburg, 1853-1854

VIENNA

FOR the 1853 Season in Vienna (April-May), the impresario Merelli had again engaged Mlle. de Méric. Another contralto, Mlle. Ida Bertrand, who had been acclaimed in Paris for her Arsace, had also been recruited. Mme. Medori was among the sopranos.

Rigoletto proved to be one of the most popular operas in the repertory of the Italian Company and Emilie played her part in its success. At every performance people had to be turned away. The most prestigious occasion was when the Emperor, the King of Prussia and the King of the Belgians were all in the theatre. Since, in their presence, all public manifestations were forbidden, the Emperor had demonstrated his approbation by having gifts conveyed to each of the singers.

Emilie also sang in *Linda di Chamounix* and in a new comic opera by F. Ricci called *Il Paniere d'Amore*, based on the French play *Bonsoir, Monsieur Pantalon*. This was not particularly successful, but there were demands for an encore of the quintet *Buona Notte, Signor Bernabo*, which Emilie sang with Medori, Fraschini, De Bassini and Scalese.

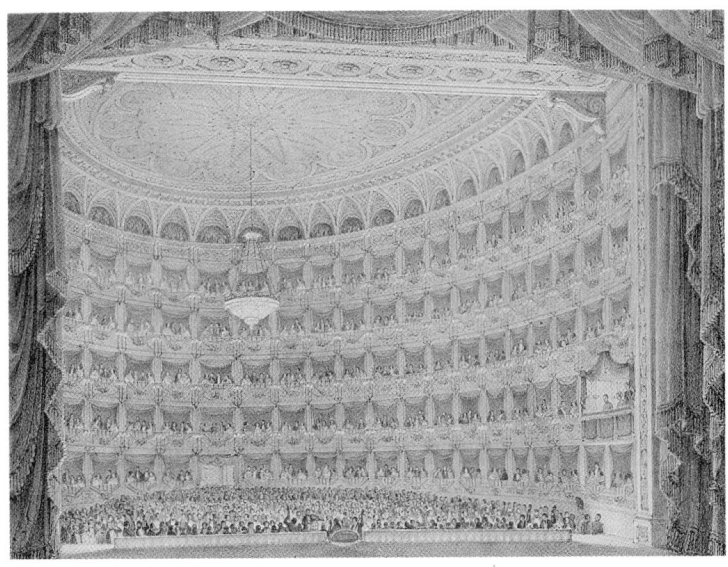

The Teatro Grande, Trieste.

(By courtesy of the Civici Musei di Storia ed Arte and the Civico Museo Teatrale C. Schmidt, Trieste.)

Billed as Emilia de Meric, Emilie almost certainly made her first public appearance in Italy in the Summer of 1853, at the *Teatro Grande* in Trieste. Trieste was at the time in the Austrian Empire.

She played her part in a very full programme, singing in *Linda, Lucia, Cenerentola, Capuleti e Montecchi, Rigoletto, Semiramide* and *Luisa Miller.*

The Teatro Grande, Trieste.

(By courtesy of the Civici Musei di Storia ed Arte and the Civico Museo Teatrale C. Schmidt, Trieste.)

In *Linda*, her resonant and robust voice had brought to mind the famous contralto singers of the golden days of the past and she enjoyed success in all the operas in which she performed. *Lucia* (2 July) was received with the utmost enthusiasm. *Rigoletto*, although well sung by Emilie and some others, was a failure when first produced on 6 July. *Semiramide* (12 July), on the other hand, was a triumph. Then, with Bozzetti, Everardi and Scalese, Emilie had delighted the audience in a scintillating production of *Cenerentola* (30 July). *Luisa Millar* (6 August) was not well received, despite good renderings by Emilie, as Federica, and by the *prima donna assoluta* Maddalena Vetturi-Olivi in the name part. On the other hand, *Capuleti* (14 August), including the third Act by Vaccai, was highly successful and Emilie distinguished herself above all the rest as an excellent Romeo. Virginia Pozzi played Giuletta.

The courageous impresario Antonio Traversari had presented a truly exceptional season of forty-seven nights, with twelve different operas. There had been full houses despite the scorching heat to applaud the galaxy of fine artists. The maestro in charge of the orchestra was Luigi Ricci (1805-1859).

These must have been heady days for the young singer, still only twenty-three. Emilie then moved on to a further season in Russia.

ST. PETERSBURG

The eleventh Italian Season in St. Petersburg (1853-1854) opened under the shadow of the impending Crimean War. However, for a time the opera was little affected. Even when war broke out with France, the French performers continued with their work in Russia. As for the Italians, Italy did not then exist as a political entity and Sardinia's stand as an ally of France and Britain did not disturb the opera world. There were in any case very few Sardinians in the Company. Joséphine and Timoleone were with Emilie.

Attendance at the Opera was actually higher than in the previous Season. Many people came because they feared that the theatres might soon be closed. There was plenty of money about, and in the first year of the war the general belief in a Russian victory only added to the enthusiasm of the Petersburg public for theatrical performances. Financially, the Italian Opera even avoided a deficit.

Once again, Luigi Lablache had come to Russia. Nicolas was with him, but not Luigi's daughter. Marie had indeed been invited, but she had just been married. In Paris, on 29 September 1853, a few days before Luigi left, the contract was signed whereby she became the wife of the Belgian business-man Baron Ernest de Caters.

Emilie appeared in seven different operas, the first being *Lucrezia Borgia*. The other female stars were Mme. de la Grange and La Medori, who had taken over all Grisi's repertoire. The company was particularly strong in tenors, with Tamberlik and three newcomers, Emilio Naudin, Enrico Calzolari and Stigelli. Calzolari became very popular, though nothing could weaken the public's attachment to Tamberlik, who succeeded in *Le Prophète* in eclipsing even the recent memory of Mario (*Le Menestrel*).

Emilie made something of a comeback. After praising her for being charming as Pierotto in *Linda*, the *Northern Bee* noted with pleasure that she had not forced her voice or strained after false effects, but had sung correctly and with sincere feeling. Her pleasant voice appealed to the audiences. All the same, there were still times when she tried to sing notes above her natural range and there was some monotony in the way she tended to prolong notes or add ornamentation. In *Linda*, she had sung with Lablache and she also sang with him in *Don Giovanni*.

After taking the part of Maddalena in another successful production of *Rigoletto*, Emilie sang in the local *première* of Federico Ricci's opera *Il Marito e l'Amante*. Ricci conducted the orchestra during this Season.

Under the title *Zora*, a new adaptation of Rossini's *Moïse* had been delighting the audiences. It was described as the most satisfying opera of the Season from the point of view of the ensemble. The quartet *Mi manca la voce* had been sung 'with a rare perfection' by Mme. de la Grange, Mlle. de Méric and the bass Didot (*Gazette Musicale de Paris*). Finally, Emilie played in *Anna Bolena*. Strangely, she does not appear to have been given a benefit performance in this Season. However, she was duly re-engaged for 1854-1855.

For the latter part of 1853, there are some private papers in the possession of Madame Balsan in Paris which throw some light on the Lablache and de Méric families at the time. Two letters written by Luigi Lablache show that at first he had some misgivings about the marriage of his daughter to Ernest de Caters. On 29 August 1853, he wrote somewhat haughtily to his future son-in-law. Ernest's father had evidently enquired about Luigi's worldly wealth. After giving a list of his considerable possessions and income and adding that he was engaged in building a house at Maisons-Lafitte, Luigi concluded by saying that if Ernest's father attached so much importance to material possessions, it might be better to forget about the wedding. However, by 2 November, Luigi was writing to his wife to assure her that the de Caters were nice people and good Catholics, so they must trust in God about Marie's marriage.

On 8 November, Nicolas wrote to his mother, in Italian, to tell her how he and his father spent their evenings in St. Petersburg: 'At 4 o'clock we go to the Demerics' for dinner. The mother [Joséphine] and daughter [Emilie] send you their regards. At this moment they are in deepest distress because Timoleone, Demeric's husband, is seriously ill and the doctors say it is very grave. The poor daughter [step-daughter] and mother attend to him like two angels, but God knows what will happen. At 8 o'clock we come back home'.

Luigi, writing on the same day to his wife, said that when he and Nicolas had returned home, they played 10-15 rounds of picquet, with Nicolas' cigarettes and his own snuff-box on the table. They went to bed at 11.30. (Luigi collected snuff-boxes and had a large number which were sold after his death).

The weather in St. Petersburg had been exceptionally mild in October 1853, but for Italians any Winter there was a severe trial. Timoleone was to die in the following year and Lablache attributed his own final illness to the effects of the Russian climate.

28

CHAPTER

*Vienna, Paris and St. Petersburg,
1854-1855:
marriage to Nicholas Lablache*

VIENNA

IN the Spring Season of the Italian Opera in Vienna in 1854, it was
the operas of Verdi which enjoyed by far the greatest success: above
all the revival of *Rigoletto* and the triumphant Viennese *première* of
Il Trovatore.

Emilie played a major rôle in both. In *Il Trovatore*, she gave her
striking impersonation of Azucena in company with Bettini, Ferri
and Madame Bendazzi. She sang in the productions of *Maria di
Rohan* and *Anna Bolena*. She also took part in Rossini's *Il Viaggio a
Vienna*, which was performed just once, on the evening of the
marriage of the Emperor Franz Joseph.

The other contralto in the Italian Company was Mme. Borghi-
Mamo. The soprano *prima donna* who caused the greatest excitement
at the Opera was Mme. Medori, but Jenny Lind was also singing in
Vienna at the time. Mme. Lind-Goldschmidt, as she had become,
gave a well-attended series of concerts. As usual, Emilie made some
concert appearances, for example on 7 May when she sang in a duet
from *Don Giovanni.*

PARIS

By 1854, Mlle. de Méric's career had settled into a regular pattern,
with Seasons in Vienna and St. Petersburg. This was to continue for
several years more, but she would be featuring on the playbills under
another name. The young angel by Timoleone's sick-bed of whom
Nicolas Lablache wrote from St. Petersburg was to become his wife.

The marriage took place at Maisons-sur-Seine (Maisons Lafitte)
on 7 September 1854. The husband's full name was Nicolas Pierre
André Lablache and he was the second son of Luigi and his wife
Thérèse, née Pinotti.

Nicolas was described in the marriage documents as an artiste,
meaning a singer. He seems to have been a performer of some ability,
but he was always overshadowed by his father and elder brother,
Frédéric. Furthermore, he never achieved the renown enjoyed by his

243

wife. According to the *Manchester Guardian*, his introduction to musical society had taken place on 22 February 1849 when he sang at a Dress Concert of the Hargreaves Choral Society in the Free Trade Hall in Manchester. The stars on that occasion had been Luigi Lablache and Thalberg. Nicolas was described as young (actually 27), with talents which, though promising, needed maturing. He had sung the duet *Per piacere* from *Il Turco in Italia*, with Mlle. Vera, and the Rossini quartet *Cantiamo, ridiamo* with Mlle. Vera, Mlle. Bassano and Signor Vera.

The Manchester correspondent of the *Musical World*, reviewing the above concert, wrote that Nicolas' voice did not yet possess much power, as a baritone, but was of a musical quality, 'and we think he promises even better than Signor F. Lablache did at that age.' In *Per piacere*, the voices of both Mlle. Vera and Nicolas had been pleasing and the baritone's 'showed that agreeable quality of mixing well, which, when he acquires more force in his lower tones, will be a most valuable addition to the Italian baritones – a class much more numerous, by the way, than our English ones.' Nicolas had also sung two duets with his famous father: *Un segreto*, from *Cenerentola*, and *Se fiato in corpo avete*, from *Il Matrimonio Segreto*, in which Luigi's *buffo* singing had evoked peals of laughter.

The singing career of Nicolas was not distinguished enough to be traceable at all completely. It is clear that at one time and another he filled managerial posts connected with opera.

THE WEDDING

The civil ceremony took place at the *Mairie* at Maisons in the morning. The bridegroom was stated to be living at the home of his parents in Paris, at No.16 rue Taitbout. He had been born in Rome on 5 February 1822. The bride, named as Emilie Marthe Marguerite Glossop, was living at Maisons with her mother. She had been born in Paris, in the Second *Arrondissement*, on 6 October 1830 and was declared to be the legitimate eldest daughter of Joseph Gapper Glossop, deceased, and his surviving widow Joséphine Bonnaud de Méric. The banns had been duly published at the *Mairie* in the Second *Arrondissement* and the three parents present had each signified their consent to the marriage.

All the necessary certificates had been provided, except one. Emilie had not produced any certification of her father's death. As we know, Joseph had died in Florence in 1850, but Emilie declared under oath that she did not know where he had died or what his last domicile had been. In support, four witnesses swore that although they were acquainted with the bride and knew her father was dead, they were equally in the dark about when and where the death had occurred. Two of these witnesses were listed as friends of the bridegroom. The other two, friends of the bride, were Dr. med. François Maroncelli, 57, living at Nice, in Sardinia, and Sigismond Thalberg, 41, *chevalier de la Légion d'Honneur*, the celebrated pianist who married one of the daughters of Luigi Lablache.

Joséphine, it seems, had not been called upon to make a statement about the death of Joseph Glossop. She signed the register as J. G. de Méric veuve Alexandre, thus as a widow establishing that Timoleone, who had for many years been generally regarded as her husband, was not alive in September 1854. Emilie signed as Emilie Glossop de Méric.

The bridal couple had informed the Mayor that they had concluded a marriage contract and this was confirmed in a certificate issued by the Paris notary, Maître Roquebert.

Church Registration of Emilie's marriage to Nicolas Lablache, 1854.
(By courtesy of the Bishopric of Versailles.)

The religious ceremony followed on the same day, at the Roman Catholic Church of St. Nicholas, Maisons-Lafitte. This, again, had presented some problems. Emilie being a Protestant, Nicolas had been obliged to get a papal dispensation for the marriage. On 5 September this had been duly obtained through the Bishop of Versailles. As was to be expected, it was granted subject to some conditions. Children of either sex were to be brought up in the Catholic Religion and the husband was constantly to strive, 'as far as prudence permitted' (*selon les règles de la prudence*), to convert his wife to the same faith.

The Church Register gives Emilie's name as Emilie Marthe Marguerite Gapper-Glossop de Méric. As at the civil ceremony, she signed Emilie Glossop de Méric. A feature of this Register is the predominance among the witnesses of members of the Lablache clan to which Emilie was henceforward to belong. Apart from Joséphine and Settimio Alexandre, there appears to be no-one from the de Méric or Glossop side. Frédéric Lablache signed, as did his younger brother Dominique Lablache, who was an officer in the French Army. Daughters of Luigi signed as Anna Singer and Marie de Caters.

It will have been a stylish wedding. By the middle of the century, Maisons-Lafitte had become a very fashionable residential area. The magnificent Château Maisons had been built by Mansart between 1634-1636 and by 1658 it was surrounded by a large walled park.

The banker and politician Jacques Laffitte had bought the estate in 1818, but in 1833 financial troubles induced him to split the park up into a collection of country villas. A railway station, the first outside Paris, was opened in 1847 and Maisons became a convenient and extremely pleasant retreat for well-to-do Parisians. There was a strong contingent from the *Bourse* and the *Opéra* and Lablache probably acquired his property in 1850 or thereabouts. A train left Paris at half-past midnight which was so full of artistes that it became known as *le train des théâtres*. The fine property which Lablache owned was in the Avenue Albine and this was inherited by Nicolas after his father died in 1858. Luigi's eldest son Frédéric lived in London. An Avenue Lablache, at Maisons, perpetuates the memory of the great singer and there is a Lablache and a de Caters family crypt in the Maisons cemetery.

ST. PETERSBURG

By the Winter of 1854, Emilie was a fully-integrated member of the Lablache family and would usually be known professionally as

Madame de Méric Lablache. She was with her husband and Luigi in St. Petersburg when the twelfth Italian Season opened in September.

Medori had declined to return to Russia after her triumphs in Vienna, but in her place the soprano Mme. Tedesco was evoking gales of enthusiasm and electrifying both the public and the other singers. She made her *début* in St. Petersburg in Donizetti's *La Favorita*, in early October. The other principal newcomer was the tenor Alessandro Bettini, from Rome.

Emilie appeared in four operas during the Season: *Lucrezia Borgia, Der Freischütz, Rigoletto* and the unpopular, 'old-fashioned' *Mathilde di Shabran*. In this latter, however, Mme. de La Grange and Calzolari proved that there were still singers who could meet the demands of the *grande école*. Emilie's aria was an insertion, by Mercadante.

On 11 December, the performance of *Der Freischütz* was given for Emilie's benefit, the part of Anneta having been transposed for her. The small rôle of the hermit was taken by Lablache, whose voice 'like a clear bell overcoming all other noise on a busy street brought peace and harmony to the last scene of the work, turning everything it touched to gold'.

This was the Winter when the terrible events in the Crimea were filling all Russia with desperation. When a *Concert Patriotique* for the widows and orphans of the soldiers killed at Sebastopol was given in the Hall of the Nobles in December, all the artistes from the Italian Company took part. The concert ended with the Russian National Anthem, sung by the Italians. There was a strong feeling in Russia against what was considered to be an unholy alliance between the British and French to join with the Turks in fighting against their fellow-Christians, the Russians. Nevertheless, the attitude towards non-combatant enemy nationals remained very civilised. Emilie was Anglo-French and her brother-in-law Dominique Lablache was in the French Army in the Crimea, but there is no reason to believe that this in any way affected her in St.Petersburg. The Anthem 'had made all Russian hearts quiver with enthusiasm': *God the Omnipotent, mighty Avenger, Watching invisible, judging unheard, Doom us not now in the day of our danger, Grant to us peace, O most merciful Lord.*

In the New Year (1855), a performance of *Rigoletto* was given for Tamberlik's benefit. This opera continued to be a favourite and there was much applause for Tamberlik appearing for the first time as the Count and for Mlle. Maray as Gilda. As the hero, Ronconi 'passed from laughter to tears in a way which gives you a shiver down the spine'. Above all, though, the concerted pieces thrilled the audiences. The quartet in the third Act between Tamberlik, Ronconi, Maray and de Méric (as Emilie was still known) had produced an electric effect.

All in all, however, the operas had been poorly attended. The war was having a baleful influence. Money was short, especially for season tickets and the more expensive seats.

A feature of the Season had been the extraordinary popularity of Madame de La Grange. The day after it had been announced that she was to have a benefit, every available ticket was sold. This had not happened for any other singer during the Season. The public took her to their heart and much regretted that she decided to go to America.

At the same time, La Grange had her critics and in the light of what had been said years before about Joséphine it is interesting to see the form which the adverse comments took. The main thrust was that Mme. de La Grange lacked 'soul' and that her vocalisation was too reminiscent of musical instruments. With Joséphine, it will be remembered, it was 'ma voix de clarinette'. According to Rostisleff, in the *Journal de St. Pétersbourg*, many of the effects which La Grange achieved recalled the sounds of wind or stringed instruments. At one time she would be like a flageolet, producing diaphanous notes, taken *pianissimo* with the greatest softness. At another, her voice would fly with the speed of an arrow up to the very highest regions. She could sound like an Aeolian harp, a hand-bell or even the sweetest of flutes.

Rostisleff agreed that the critics had some justice on their side, but maintained that it would be wrong to compare La Grange's vocalisation with that of other great singers, because hers was a thing apart. It did not derive from any lack of taste or training. The very quality of the voice resulted in most of her melodic passages being comparable with musical instruments rather than with the normal human voice. That voice might not always please, but its exceptional and wonderful quality must strike everyone who heard it. Her singing and technique were in a class of their own.

That said, Rostisleff conceded that there was indeed one aspect of La Grange's performance which was open to valid reproach: the lack of clarity in her pronunciation. Joséphine, too, had been criticised on this score. Is it, perhaps, a fault to which those with 'instrumental' voices are especially prone? Then La Grange, too, apparently never succeeded in ridding herself of her *grasseyement*, that dreaded uvular rolling of the 'r'. Rostisleff deplored this, but La Grange was to be excused because she was a Parisian and because such a nightingale of song should not be denied the occasional 'ornithological embell-ishment'. Joséphine's *grasseyement*, it may be recalled, was ascribed to her being from the Provinces and not from Paris.

CHAPTER 29

Vienna, Paris and St. Petersburg, 1855-1856: birth of Louise Lablache

VIENNA

IN 1855, Emilie was engaged in Vienna with Mme. Medori, Mme. Bendazzi and the mezzo-soprano Mme. Borghi-Mamo.

12. April 1855.

K. K. Hoftheater nächst dem Kärnthnerthore.

4te italienische Opern-Vorstellung.

Rigoletto.

Melodramma in tre Atti con Prologo, di F. M. Piave.

Musica del Sig. Maestro Giuseppe Verdi.

Personaggi:

Il Duca di Mantova	— —	Sig. Sachero Melchiore.
Rigoletto, suo buffone di corte	— —	Sig. Ferri Gaetano.
Gilda, di lui figlia	— —	Sigra. Lesniewska-Corelli Luigia.
Sparafucile, bravo	— —	Sig. Benedetti Nicola.
Maddalena, sua sorella	— —	Sigra. Lablache-Demeric Emilia.
Giovanna, custode di Gilda	— —	Sigra. Müller.
Il Conte di Ceprano	— —	Sig. Bundsmann.
La Contessa, sua sposa	— —	Sigra. Weis.
Il Conte di Monterone	— —	Sig. Demi Stanislao.
Marullo, Cavaliere	— —	Sig. Liebisch.
Borsa Matteo, cortigiano	— —	Sig. Campe.
Paggio della Duchessa	— —	Sigra. Theen.
Usciere di corte	— —	Sig. Bisi.
Cavalieri. Dame, Paggi. Alabardieri.		

Poster – Rigoletto at the Kärnthnerthor Theatre, Vienna.
(By courtesy of the Österreichische National bibliothek, Vienna.)

14. April 1855.

K. K. Hoftheater nächst dem Kärnthnerthore.

6te italienische Opern-Vorstellung.

Il Trovatore.

Dramma in quattro Atti. Poesia di Salvatore Cammarano.

Musica del Sig. Maestro Giuseppe Verdi.

Personaggi:

Conte di Luna — — —	Sig. Ferri Gaetano.
Leonora - — —	Sigra. Bendazzi Luigia.
Azucena, Zingara — — —	Sigra. Lablache–Demeric Emilia.
Manrico - — —	Sig. Bettini Geremia.
Ferrando, confidente del Conte —	Sig Benedetti Nicola.
Ines — — —	Sigra. Weis.
Ruiz — — —	Sig. Reinhold.
Un vecchio Zingaro — —	Sig. Liebisch.
Un Messo - — —	Sig Campe.

Familiari del Conte. Uomini d'arme. Damigelle. Zingari.

L'avvenimento ha luogo parte in Biscaglia, parte in Aragona.

Das Textbuch, in italienischer Sprache, ist an der Kasse für 20 kr. C. M. zu haben.

Tägliche Preise bei der italienischen Oper:

Eine Loge im 1. u. 2. Stocke, oder im Parterre 20 fl. — kr.	Ein Sperrsitz im 4. Stocke . . . . . 1 fl. 20 kr.
detto im 3. Stocke . . . . . . 12 „ — „	Eintritt in das Parterre . . . . . 1 „ 20 „
Ein Sperrsitz im Parterre . . . . . 2 „ — „	detto in den 3. Stock . . . . . 1 „ — „
detto im 3. Stocke 1. Reihe . . 2 „ — „	detto in den 4. Stock . . . . . — „ 30 „
detto im 3. Stocke 2. oder 3. Reihe 1 „ 40 „	detto in den 5. Stock . . . . . — „ 20 „

Die Cassa wird um halb 6 Uhr geöffnet. — Anfang 7 Uhr.

Emilie as Azucena in Vienna, 1855.

(By courtesy of the Österreichische National bibliothek, Vienna.)

250

Letter from Nicolas Lablache to his father, written from Vienna on 18 June 1855. The sketch portrays an exhausted Emilie, Nicolas, their baby Louise and the wet-nurse.

(By courtesy of Madame Balsan, living at Neuilly, near Paris.)

Emilie's re-appearance was warmly welcomed. The critic in the *Wiener Conversationsblatt*, writing in April, pointed out that he did not judge a singer by the importance of the rôle. So no-one should take it amiss if he returned to his *premiers amours* and began his review of *Rigoletto* with a well-loved artist-friend from earlier days: Signora Demeric. The Viennese, Dr. L. said, had the happiest memories of her and her talents. Now, on marriage, by becoming Madame Demeric-Lablache she had added another splendid artist-name to the fine one by which she had been known before. In *Rigoletto*, she had had a small part but a great success, worthy of the true artist that she was. All her skills had been brought fully into play and 'this intelligent, gracious artist had been singled out by the audience with vociferous applause and many curtain-calls.'

The same critic reported that Mme. Bendazzi and Mme. Demeric-Lablache had repeated their outstanding success of the previous year in *Il Trovatore*. This had been on 14 April. However, at subsequent performances the part of Azucena had been transferred to Mme. Borghi-Mamo, possibly because Emilie had been unwell. Bettini had been Manrico and Ferri took the part of the Conte di Luna.

No record has been found of Emilie singing between the third week in April, in an ill-received *Linda di Chamounix*, and the beginning of June. Evidence is lacking, but it is probable that this was when her first child, Louise, was born. Be that as it may, Emilie was one of the all-star cast which gave a grand charity performance at the Court *Theater am Kärntnertor* on 3 June. This was for the world *première* of the opera *Cristina di Svezia* (Christina of Sweden) which had been composed for the Theatre by the famous Viennese pianist and composer, Sigismond Thalberg. The libretto was by that most celebrated of Italian librettists, Felice Romani, 'whose work truly entitled him to be called Felicissimo.'

Thalberg himself had travelled from Naples to produce his work and the singers were Mesdames Medori and Demeric-Lablache with Signori Bettini, De Bassini and Angelini. The Emperor and Empress of Austria and the Archduke Franz Karl were in the audience. Thalberg was given an ovation after every Act, and a crowded house enthusiastically applauded the artists and the orchestra, but the opera itself was generally found to be deficient in dramatic effect. Emilie had the rôle of Paola and sang her aria in Act III 'with beautiful expression'.

The following is a translation by Mr Brian Meringo of the letter on the previous page:

Dearest Papa,

I am scribbling these few lines to you above all to wish you, on behalf of Emilie and myself, a thousand happinesses; many, many years to come, and that you have on hand everything that you desire. We are sorry to be far from you on the occasion of your Saint's Day but we are saying prayers for your precious conservation from afar, as we would from close by.

My good Emilie is well - relatively - after the birth. Mam'zelle Louise enjoys perfect health so far and at this moment is besieging a fortress of a German wet-nurse who possesses two "mamelons" which would make the mouth of a Guards corporal water.

This escapade of Emilie's will make us remain in Vienna more than we thought but one must be patient. It is never possible to have complete happiness in this world. I cannot say what emotion I experience when I hear another voice in the house - when I say "voice" I am mistaken, I should say "crying", shrieks which nevertheless scratch on my ears sweetly. It is true however that sometimes especially at night time this scratching becomes a demanding disturbance. But I am a father and because of that I consent to suffer a thousand times more, because God accords me the grace to look after a daughter.

You know (I think I mentioned it) that Emilie gave birth at least 20 days before term but I am informed by the doctors and the midwife that this happens almost always with first births. Give us your news, dear Papa, because we are very anxious to hear from you. Embrace Frédéric, Fanny and the children also on behalf of my wife.

A thousand good wishes and a thousand kisses from your son,

Nicola.

The Season as a whole had been a success. The Italian Company had been particularly well received by the Viennese public and were thought to have sung better than any of their predecessors since the days of Barbaja, the impresario who had recruited Lablache, Tamburini and Madame Fodor. Merelli was concurrently Director of *La Scala*, so that operas given their *première* there were sometimes produced with essentially the same cast in Vienna. The Season had closed on 30 June, with a pot-pourri from various operas and a dance divertissement.

PARIS

It is recorded in the *Revue et Gazette Musicale de Paris* that 'the experienced singer Madame de Méric' sang at a concert given in the Summer by the guitarist Jean Wiesen. This seems likely to have been Joséphine, but it could have been Emilie. The pieces were an aria from *Robin des Bois*, one by Handel and a dramatic ballad by Monsieur Lentz.

ST. PETERSBURG

After several years in St. Petersburg, Damcke had moved in the Autumn of 1855 to Brussels, as the music critic for the *Revue et Gazette Musicale de Paris*. He considered that the music performed in St. Petersburg was just as worthy of notice as the music in any of the other great European centres, but maintained that none of his successors in the Russian capital had carried on his work of sending out regular and detailed reports on the artistic life there. So Damcke arranged to receive his own letters from St. Petersburg and to compose a *Russian Chronicle* from Brussels.

The thirteenth Italian Season opened in the splendour of the newly-decorated Grand Theatre. Not only was the ornamentation, *à la Pompadour*, most sumptuous, water-pipes had been installed throughout so that in case of fire it would only be a matter of turning on a tap.

Once again, Emilie was the principal contralto. Much as the loss of Mme. de La Grange was regretted, the audiences were delighted to welcome a new soprano, Angelina Bosio, a native of Turin, who charmed them with her soft, lyrical voice. She was paid Fcs. 100,000, with a benefit of Fcs.15,000. Another new recruit was Mme. Lotti, 'straight from Italy.' Ronconi was very sadly missed. He had been engaged, but fell seriously ill in Spain. His place, as baritone, was taken by De Bassini and by Bartolini, who do not seem to have made any great impression. Lablache was again with the Company.

As public enthusiasm for Italian opera had been showing signs of cooling again, the Company decided to introduce more variety into their repertoire. More than a score of operas were put on, including two new to St. Petersburg: *Il Trovatore* and Meyerbeer's *L'Etoile du Nord* (The Northern Star). While Verdi was becoming the most popular Italian composer, native Russian opera was also returning to favour. No doubt this was due, in part at least, to the mood of patriotism induced by the war. Some twenty years earlier, the operas of Glinka had excited nobles and common people alike, but his successors had lacked his genius and the Russians had been forced to have recourse to foreign works. These presented formidable difficulties to native singers, who found that they could not compete with great artists schooled in the Italian tradition.

By 1855, the Direction of the Imperial Theatres had decided to send some of the most promising Russian singers to Italy for training. One of these, the young singer Setoff, had a sensational success when he returned and made his *début* as Edgardo in *Lucia di Lammermoor*. The audience in the vast hall of The Circus rose to its feet, threw flowers and screamed with patriotic joy that Russia could dare to produce a rival to Rubini and Mario. *Lucia* was performed five times in a week. In that same first week of October, too, a short comic opera called *Le Sorcier*, by the Russian composer Prince Wiasemsky, was very favourably received. Thus, after many years, the Italian Opera faced some serious competition in St. Petersburg.

The Season had opened with Verdi's *Macbeth*, disguised as *Sivardo il Sassone* (Seward the Saxon). This opera had been put on the year before, but had not then attracted full houses, partly because of the influence of Lablache and the 'old school', who were vehemently opposed to the 'new-fangled' works of Verdi. However, the public liked *Macbeth* and it found a secure position in the repertoire.

The public indeed liked Verdi and the whole of St. Petersburg high society flocked to hear Mme. Bosio in *Rigoletto*. The Italians had made a comeback. All the performers in *Rigoletto* had been at the height of their powers (Marie Escudier). There had been an encore for the quartet in the final Act in which Emilie sang with Bosio, De Bassini and Tamberlik.

After singing in *Lucrezia Borgia*, Emilie shared in the acclaim which greeted the St. Petersburg *première* in November of *Il Trovatore*. Despite what many critics had to say about the weaknesses of this opera, it triumphed, both from its novelty and from the manner in which it was performed (*Musical World*). The singers were Bosio (Leonora), De Bassini, Tamberlik and Emilie (Azucena).

Exceptionally, the contralto part is central to the highly romantic theme of *Il Trovatore*. Rostisleff indeed considered that the opera should be called *La Bohémienne* rather than *Le Troubadour*, especially in view of the striking and realistic way in which Emilie interpreted the rôle. The youthful and pretty Madame Lablache Deméric, he wrote, had demonstrated her respect for dramatic art by setting all coquettishness aside and appearing as an almost repulsive old crone. She could not have looked more like one of those gipsies who give us a fright when we meet them. Above all, she was in every look and gesture the very embodiment of a creature consumed with the burning desire for vengeance. In her first scene, with all its difficulties, Emilie had acted and sung in the most remarkable way, worthy of the highest praise. Later she had been no less moving in the nostalgic air *Ai nostri monti ritorneremmo*, the dream of enjoying again the peace of the mountain-country of her youth.

The *mise-en-scène* and the costumes received high praise. At the end of the Season, the Czar Alexander commanded a gala performance of *Il Trovatore* at the Imperial Theatre, to be followed the next day by *Rigoletto* at the Hermitage.

In December 1855, a performance of Weber's *Der Freischütz* was staged to give Emilie the chance to play Aennchen. This was not wholly successful. The critic, A. N. Serov, who was not a great friend of Italian opera, argued that the Italians were not capable of bringing out all the beauty and nuances of Weber's German music. He complained, with some justice, that as the rôle of Aennchen had been written for a high soprano it lost much of its effect when transposed by almost two tones to suit Emilie's 'low mezzo-soprano, close to contralto'. Also in December, Emilie sang in the *Barber*, with Lablache and Calzolari.

The 1855-1856 Season had been a success. Despite the fears, Italian opera had never been more popular in St. Petersburg and *La France Musicale* could maintain that the Italian Company in Russia was superior to any other in Europe.

Concurrently, during this Opera Season, there had been French classical drama in the Russian capital and *Le Théâtre Français de St. Pétersbourg* was receiving as much attention from the critics as the Italian opera. For several months, Mlle. Rachel dominated the reviews.

There is a pleasing instance of co-operation between the two foreign Companies. In October 1855, at the *Théâtre Français*, singers from the Italian Opera took part in a benefit for one of the *comédiens*, Varlet. St. Julien recorded that Mme. Lablache-de-Méric had charmed the public with her soft and flexible voice, which was just right for the final *rondo* of *La Cenerentola*.

The centenary of the birth of Mozart was celebrated in a Grand Concert in the Hall of the Nobles on 15 January 1856. Emilie, with her *Voi che sapete*, repeated the success she had enjoyed as Cherubino in 1851 and 1852. However, as before, and in defiance of Mozart, she had introduced a change at the end of the aria 'to demonstrate her fine high note'. Emilie sang excerpts from Mozart at other concerts during the Season, sometimes with Lablache.

Emilie's husband Nicolas was with her in St. Petersburg. A letter from Luigi of 27 January 1856 to his son-in-law Ernest de Caters includes a greeting from Nicolas.

Both Luigi and Emilie were re-engaged for the following Opera Season. Tamberlik had decided to betake himself to Rio de Janeiro.

At the end of March 1856, Emilie was with her mother in Strasbourg.

CHAPTER 30
Vienna, Moscow and St. Petersburg, 1856-1857

VIENNA

EMILIE returned to Vienna for the 1856 Spring Season. So did Mme. Borghi-Mamo. Emilie appeared in a successful revival of *Il Trovatore* and in three other operas: *Rigoletto*, *Zelmira* and a work by the Chevalier Tommasi called *Guido e Ginevra*, which was being given its Viennese *première*. In all, Emilie sang twenty-two times, as against twenty-eight by Mme. Borghi-Mamo.

Emilie in costume.
Presumably as Azucena.
(By courtesy of the Bibliothèque de l' Opéra, Paris.)

In May, it was announced from St. Petersburg that three singers from the Italian Opera in Vienna – Bettini, De Bassini and Madame de Méric-Lablache – had been invited to sing during the ceremonies for the coronation in Moscow of the Czar Alexander II.

Luigi's wife Teresa died at Maisons-Lafitte in July 1856 and her funeral took place there.

MOSCOW (20 AUGUST – 27 SEPTEMBER 1856)

The fourteenth Italian Season in Russia opened in auspicious circumstances. In March 1856 the Crimean War had been brought to an end. The new Czar was to be crowned in Moscow on 26 August and he had decided to include in the coronation festivities both the Italian Opera and the *Théâtre Français*.

Festivities began before the artistes even landed in Russia. In Stettin, on a fine Summer day (16 August), the Russian steamer *Vladimir* took on board a party for St. Petersburg which included not only companies of foreign singers and actors but Russian princes, German barons, diplomatic attachés and newspaper correspondents from several countries.

Suddenly, the following evening, word went round that there was to be a concert on deck. A milling crowd assembled. Then, spectacle-case in hand, Lablache gave the signal for the music to begin: it was the Italian Opera Company, performing above the placid sea - Mesdames Bosio, Lotti, Maray and de Méric-Lablache, with Signori Lablache, Bettini and Tagliafico. They opened with Rossini's *Carnaval*, followed by the prayer from *Comte Ory*. A trio by Martini led to a canon by Salieri and then to the finale of the *Barber*. The enthusiasm was boundless and the demands for encores were not brought to an end until Mme. Tagliafico went round to make a collection for the benefit of the crew (*Le Menestrel*).

In Moscow, preparations had been on a lavish scale. The singers in the Italian Company were given free accommodation in premises at the Imperial Court and Court vehicles were placed at their disposal. The old Bolshoi Theatre had been burnt out in 1853 and a vast new edifice had replaced it. Resplendent in red, white and gold, it defied all description. It could seat 2,500 and was far higher than the *San Carlo* in Naples. The cost of a box for six was a 'fabulous' twenty-five roubles and four hundred roubles was the price for the eighteen performances which were promised. In the Summer of 1856, the talk in Moscow and St. Petersburg was of nothing but the Coronation and the attendant festivities. These were organised for notables and public alike.

The Bolshoi Theatre, Moscow.

At the Opera in Moscow, the great gala performance was on 30 August when Lablache appeared in *L'Elisir d'Amore* and Ceritto danced in the ballet. Emilie's Moscow *début* was on the following evening in *Il Trovatore*, the opera which proved to be the most successful of all (*La France Musicale*). Critics went so far as to say that Bettini was even better than Tamberlik as Manrico. The singers in *Lucrezia Borgia* were given a great ovation and Emilie's *Brindisi* was encored. Emilie also sang in *Rigoletto*, but not in the Russian *première* of *La Traviata*.

During this special Moscow Season, the concerts included a notable one given on 12 / 24 September by the Grand Duchess Hélène in which Emilie played a prominent part. Her solo aria was from *Le Prophète* and she sang in concerted pieces from *Maria Stuarda* (Niedermeyer), *Alla Trinità beata* (1545) *Così fan tutte* and *Il Trovatore*. All the artists received rich presents, from both the Czar and the Grand Duchess.

On 5 September, Luigi wrote from Moscow to his daughter Marie de Caters describing the entrance of the Czar into Moscow and marvelling at the splendour of the uniforms and dresses. He asked Marie to have a Mass said for his late wife at the Church at Maisons. Luigi had managed to make the journey to Russia, despite being unwell.

ST. PETERSBURG

The Czar and Czarina returned to St. Petersburg in October, to a tumultuous reception.

The Opera had opened the night before with *Macbeth*, followed by *Ernani*, *Il Trovatore* and *Rigoletto*. This shows the overwhelming enthusiasm for Verdi which gripped Russian audiences at the time. Above all, the public loved *Il Trovatore*. Maurice Rappaport, Director of the *Journal des Théâtres et de Musique* at St. Petersburg, as quoted in *La France Musicale*, had had this to say about Emilie's performance as Azucena in Moscow:

> 'The enormous success of the *Trovatore* with us [in Russia] is due in great part to Madame de Méric. I have observed that several foreign journals failed to mention Mme. de Méric in their reports on the performances of the *Trovatore* in Moscow. We must acknowledge, in all fairness, that it is she who has created the difficult rôle of the gipsy. She has proved that she is not only an excellent singer, but a remarkable actress as well. In her acting there is so much truth that the very sight of the sinister gipsy sends a cold shiver down the spine of everyone in the audience. In the *Trovatore*, she shares the ovations which the public unfailingly bestow on Mme. Bosio, and that says all.'

During this period, the Italian Company were giving three performances a week at the Grand Theatre in St. Petersburg, on Mondays, Wednesdays and Fridays. The *régisseur* in 1856 was Monsieur Cavos. Thanks to the munificence of the Imperial Court, the Company were able to recruit the most eminent singers in Europe and it was an accolade to be invited to sing in St. Petersburg. In 1856 – 1857, the troupe no longer included Lablache. He had been replaced by the *basso profundo serio* Marini who, physically at least, could bear comparison with the great Luigi. The chief sopranos were Bosio and Lotti. Mme. Tagliafico was the supporting contralto. The tenors were G. Bettini, Calzolari and the 'blond Bettini'. Tagliafico, De Bassini and Bartolini took the baritone parts.

With the great popularity of Verdi, *La Traviata* and *Luisa Miller* were produced after *Trovatore*. However, the repertoire was by no means confined to Verdi. It included *Les Huguenots* (*Les Guelfes et les Gibelins*), *L'Italiana in Algeri*, *Maria di Rohan*, *Semiramide* and *Lucrezia Borgia*, in all of which Emilie was given a rôle.

As the page in *Les Huguenots*, she had as usual given the part a special interest and had demonstrated yet again that she possessed quite exceptional talents. In *Maria di Rohan*, though she had only a secondary part, she rceived an ovation. *Semiramide*, strangely enough, was a fiasco and had just one performance. Even the inimitable Bosio had not had the voice or the commanding presence to do justice to the rôle of the Queen of Babylon and Emilie, 'visibly indisposed', had lacked the power which the part of Arsace demanded. *Lucrezia Borgia*, on the other hand, was a complete success, with Lotti as a charming if somewhat too young-looking Lucrezia. Emilie duly received an encore for her *Brindisi*.

The Italian Company did most of the honours at the annual concert by the Philharmonic Society in aid of widows and orphans.

In the Summer of 1857, Luigi Lablache had been at Maisons-Lafitte. On 1 July, he wrote from there to his daughter Marie de Caters to say that his health was not good. His doctors had told him that he must take the waters at Bad Kissingen and then go on to Naples for the air. He added that Nicolas and Emilie were leaving Paris that evening for Naples so that he would be feeling very much alone. By 6 July, he had heard from Nicolas that all had gone well and Naples had been reached safely. Later, Luigi duly went to stay at his Neapolitan villa at Posilippo. His illness had led to false reports of his death appearing in the press in Italy. However, by the Autumn he had had a stroke and the doctors said that he could never appear on the stage again.

While Nicolas and Emilie were in Russia, their baby Louise seems to have remained at Maisons-Lafitte in the care of her aunt, Marie de Caters. Emilie had signed for a further Season in St. Petersburg, but she did not return to Vienna in 1857.

St. Petersburg and Paris, 1857-1858: death of Luigi Lablache

THE opening of the Fifteenth Season was marked by the triumphant re-appearance of Mme. Bosio in what had become one of the public's favourite operas, *La Traviata*. Tamberlik was also back in St. Petersburg, in good health and crowned with his laurels from America. He could always be relied upon to draw the crowds, though Calzolari had many fans too.

Emilie received an enthusiastic welcome when she made her *rentrée* as Maddalena in *Rigoletto*. Rappaport was full of praise for the whole cast. Mme. Bosio was 'a Gilda without compare in the whole world' and Tamberlik was 'the greatest tenor in existence'.

The operas which commanded full houses during the Season were *Il Trovatore*, *Rigoletto*, *Guillaume Tell* and *Il Barbiere*. A performance of *Il Trovatore* for the benefit of the *régisseur-en-chef*, Cavos, was a sell-out with Bosio, Tamberlik and Emilie in the principal rôles. By this time, Rappaport maintained that it was above all as an actress that Emilie excelled in her portrayal of the gipsy: her voice perhaps needed a little more moderation.

The popularity of Verdi continued unabated, though it is noteworthy that *Les Vêpres Siciliennes* was not quite so ecstatically received as the more Italianate works. The Russians preferred *le genre italien* to *le genre français*. All the same, the rôle of Hélène had been a triumph for Mme. Lotti della Santa.

The Czar and Czarina were present on 6 December for the performance of *Les Huguenots* which was given for the benefit of Mme. Lotti, who evoked 'fanatisme' for her portrayal of Valentine. Emilie had been full of grace and charm as the page (Rappaport). Next, she appeared in Verdi's *Luisa Miller*, which was given as a benefit for her on 21 December. It seems to have been during this Season that Emilie first performed in Auber's *Fra Diavolo*, in the main contralto part of Lady Pamela.

At the close of the Opera Season, a new concert hall 'the Vauxhall' had been inaugurated and Emilie took part with other members of the Italian Company in three charity concerts there. As the Italians were the focus of the musical life of St. Petersburg, they were expected to perform whatever type of music was in demand. In

1856, for example, the Director of the Philharmonic Society had turned to the Italians, not the Russians, when he was organising the Mozart Jubilee.

DEATH OF LUIGI LABLACHE

On 25 January 1858, Luigi Lablache died of bronchitis at his villa in Posilippo. The following day, a solemn funeral, with music, took place at the Church of St. Ferdinand. Later he was buried, as he had wished, at Maisons-Lafitte. A Requiem Mass was celebrated at the Madeleine in Paris on Saturday 20 February 1858. The *'faire-part'* included *'Monsieur et Madame Nicole Lablache et leur fille* [Louise]'. Rossini said that of the singers of his time many were great artists, but only three were real geniuses: Papa Lablache; that true ruby of song Rubini, and that spoiled child of nature, Malibran.

There was an auction of Lablache's belongings in May 1858. There were 352 items, including his vast collection of snuff-boxes, English silver, bronzes, furniture and pictures, one a Veronese, *Jesus at the Pharisee's Banquet*, from the Wilmore Collection in England.

The death of Luigi inevitably involved a change in the life of Emilie and her husband. Nicolas now had a more important rôle in the family affairs. True, Frédéric as the eldest son had become the head of the clan, but he had married an Englishwoman and made his home in London. Nicolas, the second son, was based in Paris and many of the family responsibilities fell on him.

PARIS

Equally, 1858 marked an important change in the pattern of Emilie's career. She was indeed to have one more Season in Russia, but that was to be the end of the series. The new departure was a spectacular return to the stage in Paris, this time at the *Opéra*.

On 22 August, *Le Menestrel* announced that there was to be a performance of *Le Trouvère* (*Il Trovatore*) for the benefit of the first tenor at the *Opéra*, Gustave Roger, in which he would for the first time sing the part of the troubadour. The rôle of Azucena would be taken by Madame Méric-Lablache. In that rôle, Emilie would be succeeding Adélaïde Borghi-Mamo, that celebrated Italian mezzo-soprano who owed her fame in Paris to her Azucena – (she was also renowned for having given birth to a daughter in 1855 only an hour after playing that same part). Madame Ugalde would be the Eléonore.

The performance duly took place on the evening of Saturday 28 August before a crowded house. As was to have been expected, Roger and Mme. Ugalde delighted the audience; but it also had the exciting new experience of enjoying the powerful and brilliant mezzo-soprano of 'that European star' and artiste of the *grande école*, Madame de Méric-Lablache. As Escudier admitted, she had indeed appeared on the Parisian stage several years earlier, but that had been at the *Théâtre Italien*. Now, she was venturing on to the essentially French scene. This, combined with the maturity of her voice and dramatic talent, was the equivalent of a *début*.

Emilie captivated the house. To quote Escudier, her Azucena had shown a rare sureness of touch, even though the ardour of her emotion had at times almost carried her away. Her singing of the ballad in the first Act had sent a thrill throughout the audience and from then on ovation succeeded ovation. This had been all the more to her glory because the memory of Mme. Borghi-Mamo was still so very fresh in the memory. It was above all as a *tragédienne*, both passionate and tender, that Emilie had fascinated the public, but she had also been acclaimed as a *cantatrice de premier ordre*, endowed with both the high notes of the mezzo-soprano and the deep ones of the contralto. In a word, her triumph had been complete.

This success in Paris must have been particularly sweet after the disappointments which Emilie's mother had suffered there. Happily, Joséphine was alive to share in the pleasure. However, not even a public triumph will silence all criticism. S.D., in the *Revue et Gazette Musicale*, expressed some reservations. He recalled that in November 1848 Emilie had sung in a few concerts in Paris and, just once, had taken the part of Gondi in *Maria di Rohan*. Her voice certainly had a wide compass and did not lack either tone or power. She had clearly had the benefit of a sound musical education. Furthermore, her face was full of expression. Her beautiful eyes and somewhat pronounced features lent themselves to dramatic situations. That said, she unfortunately erred on the side of exaggeration and this was exemplified by the manner in which she had interpreted the rôle of Azucena. She had made Manrico's mother have the body of an old crone with a still youthful face. She had portrayed with the gestures of a maniac the sombre grief and thirst for vengeance which consumed her. These were contradictions to which the critic was in duty bound to draw attention in the interest of the artist herself. All in all, though, there could be nothing but praise for the way Emilie had sung. The audience had often been moved and had applauded her most warmly.

Finally, though, the critic sounded a warning: Madame Méric-Lablache was engaged for several more years [sic] at the theatre in St. Petersburg, but if she was to have a career in Paris she must get rid of that marked *grasséyement* which was so particularly grating to French ears. Was this, one wonders, an hereditary affliction? Could it be due to childhood in Alsace and the influence of German?

Prior to this second *début* in Paris, Emilie may have had a short tour in Germany. *La France Musicale* had announced on 2 May 1858 that a Monsieur Holding had assumed the direction of a *Théâtre Italien* which would be giving performances in Germany from 1 July to 10 September. Demeric-Lablache is included in the list of the names of the artists engaged, but no information has been obtained about this tour, if indeed it took place.

CHAPTER
32

St. Petersburg and Paris, 1858-1860: birth of Henri

ST. PETERSBURG

IN September 1858, Emilie's *rentrée* in St. Petersburg was in *Maria di Rohan*. This was a great success. She seemed to have a special talent for the minor rôle of Gondi and was received by the audience as a good old friend. Madame Bosio remained the diva and she made a triumphant *rentrée* in *Rigoletto*. Ronconi was back after three years.

The Grand (Bolshoi) Theatre, St. Petersburg.
(By courtesy of The Theatre Museum, Victoria and Abert Museum.)

On 23 October, Emilie sang in a performance of *Luisa Miller* which Rappaport described as one long ovation. Yet again, *Il Trovatore* played to packed houses, superbly interpreted by Mme. Bosio, Emilie, Tamberlik, De Bassini and Everardi. Rappaport remarked that Paris had now seen Emilie as Azucena and he liked to think that the Parisians would fully share his view of that excellent artist.

Emilie is described as having enjoyed a striking success in a fine performance of *Lucrezia Borgia*. The novelty of this sixteenth Season (1858-1859) was Flotow's *Marta*, with Bosio in the principal part, one which she had just created in London. Emilie had the contralto rôle of the waiting-maid Nancy and shared in the 'brilliant success' of the opera.

Emilie chose *Il Trovatore* for her benefit, on 7 February 1859. This was also her farewell to opera in St. Petersburg. After so many Seasons, her final operatic performance was in one of her finest creations, Azucena.

However, as was customary, the Opera Season was followed by a series of concerts. One of the most brilliant, that year, was given by Monsieur de Sabouroff, with performances by Emilie, Bosio, Tamberlik, De Bassini and Calzolari. Also, before leaving Russia, Emilie had revisited Moscow, where she reportedly had much success and received magnificent presents.

Unhappily, there is a sad and seemingly uncharacteristic postscript to Emilie's trip to Moscow. On the return journey to St. Petersburg, she and Mme. Bosio apparently had a quarrel. Bosio, in her annoyance, left the warm railway carriage in which they were travelling and went to another one which was unfortunately unheated. She caught a severe chill. She was already suffering from a liver complaint, which was being treated by the French doctor who accompanied the Italian Company, but she now contracted pneumonia from which she died. The Russians felt that they had lost a highly-valued friend and gave her a magnificent funeral.

On leaving Russia, Emilie returned to the Lablache villa at Maisons-Lafitte.

PARIS

In the apparent absence of reports of stage performances, it seems probable that Emilie spent much of 1859 at Maisons. She was certainly there in July, when a Mass was celebrated in the local Church in aid of the infants' school. This was very much a Lablache family occasion, the principal singers being Emilie, Nicolas, Mme. de Caters and a Monsieur Aymès. By this period, Maisons-Lafitte had become a favourite Summer retreat for rich Parisian families and *La France Musicale* had no doubt that the Mass would be a financial as well as an artistic success.

In April 1860, the same journal announced that Mme. de Méric-Lablache, who had been absent from the theatre for several months, had given birth to a son; however, she intended shortly to resume 'the course of her brilliant successes on the lyric stage'.

The son was Henri Louis, born on 15 March 1860 at the home of his parents in the Avenue Albine at Maisons-sur-Seine. At the registration, a witness was Henry Singer, one of the child's uncles by marriage. The child received a Roman Catholic baptism at the Church of St. Nicholas, Maisons, on Wednesday, 20 April. The godparents were Tamberlik and Marie de Caters, his aunt. The father was described as a landowner in the Parc de Maisons. As already indicated, the career of Nicolas has not proved easy to follow in any sustained fashion. He cannot have been much of a success as a singer and he surfaces mainly in administrative or managerial capacities, albeit in musical contexts. In December 1860, when a *Cercle de l'Union Artistique* was formed in Paris to promote the arts and offer practical help to aspirants, the name of Lablache (Nicol) appears in the list of Founder Members. The President was Prince Poniatowski and Charles Gounod was one of the Vice-Presidents.

CHAPTER

33

Madrid, Barcelona and Paris, 1860-1862: birth of Anna

EMILIE next moved to an entirely new scene, Spain. In August 1860, *La France Musicale* was able to announce the names of the Italian Company which would be performing that Autumn at the *Teatro de l'Oriente* in Madrid. It was an ensemble which the journal believed had no equal elsewhere in Europe: Mesdames Julienne Dejean, Charton-Demeur, Sarolta, de Méric-Lablache and Calderon; Messieurs Fraschini, Morini, Ronzi, Giraldoni, Marra, Bouché, Manfredi and Rovere. *La France Musicale* was at a loss to understand how the theatre in Madrid could afford the cost of such a constellation of talent. The man behind this recruitment was that *emperador de los empresarios*, that man of great taste, Monsieur Bagier. (At this period the majority of 'Italian' companies were engaged in Paris, largely by the Agency founded by Edouard Duprez).

Emilie had left Paris for Madrid in mid-September. On 20, 21 and 23 October, she appeared as Orsini in *Lucrezia Borgia*, to receive congratulations from all sides. According to *La France Musicale*, everyone wanted to hear 'this famous artist who had been fêted in St. Petersburg and applauded on the principal stages of Europe.' Their expectations had been not only fulfilled but surpassed. Never before in Madrid had been heard such a beautiful contralto voice combined with such a dramatically expressive appearance and so perfect a singing technique. Consummate *tragédienne* that she was, Emilie had given the rôle of Orsini a most original character. She had both played and sung the famous *Brindisi* so appealingly that she was interrupted after every bar with bravos. Her success could not have been more striking or more deserved. Mme.de Méric-Lablache was indeed a precious acquisition for the royal theatre in Madrid.

Iberia, after praising the performance of *Lucrezia Borgia* as a whole and saying how admirable Fraschini (tenor) and Mme. Dejean (soprano) had been, went on:

> 'Madame Lablache de Méric, who was appearing for the first time before the public in Madrid, at once captured all their sympathy. Her voice is superb, her singing masterly. One could not but be struck too by the distinction of her manners and her beautiful bearing on the stage. She was called before the curtain several times, with Mme. Dejean,

Fraschini and Bouché. The *Brindisi* was sung with irresistible zest. She is regarded here as one of the most perfect artistes who has ever appeared on the Italian stage in Madrid.'

Emilie received an ovation for her performance in *Il Trovatore* and appeared in a production of *Marta* which was very warmly greeted. In *La Fille du Régiment* it was Mme. Charton-Demeur who deservedly triumphed, but Emilie also made a hit. 'Out of sheer camaraderie' she had undertaken the minor rôle of the Marquise, but 'as there are no small parts for talents of the first order, she had raised it to the height of her talent – which is to say all' (*La France Musicale*). The Madrid correspondent of the paper had expressed surprise that such a great artist as Emilie had not been recruited by the *Théâtre Italien* in Paris long ago. *La Fille du Régiment* proved to be one of the greatest successes of the Season, being performed nine times in three weeks and always to full houses.

Emilie appeared also in *Il Giuramento*, with Mme. Dejean and the tenor Morini; in Donizetti's *La Favorita*; in *Maria di Rohan* and in *Rigoletto*. The sensation of the Season, however, was the Madrid *première* of *Un Ballo in Maschera*, on 5 March 1861. No-one could remember a more complete triumph than was achieved by Verdi's new *chef-d'oeuvre*. The singers Mme Dejean, Fraschini and Giraldoni, for whom the opera had been written (Rome 1859), held the audience spellbound for five hours. Emilie made her due contribution with a fine rendering of the part of Ulrica, 'an interpretation which did her much honour.' This rôle was said to have been 'sacrificed', in Paris, by the indifferent performance of Alboni.

The success of *Ballo*, which went to eighteen performances, caused Bagier to extend the Season by two months, to the beginning of June. Emilie remained with the Company. Altogether, there had been eight months of full houses in Madrid. It had been a memorable Season and even the receipts had been a record. Mme. Charton-Demeur was being described as another Grisi, with the addition of *l'élégance française*. Mme. De Lagrange had inherited the finest qualities of Mme. Sontag and Mme. de Méric-Lablache was the rival of Alboni and Borghi-Mamo.

By the end of the second week in June 1861, Emilie was back in Paris, as was the impresario, Bagier.

The Lablache family bestirred themselves to bring music to their retreat at Maisons. On a Sunday early in July, they gave a concert in the great gallery of Mansard's former royal *château* there, which had been put at their disposal by that 'prince of financiers' Monsieur Thomas. This was a grand affair. Nicolas was in charge of the organisation. The invitations were issued in the names of Madame de Méric-Lablache and Madame de Caters, described in the press as the most charming ladies in Paris. Undaunted by the pouring rain, 'toute l'aristocratie parisienne', in full dress, had filled the train to Maisons to capacity. On their arrival at the entrance to the Park, the guests were greeted by a military fanfare.

The concert included both vocal and instrumental music, some of which was unfamiliar. The singers were Emilie, Marie de Caters, Nicolas Lablache and Morini (from Madrid). The pianist Mme. Camille Dubois played Chopin and the young prodigy Sarasate electrified everyone by his virtuosity on the violin.

Emilie had chosen to sing the *Brindisi* from *Lucrezia* and the *arioso* from *Le Prophète*. Her performance led more than one critic to express regret that she was not appearing on the stage in Paris. Could it just be that she had the misfortune to be French? Paris, alas, was not being allowed to hear Madame De Lagrange or Madame Charton-Demeur either.

As for the singers, it was plain to *Le Menestrel* that Emilie was without question an artist to her fingertips, pre-eminent for her voice, style and dramatic talent. Madame de Caters, for her part, was an elegant *femme du monde* who was clearly at the same time the daughter of an artist, brought up in the atmosphere of great music. Nicolas had inherited the qualities of style and good taste from his father and had everything needed to make a singer – except, alas, the voice. (Mme. de Caters had been the moving spirit behind the charitable purpose of the concert, which was to pay for a second infants' school. A large sum was collected.)

The concert over, Emilie and her husband went to Boulogne for the sea-bathing. *Le Menestrel* hoped that the *Société Philharmonique* at that resort would have the honour and pleasure of hearing 'the great *cantatrice* whom our *Académie Impériale de Musique* ought to take away from the Italian Theatre in Madrid'. Boulogne was a favourite meeting-place for the Lablache family. In 1862, Frédéric, from London, was there with his brother Dominique, the military officer. They stayed variously at the Hôtel Royal, the Hôtel Impérial and the Hôtel du Nord.

The astute Bagier, always loath to lose popular members of his Company, had not failed to re-engage Emilie for Madrid. She was given the rank of *prima donna assoluta*, which she shared with Mmes. De La Grange and Dejean.

BIRTH OF ANNA

Emilie arrived back in Madrid in mid-September 1861 after, it seems, an appearance at the *Teatro Regio in Turin*, in *Il Trovatore*.

Unfortunately, the Madrid Season had been heralded by a public dispute between Bagier and a small number of the subscribers to the theatre. The impresario was accused of raising prices unduly, making unacceptable changes in the seating arrangements and the like. Above all, it was alleged that he had assembled a third-class Company, unworthy of the royal theatre.

Nonetheless, the theatre duly opened on 5 October and the production of *Lucrezia Borgia*, with Emilie in her usual part, was a stupendous success. The number of subscribers increased greatly and it seemed to be generally agreed that the accusations had come mainly from rivals who were jealous of the success of a foreigner at the royal theatre and from opponents of the Government, which had authorised Bagier's changes.

Emilie appeared in *Il Trovatore* and *Un Ballo in Maschera*, both of which played to full and enthusiastic houses. *Ballo* was the hit of the moment, with Emilie, Dejean, Bettini and Coletti 'defying comparison' (*La France Musicale*). After *Linda di Chamounix*, there was a well-staged production of Flotow's *Marta*. The King and Queen of Spain attended both *Ballo* and *Marta*.

At this period, if we may believe *L'Art Musical*, the *Teatro de l'Oriente* in Madrid could lay claim to one of the first positions among the great 'Italian' stages in the world and their Company of *artistes d'élite* had hardly a rival. If the highest honours had to be bestowed on Mesdames De Lagrange and Dejean, and to Bettini, Emilie was by no means far behind. Her perfect artistry and warmth were infectious enough to make the coldest of audiences applaud.

From Madrid, Emilie went to the *Teatro del Liceo* in Barcelona for the Carnival Season, but was then obliged to absent herself from the stage to give birth to her third child. This was Anne Marie (Anna or Nina), born in Madrid on 6 February 1862. Her father Nicolas described himself then, not as a singer, but as a man of private means (*rentier*).

By Holy Week, Emilie was able to sing in a performance of Rossini's *Stabat Mater*, which was received with general acclaim. The Opera Season closed on 4 May after scenes of triumph for Mme. De Lagrange in the final productions of *La Traviata* and *Norma*. Once again, too, the Season had been a financial as well as an artistic success. Over a million francs had been taken and Bagier had recouped his outlay.

In June 1862, Emilie was back in France, taking her ease at the villa at Maisons which had come to Nicolas as part of his father's inheritance. The respite did not prevent her from taking part again in a Sunday concert at the *château* which her sister-in-law had set in motion for the benefit, this time, of the now-completed poor-children's school. The event was publicised as a golden opportunity of doing good and at the same time enjoying excellent music in one of the finest houses in France. Sarasate had been recruited again. Mme. de Caters sang the *cavatina* from Prince Poniatowski's *Pierre de Médicis* 'with her father Lablache's method and the voice of Giulia Grisi at her best.' Emilie had an immense success with the *Brindisi* from *Lucrezia* and sang duets with Marie de Caters from *L'Elisir d'Amore* and *Il Trovatore*. The collection was said to have amounted to as much as Fcs.8,000.

Bagier had engaged Emilie again as the leading contralto for the 1862-1863 Season in Madrid, which was to open on 1 October. *L'Art Musical* credited him with having once more assembled the most brilliant and complete company of 'Italian' singers in the whole of Europe. In that journal's view, the Italian companies in both St. Petersburg and Madrid were superior, in their ensemble, to the best which Paris could offer at either the *Académie Impériale de Musique* (the *Opéra*) or the *Théâtre Italien*. The public in Madrid were so impressed by the names in Bagier's troupe that the number of subscribers was even higher than the year before, which had itself been exceptional.

Escalier d'honneur, Château Maisons.
(By courtesy of the Caisse nationale des Monuments historiques et des Sites.)

Madrid, Barcelona, Baden-Baden and Paris, 1862-1863

MADRID

EMILIE left Paris in mid-September 1862 for Madrid and played her part in the successful production of *Il Trovatore* with which the Season opened on 27 September. Mme. Carlotta Carozzi-Zucchi, the Leonora, was making her *début* in Madrid and was warmly received. However, the main honours went to the baritone Giraldoni as the Conte di Luna. By this time, Emilie had become well known and well loved by the Madrid audiences and she was applauded after every song. Through the artistry of her singing and acting, she was regarded as the model of a *Bohémienne*. Her next appearance was in *Il Barbiere*, with the tenor Baragli: he was being credited with charms of voice and person which almost equalled those of the great Rubini.

In mid-October, the Company staged Donizetti's *La Favorita*, in which the action takes place in mediaeval Spain and tells of the unhappy love of Fernando, a novice monk, for the mistress (Leonora) of the King of Castile. All the singers gave satisfaction, but it was Emilie and G. Bettini who were most frequently recalled for acclaim.

Flotow's *Marta*, though it had been given nineteen times the previous year, was revived with all the excitement of a novelty. Then, after an appearance in *Ballo*, Emilie proved once again, in *Lucrezia*, that she was 'the most charming Orsini imaginable'. Next, *Maria di Rohan* had given all the artistes the chance to surpass themselves (*La France Musicale*). *Les Huguenots* seems to have been sung in Italian, as *Gli Ugonotti*.

In November, Verdi left St. Petersburg, where he had presided over the first production there of his new opera *La Forza del Destino*, in order to prepare for the *première* of this work in Madrid. It is reported that having come to know Emilie in St. Petersburg he was determined to choose her to take the part of the gipsy, Preziosilla. Verdi arrived in Madrid towards the end of January 1863. He attended a performance of *Rigoletto* and when the audience discovered that he was in the house they acclaimed him 'with an enthusiasm which could not be imagined outside a Mediterranean country'.

La Forza del Destino, based as it is on a Spanish drama, was followed with the closest attention and both the *maestro* and the singers were given multiple ovations. The *rataplan*, sung by Emilie and the choruses, was encored amid frenzied applause. Verdi had to come forward three times and it fell to Emilie to present him with a silver garland on a satin cushion. On each leaf had been engraved the title of one of Verdi's masterpieces.

The *mise-en-scène* of the new opera – *à la parisienne* – the decorations and the costumes had all been exceptionally fine. Bagier received due recognition for his achievement. The Madrileños found it difficult to forgive him for not being Spanish, but then he was after all rich, generous, clever and loyal, altogether an impresario of a rare breed.

At this period, early 1863, two other lady members of the Lablache family were giving vocal performances. Madame Brayda Lablache, a niece of Luigi, took the part of Bertha (soprano) in the Spanish *première* of Meyerbeer's *Le Prophète* at the *Teatro Liceo* in Barcelona and la Baronne de Caters had been invited to sing at a *soirée intime* in the *Tuileries* in Paris at which the Empress Eugénie asked her to include some Spanish airs. Mme. de Caters also sang at a charity concert in the *Salle Herz* where she reportedly delighted the audience with the *cavatina* from *Pierre de Médicis* and the *Inflammatus* from Rossini's *Stabat*.

From Madrid, Emilie returned to Maisons-Lafitte where she was to spend part of the Summer. As in the previous years, a charity concert was given at the *château*, this time for Church construction. Emilie and Mme. de Caters were assisted by Nicolini, Rossi and Agnesi, while Sarasate once again demonstrated his skill on the violin. Emilie's main contribution was an aria from *Le Prophète*.

BADEN-BADEN – SUMMER 1863

The elegant spa town of Baden-Baden, on the fringe of the Black Forest in Southern Germany, was a favourite Summer resort of high society and the list of the aristocrats who were there in 1863 'read like a supplement to the *Almanach de Gotha*'. The King and Queen of Prussia had as their guest the music-loving King William III of the Netherlands.

A major diversion at Baden-Baden was provided by the race-course. However, in 1863 a new Court Theatre had been opened, promising grand opera with stars from the *Théâtre Italien* in Paris. The Season opened on 21 August with *Lucia di Lammermoor*, in which Emilie's sister-in-law Mlle. Marie Battu (Madame Dominique Lablache) was said to have been adorable in the name part. The tenor Emilio Naudin, as Edgardo, was hailed with the greatest possible praise as a new Rubini.

L'ILLUSTRATION DE BADE

JOURNAL LITTÉRAIRE ET ARTISTIQUE DE LA VALLÉE DU RHIN ET DE LA FORÊT-NOIRE.

DIRECTION : A BADE, place de la Croix, 163.
Conditions d'abonnement : Pour la ville de Bade , 4 florins.
— Pour Strasbourg , 8 fr. 50 c. — Pour le Bas-Rhin, le Haut-Rhin, les Vosges, la Meurthe et la Moselle, 9 fr. — Pour Paris et le reste de la France , 9 fr. 50 c. — Pour l'étranger, le port en sus, suivant les taxes postales.
LE NUMÉRO : 40 CENTIMES OU 12 KREUTZER.

sixième année.

N° 6.

9 JUILLET
1863.

LES ABONNEMENTS SONT REÇUS
A Bade , au bureau du journal, place de la Croix, 163, vis-à-vis la maison Herzer ; à la librairie Marx et sous la colonnade de la Conversation. — A Carlsruhe, chez M. Bielefeld, éditeur. — A Paris, au bureau du Passage-des-Princes. — A Vienne, chez MM. Miethke et Wawra, éditeurs, Singerstrasse. — A Strasbourg, à l'imprimerie Silbermann.

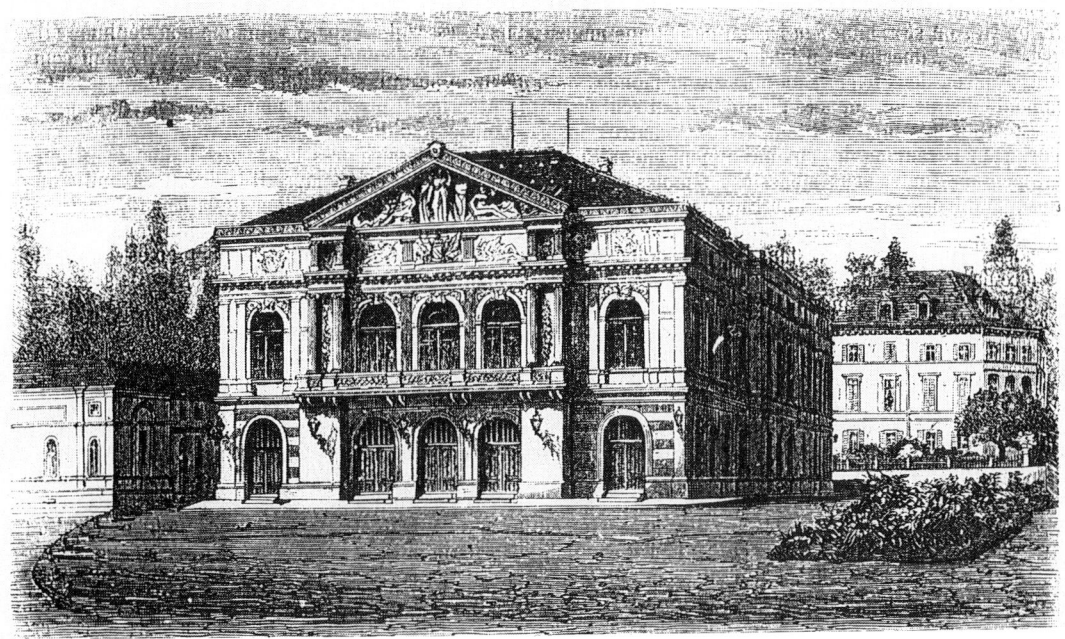

View of Baden-Baden, with the Theatre.

(By courtesy of the Bibliothèque Nationale, Paris.)

277

Emilie came into her own in *Il Trovatore*. In *L'Illustration de Bade*, the critic Méry wrote of her as follows:

> 'Madame Lablache de Méric, whose name is of all names the most dear, played and sang as Azucena, the passionate gipsy – the dramatic rôle *par excellence* which cries out for a Rachel and a Malibran combined. Mme. Lablache de Méric successfully performs this double task with splendid versatility: she moved, charmed and uplifted the audience, interpreting Verdi exactly as Verdi himself would wish.'

This rings true because the composer is believed to have made some changes in the part for Emilie's benefit.

When it came to *Rigoletto*, Emilie's acting as Maddalena made a deep impression. In the famous quartet in Act III her shrill and sarcastic laughter had sent a shudder through the audience. Meyerbeer was in Baden-Baden at the time and is reported to have been liberal with his applause for both *Trovatore* and *Rigoletto*. Wagner was also there, but it has not been discovered how he responded.

MAISON DE CONVERSATION.

A l'occasion de la fête anniversaire de S. A. R.

Le Grand-Duc Frédéric de Bade

Mercredi 9 Septembre 1863 :

GRAND CONCERT

dans les nouveaux salons

AU PROFIT DE L'HOPITAL DE BADE.

EXÉCUTANTS.

Chant . . . . . . Mlle **Marie Battu.**
  „ . . . . . . Mme **Lablache de Meric.**
  „ . . . . . M. **Delle Sedie.**
Violon . . . . . . M. **Alard.**
Violoncelle . . . M. **Seligmann.**
Piano . . . . . . M. **A. Jaell.**
Harpe . . . . . . M. **Krüger.**

Notice of Charity Concert at Baden-Baden.
(By courtesy of the Bibliothèque de l' Opéra, Paris.)

The Opera Season closed with *Ballo*, 'brilliantly executed'. Another musical highlight was the Grand Concert on 9 September, to celebrate the birthday of the Grand Duke of Baden. This Duke was that reputedly wise and statesmanlike Frederick I, whose consort was the Princess Louise, daughter of the King of Prussia. Both Emilie and Mlle. Battu took a prominent part. Together, they sang the duet from Rossini's *Stabat Mater*, to thunderous applause. François Schwab, writing in *L'Illustration de Bade*, described Emilie as a powerful contralto whose deep notes penetrated the hearer with a strange emotion. She had been truly magnificent in her rendering of the *arioso* from *Le Prophète*.

CHAPTER 35

Paris and Germany, 1863-1865: Escudier's vendetta

A significant event for Emilie was the decree of 25 March 1863 whereby Bagier was appointed in place of Calzado as Director of the *Théâtre Italien* at the refurbished *Salle Ventadour* in Paris. This took effect from 1 May. Bagier had accepted the post despite the prospect of the discontinuance of the Government subsidy and he remained in charge of the Italian Company in Madrid as well.

The French at once began to congratulate themselves with the expectation that they would soon be welcoming famous singers hitherto unseen on the Parisian stage. *L'Art Musical* was confident that the change in the Direction would lead to great improvements in the way the theatre was managed and in the range and quality of the productions. All the same, the paper feared that there might not be a public for the performances five days a week which were planned.

In August, the names of the artistes who had been engaged were officially announced. These included Mesdames De Lagrange, Borghi-Mamo and de Méric-Lablache, with Messieurs Fraschini, Baragli and Nicolini (tenor), Delle Sedie and Guicciardi (baritone), Bouché and Antonucci (bass) and Scalese (*basse bouffe*). Above all, though, Bagier had secured, at great expense, the young star Adelina Patti whose contract was to run from 15 December 1863 to 5 February 1864.

A general atmosphere of *bienveillance* prevailed. It was hoped that the uncertainties of the years since 1848 might be at an end. At least there would be a man of taste at the helm who could be expected not only to recruit first-class singers but to engender a sense of unity in the Company as a whole. Also, be it admitted, a nostalgia for former glories evoked sighs of happy relief when the doors of the *Salle Ventadour* opened in October to 'cascades of gauze and rivers of diamonds' swirling past mountains of exotic plants.

The Season began, though, with some hiccups. Mme De Lagrange had hoped to open in her favourite opera, *Norma*. Emilie wanted to make her first appearance in *Il Trovatore*. In the event, the first production was *La Traviata*. Emilie made her *rentrée* in *Rigoletto*, as Maddalena. Though this part did not give her much scope, she made the most of it and gave every sign that she would 'burst forth in all her glory' when cast in a suitable major rôle. She had played a full part in the resounding success of the quartet in the fourth Act. *L'Illustration*, while praising her voice and spirited acting, reverted to the old complaint about her *grasseyement*, but added that it at least proved that she was not Italian.

Emilie made her real *début* of the Season on 15 November, as Azucena. As a whole, this production of *Il Trovatore* was not regarded as a great success 'except for Mme. de Méric-Lablache and Fraschini'. The critics were at one in praising Emilie's performance. Her success had been complete and well deserved (*L'Illustration*). Her voice was vibrant, sonorous, penetrating and full of feeling. She could rise easily to notes beyond her normal pitch. She was indeed a worthy daughter of the famous singer whose name she bore and a worthy daughter-in-law of the great Lablache, who had given her invaluable advice. Thus she came with the advantage of a fine style and a sound knowledge of the traditions of the stage. The public had recognised this and rediscovered, in her, two names long held in fond remembrance. Emilie's success had been assured from her first aria and the following recitative and aria with Fraschini had won her the sympathy of the whole house.

As an actress, Emilie was welcomed as a true *tragédienne*, full of understanding for the rôle of Azucena. Yet she had the defects of her qualities. She was so anxious to be dramatic that, to Parisian eyes at least, she tended to overplay the part. It was also objected that she portrayed the gipsy as too decrepit and too swarthy: so much so that her complexion looked as though it might have been reddened not by the sun but by wine . . . . Then there was still that terrible *grasseyement*.

Il Trovatore drew the crowds and was repeated several times. The Emperor Napoleon III and the Empress attended a memorable performance in December at which Emilie had been 'superb'.

Emilie was not given a part in *La Sonnambula*, in which Mme. Borghi-Mamo had the rôle of Amina, but she appeared in *Lucrezia Borgia* at the end of November. *Sonnambula* was not well received, but *Lucrezia* was a brilliant success. Emilie was seen to have just the figure for the rôle of a young Venetian nobleman and her singing of the *Brindisi* earned her many bravos. The audience had been disappointed to miss the trill on the high E to which Alboni had accustomed them, but Emilie had adhered to the score as written. In other places, however, she had introduced some variations of her own which were condemned.

L'Art Musical was sufficiently impressed by Emilie to ask why not she but Borghi-Mamo had been chosen to sing the contralto part in the forthcoming production of *La Cenerentola*. Emilie next appeared as Ulrica, the fortune-teller, in Verdi's *Un Ballo in Maschera*. According to *Le Menestrel*, her performance was masterly, and

Fraschini, as always, was incomparable, but the opera nevertheless failed. Giraldoni had not fully recovered from illness, Madame Dejean had not come up to expectations, the work had been under-rehearsed and the orchestra was too loud. This proved to be the beginning of troubles for Bagier. He felt obliged to publish a letter of apology in the *Gazette des Etrangers*. He admitted that there was some justice in the criticisms. Unfortunately, he had been pre-occupied by the death of a young niece who had been married for only a year. This had prevented him from supervising rehearsals and the day when the opera was put on had coincided with his niece's funeral. Many of the singers had attended to pay their last respects and this had no doubt affected them emotionally, caused them fatigue and so impaired their performance.

In the Winter of 1863-1864, sickness was rampant. In January 1864, when Emilie was ill, her place in *Il Trovatore* was taken by Miss Lumley and Emilie was still hoarse when she returned.

By this time there was a crescendo of criticism directed at Bagier and most of his Company. It was being said that apart from Fraschini his Company was third-rate and a disgrace to the great tradition of the *Théâtre Italien*. In particular, the female singers were below standard. Emilie was no Alboni and only the arrival of Mlle. Patti held out any hope of Bagier saving the day. As it turned out, Patti triumphed in *La Sonnambula*.

Emilie was now singled out by Escudier for an attack of great virulence. This seemed to amount almost to a vendetta. The full force of the barrage will unfold as the Season progresses, but as a first shot Escudier criticised her performance as Gondi in *Maria di Rohan*, a rôle with which she had been familiar from the earliest days. She transgressed, he claimed, by inserting an aria which was entirely out of place, thereby showing disrespect for Donizetti. She had given a desperately lustreless performance. In Escudier's opinion, Bagier had no contralto in his Company until February 1864 when he recruited Mlle. Barbara Marchisio: his only hope was that, with Patti, the two Marchisio sisters and Mme. Spezia-Aldighieri, the Italians might regain the stature they had lost.

In the event, Mario also came to Bagier's rescue. On 21 February, Patti, Emilie, Mario, Delle Sedie and Scalese appeared in Flotow's *Marta*. This was a triumph for Patti, who was singing the title-rôle for the first time in Paris, and Mario was singing as of old. Escudier thought that Emilie lacked lightness, but others praised her as an ideal Nancy, gay, droll and as sprightly as could be. She had played her full part in the success of the spinning-wheel quartet and had been much applauded for her aria in the third Act. The quartet had so pleased the Empress that she invited the singers to include it in the Court Concert on 7 March. The four singers were Patti, Emilie,

Mario and Delle Sedie. Eugénie had received Bagier after the performance of *Marta*, expressed her pleasure at being with the *Italiens* and offered to help Bagier if the need should arise. The Court Concert was arranged by the French opera composer Jules (Giulio) Alary (1814-1891). The programme included the *rataplan* from *La Forza del Destino* which Emilie and the chorus performed to acclaim.

Emilie was unwell again in March, when her place in *Il Trovatore* was taken by Barbara Marchisio, who was very warmly received. However, by the end of the month Emilie was once again playing Azucena 'with her well-known intelligence and delicate care' and Fraschini was delighting audience and critics alike. Fraschini also achieved success as the Duke of Mantua in *Rigoletto* and the quartet in which he sang with Delle Sedie, Carlotta Marchisio and Emilie gave great satisfaction.

At this juncture, Escudier publicly urged Bagier to get rid of Mme. de Méric-Lablache. Bagier did no such thing, but some colour was given to the suggestion that she might be demoted when it was announced that in *Cenerentola* she would not be given the title-part, but, with Carlotta Marchisio, would be one of Cinderella's two sisters. The truth, it seems, was that Emilie was genuinely being obliging. She and the Marchisio sisters had agreed to a reciprocal arrangement which would favour Emilie in the forthcoming production of *L'Italiana in Algeri*. *Le Menestrel* reported this as a rare example in opera of such goodwill, which it hoped would set a precedent.

Meanwhile, *Ballo*, which had 'suffered shipwreck' at the start of the Season, was revived with success in April. As Ulrica, Emilie had either 'sung with her customary talent' (*Le Menestrel*) or just 'done her best and not spoilt anything' (*L'Art Musical*). The Empress had been present and the revival proved highly popular.

A very different fate awaited *L'Italiana in Algeri*. As for the work itself, *Le Menestrel* described it as a *chef d'oeuvre* in the *opéra bouffe* class, but that type of opera was difficult to mount and melodrama seemed to be more to the public taste. Though there had been some good moments in the performance, the critic preferred not to go into detail, but to hope for better things next year . . . . The *Gazette* wrote that the opera had been performed and the offence was fortunately not to be repeated. *L'Art Musical* roundly declared that the evening had been a disaster. Apart from the tenor, Bettini, all the singers had been deplorable; Mme. de Méric-Lablache had obviously been indisposed and had completely failed.

Escudier, in *La France Musicale*, seized the opportunity to turn all his guns against Emilie. In a tirade filling a whole column, he said that till then she had played only secondary parts. That showed her cunning. She must know that she would not have been accepted if she had put herself forward as a replacement for Mme. Alboni or even Mme. Trebelli. Yet now she had all of a sudden taken it into her head to tackle a great rôle and to pose as a star with attendant satellites. And what satellites? Why, two artists of the first rank, the Marchisio sisters! This was an error which might well cost Mme. Lablache dear. If it was repeated, Bagier's reputation as an able director was likely to suffer.

Escudier went on to suggest that Emilie should not hope to trade on the appeal of the Lablache name. When she appeared in *L'Italiana in Algeri*, as Isabella, all the friends of the Lablache family, who were numerous, had arranged to occupy the orchestra stalls. They had displayed much goodwill and even courage by applauding their favourite for whatever she sang. Yet even they had been forced to beat a retreat in the face of hostile demonstrations which they were powerless to stifle. The barrage continued:

> 'True, one must have deep admiration for anything which awakens memories of the great, illustrious and immortal Lablache; but that was no reason why one should be party to a blind infatuation, unjustifiable by even the most devoted affection. We appeal to all disinterested members of the audience who witnessed this production of *L'Italiana in Algeri*. We ask them: do you think Mme. Deméric-Lablache sings in tune? Do you think she has an agreeable voice and acts naturally?'

> 'For our part, we consider that her voice is neither a soprano, a mezzo-soprano nor a contralto. It is a voice which defies all classification. She usually seems to be off key and that is far from pleasing to discerning ears. Our impression is that when she wishes to change passages which are beyond the powers of her organ she distorts them with tricks at odds with both the style and intentions of the composer. On the pretext of being an expressive mimic, she gesticulates without rhyme or reason and finishes by guying her characters.'

> 'Such is our opinion and we believe that it is also that of the public. Let Mme. Deméric-Lablache but return to the minor rôles to which she confined herself hitherto and she will have the benefit of our indulgence. If she persists in trying to climb up to higher rungs, she will risk some serious falls. Then she may find it hard to recover. The *habitués* of the *Théâtre Italien* may not make their protest by unseemly demonstrations, but they will assuredly stay away and that will be very unfortunate

for Monsieur Bagier. Without Mme. Lablache, the production of *L'Italiana* would have gone swimmingly. Agnesi was excellent as Mustafa and Scalese brought a fine comic attack to the rôle of Taddeo. Bettini is blameless. The Marchisio sisters, who had nothing to sing except the famous septet in Act II, contributed greatly to a fine performance of this admirable piece, which was encored by acclamation.'

At this distance, it is very difficult to know how much weight to give to these comprehensive strictures. Perhaps, despite the dispassionate tone, there was some element of personal malice. One can only set against Escudier the evidence of others and the record of Emilie's subsequent career. On one point, the exceptional character of her voice, it may be that, like her mother, Emilie had a voice apt either to delight or disconcert. Certainly the range must have been exceptionally wide.

As regards acting, there seems little doubt that Emilie's forceful style had greater appeal in other countries than in France. Health must also be taken into account. It seems more than likely that Emilie had not fully recovered from her illnesses when she sang in *L'Italiana in Algeri*.

The Opera Season, having started late, had been extended and finally closed on 15 May. The subscribers had paid for seven months. As was customary, the last regular performance was composed of sections from various operas – on this occasion *Rigoletto*, *Ballo*, *Lucrezia* and *Lucia*. Bagier then put on a special performance of *Trovatore* for the benefit of the choral singers.

Bagier had had his troubles, but it was generally agreed that his Season had risen to a successful climax with *Ballo*. The chief criticism was that he had tried too hard, shown *trop de zèle*. In theory, his control of the two theatres, in Paris and Madrid, gave him flexibility in moving his artists from one stage to the other. In practice, he had engaged rather too many singers and had found that he could not make ends meet without the State subsidy. He had erred, it was felt, by trying to put on too many different operas and by having five instead of three performances per week. He had sacrificed quality to quantity. That was fatal for the *Théâtre Italien*, whose very *raison d'être* was to give definitive performances, impeccably produced. Bagier, it was argued, had depended too heavily on Fraschini and Patti and had not fulfilled his promise of a well-balanced, well-rehearsed troupe. As for his repertoire, a third of the operas had been by Verdi and there had not been any Mozart at all.

As was normal, Emilie had not sung just in opera. On 15

February, Rossini held his first *soirée* of the Season, at his house, with Meyerbeer present and applauding. Emilie sang with Patti, Gardoni and Delle Sedie. All the songs and instrumental pieces were by Rossini, who sat apart in his little study while Madame Rossini did the honours. Emilie's solo was from *Tancredi*. One of the greatest successes of the evening was the quartet from *Moïse* in which she took part.

Mario was back in Paris in February and Emilie, Patti and Delle Sedie joined him in performing the vocal parts in a high-society *soirée* given by M. Isaac Pereire. In Holy Week (24 and 26 March), Bagier arranged two fine concerts of religious music at the *Salle Ventadour*. Members of the Italian Company sang excerpts from the *Stabats* of Haydn, Pergolesi and Rossini. Emilie's main contributions were the *Quae maerebat* and the *Quando corpus* by Pergolesi and the *cavatina Fac ut portem* by Rossini.

At the end of March 'the famous Dr. Trousseau' gave a *soirée musicale* in his salons at which both Emilie and Madame de Caters sang. *Le Menestrel* was full of praise for Mme. de Caters' voice and dramatic talent and only wished that she had been willing to appear on the stage. '*La belle voix*' of Madame de Méric-Lablache had been applauded by the '*public élégant*' at a concert given by Madame Ronzi.

Good works were not neglected. In April, the *Italiens* staged a special performance for the benefit of the Charity for Convalescent Children. The main offering was Act III of Gounod's *Faust*, in Italian, with Patti as Marguerite, Morini as Faust, Agnesi as Mephistopheles and Emilie as Siebel, the village youth in love with Marguerite. This had delighted the audience. Later, in the torrid heat of an early Summer evening, a charity event took place at the *Opéra* for the composers of dramatic works. Emilie sang with Fraschini in Act II of *Ballo* and Act IV of *Rigoletto*.

GERMANY

In the Summer of 1864, the Italian Company from Paris had a short Season in Germany. Emilie was with them.

They opened on 16 June, at the *Stadt-theater* in Cologne, with *Sonnambula*. The productions were well received, *Trovatore* and *Lucia* proving to be the most popular.

The Company proceeded to Bad Homburg, where the public warmed particularly to Madame de Méric-Lablache, Sterbini and Antonucci. The advertisements had been published by the *Neue Frankfurter Zeitung* in French under the title '*Hombourg ès Monts, Théâtre du Kurhaus*'. The Season opened on 16 July with *Il Trovatore*, Azucena being entrusted to 'Sgra De Meric-Lablache'. Emilie was billed to play Rosina in the *Barber* (26 July) and to sing a Spanish song and Arditi's *Il Bacio*. To close the Season, on 15 August, the Company staged *Sonnambula*, with Emilie as Lisa, and Act IV of *Rigoletto* in which Emilie played Maddalena. The troupe was under the direction of Antonio Ronzi, with Orsini leading the orchestra. Performances were also given in Frankfurt and Bonn.

HOMBOURG ES MONTS.
Théatre du Kurhaus.

Samedi 16 Juillet 1864:
Première Réprésentation
de la troupe du Théâtre Impérial Italien de Paris.

IL TROVATORE.

Grande Opéra en 4 actes de J. Cammarano. Musique de G. VERDI.

Chef d'Orchestre: Signor Orsini.

Le comte de Luna	Sgr. T. STERBINI.
Leonore	Sgra. G. VITALI.
Azucena, Bohémienne	Sgra. DE MERIC-LABLACHE.
Maurico	Sgr. J. BARAGLI.
Fernando	Sgr. G. ANTONNUCCI.
Inez	Sgra. CHAPISSON.
Ruiz	Mr. ENDERS.
Choeur	

Les Bureaux ouvriront à 6 h. ½.

Le Spectacle commencera à 7 heures.

2388

Notice from – Neue Frankfurter Zeitung.
(By courtesy of the Bibliothèque de l' Opera, Paris.)

A bizarre feature of the 1864 Summer in Bad Homburg, which however presumably did not involve the Italian Company as principals, was a cricket match in the Park between Eleven Gentlemen of the Hombourg Cricket Club and the same number from the Paris Cricket Club. This took place on 10 and 11 August and the announcement about it was given by the German paper in English.

PARIS (1864-1865)

In September 1864, Bagier announced that the *Théâtre Impérial Italien* would open in Paris on 1 October and close on 4 May in the following year. Undeterred by Escudier, he had re-engaged Mme. de Méric-Lablache as a *prima donna*. Other ladies included Mmes. Charton-Demeur, De la Grange, Patti, Penco and the sisters Marchisio. There were six *primi tenori*, notably Fraschini, Naudin, Nicolini and Baragli. The baritones were Agnesi, Delle Sedie and Sterbini; the basses Antonucci, Foli and Marchetti. Bagier had intended to provide a high-class ballet in addition to the opera, but this plan had to be abandoned because of the expense.

DES ARTISTES ENGAGÉS JUSQU'A CE JOUR

Pour Paris et Madrid

Prime donne soprani, mezzo soprani e contralti :

Mmes ADOMALI (Maria),	DE BRIGNI (Clara),
CHARTON-DEMEUR,	DE LA GRANGE (Anna).
DE MÉRIC-LABLACHE,	MARCHISIO (Carlotta),
MARCHISIO (Barbara),	PATTI (Adelina),
PENCO (Rosina),	SPEZIA,
TALVO-BEDOGNI,	VANDER-BEEK (Sidonie),
VITALI (Giuseppina).	

Comprimarie :

Mmes CARANTI-VITA, MOYA, VESTRI.

Primi tenori :

MM. BARAGLI, CORSI, FRASCHINI, NAUDIN.
NEGRINI, NICOLINI.

Tenori comprimari :

MM. ARNOLDI, CAPELLO, LEROY.

Primi baritoni :

MM. ALDIGHIERI, AGNESI, DELLE-SEDIE,
FAGOTTI, STERBINI, ZACCHI.

Primi bassi profondi :

MM. ANTONUCCI, FOLI, MARCHETTI, SELVA, VAIRO.

Altri bassi :

MM. MERCURIALI, PADOVANI.

Buffi :

MM. SCALESE, ZUCCHINI.

Coreografo : M. COSTA.

Primi e secondi Ballerini. — Prime e seconde Ballerine. — Corifee e Corpo di Ballo.

Direttori d'Orchestra e Maestri al cembalo :

MM. BOSONI, GRAFFIGNA, PORTEHAUT.

Direttori del Canto : M. ALARY.

Direttori dei Cori : M. EURAND.

Pittori scenografi : MM. FERRY, BUSATO.

NOTA. La Liste des Artistes de la Danse, composant le Corps de Ballet, sera publiée prochainement.

Part of the prospectus of the Italian Opera Company in Paris, 1864-1865.
(By courtesy of the Bibliothèque Nationale.)

A sore throat having prevented Patti from singing, Bagier postponed his production of *Sonnambula* and the Season opened with *Rigoletto*. The tenor Sarti, from Florence, made a disappointing *début* as the Duke of Mantua. Emilie, though apparently still tired from her exertions in Germany, did well as Maddalena. Appearing next in *Lucrezia Borgia*, she sang the *Brindisi* 'with remarkable brio'. Then, as Azucena, she repeated her success of the previous year and received a curtain call after her scene in Act II. Escudier alone declared that she was the same as ever, exaggerating, but full of zeal – it must be her zeal, he supposed, that her friends applauded, he would do the same in their place. The *Art Musical* pronounced succinctly that she had both sung and acted the part to perfection. This paper also praised her performance as Maddalena after *Rigoletto* had been put on again.

At the end of November, Bagier staged *Ballo* with Emilie, Mme. Charton-Demeur and Fraschini. Verdi's operas were all becoming increasingly popular in Paris and this 1864 *Ballo* was considered to have more than made up for the disaster of the 1863 production. Emilie missed the final performance, through indisposition, being replaced by Mme. Talvo-Bedogni.

Bagier's critics were now complaining not that he was putting on too many operas, but that he was offering no new works. Even Patti, though still much praised, was no longer universally popular and Bagier's expensive 'star system' was blamed for being responsible, in part at least, for his financial difficulties. However, *Marta* was revived, successfully, in November for the *début* of Brignoli, with Emilie, Patti, Delle Sedie and Scalese. Brignoli had been hissed in Madrid, but was acclaimed in Paris.

For Emilie and for Patti, a significant event took place on 18 December, with the revival of *Linda di Chamounix*. This opera, in which Emilie had enjoyed one of her earliest successes, had not been staged in Paris for some fifteen years. Patti was making her European *début* in the title rôle. She excelled herself and *Linda* was exceptionally well received. Even Escudier conceded that Emilie had given general satisfaction as Pierotto. The box-office receipts were the highest of the Season.

This period, the end of 1864, was an important one for the Lablache family as a whole. Nicolas sold, for Fcs.130,000, the splendid property at Maisons-Lafitte which he had inherited from his father.

With the news of this historic sale, *Le Menestrel* ran a series of articles about the great Luigi. Way back in 1846, Lablache and his family had been living in Paris at 14, rue Taitbout. The singer was above all a family man and there was nothing he had liked better than to entertain his close relations and special friends at intimate dinners on the first floor of his apartment. There, the salons were luxuriously furnished. Opposite a picture by Paolo Veronese stood the cabinet which contained the fabulous collection of jewelled snuff-boxes, said to be worth some Fcs.200,000, which Luigi had either been given by Monarchs, Ministers and other high personages throughout Europe or had himself bought. At the dinners, his eldest daughter (Marie) did the honours as hostess, while his wife remained in the background, active in making sure that the domestic arrangements went smoothly. The family living in Paris consisted of his sons Henri, Nicolas and Dominique and the two younger daughters Noninna and Mimi, 'two charming heads *à la Greuze*'. Sometimes they would be joined by Frédéric and his wife and children, when they came over from London. There was a house rule that no 'shop' must be spoken – not a word about music or the theatre.

At Maisons-Lafitte, things were on a grander scale, but no doubt the same atmosphere of luxury combined with homeliness will have greeted Emilie when she married Nicolas there in 1854.

Luigi's well-loved villa in Italy, at Posillipo, had passed after his death to his son-in-law Thalberg. Thalberg was much attached to this property, where he liked to spend the Winter. He prided himself on maintaining the vineyard attached to the villa and enjoyed drinking the Burgundy wines with which Lablache had stocked his cellar.

But to revert to the 1864-1865 Opera Season: when *Rigoletto* was put on again in February, a young *débutante* took the part of Gilda. This was Mlle. Vitali, a niece of Fraschini. The *Revue et Gazette Musicale* said that she did full justice to the rôle and credited her, Fraschini himself, Delle Sedie and Emilie with the success which the performance achieved.

Before the Season closed, Bagier did produce an opera new to Paris. This, in which Emilie played a central rôle, was a melodramatic piece called *La Duchesse de San Giuliano*, by the composer Achille Graffigna. It was based on a fifth-century Florentine legend about a betrayed wife, Veronica, who had her rival's head cut off and served up, with parsley, to her unfaithful ducal husband. All this took place in the Villa Salviati at Fiesole, the magnificent estate near Florence subsequently acquired by Mario. In the opera, Emilie was the victim (Caterina) and Mme. Charton-Demeur the jealous wife. However, in deference to French sensibilities, it was not the severed head which was displayed to the Duke's horrified gaze, but a lifeless corpse on her lover's bed.

The composer was the second *chef d'orchestre* at the *Théâtre Italien* in Paris. His music was described as eminently musicianly and singable, though too reminiscent of Donizetti and Verdi. The cast were praised for interpretations which did justice both to the opera and to themselves. Mme. Charton-Demeur was a splendid Duchess, looking for all the world like one of the fine portraits which enrich the museums of Italy. Mme. de Méric-Lablache put the critic on the *Revue et Gazette Musicale* in mind of Goethe's Marguerite [the innocent girl in his *Faust*]. With her blonde hair and tight-fitting *juste-au-corps*, she had a figure which had never looked younger or more elegant. Vocally, one of her finest pieces had been the touching prayer in the third Act, which she had sung perfectly. This had been encored.

Le Menestrel complained that one of Emilie's arias had been drowned by the orchestra, but considered that hers had been the greatest success of the evening. The romance in Act II, *Sulla deserta coltrice*, was very graceful and had been sung with rare taste and feeling. In the part of Caterina, Emilie had pleased the *Menestrel* critic more than in any other. Similarly, *L'Art Musical* wrote that Emilie had never before been given a part better suited to her talents. She had been touching and *sympathique* and had not suffered a single lapse. The whole audience had responded with rapturous applause. In the pathetic prayer in Act III, she had been beyond praise and her success had assumed the proportions of a triumph.

Graffigna was judged to have done well, though Escudier remarked acidly that such a story, with all its gory horrors, was bound to attract a composer of the Verdi school. The cast, with the composer, were given two curtain calls and the opera ran to seven performances (as against one each for *Don Giovanni* and *Norma*), but it disappeared from the repertoire.

In *Don Giovanni*, Emilie took the part of Zerlina, with Mme. Frezzolini as Donna Anna.

Emilie's singing apart from opera included, at the end of March 1865, one of Rossini's famous 'Saturdays'. She sang Gounod's *Ave Maria*, accompanied by Diémer and Sarasate. Rossini made her promise to come another Saturday to sing the romance from *La Duchesse de San Giuliano* of which he had heard so much praise. This was indeed generous, because Rossini was notorious for claiming that France was the land of pretty women, little *pâtés* and good wine – a charming country that only needed contraltos to make it perfect. Perhaps Emilie was the exception to prove the rule.

The singers and orchestra of the *Théâtre Italien* had been invited to perform at the third concert of the Season at the Imperial Court. Emilie sang an *arioso* from *Le Prophète*, a duet from Mercadante's *Giuramento*, with Mlle. Vitali, and the quintet *E scherzo e follia* from *Ballo* with Mlle. Vitali, Fraschini, Delle Sedie and Zucchini. *La France Musicale* reported that the *arioso*, sung with great feeling by Mme. de Méric-Lablache, had been particularly appreciated, but the honours of the evening had gone to the quintet. At a private concert given by Mme. de Biré in the Faubourg Saint-Germain, Emilie sang in quartets from *Rigoletto* and *Marta* with Mlle. Vitali, Gardoni and Delle Sedie.

THÉÂTRE IMPÉRIAL ITALIEN

1865

JEUDI 13 Avril, à 8 heures du soir

CONCERT SPIRITUEL

STABAT MATER

De ROSSINI

PROGRAMME

PREMIÈRE PARTIE

1. **Chœur** et **Soli** : *Stabat Mater*.
   Mmes VANDERBECK, TALVO-BEDOGNI, MM. CORSI et FOLY.

2. **Air** : *Cujus animam gementem*.
   M. BRIGNOLI.

3. **Duo** : *Quis est Homo!*
   Mmes CHARTON-DEMEUR et DE MÉRIC-LABLACHE.

4. **Air** : *Pro peccatis*.
   M. AGNESI.

5. **Chœur** et **Récit** : *Eja Mater fons amoris*.
   M. FOLY.

DEUXIÈME PARTIE

6. **Quatuor** : *Sancta Mater*.
   Mmes CHARTON-DEMEUR, TALVO-BEDOGNI, MM. CORSI, AGNESI.

7. **Cavatine** : *Fac ut portem*.
   Mme TALVO-BEDOGNI.

8. **Quatuor** : *Quando Corpus*.
   Mmes CHARTON-DEMEUR, DE MÉRIC-LABLACHE, MM. BRIGNOLI, AGNESI.

9. **Air** et **Chœur** : *Inflammatus*.
   Mme CHARTON-DEMEUR.

10. **Finale** : *Amen*.
    TUTTI.

Programme of Sacred Concert at the Théâtre Italien in April 1865.

(By courtesy of the Bibliothèque de l' Opéra, Paris.)

292

In Holy Week 1865, the Italian Company performed Rossini's *Stabat*, as they had for the past twenty-five years. They also gave a rendering of Alary's popular oratorio *Redenzione*. This had been sung in French, which *Le Menestrel* thought had put Mmes. Charton-Demeur, de Méric-Lablache and Talvo-Bedogni 'a little more at their ease than usual'.

SAMEDI 15 AVRIL
à 8 heures du soir

LA RÉDEMPTION

Mystère en cinq parties, avec Prologue et Épilogue,

Poëme de MM. ÉMILE DESCHAMPS et ÉMILIEN PACINI, Musique de GIULIO ALARY

PROGRAMME

PROLOGUE : LA CÈNE

Le Chœur récitant — **M. JOUANNI** — Les Apôtres.

1re PARTIE
LE JARDIN DES OLIVIERS

Le Messie...........	**M. FRASCHINI**
Judas Iscariotte.......	**M. AGNESI**
Jean...............	**M. VERGER**
Pierre.............	**M. LEROY**
	Mlle VITALI
Quatre Anges........	**Mlle VANDERBECK**
	Mme DE MÉRIC-LABLACHE
	Mme TALVO-BEDOGNI

Les Apôtres, Chœur de Soldats.

2me PARTIE
LE SANHEDRIN

Strophes............	**M. JOUANNI**
Pierre.............	**M. FRASCHINI**
Judas...............	**M. AGNESI**
Caïphe.............	

Les Apôtres, Chœurs de Soldats.

3me PARTIE
LE JUGEMENT

Strophes............	**M. JOUANNI**
Le Messie...........	**M. FRASCHINI**
Caïphe.............	**M. AGNESI**
Ponce Pilate........	**M. VERGER**
La Foi..............	**Mme CHARTON-DEMEUR**
L'Espérance.........	**Mlle VANDERBECK**
La Charité..........	**Mme TALVO-BEDOGNI**

Chœurs de Prêtres, Soldats, Peuple.

4me PARTIE
LE GOLGOTHA — LES STATIONS

Strophes...........	**M. JOUANNI**
Le Messie...........	**M. FRASCHINI**
Le Juif Errant.......	
Un Héraut...........	
Un Centurion........	**M. AGNESI**
Un Soldat Romain....	
Premier Juif........	**M. MERCURIALI**
Simon le Cyrénéen....	**M. VERGER**
Deuxième Juif.......	**M. LEROY**
La Vierge Marie.....	**Mme CHARTON-DEMEUR**
Une jeune Fille......	**Mlle VITALI**

5me PARTIE
LES SEPT PAROLES

Strophes............	**M. JOUANNI**
Le Messie...........	**M. FRASCHINI**
Jean...............	**M. VERGER**
Dismas le bon Larron	**M. GHISLANI**
Troisième Soldat....	
Gesmas le mauvais Lar.	**M. AGNESI**
Le Centurion........	
Premier Soldat......	**M. MERCURIALI**
Deuxième Soldat....	**M. LEROY**
La Vierge Marie.....	**Mme CHARTON-DEMEUR**
Marie Cléophas.......	**Mme TALVO-BEDOGNI**
Madeleine...........	**Mme DE MÉRIC-LABLACHE**

ÉPILOGUE : LA RÉSURRECTION

Voix du Ciel, Mmes **VITALI, VANDERBECK, DE MÉRIC-LABLACHE, TALVO-BEDOGNI**

Programme of Sacred Concert given by the Italian Opera Company in Paris on 15 April 1865.
(By courtesy of the Bibliothèque de l' Opéra, Paris.)

Britain and Ireland, 1865

FOR whatever reasons, Emilie left Paris in 1865. The villa at Maisons had been sold and it was announced in August that Nicolas Lablache had resigned from the functions which he had been performing at the *Théâtre Italien*. The Electoral Roll at Maisons-Lafitte lists Nicolas Lablache as a *propriétaire* there from 1860 to 1864 only. From that date it becomes increasingly difficult to follow Nicolas or to determine how much he and Emilie were together. Emilie's singing career is quite well documented and it is clear that in 1865 she embarked on what proved to be a prolonged 'Anglo-Saxon' period which was to take her all over the British Isles and much of the United States of America.

The ambitious English impresario 'Colonel' James Henry Mapleson (1830-1901) had recruited Emilie to join the Company from Her Majesty's Theatre in London which was to embark on a provincial tour in Britain and Ireland in the Autumn of 1865. (In Paris, Bagier had engaged Mlle. Grossi, from London, to take Emilie's place. That young lady was to be praised by French critics for her trim figure and for legs as well turned as those of Madame de Méric-Lablache.)

The music critic Joseph Bennett (1831-1911) recounts in his *Forty Years of Music* that his editor had asked him to cover a concert in the early Spring of 1865. This, he thought, had been in the newly-erected St. James's Hall. 'The only points I clearly recall in connection with it', he wrote, 'are the appearance of Madame de Méric-Lablache and the sense of responsibility with which I prepared a notice for my chief [Henry Coleman.]' No other reference to this concert has been discovered. Certainly the date is doubtful, as Emilie was still in Paris in the early part of 1865.

Mapleson's principal contralto in London had been Mme. Trebelli. He could not engage her for his touring company because of her engagements in Germany and he recruited Emilie in her place. The tour opened in September 1865 with six nights in Manchester. Mapleson had a strong team. Mlle. Tietjens and Mario were his two stars and the Company included Madame Sinico, Mlle. Sarolta, Bossi and Santley. Arditi conducted.

St. James's *Hall.*
(By courtesy of Illustrated London News, 1856.)

In Manchester, Emilie duly played Azucena (9 September) and Maddalena 'in which she was above the requirements of the part' (*Manchester Daily Examiner and Times*), but the rôles of Siebel, Adalgisa and Zerlina were entrusted to Mlle. Sarolta.

L. Haase & Comp.
Königl. Hof-Photographen
und Hof-Photographen I. K. Hoheit der Frau
Kronprinzessin v. Preussen.
Berlin   Breslau
178. Friedrichsstr. 178.   10. Tauenzienstr. 10.
Cöln
Königin-Augusta-Halle (Passage) 39.

Emilie de Méric Lablache, about 1865.
Carte-de-visite photograph in the author's possession.

Before the end of September, Mapleson and his Company were in Dublin, a city with a long and distinguished musical tradition. For Emilie it had the further great advantage of being the home of some of her closest relations. Her maternal uncle Eugène de Méric (1809-1875), sometimes honoured with the title of Count, had been *chancelier* at the French Consulate there since 1853. By then he had already been living in Dublin for many years, teaching. Back in May 1839 he had married Rosalie d'Arenberg (or Abeltshauser), the daughter of another French family which for reasons not altogether clear had also moved from Strasbourg to Ireland. So when Emilie arrived in Dublin she found a well-established family to welcome her. Eugène's daughters Sophie (26) and Marie Clémentine (23), known in the family as Mysie, were there and Emilie gave a photograph of herself to them inscribed, in French, 'to my dear nieces'. This is now in the possession of the author. Nephew Eugène Victor (19), grandfather of the author's late wife, did not become an Assistant Surgeon in the Royal Navy until 1866 and he was also in Dublin to greet his aunt Emilie in 1865.

Two manuscript letters dated 1865 and 1866 which Joséphine wrote from Paris to her sister-in-law Rosalie de Méric in Dublin have survived. They are reproduced here by courtesy of Lieut-Commander M.A. de Méric R.N. (retd).

The first explains that Emilie had written to her aunt Rosalie to announce her impending arrival in Dublin but had inadvertently posted the letter in an envelope addressed to her Mother. In passing the letter on, Joséphine apologises for not having written to Rosalie sooner, but she had been in low spirits. She was finding it most difficult to get used to Emilie being away. She was also short of money and having to think of taking up teaching again: she only hoped that pupils would not desert her, the French were so fickle. Were she but rich, she would go off to Nice for six months and take Rosalies's two daughters with her.

As it was, Emilie and Emilie's children were her consolation. Emilie seemed to have been highly successful in England and was surely now 'a great artist'. The three children (Louise, Henri and Anna) were adorable and affectionate – Louise (then aged about ten) was 'grace personified'. Joséphine's great joy was to be able to spend a day with them.

The letter is evidence of Joséphine's attachment to the wide circle of her family. If niece Mysie wanted a job, let her come to Paris: Joséphine had many contacts and felt sure she could help. Brother Eugène was hoping for promotion in the Consular Service: she had lobbied an official who had assured her that the matter was going well at the Ministry (actually Eugène was to be disappointed). She was gratified that young nephew Eugène was showing an interest in Italian music. Finally, Emilie's 'distinguished' husband, Nicolas, was being very kind to her in her old age (64).

There was also another family connexion which may have smoothed Emilie's path on her first appearance in the Irish capital. By arrangement, presumably, with Mapleson, the Italian operas were being presented by Augustus Glossop Harris, Emilie's half-brother. The *Irish Times* of 14 September 1865 contained an announcement by Harris giving a full list of the artistes engaged and promising a two-week programme.

The Season at the Theatre Royal opened on 20 September with *Rigoletto*. This opera had been very seldom produced in Dublin. By 1865 the 'Verdi fever' was subsiding and the *Irish Times* thought that the main reason for including it in the repertoire was to show Mario (the Duke) and Mlle. Sarolta (Gilda) to the best advantage. Emilie played Maddalena and according to the *Freeman's Journal* acquitted herself admirably. The *Irish Times* considered that the gem of the opera had been the quartet *Bella figlia* sung by Mario, Santley, Madame Lablache and Mlle. Sarolta.

For her Azucena (27 September), Emilie received rather less than the customary praise. Despite her admirable taste and judgment, her voice lacked the power which had made Alboni and Viardot Garcia so famous as the gipsy (*The Freeman's Journal*). The *Irish Times* gave her only second rating as a singer, 'but her judicious and vigorous acting made her version of *Stride la vampa* more than usually successful' and she had exhibited singular declamatory power in the descriptive passage which followed.

Again, as Maffeo Orsini in *Lucrezia Borgia*, Emilie seemed to the *Irish Times* to be inferior in voice to the singers Dublin had heard in the part. However, 'Madame De Méric Lablache is a very clever actress . . . [and] her acting carried off whatever deficiences were discovered in her vocalism, and her version of the familiar *Il segreto* thoroughly deserved the encore which it received.' Mario had declined to respond to demands for encores, to save his voice.

The other operas in which Emilie appeared in Dublin were *Marta* (as Nancy) and *Ballo* (Ulrica). *Marta* was a prime favourite there. This was due, no doubt, to the many well-known Irish melodies which it contains, particularly *The Last Rose of Summer*. *Ballo* had only been produced once or twice before in Dublin. According to the *Irish Times*, Emilie had acted very finely and had declaimed with great energy and effect the difficult theme *Re dell'abisso*.

The *Annals of the Theatre Royal, Dublin* speak of Madame de Méric Lablache 'coming out' during this engagement:

> 'And a more substantial, universally-accomplished lady could hardly be found, with a voice (mezzo-soprano) almost contralto in quality and in general fulfilling parts of this class. Mdme. De Méric Lablache is "under studied" in almost every part in the Operatic Calendar, and therefore, in cases of illness or disappointment, from whatever cause, this most useful of "members" is ready at a moment's notice to become the *prima* or *seconda donna*, and has often, by so doing, relieved the management of much embarrassment.'

The Company gave a Morning Concert in the Antient [sic] Concert Rooms on Friday 6 October 1865.

From Dublin, the Company moved to Glasgow where the city's *première* of *Faust* was given at the Theatre Royal on 9 October. Emilie was not in that cast, but appeared as Azucena on 11 October and took part in the Grand Morning Concert two days later, being described as Mdlle. Demeric-Lablache.

There followed a programme of five nights (16-20 October) at the Theatre Royal in Liverpool. Emilie was billed to sing Azucena on 17 October, but was not in the casts of *Faust*, *Norma* or *Don Giovanni*. A Saturday Morning Concert was given at the Philharmonic Hall (beginning at three o'clock). The advertisement for this concert placed Emilie's name below those of Tietjens, Sinico and Sarolta. The highest admission charges in Liverpool were 10s.6d. for the operas and 5s. for the concert.

In November 1865 both Emilie and her husband were in

London. They were present as witnesses at an important occasion for the Lablache family. As recorded in the Roman Catholic Register held at Archbishop's House, Westminster Cathedral: on 8 November, in the French Chapel, Johann Rokitansky [the Austrian bass] married Thérèse Lablache, eldest daughter of Frédéric Lablache and his wife Fanny Wyndham. Emilie signed 'E. Lablache de Méric'. Other witnesses were Julius Benedict and the baritone Ciabatta. Virginia Arditi represented the conductor's family.

A week later, Emilie was down on the coast in Brighton where, on 15 November, the composer and pianist Wilhelm Kuhe gave his annual concert in the Town Hall. He was supported by several other members of Mapleson's Company, including Tietjens, Gardoni and Santley. One of the chief honours went to the organist, Louis Engel, who is credited with having 'established' the harmonium in England. The *Brighton Gazette* described Emilie as a contralto of great power. She had been encored for *Ah, mon fils*, which she had sung with much feeling and expression.

Brighton Town Hall.
(By courtesy of The East Sussex County Library.)

Provincial concert tour, 1866

Emilie in 1866. Photograph by
A. Graves et Cie.
(By courtesy of The Cabinet des Estampes,
Bibliothèque Nationale, Paris.)

THE small group from Her Majesty's Theatre which Mapleson had
collected for his provincial concert tour in 1866 consisted of Mario,
Grisi, Emilie and the Irish bass Allan James Foley (1835-1899),

known as Signor Foli, who had made his London *début* at Her Majesty's in 1865. The conductor was Luigi Arditi and he was accompanied by his daughter, the violin soloist Emilia. Arditi had been approached by Bagier, but the salary which Bagier could offer in Paris had not proved sufficiently attractive.

Emilie was to have a long professional association with both Mapleson and Arditi. With Arditi there was also a personal connexion. As he was to recall many years later in 'My Reminiscences' (1896): 'Of my old friend, and godmother to my son, Madame Demeric Lablache, I think with much affection . . . . Everyone knew her to be an artist to her finger-tips, besides being a woman of extraordinary charm, intelligence and ability.' The son to whom Arditi referred was born in July 1866.

The Mapleson tour began in Nottingham on 10 January. There could be no question of such a small group staging operas and they confined themselves to concerts. In Nottingham, the concert was under the auspices of the city's Sacred Harmonic Society which enjoyed 'the immediate and distinguished patronage of the Duke of Newcastle and several members of the Clinton family'. However, unforeseen circumstances had prevented these noble personages from being present and it had also been feared that the principal singers would fail to appear. A snowstorm in London the previous day had thrown the cab service out of gear and Mapleson's group had missed the train by which they would have reached Grantham by the appointed time. As the *Nottingham Journal* reported, 'The officials at that station, on learning the state of things, courteously allowed a carriage or two to be attached to a coal train to Nottingham' and it was in that way that the singers were able to reach their destination.

The concert was in two parts. First, Rossini's *Stabat Mater*, 'which has so long and deservedly held a high place among the admirers of classical music' and secondly 'a selection of charming miscellaneous secular pieces.'

The audience proved appreciative. Mario and Grisi naturally had to give encores. Foli had used his powerful bass voice 'with great taste and judgment'. Emilie had displayed her voice with great ability in the solo *cavatina Fac ut portem* and had sung Donizetti's ballad *Il Segreto* with much sweetness. Even the *Revue et Gazette Musicale de Paris* devoted a short paragraph to the 'immense success' of the performance of the *Stabat* in Nottingham.

After Nottingham, it was Leeds. The *Leeds Mercury* had advertised a Great Musical Treat at the Town Hall on Wednesday 17 January which was to be 'positively the LAST TIME of GRISI and MARIO in Leeds'. To judge from an article in the *Leeds Intelligencer* of 20 January, these two famous singers had failed to fulfil their engagements in the city on more than one previous occasion. That, the paper remarked, might explain why the room had not been crowded as it deserved.

Leeds Town Hall, by C. Fenn.
(By courtesy of Leeds City Libraries.)

This time, Mario and Grisi had duly appeared and 'No one could have listened to the concert last Wednesday without the greatest pleasure possible. A more delightful one we have scarcely ever heard; it seemed to be the aim of all the artistes to do their utmost to gratify the audience'.

Emilie had sung very pleasingly and received a well-deserved encore for *Voi che sapete*. She sang the trio from *Semiramide* with Grisi and Foli and took part in the quartet from Rossini's *Conte Ory*. Mario had obliged, as an encore, with *Come into the garden, Maud*.

After, it seems, a concert in Newcastle (19 January), the group went on to Scotland, where performances were given in Glasgow, Greenock, Dundee, Aberdeen, Perth and Edinburgh. In Aberdeen, the public had been offered as a special attraction a rendering by Mario of *Comè gentil*, from *Don Pasquale*, described as *Oh, Summer Night*. The most expensive seats there were five shillings and the *Aberdeen Herald* reported with satisfaction that the concert had been remunerative to the organiser.

303

Theatre Royal, Newcastle on Tyne.
(By courtesy of The Theatre Museum, Victoria and Albert Museum.)

After the concert in Edinburgh (27 January), the *Evening Courant* devoted a paragraph to Emilie which was not entirely flattering:

> 'Madame Demeric Lablache has a contralto voice of considerable richness and flexibility, and a pleasing appearance and manner, but her singing is greatly marred by an unpleasant habit of indulging in tremolo. She might take example in this matter from Madame Grisi, who, with all the wear and tear that her voice has gone through, never shows the slightest tendency to vibration. We would be inclined to look with leniency on this failing in a singer whose best days are past, but can hardly show it the same toleration when deliberately adopted as a trick of fashion. A little more distinctness in enunciating her words would also be an improvement. Madame Lablache's solo songs were *Ah quel giorno* (*Semiramide*), *Voi che sapete* (*Le Nozze di Figaro*) and *Il Segreto* (*Lucrezia*), the latter given after an "encore"'.

Was the tremolo indeed fashionable?

Emilia Arditi had played three violin solos. A comment by the *Evening Courant* casts light on an attitude towards women prevalent at the time:

> 'The performances of the Miss Drechsler-Hamiltons have already habituated the Edinburgh public to the idea of violin playing as an accomplishment not inconsistent with feminine gracefulness of deportment . . . .'

From Edinburgh, the group gave a performance in Dumfries and then returned to England.

The *Wiltshire County Mirror* informed its readers that a Grand Concert would be given in the Assembly Rooms in Salisbury on 2 February at which the vocalists would be Mme. Grisi, Mme. De Méric-Lablache, Foli and Mario. The solo violinist would be Mlle. Arditi and Arditi would conduct. The concert would commence at eight o'clock and carriages might be ordered for ten. The most expensive seats would cost five shillings.

The Salisbury paper gave a glowing account of the way the concert had gone. The two great singers of the age had been in splendid voice. When Mario gave an encore, singing the elegant serenade from *Don Pasquale Comè gentil*, with the other artistes supplying the chorus, there had been a torrent of applause and 'the frigid propriety which usually rules in this class of concert was broken through during the evening.' Emilie's 'mellow mezzo-soprano' had told well both in *Voi che sapete* and in the concerted pieces.

The next day, Saturday 3 February, the group gave a matinée performance at the Philharmonic Rooms in Southampton, where the most expensive seats were six shillings.

From Southampton it was no great distance to Bath and the next concert was given at the Assembly Rooms there on 6 February. The *Bath Chronicle* of 8 February drew attention to the exhibition in the Assembly Rooms of a curious creature called the Yahmo, or man-fish, which was said to be a veritable merman. On the same page, the paper devoted a column to the Evening Concert. This had been organised by Mr. H. N. King, who, curiously enough, was both Photographer to the Queen and the composer of a ballad called 'Today and Tomorrow'. This ballad was one of Grisi's 'encore' pieces.

The *Chronicle* emphasised that the appearance of two artists such as Mario and Grisi 'in a city like this where the art to which they have devoted themselves is so highly appreciated' was sure to bring together a large audience. The house had indeed been full. All the same, the paper found it difficult to reconcile itself to the spectacle of a lady playing the violin. Evidently Bath had not had the conditioning experience which had helped the good people of Edinburgh to accept the phenomenon. 'Custom has confined its use to men, and one of the gentle sex who plays it in public has the air of one defying custom and vindicating women's rights.' Romantic heroines 'should bend gracefully over the harp or sit as gracefully at the piano . . . . Venus herself would hardly look engaging if she were playing the fiddle.' Engaging or not, Mlle Arditi was admitted to have given great pleasure by her performance.

The concert as a whole evoked a mixed response from the *Chronicle*. It had started 'with something less than precise punctuality'. Much of the performance had consisted of familiar music, with Rossini furnishing the largest share. Emilie had sung *Ah quel giorno* from *Semiramide* and was found to have a pleasant voice and good method, but to be somewhat inexpressive. Her performance had obtained 'only complimentary notice'. She and Foli had executed the duet *Dunque io son,* from *Il Barbiere,* 'fairly enough'. After Grisi's rendering of *Home, sweet home,* the duet from *Trovatore Se m'ami ancor,* by Mario and Mme. Lablache 'had seemed tame' and even the excellent trio from *Semiramide L'usato ardir* had attracted little attention, though the singers had been Madame Grisi, Madame Demeric-Lablache and Signor Foli.

The second part of the concert had begun with a quartet, the prayer from Rossini's *Conte Ory,* 'an opera almost unknown in this country'. Then Emilie had sung *Voi che sapete,* transposed, of course, to suit her range of voice. With Grisi, she had sung *Giorno d'orrore,* from *Semiramide.* Foli had sung Arditi's spirited song *The Stirrup Cup,* but that had been somewhat spoilt because many of the audience were already hurrying away. The concert had ended with the 'inevitable' spinning quartet from *Marta.* (All in all, one is left wondering whether the singers had not been on top of their form or whether the Bath audience were not quite as musical as they thought themselves.)

Press reporting on the concerts and operas during the period under review seldom gave any personal notes about the performers. In Bath, though, the *Chronicle* stated that the group had all stayed at the York House Hotel. Emilie had with her there 'Mlle. Lablache', presumably her ten-year-old daughter Louise.

The group were now nearing the end of their concert tour and preparing for seasons of Italian opera, to start in Scotland. En route, they gave a Morning Concert at the New Town Hall in Newcastle on 17 February 1866. Here they were joined by Tietjens, Bossi and the 25-year-old Sicilian tenor Roberto Stagno. The *Newcastle Weekly* declared that such a galaxy of talent had seldom if ever been equalled in Newcastle. The programme included a recital from Gounod's *Faust,* with Emilie as Siebel. Mario had not been well enough to take his place as Faust and Stagno had stepped in at short notice, 'with marked success'. Bossi was Mephistopheles.

CHAPTER 38

Mapleson's Operatic Company, 1866

WITHOUT respite, the Mapleson Company gave a nine-night Season of opera at the Theatre Royal in Edinburgh beginning on Monday 19 February 1866. They opened with Gounod's *Faust*, the first time that that opera had been performed in Scotland. Arditi conducted.

No Italian opera had been produced in Edinburgh for several years and the *Edinburgh Courant* hoped that 'the enterprise of Mr. Wood in bringing together so excellent a company will meet with such unequivocal encouragement from the public that opera will once more be considered as permanently established in Edinburgh.'

On the first night there was 'a brilliant audience in the stalls and boxes' and every part of the house was filled to overflowing. Most of the limelight naturally fell on Mario, Grisi and Tietjens.

Emilie seems to have pleased the public more than the critics. In *Faust*, she played Siebel, the respectable lover of Gretchen (Tietjens) whom Mephistopheles tries to keep out of her way. The *Courant* thought that Emilie's acting was better than her singing, which was marred by 'a constant indulgence in tremolo effects'.

As Azucena (21 February), Emilie gave what the *Scotsman* described as a very praiseworthy performance. This part was a great mainstay throughout her career and the *Scotsman* drew attention to her good conception of the character. In the scene where she is dragged before the Count, her acting and singing had been full of true dramatic fire. The duet with Mario in the prison had been beautifully sung by both artists.

After an appearance in *Lucrezia*, Emilie played Zerlina in a memorable production of *Don Giovanni* (24 February). According to the critic on the *Scotsman*, this was only the second time that the Edinburgh public had had the opportunity of witnessing Mozart's *chef d'oeuvre* in anything approaching its integrity. The only other occasion had been in 1853, the year when Mr. Wood had inaugurated a successful series of annual opera Seasons. Even in London, the critic said, *Don Giovanni* had not been given with the whole of the music until 1833. Then, he himself had had the good fortune to hear it at Drury Lane 'with a great cast'. That cast, it may be remembered, included Joséphine de Méric as Donna Anna.

Emilie was praised for her acting as the coquettish *paysanne*; 'she had looked the part to perfection', but fault was found with her singing. Her voice and style did not do justice to Zerlina's lovely arias and the tremolo tarnished her best efforts (the *Scotsman*). The *Courant* complained that her singing occasionally lacked finish and was at times injured by a disagreeable throatiness of tone. Opinions differed about the effectiveness of *Là ci darem*, which Emilie sang with Caravoglio as the Don, but *Batti, batti* seems to have gone down well and *Vedrai carino* was encored. 'Zerlina's tender cajoling was sufficient to have disarmed the most strongheaded Masetto' (the *Courant*).

When *Semiramide* was performed, by special desire, on 26 February, Emilie had the breeches part of Arsace. Again, the *Courant* wished that her singing had been as good as her acting, but admitted that she had several times 'received unequivocal marks of approbation from the audience.'

From Edinburgh, the opera company moved to Glasgow for an eight-night Season opening on 1 March 1866. The programme was virtually the same as in Edinburgh, with a full orchestra and chorus, conducted by Arditi. The most expensive seats were 8s.6d.

Emilie received good notices for her Siebel and Azucena. In praise of her singing, the *Glasgow Morning Journal* singled out her duet with Mario in *Trovatore* (*Si, la stanchezza*), where she implores Manrico to return to 'our mountain'; and the *North British Daily Mail* said that she had sung the Orsini air *Il segreto*, in *Lucia*, delightfully.

Semiramide was given its Glasgow *première*. Both Tietjens and Emilie were repeatedly applauded. The duet *Giorno d'orrore* brought the house down. Between the Acts and at the end of the performance the two singers were showered with bouquets. The *Morning Journal* had been impressed by Emilie's Arsace:

> 'The heaviest portion of the work fell to Madame Lablache, and she sustained herself with great consistency throughout. In some of the many airs set down for Arsace she surpassed any of her former appearances in this city, and her every effort was deservedly followed by enthusiastic applause. A special compliment is due to Madame Lablache for her tasteful and handsome "make-up".'

However, *Semiramide* had given the Glasgow audience some amusement which was far removed from the opera's tragic theme. The slaves were seen to have black faces but white necks. One of the fair singers performed a pirouette when she found to her surprise that she was on stage and not in the wings: this had been rendered all the more attractive by the shortness of her Babylonian costume. Then there had been an audible titter when Semiramide was observed to be reading some very affecting news from a scroll held well away from her face and obviously containing no legible writing.

As in Edinburgh, Emilie's Zerlina was regarded as a weak link in the cast of *Don Giovanni*, but the *North British Daily Mail* wrote that her vocalisation had been marked by genuine artistic taste 'and might have been better appreciated had Zerlina not been so generally heard as a soprano part.'

Emilie. Photograph by Disdéri.
(By courtesy of the Musée Carnavalet, Paris.)

From Glasgow to Dublin, which brings us to the second letter from Joséphine to her sister-in-law. This is dated 8 March 1866 and announces that Emilie will be sailing from Glascow [sic] to Dublin on 10 March, for a stay of a fortnight. Joséphine fully expects the whole of her brother's family to be gathered to welcome Emilie again.

Joséphine says how glad she is that Emilie has been making 'a truly triumphal tour' throughout England, but she feels sad for the 'poor child' being separated from her husband and children and being obliged by her exhausting profession to spend half her time in trains.

Both Joséphine and Nicolas had been distraught because of the vagaries of the post: so many letters had gone missing and there had been no news of Emilie.

In her widowhood, Joséphine evidently felt very lonely at this period. In one telling sentence, she speaks of her sadness at living in the same city as a brother and other close relations 'and being completely forgotten'. Her chief contact with her brother Hector Alexandre appears to have been in connexion with a family lawsuit in Strasbourg. This had been won, but had produced little financial benefit. Even over this matter, her brother had left a letter unanswered for two months.

It was apparently a journey of twelve hours from Glasgow to Dublin and Joséphine characteristically wondered how well Emilie would withstand such a sea-voyage.

Letter written by Joséphine in 1866.
(By courtesy of Lieut-Commander M.A. de Méric R.N. (retd).

310

On 12 March 1866 a crowded and fashionable first-night audience enjoyed a performance of *Faust*. The Lord Lieutenant and Lady Wodehouse were in the State Box. The *Freeman's Journal* described *Faust* as 'one of those things that is destined to endure and to be classed among the highest achievements of the composers of lyric drama'. Emilie, as Siebel, had fully sustained her high reputation as an accomplished musician and vocalist.

In *Lucrezia Borgia*, which followed, Emilie gave what the *Journal* described as a charming personation of Orsini:

> 'Her voice possessed all the rich sweetness of the true contralto, and she used it throughout . . . with all the grace and expressive power of a genuine artist. She was most happy in her rendering of the famous '*Brindisi*' '*Il Segreto*', which she had to repeat at the unanimous call of the house.'

Emilie appeared next as Nancy in *Marta*. There is nothing more deservedly popular, declared the *Journal*, than Flotow's delicious opera. Yet, in the 1990s, how many opera-lovers are familiar with it? This light-hearted piece, subtitled *Richmond Fair*, recounts the adventures of a Maid of Honour to Queen Anne (Lady Harriet) and her maid (Nancy) who, as a joke, go to the Fair disguised as country girls (Martha and Julia) and then find that they have let themselves become bound by contracts to enter the service of two farmers (Lionel and Plunkett). The farmers of course fall in love with them, but Lionel turns out to be a nobleman, his love is returned and the opera ends with two happy marriages.

Over five years had passed since *Marta* was first performed in Dublin. Then, the stars had been Grisi, Viardot Garcia, Mario and Graziani. That had been one of the finest casts the opera can ever have enjoyed (Elizabeth Forbes). By 1866, Grisi and Mario were still most accomplished actors, but their voices, alas, seemed 'but a memory of their former selves'.

As Nancy, Emilie was spared comparisons with Viardot:

> 'There is nothing that gives us more sincere pleasure than to be called to give exalted merit its reward and indeed we have no hesitation in now stating that Madame De Méric Lablache was fully entitled to the cordial expressions of approbation which were called forth by her efforts last evening. In addition to a magnificent contralto voice, not, perhaps, as remarkable for power as for a mellow richness of tone, she possess an exquisite ear, refined taste and

musical knowledge . . . in her aria *Il tuo stral* she threw a grace and vivacity into her vocalism and acting that won for her golden opinions. In the concerted pieces generally, she was most effective and did much to "bring the house down" in an unanimous call for an encore of the celebrated "Spinning Wheel Quartet".'

St. Patrick's Ball at the Castle took much of the limelight from the first night of *Il Trovatore*, but there was also 'the fact that the music of Verdi is not as popular now as it was a few years ago, and is fast finding its proper level in public estimation'. Thus the *Freeman's Journal*. 'The opera on which the fame of Verdi principally rests,' the *Journal* continued, 'is not likely to prove a permanent basis, if we are to judge by its decline in general favour, which is more rapid than its rise has been. Amongst the lovers of genuine music it had few admirers, but amongst the brilliant novelties of its time it must be assigned a prominent position'.

A major attraction of the Season was to be *Don Giovanni*. For the performance on 17 March the house was well and fashionably filled and as it was St. Patrick's night 'the celestials' were in the best possible humour. As soon as Arditi appeared with the orchestra, everyone called out for "Patrick's Day", which was then played amidst a storm of applause. For the opera, the instrumentalists received more praise than the singers. If we are to believe the *Journal*, Mario was miscast as Don Ottavio [!], the music of Donna Anna was too much for Grisi, particularly in the higher register, and Caravoglio was an utter failure as the Don. Only Bossi (Leporello) and Emilie escaped the strictures. The *Journal* 'had the most pleasing duty to refer in the terms of warm praise to the singing of Mdlle. [sic] de Méric Lablache in the role of Zerlina. Her acting was most natural and her rendering of the famous *Batti, batti* won an imperative demand for its repetition.' With her 'finely-educated and sweet-toned contralto voice', she had sung *Vedrai carino* charmingly and this too had been encored. The *Journal* felt that it had every reason to expect Emilie's career to be a briliant one. She was then thirty-five.

Don Giovanni was repeated at the end of the second week, on both the Friday and Saturday. The *Annals* said this marked the third and final "last appearance" of Grisi.

As a break in the provincial tour, Mapleson had a Season in London, at Her Majesty's, in the Spring and Summer of 1866. Emilie remained with him. By this time, she had more than one family connexion in London. Her mother's brother, Dr. Victor de Méric FRCS.,MD., had been living in Upper Baker Street since 1852 and remained in the Marylebone area until his death in 1876. Her brother-in-law, the singer Frédéric Lablache, had been domiciled in London since 1848, residing at various addresses in Albany Street. He lived until 1887, then his son Luigi remained in the same house. Emilie's half-brother Augustus had by 1866 become Administrator at Covent Garden, under the Director, Gye. Harris' company included Adelina Patti, with Costa as the conductor.

In August, Harris was in Paris where his daughter, the brunette Mary Harris, was on the stage at the Porte Saint-Martin in a *fantaisie à grand spectacle*, with singing and dancing, called *Les Parisiens à Londres*. According to the *Revue et Gazette Musicale de Paris*, she played with infinite sweetness and grace a part half in English and half in French which had been specially written for her.

In 1867, Arditi and his wife went to live at 41, Albany Street, where Arditi recalled that they had often had the pleasure of entertaining Frédéric Lablache and his wife (Fanny Wyndham). No doubt Emilie would also have been a guest there.

Emilie in one of her fine gowns.

(*By courtesy of The Columbia University Library – Dramatic Museum Portraits.*)

Then there was Johann Rokitansky, who had married Frédéric's daughter Thérèse. That *primo basso profundo* 'from the Imperial Opera, Vienna and the principal theatres of Italy' performed at Her Majesty's in 1866 as Osmin in *Il Seraglio*, as the Commendatore in *Don Giovanni* and in the title rôle in Nicolai's *Falstaff*. Rokitansky had made his London *début* the year before as Marcel in *Les Huguenots*.

For Emilie, April 1866 marked her London *début* as Azucena. The *Musical Times* hailed her arrival, with that of Mr. Hohler, as the event of the season at Her Majesty's and said that Emilie had 'stamped herself at once as a genuine artist by her excellent impersonation of Azucena'. The critics were unanimous in her praise, speaking of her enjoying a triple triumph, as woman, singer and actress. The *Illustrated London News* greeted her performance enthusiastically in the following terms:

> 'Mme. de Méric Lablache is not entirely a stranger to the public. She is the daughter of Mme. Demeric, a celebrated performer of her day, and, when very young, appeared at Covent Garden some dozen years ago. Since then she has ripened into an accomplished artist; and judging from her appearance on Saturday, we would say that she has no superior among the contralti of the present opera stage. Her Azucena struck us as being the finest performance of the character, both dramatic and vocal, that we have met with since that of Mdme. Viardot Garcia, its original representative. The wild grandeur of her aspect, the tragic force and pathos of her acting, were all in the highest style of art. Her merits were fully appreciated by the audience. She was vehemently applauded, and repeatedly called before the curtain with acclamations.'

Later, Emilie sang as *secondo capraio* (second goatherd) in Meyerbeer's slight pastoral opera *Dinorah*, also known as *Le Pardon de Ploërmel*, about a peasant girl and hidden treasure. This work is rarely performed, but it was popular in its time and includes a great *coloratura* soprano showpiece, the *Shadow Song*. For the contralto, there is a duet in the third Act with the soprano goatherd. In reference to this, the *Gazette Musicale de Paris* said that Emilie had proved that for her talent no part was a small one.

The Times reported that Emilie had done full justice to the music of Puck in the performance of Weber's last opera *Oberon* which was given in June. This was despite Puck being a soprano rôle.

Apart from opera, Emilie sang, as usual, in several major

concerts. In 1866, the New Philharmonic Concerts were given at the St. James's Hall, under the direction of Professor Wylde. In April, at the first of the series, Emilie sang with Mme. Lemmens-Sherrington and Signor Bossi. The Hall had been crowded and the *Illustrated London News* described the performance as successful in every respect.

Emilie, Santley and Cummings were the principal singers at a Crystal Palace Concert on 30 June in Mendelssohn's 'celebrated cantata' *Die Walpurgis Nacht.*

The residence of the Marquis of Downshire in Belgrave Square was the scene of a *matinée musicale* on 9 July 1866 given by Signor Pezze and Signor Traventi. The *Illustrated London News* reported that this had been an elegant and successful entertainment:

> 'Signor Pezze (we need scarcely tell our musical readers) is the principal violoncello at Her Majesty's Theatre and an accomplished performer, and Signor Traventi is a distinguished composer of Italian vocal music. On this occasion, several charming vocal pieces from his pen were sung with great effect by Mme. Parepa, Mlle. Linas Martorelli, Mdme. Demeric-Lablache, Mdlle. Liebhart, Miss Louisa Pyne, and other favourite vocalists.'

Both Emilie and Rokitansky were billed to sing at Arditi's concert at Her Majesty's on 15 July.

Emilie and Hohler were singled out by the *Musical Times* as the newcomers who had made a highly favourable impression during the London Musical Season of 1866.

In September, there was a second 1866 Opera Season in Dublin. The arrangements had again been made by Augustus Harris and Arditi conducted. This time, the company included Mario, Santley, Tietjens, Mlle. Zandrina and Mlle. Bauermeister, who was making her Dublin *début.* Zandrina was to be given the part of Zerlina and Bauermeister took over as Martha, in *Faust.* However, Emilie duly appeared as Maffeo Orsini, Nancy, Azucena and Maddalena and sustained the demanding rôle of Arsace in *Semiramide.*

The Season opened on 17 September. The 'melancholy *Lucia* and the profound *Faust,* full of the weird and mystic ideas peculiar to Germany' had been followed by the 'sparkling but genuine *Marta*'. So wrote the critic in the *Irish Times.* He did not claim any originality for the melodies in *Marta,* but emphasised the excellence of the orchestral parts, particularly the violin and the harp. As for Emilie, her Nancy was:

'the very ideal of that character – the merry sauciness of her acting and the picturesqueness of her costume making it impossible to believe that she was the same person who appeared as Azucena last season; while, above all, the magnificent tone of her contralto voice, extending with ease over a compass of two octaves, and her unfailing command of it make a combination rarely to be met. Her singing of the *scena*, commencing at *Esser mesto* and ending with the aria *Il tuo stral nel lancian*, won the hearty acknowledgments of the audience, while in the concerted music her soft mellowness of tone made the harmonies full and completely satisfying. Taking all in all, *Marta* was the most successful opera yet produced.'

The Lord Lieutenant and the Marchioness of Abercorn had chosen to attend the performance of *Il Trovatore* which was given on 22 September. Mario had had one of his good nights. Mlle. Tietjens had sung Leonora as a great artist should. Santley, as the Count, had performed with vigour and judgment throughout. Emilie, 'though by no means equal to the great artistes with whom the part of Azucena is identified, was careful, effective, and now and then most impressive.'

Semiramide had not been produced in Dublin for eight or nine years and was considered to be in 'a style which was far more popular thirty years ago'. Nevertheless, it contained 'some very fine concerted music' and gave 'a splendid opportunity for good acting and spectacular effect'. Tietjens had never sung 'with more exquisite purity or thrilling power than in the fine air *Dolce pensiero*, in which the proud queen expresses her consuming passion for Arsaces. . . . She was fortunate in having the aid of such an accomplished vocalist as Madame De Méric Lablache in the trying duet for which the opera is noted.'

In October 1866, Emilie was at the Royal Amphitheatre in Leeds for three nights of Italian Opera. Mapleson had made the arrangements with a Mr. Loraine. The company included Mme. Sinico as well as Tietjens and Bauermeister. Among the men were Mario and Santley. Arditi had the assistance of Grua and de Rialp at the podium. Emilie played Azucena and Siebel.

From Leeds to Hull. Hull, proclaimed the *Hull and North Lincolnshire Times*, 'has long held a foremost place among provincial towns in its love of music. And an experience extending over a quarter of a century does not furnish us with a precedent for such a powerful and complete operatic entertainment as that with which we are promised next week'. Such was the puff for two nights of opera at the 'beautiful new' Theatre Royal. (11-12 October).

The stock company of the theatre had agreed to give their performances in the daytime in order to give place to the Grand Italian Opera Company from Her Majesty's Theatre, London, in the evening. The operas to be staged were *Il Trovatore* and *Don Giovanni.* Mdlle. [sic] Demeric Lablache was presented to the public as possibly the best living contralto. It has not been discovered how the performances were received. For Emilie, Hull must have seemed a far cry from St. Petersburg where she had been singing in October ten years before.

Travel weary though they might be, the singers had engagements in Liverpool and Norwich before they returned to London for a brief Winter Season.

On 15 October, there was a crowded house in Liverpool for the opening of the new Prince of Wales Theatre. The manager, Mr. Henderson, had made arrangements with Mapleson for a twelve-night opera season.

The first night gave the public the chance to see Mario as Faust and Tietjens as Marguerite. Emilie gave what the *Daily Courier* described as a graceful and truthful rendering of the part of Siebel. In *Trovatore* (18 October), 'the dreadful, vindictive, and even blood-thirsty gipsy, Azucena, was played by Madame Demeric-Lablache, whose efforts were continually and occasionally tremendously app-lauded.'

On 24 October Emilie appeared in *Marta.* The following evening she played Arsace 'with rare ability and artistic conception, and we shall not be surprised' the *Courier* wrote, 'to find her taking a very high position in this character, for which in voice, style and acting she seems particularly fitted.' However, the opera had been ruthlessly curtailed and the *Courier* complained that the character of Azema, the Princess, 'upon whom depends a considerable share of the plot' had been left out altogether. At a final Morning Concert, Emilie sang an aria by Mercadante and *Voi che sapete.*

The *Illustrated London News* of 13 October had given notice that the 1866 Triennial Norwich Festival would be held throughout the week beginning on Monday 29 October. The Festival was later in the season than usual, it was explained, to suit the convenience of the Prince and Princess of Wales, who were to honour it with their presence. Mr. Julius Benedict, as before, was to be the conductor. The singers Tietjens, Sinico, de Méric Lablache, Sims-Reeves and Santley had been engaged.

It has not been determined what Emilie herself sang, but the works offered during the week included Handel's *Israel* and *Messiah,* with fragments from his *Passion* never before performed anywhere; Haydyn's *Creation;* the cantata *St Cecilia,* which Benedict had com-posed specially for the Festival; and an oratorio by da Costa called *Naaman.*

Costa's oratorio had been dedicated to the memory of Prince Albert. The composer, who conducted it, received compliments from the Prince and Princess of Wales, the Duke of Edinburgh (Prince Alfred) and the Queen of Denmark. However, the audience showed most enthusiasm for Benedict's *St. Cecilia*. Though clapping had been banned, the cantata was frequently applauded.

Mapleson had announced that he would give a short Winter Season of Italian opera at Her Majesty's lasting for no more than a fortnight. Emilie was among the singers engaged. Others were Tietjens, Bauermeister, Santley, Morini and Gassier. To general surprise, the advertisements stated that the 'fashionable' tariff would be reduced and that the normal strict regulations governing evening dress would be lifted in their entirety for the period. The house was full on the first night and the audience were pleased to find that the stage had been considerably enlarged. The footlights had been pushed ten feet into the auditorium, to the advantage of the singers. The Season opened with *Faust*, followed by *Norma*, *Freyschütz*, *Trovatore*, *Nozze di Figaro* and *Don Giovanni*.

The provinces and London, 1867

At the beginning of 1867, the opera world was shaken by an announcement that the Czar had decided to withdraw his subsidy from the Italian Opera in St. Petersburg. This would in effect have meant its closure because it was dependent on the Imperial bounty.

Emilie, by Disdéri.
(By courtesy of the Bibliothèque Nationale, Paris.)

The Czar's munificence had enabled the Italian Opera in St. Petersburg to reach such heights that even the French had been prepared to admit that the Russian capital had taken over from Paris as the centre of Italian dramatic music in Europe. This had had the unfortunate result, elsewhere, of giving singers the chance to demand exorbitant fees 'or we shall go to Russia'. On the other hand, if a withdrawal of the Czar's subsidy had a nationalistic motive, and was designed to encourage native music, it carried with it the danger that rulers in other countries might follow the Czar's lead and cut the subsidies on which the very survival of Italian Opera depended.

In the event, the outcome, in St. Petersburg, was not as drastic as had been feared. In August 1867 it was being reported that the Imperial Administration proposed after all to have a short Winter Season and that they had engaged Augustus Harris to run it. Harris undertook the task, but made what must be regarded as the mistake of engaging Mario, by then well past his prime, to sing in the *Barber*.

MAPLESON'S 1867 TOUR

Mapleson's Company took to the road again, for three months, in January 1867. Arditi records that his place as conductor had been taken over by the Neapolitan Enrico Bevignani (1841-1903). Bevignani had a long and distinguished career at Her Majesty's, at Covent Garden and at the Met in New York. Adelina Patti chose him to conduct for her whenever she could. Bevignani married a niece of Mlle. Tietjens.

The Mapleson tour began in Nottingham. When Emilie paid this return visit to the Midland city, the weather was once again inclement. Nevertheless, and despite the 'somewhat high prices', there was a large and fashionable audience in the Mechanics Hall for Mendelssohn's Oratorio *Elijah*. This 'well-known and much admired' work was performed by the Nottingham Sacred Harmonic Society in collaboration with Mapleson.

Among the guest artists, the lion's share had fallen to Santley and Tietjens. The *Nottingham Journal* reported that they had both acquitted themselves admirably. Madame Lablache had previously achieved a local reputation for herself, one 'which will certainly not be rendered less by her last night's performance [21 January]. The manner in which she rendered the air *O rest in the Lord* especially attracted well-deserved attention.' The *Journal* remarked that none of the artists had come in for an encore. However, this was not because the singing was unappreciated, but 'owing to the fact that the public have learned that repetitions of this kind are contrary to good taste.'

On this tour, the operas in which Emilie took part were *Faust*, *Lucrezia Borgia*, *Marta*, *Il Trovatore* and *Gli Ugonotti*. Twelve nights at the Theatre Royal in Edinburgh in March opened with *Faust*. The *Scotsman* considered that the part of Siebel was an unnecessary one, but Emilie had sung her air *Partatele d'amor* very tastefully. Flotow's *Marta* had been given its first performance in Edinburgh and had proved successful. Emilie was praised for the spirited manner in which she had enacted the part of the coquettish maid. In *Il Trovatore* (21 March), both her singing and acting had been full of true dramatic fire.

This provincial tour, which had concluded with a fortnight at the Theatre Royal in Liverpool, was the prelude to Mapleson's final Season at Her Majesty's in London. This opened on 27 April with *Le Nozze di Figaro*. *The Times* critic noted that the cast was the same as that of the previous year, except that Madame de Meric Lablache had taken the place of Madame Trebelli Bettini as the naughty page, Cherubino. Being, like her predecessor, a contralto, Emilie had, as a matter of course, had the music accommodated to her means. 'Mme. de Meric gave both her songs with real feeling, and, though she a little overacted the part, the best intentions were evident throughout her performance, which was always intelligent, if occasionally, in its histrionic development overstepping the boundaries of strict taste. The incomparable romance *Voi che sapete* was unanimously called for again'. The *Illustrated London News* said that there had been an unusually strong cast, with Emilie being a charming page. Tietjens had played the Countess, with Gassier as Figaro, Santley as Almaviva and Foli as Bartolo. Mlle. Sinico was Susanna. Arditi was back as conductor. The opera was repeated several times, with 'extra nights' on 9 and 25 May. Concurrently, the *Marriage of Figaro* was being performed by the Royal Italian Opera at Covent Garden, with Pauline Lucca as Cherubino.

During the Season there were some changes in the casting. Emilie took her usual part of Azucena in *Il Trovatore* (13 May), but Mme. Trebelli Bettini was Maffeo Orsini in *Lucrezia* (18 May) and she replaced Emilie as Siebel after the initial performance of *Faust* on 25 May.

It has not been discovered whether Emilie became unwell after the early days of the Season, but after she had played Urbano in *Gli Ugonotti* on 4 May she was replaced in the part by Trebelli Bettini. Emilie's relation by marriage, Johann Rokitansky, came in for high praise from *The Times* for his performance in *Gli Ugonotti*. ' . . . it would hardly be possible now-a-days to find a better Marcel than Herr Rokitansky, who exults in one of those noble and deep-toned bass voices in which Germany has always been so rich.' The critic could not recall a better Marcel since Herr Formes.

On 14 May, Nicolai's German opera *Die lustigen Weiber von Windsor* was given in its Italian version under the title of *Falstaff*. The cast was excellent (*ILN*) and the production met with con-

Emilie in a crinoline.
(By courtesy of the Cabinet des Estampes, Bibliothèque Nationale, Paris.)

siderable success. 'Tietjens's Mrs. Ford . . . was a delightful piece of Shakespearean comedy. Nor did Mlle. Sinico and Mme. Demeric-Lablache, as Mrs. Page and Ann, leave anything to desire, either in acting or singing.' *The Times*, recalling that Emilie was in the part formerly taken by Mlle. Bettelheim, was inclined to think that the change, on the whole, had not been greatly for the worse. Rokitansky played Falstaff.

Mapleson revived Weber's *Oberon* on 1 June, with Emilie in the soprano rôle of Puck, in which she had been 'deserving of much praise' (*The Court Journal*). She took part in a rendering of *Viva la Libertà* which followed the performance of *Don Giovanni* on 13 July.

The Summer had been marked by several notable musical events outside the theatre, in which Emilie participated.

One evening in mid-June, the Prince of Wales was host at a State Concert at Buckingham Palace at which a galaxy of artists, including Mario, took part. Pride of place among the ladies was enjoyed by Paolina Lucca and Adelina Patti, but Emilie also had the honour to be included. She was not given a solo, but sang in the quintet *Di scrivermi ogni giorno*, from *Così fan tutte*, a trio from the Prince Consort's *L'Invocazione all'Armonia*, the duet *Conversation Alsacienne* from Offenbach's *Lischen und Fritzchen* and a quartet by Flotow. Some seven hundred guests had been invited, including many Royal personages, members of the Diplomatic Corps, peers and senior officers of the Armed Forces (*The Court Journal*).

An extraordinary Musical Festival took place at the Crystal Palace on 16 July in honour of the Sultan of Turkey who was paying a visit to London. Arditi has left an account. The Sultan apparently kept the audience waiting for over six hours. This 'caused a slight curtailment of the programme'. One of the items omitted was the *Spinning Quartet* from *Marta*, which Emilie was to have sung with Mlle. Sinico, Gardoni and Gassier. A highlight seems to have been the finale of *Don Giovanni*, with Rokitansky as the Commendatore.

Meanwhile, Emilie had sung, by permission of Colonel Mapleson, at the Fifth Concert of the Philharmonic Society. The aria chosen was *Vedrai carino*, from *Don Giovanni*. This is a soprano song and Emilie was described in this context as a soprano. At this time, Emilie's husband appears to have been in Paris. It is recorded that he sang with his sister Mme. de Caters at a *soirée* given by a Mme. de Verville.

Emilie was in Dublin again for the Season of Italian Opera which Harris opened at the Theatre Royal on 16 September 1867 with the *Nozze di Figaro*. She was given the part of Cherubino which had been taken in the previous year by Mlle. Zandrina. The conductor was Bevignani. Mario had been expressly engaged, on his way to St.

Petersburg, but indisposition had prevented him from going to Dublin.

According to the *Annals*, interest in opera in Dublin had been tending to flag until it was pulled up by Signor Bettini and his wife. She had been summoned at short notice from Paris. The great event of the fortnight was to have been the local *première* of Nicolai's *Falstaff* (24 September) – in which Emilie played the part of the page – but 'as is very often the case in Dublin with new works, the public did not come to judge; the house being about half full, if so much.' The *Freeman's Journal* condemned the opera as musically worthless and a repetition was not risked.

Emilie took her usual parts in *Marta* and *Trovatore*, but gave way to Mme. Trebelli Bettini in *Faust*, the *Barber* and *Lucrezia*. In the *Nozze di Figaro*, Emilie had some success as Cherubino. The *Freeman's Journal* wrote that she must have been aware, when she appeared in this rôle, 'that she was a great favourite by the gracious reception she met with, and she continues to be as charming an actress and singer as ever'. As Cherubino, her rendering of the celebrated *Non so più cosa* had been most graceful and artistic, though it 'lacked vocal power to some extent.' However, during the evening she had given most satisfactory evidence 'that she was well entitled to the high position which she holds on the lyric stage.' The *Journal* also spoke of Emilie's artistic grace and skill in her performance as Puck in *Oberon* (27 September).

At the Grand Concert [concerts in those days had a way of being grand] on the final Saturday (4 October), Emilie had sung *Ah, mon fils* from *Le Prophète*, with genuine dramatic feeling, imparting to that 'spasmodic composition much more merit than it deserved.' The *Freeman's Journal* regretted that she and Tom Hohler had chosen to sing the 'done-to-death' gipsy duet from *Trovatore*.

In October, Emilie was in another Season of opera in Liverpool. This was at the Alexandra Theatre. The *Daily Post* of 8 October describes a performance of *Le Nozze di Figaro* saying that 'with such executants it is no wonder it was a success.' Tietjens took the part of the Countess, 'one for which she is eminently fitted' and Mlle. Sinico was 'as charming as last year as Susanna.' The cast had been 'immensely strengthened by Madame Demeric-Lablache's impersonation of Cherubino.' Evidently Emilie was regarded as a much more finished artiste than Wiziak who must have taken the part the previous year. The other main rôles were taken by Mlle. Bauermeister (Marcellina), Santley (the Count), Gassier (Figaro), Foli (Bartholo) and Lyall (Basilio).

Figaro was followed by *Il Trovatore* (10 October) which, to the regret of the *Daily Post*, drew larger houses.

Emilie's Azuzena 'possessed the same excellencies and defects which we noticed on her last appearance in the character. Her action poses and facial expression were perfect, and a great deal of the music left little to desire, but we observed the same excess of tremolo as when last here, which gave great uncertainty to her intonation. At the same time, in situations evoking intense mental anguish, or fierce hate and defiance, it is not to be wondered at if the voice give an unmistakable indication of the tempestuous state of the mind. In her chief scenes . . . she rendered all the music with thrilling power, and in the last scene of all was most effective'.

When Mapleson was back at Her Majesty's, Emilie returned to the part of Pierotto in Donizetti's *Linda di Chamounix* and sang Nancy in *Marta*. This was in November.

CHAPTER
40

England, France and Portugal: *family events, 1868-1873*

NOT much evidence has so far come to light about Emilie's activities in the early part of 1868 or indeed for much of 1868-1870. Certainly, from May to July 1868 she must have been mostly in London. At the Theatre Royal, Drury Lane, she sang with Rokitansky in *Don Giovanni* and with Santley in *Marta*. This was in May. In July, she had a part in *La Fille du Régiment*.

Apart from Opera, she took part in the concert which the Metropolitan Choral Society gave at the Crystal Palace on 25 May then sang *Donzella nata in sen*, from *Oberon*, at the Seventh Concert of the Philharmonic Society of London on 22 June.

A social event of importance in the operatic calendar of the year occurred on 29 July. Immediately after the end of the Covent Garden Season, Adelina Patti married the Marquis de Caux at the Roman Catholic Church on Clapham Common. The Church was crowded for the ceremony, which took place at eleven in the morning. It is highly probable that Emile attended.

In September 1868 the Italian Opera Company once again put on a Season in Dublin. It is to be presumed that, after London, Emilie will have felt most at home in Dublin, with her relations there, but it is by no means clear whether she was with the Company in the Autumn of 1868. *Trovatore* had been announced for the first night (14 September), with Emilie as Azucena, but in the event the part was taken 'at a moment's notice' by Sofia Scalchi (1850-1922). It seems from such records as have been consulted that Emilie did not perform in Dublin during the Season in question.

By November, she was in Paris. On the 21st, Rossini's funeral was preceded by a musical service at the newly-erected *Eglise de la Trinité* at which a long list of distinguished singers took part. Emilie was among them, as were Marietta Alboni and Adelina Patti.

In 1869 there is one of the rare glimpses of Nicolas Lablache. According to the *Gazette Musicale de Paris*, the superintendent of the theatres of Cairo, in Egypt, engaged him in May as administrator of the Italian Opera and Vaudeville there. Nicolas was to share duties with Monsieur Thibaut under the general direction of that veteran impresario, Bagier. It is recorded that when a fire broke out during a performance of *Rigoletto*, Nicolas was active in helping to extinguish it. If Dwight's *Journal of Music* is correct, Nicolas was still in Cairo in 1871, and was directing the opera there on the celebrated occasion of the world *première* of *Aïda* on Christmas Eve in that year. It has not been discovered whether at any time Emilie was with her husband in Egypt.

In 1869-70, Emilie had a Season in Portugal. She had been engaged by the Sao Carlo Theatre in Lisbon to sing in *Il Trovatore*, *Ballo in Maschera* and *La Favorita*. On 26 January 1870, she took part in the world *première* of Angelo's opera *Enrico*. The Portuguese Season included Oporto, where a performance of *Trovatore* was given at the *Teatro São João* on 8 November 1869.

Rivière's Concerts in London, 1871.
*(By courtesy of The New York Public Library, Music Division.. NYPL - (Music): MusicRes. *MBD (uncat), 19c. programs.)*

All that can be stated with any certainty about Emilie in 1871 is that she was probably in the cast of *Fra Diavolo* when that opera was performed at Covent Garden, under Gye, at the end of March and that she took part in the six-week series of Grand Instrumental and Vocal Promenade Concerts which the conductor Monsieur Rivière gave at the Theatre Royal, Covent Garden from 25 August. One of the attractions which Rivière promised was a new Grand Triumphal March *The Return of Richard Coeur de Lion*, for full orchestra,

Military Band and chorus, which had been composed expressly for the concerts by Prince Poniatowski (1816-1873).

On the opening night, which was crowded, Emilie took part in a performance of Rossini's *Stabat Mater*, conducted by Arthur Sullivan. Her solo was the *cavatina Fac ut portem*. Midway through the programme she sang the *Brindisi* from *Lucrezia*.

If Emilie stayed until the end of the evening, which was billed to last from 8 to 11.30 p.m., she would have heard a Mr. Arthur Lincoln, from New Orleans, playing for the first time in Europe 'an Instrument of the most novel and extraordinary description, called THE CRYSTALPHONICON' upon which he would be performing 'with his right hand a Solo and Variations, accompanying the same, with his left hand, on the Pianoforte.'

The eclectic programme concluded with a fantasia on Irish melodies and a quick march *Lusitania*, composed by Sir Julius Benedict and dedicated to the King of Portugal.

Altogether, Rivière's Promenade Concerts were on the popular side and did not receive much critical attention. However, he did not neglect the classics which featured in the first part of the programme most evenings. The practice was to give the classical concerts on the Wednesdays and sacred ones on the Fridays.

Emilie sang the aria *In questa tomba* on the Beethoven Night (30 August), when the orchestra played the *Pastoral Symphony*. She was billed as one of the principal vocalists in *The Messiah* (1 September) and on 8 September, when Mendelssohn's *Elijah* was performed, her solo was *O rest in the Lord*. In the quartet *Cast thy burden*, she sang with Madame Rudersdorff, Mr J. H. Pearson and Mr Whitney. Her partners in *Lift Thine Eyes* were Mme. Rudersdorff and Miss Jenny Pratt. Arthur Sullivan conducted.

Madame de Méric Lablache, 'from the Royal Opera, Covent Garden', was among the artistes who had graciously promised their services on Rivière's benefit night on Saturday 14 October. This was a Floral Festival. Three thousand bouquets were to be distributed to the audience, each lady and gentleman receiving one together with a *carte-de-visite* of Monsieur Rivière, photographed by Elliot and Fry of Baker Street. The Grand Orchestra was to be decorated with REAL FLOWERS and the whole theatre was to be transformed into a LUXURIANT GARDEN (by J.H. Wills, F.R.H.S., Royal Exotic Nursery and Floral Depôt, Sussex Place, Old Brompton). The artistes seem to have been called upon for only one offering and Emilie's was *Il segreto per esser felice*. Prices of admission for Rivière's concerts ranged from two guineas for private boxes to one shilling for the amphitheatre and promenade.

Nicolas Lablache had returned to Paris by 1872, when he is recorded as running a singing course at the *Théâtre Italien* (*Gazette*

Musicale de Paris). He is listed as *Direttorre Generale della Scena* at the *Théâtre Italien* for the 1872-1873 Season.

The main family events for Emily in 1873 were the death of her half-brother, at the relatively young age of 58, and the marriage of her daughter Louise.

Augustus Glossop Harris died in London on 19 April 1873 and was buried in Brompton Cemetery. His life had been spent in the theatre and he was connected, as has been seen, with Emilie's professional career. Unfortunately no record has been traced of the personal relations between them.

As a young man, Augustus Harris was sent to Paris to study *Les Danicheff*, which was having a long run at the *Odéon*. This had been arranged by Mrs. Wood, who briefly managed the St. James's Theatre, and the owner of that theatre, Viscount Newry (later Earl of Kilmorey).

Following the retirement of Charles Keane in 1859, Harris had become the manager of the Princess's Theatre and it was under him that Henry Irving made his first appearance in London, in Oxenford's *Ivy Hall*. Harris also introduced the actor Charles Albert Fechtler (1824-1879) to the London stage. However, he is chiefly remembered as having been the manager responsible for opera and ballet at Covent Garden, with only one break, for twenty-seven years. He is credited with having had an admirable eye for colour and a great capacity for stage management. He directed opera as far afield as Madrid, Paris, Berlin and St. Petersburg. His daughters Maria and Nelly were well known in the theatrical profession. Harris's widow, Maria, went into the costumier business in Regent Street as Auguste et Compagnie.

The marriage of Emilie's daughter Louise, at the stated age of seventeen, was celebrated on 26 May 1873 at St. Paul's Church, Avenue Road, Hampstead, North London. The bridegroom was James Hamilton Cobley, aged twenty-seven, bachelor, described simply as a gentleman.

The bride's full name as given in the marriage certificate was Louise Emily Colette Joséphine Thérèse Marguerite Lablache, thus showing that respect had been accorded at her birth to the mothers of both Emilie and Nicolas.

Three years after the marriage, on 23 May 1876, a daughter, also named Louise Emily (Louie) was born. Cobley and his wife had remained in much the same district of London and were living in Springfield Road, Marylebone, when their daughter was born there.

Returning to Emilie's career, we find that by the Autumn of 1873 it was Augustus Glossop Harris II, later to become Sir Augustus, who was putting on opera in Dublin. He announced a series of

Italian operas for three weeks, at the Gaiety Theatre, from 15 September to 4 October. This engagement had been effected through the enterprise of Messrs. Gunn and Sons, musical instrument warehousemen of 61, Grafton Street, Dublin. On the opening night, Mr. M. Gunn himself appeared on the stage, but only to apologise for Signor Bettini, who was 'fatigued after a hurried journey from Paris'. Emilie sang in *Lucrezia, Trovatore* and *Faust.* In *Faust* she displayed her ability to show what can be done with the minor part of Siebel. 'This gifted artiste', wrote the *Freeman's Journal*, 'always sings feelingly, always shows an appreciative spirit, and she plays with grace and *verve.*'

Later in 1873, Emilie was engaged by the American impresario M. B. Ullman(n) for a concert tour in the French provinces with the 'Concerts Ullman'. This was to include performances in Bordeaux, Marseille and Versailles. Emilie apparently had to break off in mid-tour owing to ill health (*Gazette Musicale de Paris*), but she took part in the Bordeaux concert, which was held on 10 November in the *grande salle Franklin*. She disappointed the *dilettanti*, who had been expecting to hear her with Marie Cabel in the duet from Rossini's *Stabat Mater*, but she delighted them with her part in the *trio bouffe* from the *Matrimonio Segreto (La Gironde).*

Louise Lablache
(By courtesy of the Harvard Theatre Collection.)

Britain, Denmark and Ireland, 1874-1876

BETWEEN 1874 and 1878 Emilie was mostly in Britain and Ireland. In London, in the Summer of 1874, she had a minor part at Drury Lane in *The Magic Flute* with Mlle Bauermeister and Mlle. Justine Macvity as one of the Three Geni, but her appearances were mainly in the provinces. With the Royal Italian Opera in Liverpool in the Autumn, when she played Marta in Gounod's *Faust*, she was mentioned as being too well known to require much notice, but she had sung and acted quite up to her usual standard (*Daily Post*). Then Newcastle and Bristol were followed by what was perhaps Emilie's first appearance in Portsmouth, where the Company arrived by special train. Augustus Harris brought Her Majesty's Italian Opera Company to the Theatre Royal there in December 1874, with Signor Li Calsi as conductor. It was the first time that the Italian Opera Company had been in Portsmouth, though the old Royal had in the past welcomed to its stage the greatest celebrities of the theatrical world (*The Portsmouth Times and Naval Gazette*). Emilie's only part seems to have been Azucena. After a final-day concert at the Portland Hall in Southsea, the Company went on to Brighton (Theatre Royal and Opera House), where Emilie sang Marta. The visit to Brighton ended with Mr. Chart's Grand Morning Concert on 19 December, in the Dome Assembly Room, in which Emilie took part.

In early 1875, Emilie was with Mapleson again, this time in Glasgow, where he had a strong company for a series of as many as ten operas. She was there with Tietjens, Trebelli-Bettini, Valleria and Bauermeister, to name only the female singers (*Musical World*).

Mapleson brought his Company to London in the Summer of 1875 and when Emilie appeared as Marta on 13 May she was performing with a new generation of singers in the major rôles. Jean De Reszke was the Valentine and Christine Nilsson gave a memorable portrayal of Marguerite.

In what seems to be a brief interlude in her career in opera, Emilie gave a concert in Denmark in the Autumn of 1875, at the *Folkstheater* in Copenhagen (14 September). She sang *Ah! mon fils*, Siebel's romance and the *Brindisi* from *Lucrezia*. She was accompanied by the French cellist, Albert.

However, she was back in Ireland before the end of the year, with the Italian Opera Company conducted by Li Calsi. This was for a short six-night Season, beginning on 15 November. Emilie appeared on the first night, as Marta, and as Teresa in *La Sonnambula*, with which the tour concluded.

For Emilie, a link with Ireland had been severed in 1875, her uncle having died in September. However, that in no way caused her to stop crossing the Irish Sea. In March 1876, she received an ovation in Cork. The Italian Opera Company under 'Signor' Campobello (actually Campbell) had been engaged for a week at the Opera House there. The headlines had been devoted to Madame Sinico Campobello, to Emma Howson, 'niece of the celebrated Albertazzi', to Madame Larille-Ferminet from the Theatre Royal, The Hague, making her first appearance in Ireland and to Madame Piccioli 'specially engaged to sustain the important rôle of Amina in *La Sonnambula*'. Then, on the second night, 7 March, Emilie was seen in the part of Azucena. *Trovatore* received an ecstatic review in the *Cork Daily Herald*. It had been produced in a way that it was never before listened to in Cork, 'a banquet of the immortals to appetites that must usually put up with very homely fare indeed'. In consequence of her great reception in the part, the paper declared, she had been chosen to sing as Marcellina in *Le Nozze di Figaro*, thus ousting Mlle. Bauermeister who had previously been billed.

Figaro had only once before been heard in Cork and proved a revelation to that 'music-loving city'. The new theatre had never before held so great and fashionable an audience in all its parts. There had not been a solitary seat vacant - even in the dress circles, where the varied toilettes of the ladies and the numerous brilliant uniforms of the officers in full dress made the scene fair to look at. 'No praise could be extravagant' for Emma Howson's Cherubino, but Madame de Méric Lablache had not been upstaged as the doting old Marcellina.

In *Sonnambula*, Emilie had been billed, not surprisingly, as Teresa, but the *Daily Herald* critic, probably rightly, praised her for her performance as Lisa. Madame Piccioli, as Amina, with her exquisite soprano voice, had been applauded to the echo. The house had been crowded again and any doubts about the success of such a distinguished company in Cork had been dispelled, 'the only fear remaining is that secondary performers will hardly be listened to in future.'

Les Huguenots was given its Cork *première* on 9 March, with Emilie as Urbano. The stage of the new opera house had proved rather too small for the crowd scenes, but that had not detracted from the opera's success. There had been standing room only and although the work went on till nearly twelve o'clock, it had been listened to throughout 'with untiring and breathless attention'.

Emilie's aria *Nobil Donna* had drawn forth repeated applause.

The week had proved something of a triumph for Campobello and indeed for the conductor, Li Calsi and the *régisseur*, Augustus Harris. It is of interest that arrangements had been made for people outside the city itself to visit the opera: four special trains were laid on, at 11.15 p.m., to take members of the audience home. Were the trains held back after *Les Huguenots*?

Such had been the success of the 1876 Spring Season that the Cork Opera House arranged for a series of Italian operas to be given in the Autumn of the same year. However, Emilie was not then in the Company, which was under Mapleson. The rôle of Azucena fell to Madame Trebelli.

A playbill which has survived, a copy of which is included in this book, confirms that Emilie was with Campobello's Italian Opera Company in April 1876 when they gave a Season of opera at the Royal Alexandra Theatre in Liverpool. Emilie's name appears second only to that of Madame Sinico Campobello. Emilie's rôles were Urbano in *Les Huguenots*, Edwige in Rossini's *Guglielmo Tell* and Lazarillo in *Maritana*. She was one of the Three Geni in *The Magic Flute*, but apparently had no part in *Don Giovanni* or *La Traviata*.

ALEXANDRA THEATRE.

SOLE LESSEE .. .. MR. EDWARD SAKER.

SIGNOR CAMPOBELLO'S

ITALIAN OPERA COMPANY.

Artistes :

MADAME CAMPOBELLO SINICO.

Madame DEMERIC LABLACHE.

Madame PICCIOLI,
(Her first appearance in Liverpool).

Madlle. EMMA HOWSON,
(Her first appearance in Liverpool).

Madlle. BAUERMEISTER.

Madame DE SANTE.

AND

Madame LAVILLE FERMINET,
(From the Theatre Royal, The Hague. Her First Appearance in Liverpool.)

Signor VIZZANI.

Signor DELLA ROCCA.

Signor RINALDINI.

Signor PAOLO BOLLI.

Signor MARCHETTI.

AND

Mr. ARTHUR BYRON,
(From the Principal Theatres of Italy.)

Signor FOLI,
(His First Appearance for three years.)

Signor FREDERICO FEITLINGER,
(From the Grand Opera, Paris. His First Appearance in Liverpool.)

Signor ZOBOLI.

Signor GOUNET.
(His First Appearance in Liverpool.)

Signor CASABONI.

Signor VERCELLINI.

Alexandra Theatre, Liverpool –
Campobello's Italian Opera Company.
(Playbill in the author's collection.)

The *Daily Post* (11 April) found much to criticise in *Les Huguenots*, but Raoul had been sung by Vizzani, 'than whom there is perhaps no finer tenor at present on the operatic stage' and Emilie 'had exhibited a mature sprightliness' as Urbano.

As in Cork, the *régisseur* was Augustus Harris and the *Daily Post* paid him a tribute. The stage for *William Tell*, the critic wrote, 'was arranged and the auxiliaries grouped with inherited skill and taste by Mr. Augustus Harris.' All the same, the paper considered that *Tell* was rather too ambitious a project for a provincial theatre and a travelling company. The work had not been done in Liverpool since the days of Duprez [the French tenor 1806-1896], which was sufficient proof of its formidable character. As for Emilie, she had been an excellent Edwige, but there always seemed to be something rather mechanical about her acting 'appropriate and practised' though it was.

The Company also put on the three-act opera *Maritana* (1845) by the Irish composer Vincent Wallace (1812-1865). This seems to have been translated from English into Italian for the occasion. It was a popular work at the time and was received by the Liverpool audience with great enthusiasm. Emilie had been 'a capital Lazarillo and her singing was all that could be desired; especially . . . in *Alas, those chimes*, which had been rendered with great fervour and expression.'

Emilie took part in a Holy Week Sacred Concert which included selections from Verdi's *Requiem Mass* and Rossini's *Stabat Mater*. On Good Friday, 14 April, the weather had been balmy and thousands of pleasure-seekers had 'thronged the river', but then Merseyside had been battered by gales and snowstorms such as had never been experienced at Eastertide before. Communications were seriously disrupted and the newspaper train lost an hour and a half between London and Rugby . . . .

Campobello's company went on to the New Theatre Royal in Bristol (24-27 April), where they gave *Maritana* 'for the first time in Italian', *Tell*, *Der Freyschütz* and *Trovatore*. This was when Emma Howson apparently made her first appearance in England. The *régisseur* was Charles Harris, a brother of Augustus. Li Calsi and de Rialp conducted.

The short Season in Bristol was plagued by mishaps to which travelling companies are prone. On the first night, the miserable weather was no doubt accountable for the poor attendance. On the second night, it was found that the orchestral parts for *Lucia* had gone astray, so that *Tell* had to be substituted at the last minute. Happily, then, the overture to *Tell* was so loudly applauded that de Rialp repeated it. On this second night the attendance had been better, but there had been much prompting. *The Bristol Times and Mirror* commented that the prompter had played the part of a Greek chorus. 'His voice is heard all through the opera, and if to be talked about is fame, the gentleman may flatter himself that he has been more talked about this week than all the rest of the company. He has a fine voice and knows how to use it. But perhaps without his assistance the operas might not have gone off as successfully as they have, and the artistes themselves will probably be the first to acknowledge his services.'

In *Maritana*, Emilie was given an encore for *Alas, those chimes* and in *Trovatore* her *D'amor sull'ali rosee* brought the house down (*Bristol Times and Mirror*).

It is not clear to what extent, at this period in her career, Emilie was accompanied by her husband. It seems probable that they were often apart. Only sporadic references to him have been traced. One is that on 15 September 1876 Nicolas was present at the cemetery of Père Lachaise in Paris when the ashes of Bellini were exhumed for translation to Italy.

George Bernard Shaw quotes an anecdote about Emilie. In 1876, the impresario G. J. Lee was arranging a concert. One of the leading singers was Shaw's mother, who had been trained by Lee. At a rehearsal, Madame Demeric Lablache had taken exception to something and refused to sing. Whereupon Lee shrugged his shoulders and asked Mrs. Shaw to carry on, 'which she did to such purpose that Madame Lablache took care not to give her another chance.'

CHAPTER 42

Britain and Ireland again, 1877-1878: death of Joséphine

EMILIE had a full programme of engagements in Britain and Ireland in 1877 and 1878. De Rialp had established a new Imperial Italian Opera Company for which Emilie and Emma Howson had been recruited. An early engagement was six nights from 12 March 1877 at the New Theatre Royal and Opera House in Leeds. Emilie's major rôle there was as Azucena. She also played Maddalena and the soprano part of Lisa in *Sonnambula*. The climax of the week was a Ballad and Instrumental Concert on St. Patrick's Day (17 March) in Leeds Town Hall at which Tietjens was the great draw. The *Leeds Express* had written that 'as a contralto, there is only one name upon the operatic stage that can be placed beside that of Madame Demeric-Lablache.'

Emilie was to have two Seasons at the Theatre Royal in Belfast in 1877, though not with the same company.

In March, she was still with de Rialp. His Company received a restrained welcome. As the Belfast News Letter put it, it was regrettable that the town was not accorded the privilege of an annual visit from members of Her Majesty's Opera Company. Doubtless, however, the Belfast public had only themselves to blame. The dilemma was that there was insufficient support for companies of the first rank, yet excellent concert performances had educated local musical taste and made 'an inferior performance of an opera intolerable'. Rialp's Company seemed to go a good way towards solving the perplexing problem. 'Of course there was an absence of the splendid powers of the singers of Her Majesty's Opera.' Belfast did not expect to hear wonders such as the purity of a Patti, the passion of a Tietjens or the thrilling power of a Trebelli, but the first-night performance of *Il Trovatore* had been far above the average, 'and in every scene there was evidence of the greatest culture, refinement and good taste - qualities all too rarely to be met with even in the most pretending companies.' Vizzani, the tenor well known on both sides of the Atlantic, had been the Manrico. As so often with tenors, he had had a cold, but had always hit the right note. Emilie had sung splendidly and imbued the rôle of Azucena with the finest passion. 'Her voice was wonderfully clear and faithful, and her acting . . . was powerful, without being melodramatically distasteful' (Belfast News Letter).

In *Don Giovanni*, the pleasure of the audience had been marred by the voice of the prompter which had been heard at every pause. The *News Letter* singled Emilie out as the first singer to praise. As Donna Anna she had sung so well that the critic was tempted to wish that she had had more to do. 'The same clear, rich and mellow tones that were heard on Monday evening were sustained with equal purity last night; there was just the least perceptible weakening of the highest notes in some of the airs' [But then, Emilie was not a soprano]. Mme. Lablache had also done some spirited acting, 'but indeed, to enumerate the excellent points of her performance . . . would be to catalogue all the airs that fell to her share'. Vizzani had come into his own in *Là ci darem* and Emma Howson had been delightful as Zerlina.

The *Nozze di Figaro* had struck the *News Letter* critic as the highlight of the week. The execution of Madame Demeric Lablache had been splendid. 'Her entrance was the signal for an outburst of applause, which was renewed at the conclusion of the cavatina *Porgi amor*. This was sung . . . with the purest feeling, that became at times almost passionate. The duet *Sull'aria* . . . was another example of power on the part of Madame Demeric Lablache, whose acting throughout the entire opera was of the most finished character'. It seems likely that Emilie and Emma Howson stood out among the female singers as having star quality.

A different opera had been given each evening. Rialp had apparently staged the first Belfast productions in Italian of *La Traviata*, *Le Nozze di Figaro* and *Maritana*. The week of opera ended with *Il Barbiere di Siviglia*, but there was the usual final concert. This took place in the Ulster Hall on 8 March. Emma Howson sang *Kathleen Mavourneen* and Emilie gave her renderings of *Ah, mon fils* and the *Brindisi* from *Lucrezia*.

From Belfast, de Rialp went on to give his Company their début in Dublin. The Season opened at the Theatre Royal on 2 April 1877 with *Figaro*. Campobello had been specially engaged to play the Count and Emilie was the Countess. The *Irish Times* dealt with her performance in this unaccustomed rôle with sensitivity. Madame Demeric-Lablache is so thorough an artiste, the critic wrote, so careful and conscientious in everything she attempts, that one can scarcely conceive of her doing anything badly. The part of the Countess is totally unsuited (as far as the music is concerned) to such a voice as hers. Nevertheless she succeeded by her capital acting and artistic vocalism in making the impersonation not only satisfactory, but highly attractive. The *Porgi amor* (transposed) she sang very agreeably. The audience for the opera had been appreciative, but had not been as large as might have been expected. However, a concert by Rubinstein had been a counter-attraction the same evening.

Maritana, in Italian, followed on 3 April, with Emilie as Lazarillo. The *Irish Times* considered that Wallace's melodious opera, 'so widely and justly popular,' lost nothing by being sung in Italian. Emilie had achieved a very decided success and had thoroughly earned the applause with which she was greeted. 'Her manner, appearance, acting and singing were admirable, and her singing of *Alas, those chimes* was loudly encored.

In the 'evergreen' *Trovatore*, Emilie had given a performance fully worthy of her high reputation, proving herself to be one of the best Azucenas on the stage.

In *Faust* (10 April), Emilie had shown her versatility in the part of Siebel, the music of which had been transposed. She had been encored in *La pariate*. *Traviata* had been billed, but *Rigoletto* was given instead, with Emilie as Maddalena.

The Company gave two concert performances. At the first, Emilie sang *Sleep, dearest, sleep* and *Il segreto* 'with all the culture and refinement that might be expected' (*Irish Times*). On the final night, with the second Act of *Maritana* and the last Act of *Trovatore*, Emilie sang *Alas, those chimes* and, with Vizzani and Rollo, *Turn on, old Time*.

Later in April, Emilie was in Cork again for a Season of Italian opera in which she was given star billing with Emma Howson, Vizzani and Sterbini.

The Season had been due to open on 16 April with *Le Nozze di Figaro*, Emilie being cast as the Countess. However, on the morning of that day the *Cork Daily Herald* came out with the following special notice: 'In order to meet the wishes of a great many admirers of Signor VIZZANI and Madame LABLACHE, who created so great a sensation in Cork in their great characters, Manrico and Azucena, during the visit of Signor CAMPOBELLO's Opera Company, VERDI's Tragic Opera IL TROVATORE will be produced THIS EVENING . . . .'

Maritana, again in Italian, proved to be the other favourite. Its success on 20 April led to its being repeated on 23 April. 'If there is an opera', wrote the *Daily Herald*, 'that English companies can produce which has proved that all classes can appreciate it, it is *Maritana*'. On 20 April, with a powerful cast and a crowded house, 'there was nothing more that could be desired. Madame Lablache, as Lazarillo, sang with the grace which places her in the first rank of contraltos. She was encored in the air known in English as *Alas, those chimes*, which she sang exquisitely. Madame Lablache was perfection in the part'.

Figaro was duly put on, as a matinée, and Emilie also sang in *Guglielmo Tell*.

In the Spring and Summer of 1877, Emilie returned to the mainstream, taking leading parts in operas in London at Her Majesty's Theatre in the Haymarket. This was the first Season of opera there for ten years. Sir Michael Costa directed and conducted.

In May, Verdi's *Ballo in Maschera* saw the début, as Amelia, of Mlle. Carolina Salla, but Shaw roundly declared that the main success of the evening had been Madame Lablache's striking impersonation of the fortune-teller, Ulrica, 'which was the principal feature of the first act, and indeed of the entire opera. The scena *E lui*, concluded on C in the alt, was declaimed with the fine dramatic power which especially distinguishes the artist'. The *Daily News* considered that Emilie's sorceress was as meritorious in dramatic feeling as her previous performance of Azucena.

During this Season Emilie took several parts normally sung by sopranos such as the Marchioness in Donizetti's *La Figlia del Reggimento* and Teresa in *La Sonnambula*. As Marta in Gounod's *Faust*, she sang again with Christine Nilsson, but also with Minnie Hauk who was making her English début as Marguerite.

In the Company with Emilie were her friend Tamberlik, Rokitansky and Etelka Gerster. Emilie was not one of the performers at the State Concert at Buckingham Palace on 6 July 1877, but several of her close associates were: Mlle. Zaré Thalberg, Etelka Gerster, Foli and Santley.

At the end of September 1877, Mapleson returned to Belfast, after an absence of four years, with a travelling company selected from members of Her Mjesty's Opera. Emilie was one of these. Others, among the ladies, were Carolina Salla, Mila Rodani and Anna de Belocca, who were making their first appearance in Ireland. Li Calsi conducted. Mapleson presented two operas not previously seen in Belfast: *Un Ballo in Maschera* and Les *Huguenots*. The other evenings were devoted to the *Barber*, *Trovatore*, Flotow's *Marta* and Gounod's *Faust*.

Belfast cannot be said to have risen very well to the operatic challenge. On the first night, for *Ballo*, there was an 'unsatisfactory attendance at all parts of the house but the dress circle' (*News Letter*). The critic feared that despite the activities of numerous musical societies 'the cultivation of music as an art is not very far advanced amongst us yet'. The public, it seemed, preferred to listen to their friends than to unknown artistes from far away. Yet Mapleson had always brought to Belfast singers of high calibre whose reputation had already been made.

The *News Letter* gave Emilie unstinted praise for her Ulrica. 'We quite forgot the absence of Madame Trebelli. The incantation scene was sung with the greatest power, the wonderful air *Re dell'abisso affretati . . .* was dramatic in the extreme. It is a satisfaction to hear such sound vocalization as that of Madame Lablache. The *Northern Whig* agreed that Emilie made a capital Ulrica, remarking that she stood her years and her work well. She was forty-seven.

The *Barber* was described as having had a brilliancy and 'swing' beyond anything to which the audience had been accustomed. Mlle. de Belocca had charmed everyone with her Rosina and Bettini had been admirable as the Count. In the minor part of Berta, Emilie had given an exquisitely finished performance . . . equal to anything in the opera.

As for *Il Trovatore*, the *News Letter* critic had been bowled over by the magnificence of the production. Mlle. Salla had come into her own as Leonora, 'one of the most grateful of operatic parts', and as was to be expected Emilie had given 'in point of finish . . . the most carefully-considered representatioon of the part [Azucena] we have ever seen'.

Emilie played Martha in *Faust* with delicate humour and 'we never saw so much made of the part' (*News Letter*).

It seems that the audiences had been meagre for all the operas except *Les Huguenots* (in which Emilie did not appear). The *Northern Whig* said that this was not at all creditable to a town of such musical pretensions as Belfast. Mapleson's Company had indeed been weaker than in previous years, but all the works had been produced in an admirable manner, whilst any little deficiencies in some were fully compensated by the excellence of others.

On Saturday 29 September, when the Grand Concert was given in the Ulster Hall, Emilie again sang the scena from *Le Prophète Figlio mio* (presumably this time in Italian). A critic wrote of the peculiar fulness of tone which was characteristic of Madame Lablache's contralto.

Figlio mio was Emilie's only solo, but she took her part in the quartet from Flotow's *Marta*, in the terzetto *Gratias agimus* from Rossini's *Messe Solennelle* and in the trio *L'usato ardir* from *Semiramide*, sung with Madame Marie Roze and Del Puente.

Mapleson's tour in Ireland continued with three weeks at the Theatre Royal in Dublin, from 1 October 1877, and a week in Cork. Emilie's main parts were Ulrica, Azucena, the Marchesa (in *La Figlia del Reggimento*) and Marta in *Faust*.

In Cork, the theatre had been almost totally rebuilt and in its renovated guise could claim 'with the utmost truthfulness' to be second to no provincial house in the Kingdom (*The Cork Constitution*). Furthermore, according to the paper, there was no class of performance so popular in Cork as the opera. The *Constitution* was impressed by the array of talent which Mapleson had recruited. Previously, his Company had lacked a high-class tenor, but this time he had managed to engage Giuseppe Fancelli (1833-1888), 'who doubtless possesses the finest tenor voice in Europe'. (Fancelli had become available following the closure of the Viceregal Opera in Cairo, where he had apparently been paid £120 a night). Offering a special welcome to Anna de Belocca, the *Constitution* said that at last Rossini's intentions for Rosina would be expressed in all their purity, without the inappropriate ornamentation which was Patti's great sin. As for Emilie, she was perfect in any part which she undertook.

Opera House, Cork.
(By courtesy of The National Library of Ireland.)

It is recorded that Emilie took part in a week of Italian opera at the Royal Alexandra Theatre in Liverpool from 29 October 1877, as Azucena, Marcellina, Ulrica and one of the Three Geni.

The end of the year was overshadowed by the death of her mother. Joséphine died in London on 26 December and was buried in the cemetery at Kensal Green. No recognisable memorial stone can now to be found.

With hindsight, we know that 1878 was the year in which Emilie was preparing to embark on the great new adventure in her career, the operatic tours in the United States of America. Meanwhile, there were still parts to be played on the familiar stages in such places as Leeds and Dublin.

Leeds felt that it had been falling behind in providing first-class opera. To quote the *Leeds Express* of 26 March 1878: 'It is so long since Italian opera had been given on a proper scale in Leeds that the younger generation of theatre-goers have probably forgotten all about it. Why is it that we have been so long deprived of the highest class of dramatic music it is difficult to say. In Bradford no year is allowed to pass without the appearance of the best travelling companies . . . .'

One reason was that Leeds had lacked a theatre sufficiently large to enable Italian opera to be a paying proposition. By 1878, however, the town had a theatre which was surpassed in size by few theatres in the Kingdom 'and in point of elegance and comfort can hold its own with any'. Certainly Mapleson was intrepid enough in the Spring of 1878 to take to the new theatre a company which he claimed was organised upon a scale which few travelling companies could attempt, so much so that he could change first-class singers in the principal parts almost nightly and fill even the subordinate rôles with competent artistes. Mapleson did not hide any of his lights under a bushel, but it was no doubt true that Emilie, as Martha in *Faust*, proved herself 'as much at home in that small part as she would have done in the most prominent'. Mapleson's Royal Italian Opera Company returned to Leeds at the end of October and achieved immense success in a three-night stand, with *Lucia*, *Don Giovanni* and *Faust*. Emilie's only part seems to have been Martha.

Emilie's last engagement before leaving for America must have been with Mapleson in Dublin from 2-14 September 1878, with Arditi conducting. This was the last Italian engagement at the 'Old Royal' before it was destroyed by fire in February 1880. Mapleson had also engaged Etelka Gerster, who was making her first appearance in Ireland, where her 'perfect vocalism was fully appreciated' (*Annals*). This was also when Minnie Hauk made her Irish début.

Emilie was not included in the casts of *Rigoletto* or *Don Giovanni*, but she sang on the opening night as Teresa in *Sonnambula* and on the following night as Marcellina in *Figaro*. Then she had the distinction of playing in the première in Ireland of *Carmen*. She was Mercedes, with Minnie Hauk in the name part.

The Season ended with *Faust*, Emilie playing Martha. The previous night had been *Trovatore*, but the Azucena was Madame Trebelli.

Before we follow Emilie with Mapleson to the United States, let us look briefly at the history of Italian opera there; above all at the foundations which had been laid by her predecessors in the field, not least by Elizabeth Féron after she arrived in America in 1828. This will also form the concluding chapter of Féron's life, in Italy and back in England.

43 *Elizabeth Féron in America and back in London: her death*

THE UNITED STATES OF AMERICA

STRANGELY enough, Elizabeth Féron had been immediately preceded on the operatic stage in America by a lady described by Odell as 'a sister of the great Mme. Feron, whom I shall soon have the pleasure of introducing.' This was the 'remarkably attractive' Madame Mangeon who had made her American debut on 28 September 1826 in a revival at the Park Theatre of Braham's opera *The Cabinet.* Billed as being from the Theatre Royal, Covent Garden, she had taken the part of Floretta. However, no documentary evidence has come to light to establish whether or not Mme Mangeon was in fact Féron's sister. (A Miss Mangeon had first appeared at the Theatre Royal, Drury Lane in December 1816, but she is described in *La Belle Assemblee* of April 1817 as the daughter of the late Mr William Mangeon of Clifton near Bristol).

The Wemyss Chronology informs us that Madame Fearon (Mrs. Glossop) made her *début* on the American stage as a 'star' in 1828, when she too played the part of Floretta in *The Cabinet* at the Park Theatre. Her business agent in the United States was J. M. Maddox, manager of the Princess's Theatre in London, where she had recently performed.

In the wake of Garcia, Féron must be credited with having blazed the trail for Italian opera in America. Odell devotes a whole section of his 1828-1829 chapter of the *Annals* to the impact which she made. This is what he wrote:

> 'The best thing, so far, was the appearance on November 27th [1828] of the brilliant soprano, Mme. Feron, who, after a great success in London, came here unquestionably the most noted woman singer who had approached these shores. Garcia-Malibran brought but slight reputation with her; she made hers here. Mme. Feron was the daughter of a French refugee to London; she had had the finest musical education and experience, and was a perfect exemplar of the old Italian *bel canto* of the florid type. She made her first appearance here as Floretta in

The Cabinet, "supported" by singers like Hilson, Barnes, Placide, and Mesdames Hackett, Sharpe and Wallack, and most of them could sing, in a way. The *Albion* of November 29th saves me the necessity of speculating as to the qualifications of the brilliant new songstress, or, indeed, of comparing her with the greatest among her contemporaries. Here, then, is an admirable review of her singing:

"Madame Feron's voice is one of wonderful power and flexibility, which united to her musical skill, science and taste, enables her at once to astonish and entrance her audience. Her first two songs on Thursday . . . established her at once; and her execution of *Chi dice mal d'amore*, by Meyer, proved her to be in Italian singing the legitimate successor of Madame Malibran . . . .

"The texture and quality of Madame Malibran's voice is intrinsically richer than Madame Feron's; although we are ready to admit, that the latter makes up by her skill and experience, and by art, what the other has by nature. The deep and rich tones, the melody, pathos and energy of Madame Malibran, will never be effaced from the re-collection of all who heard her. Madame Feron *astonished* us with her bold and masterly flights, but Garcia *pleases* us with her tenderness, sweetness, and passion.

"Madame Feron, then, may be summed up as a person possessing vast scope and power, great science and taste, acquired and cultivated by unremitting study – and a brilliance of execution which lays the applauses of the whole theatre under immediate and constant con-tribution. Profuse in the use of shake, and loaded with ornaments, she runs to the top of her voice – which, as we have said before, is of incomparable extent and compass – and then by some masterly and unexpected achievement, bears away all before her, and causes us in amazement to forget whatever natural defects and lack of melody we may have supposed her voice to stand charged with. Much has been said of her execution of the *Soldier Tired*. We are certainly of the opinion, that we have heard Mrs. Austin perform it with greater accuracy; but Mrs. Austin made this song her own . . . .

"We are now admirably supplied with female vocal talent. Mrs. Knight, in Ballad; Mrs. Austin, *Bravura*, and Mde. Feron in Italian and operatic singing, present a galaxy of talent which will not for a long time be exceeded, if ever equalled in this country . . . " '

Mrs. Knight had been the reigning favourite until she was eclipsed by Mrs. Austin and Mme. Féron.

Although Odell's meaning is not entirely clear, he appears to have recorded that on 29 November Féron sang in *The Haunted Tower*, by Storace, which 'oddly enough', he says, was her last for some time. He wondered why 'the gifted lady' had had so few appearances.

Certainly she returned to the stage on 24 December when she appeared with Pearman in Storace's popular ballad opera *The Siege of Belgrade*. Then, after a short illness, she took the part of Mandane in *Artaxerxes*, with Pearman as Arbaces (30 December). The Christmas Season at the Park was enlivened by a *Barber of Seville* on 3 January 1829, followed on Twelfth Night by a *Marriage of Figaro* with an exceptional cast: Charles Edward Horn (1786-1849) as Almaviva, Pearman (Figaro), Féron (Susanna), Mrs. Austin (the Countess) and Mrs. Hilson (Cherubino).

On 10 January Féron sang with Pearman in *The Cabinet* and the pair appeared as Margaretta and Robin in Storace's *No Song No Supper*. Féron enjoyed a benefit on 13 January, playing Louison in *Henri Quatre*. The evening had concluded with the third act of Rossini's *Otello*. At Pearman's benefit on 15 January, Féron was Mrs. Ford in an operatic version of *The Merry Wives of Windsor* 'as performed at the Theatre Royal, Drury Lane.' Odell hazards the opinion that much worse singing at vastly higher prices had been heard at the Academy of Music and the Metropolitan Opera House than New York heard at the old Park in the years 1825-1828.

It should perhaps just be noted that while in opera Féron's *début* in America was in November 1828, she is reported to have made a concert appearance in August of that year at the *Sans Souci*, later known as Niblo's Garden.

The reason why Féron had made so few appearances in New York in December 1828 was that she had been enticed to Philadelphia. On 9 December, at the Arch Street Theatre there, she had given her performance as Floretta in *The Cabinet*.

At the Park, Feron was playing Susanna again on 25 March 1829 and two nights later 'a great cast' performed Linley's *The Duenna*, with Féron as Clara. On 30 March Féron was with Horn and Mrs. Austin in *Native Land* and finally on 1 April she repeated her rôle as Mrs. Ford. 'I doubt' wrote Odell, 'if the music [of the *Merry Wives*] had ever before been so well sung.'

As has been seen, one of Féron's hobby-horses was that remarkable work the *Trionfo della Musica*. This had received its American *première* in New York at the Bowery Theatre on 20 April 1829. A week later Féron was given a benefit performance with the added *bonne bouche* of Horn's little operetta *The Quartetto*, sung by the composer and the beneficiary. To conclude, Féron had sung Caroline in *The Prize* (Odell).

Arch Street Theatre, Philadelphia.
(By courtesy of The Harvard Theatre Collection.)

Il Trionfo was taken from New York to Philadelphia and Féron can claim the credit of having appeared, on 5 May 1829, in the first Italian opera ever given in Philadelphia. Previously, from about 1800, the so-called ballad operas had held the stage there. The city's first extended series of 'serious opera' had been provided in 1827 by a French company from New Orleans. *Il Trionfo* was staged at the Chestnut Street Theatre. The opera, with Féron as Aristea, 'gave great satisfactioon, and in this worse than wretched season, produced four hundred dollars nightly.'

In accordance with custom, Féron sang in various concerts during the operatic season. Odell records that in 1829 the finest entertainment in the Summer in New York was in the Gardens, particularly Niblo's. He wrote:

'Much brilliancy attended the season at Niblo's. In the new and splendid saloon on 18 May appeared a remarkable group of soloists including Mme. Feron, Mrs. Austin, Mme. Brichta, Miss Pearson, Rosich, Boyle, Kyle, Angrisani, Horn, Gear, Miss Sterling, pianist, Powell, harpist, Norton, trumpeter, a chorus and a band. I am sure, if I had lived at the time, I should have considered that aggregation worth going miles to hear, even at the slow rate of progress then possible to man.'

Féron appeared again at Niblo's on several occasions during the Summer. The final night was 28 September, marking the close of what Odell believed to have been an extremely brilliant season.

A feature of the season had been the Musical Fund Concerts. An aria sung by Féron at one of these concerts was said to have been composed expressly for her by Donizetti.

A season of Italian opera and French ballet opened at the Park in New York on 22 July 1829 with *Tancredi*. Mme. Brichta was in the name part, with Mme. Féron as Aménaïde, the rôle in which Joséphine had made her début in Paris.

Feron had been at the Bowery Theater when it had re-opened on 4 June 1829, but only to sing, with Rosich, after the curtain had come down on a farce. After the death of the manager of the Bowery, Mr. Gilfert, Féron was among many who gave their services in a benefit concert for his widow (5 August 1829). A performance of the part of Susanna which Féron gave in New York in October was described by Ireland as unsurpassed in brilliance.

Theatre at Richmond, Virginia.
(By courtesy of The Harvard Theatre Collection.)

Féron was among the first to take Italian opera to provincial cities in the United States. An unconfirmed report states that she was in the first Italian opera to be staged in Savannah. Certainly she played

Susanna in Richmond, Virginia in 1829. The performance of the opera had included, by popular desire, several songs of the ballad variety. At a four-night engagement in Richmond (19-22 October 1829), Féron sang on each occasion: as Rosetta in *Love in a Village*, by Arne, as Caroline in *The Prize*, as Adela in *The Haunted Tower* and as Margaretta in *No Song No Supper*. She took her benefit on the final night, after which she gave a concert at the Capitol which 'attracted the most fashionable house of the Season.'

By the Spring of 1830, Féron was in the American home of French opera, New Orleans. In the late twenties, the impresario Davis had formed a resident opera company there and in November 1829 he had been able to enhance the appeal of his productions by recruiting a first-class corps of ballet dancers from the *Théâtre de la Monnaie* in Brussels. However, Davis faced a rival to his Orleans Theater in an American theatre on Camp Street. In February 1830, the Belgian dancers were enticed away from the French theatre to Camp Street, where the Americans had also engaged 'the renowned singer, Madame Feron'. She was introduced on 3 March 1830 as Rosina in the *Barber*. The occasion was not a great success. According to Henry Kmen, in his *Music in New Orleans 1791-1841*, the supporting cast was miserable and the orchestra poorly directed. Féron herself had been obliged to sing such songs as *The Arab Steed* and *An Old Man would be Wooing*, thereby omitting a substantial part of Rossini's music.

In an attempt to drum up support, the Camp Street managers had announced that Madame Féron would make her positively last appearance in New Orleans on 3 April. Madame, however, had other ideas. Only ten days later, she had transferred herself to the Orleans Theater, in the *Barber*, 'with the kind of support that only the French company could give.' By the end of April she had sung four more operas there, interspersed, *bien entendu*, with various ballads.

Though Elizabeth Féron was highly regarded in New Orleans, the audiences there were disposed to prefer Mlle. St. Clair. She too was a soprano, not pretty, but young and possessed of a pure, fresh voice. This was, after all, the Romantic period and Féron in more ways than one represented an older tradition.

By the Autumn of 1830 she was back in New York. On 2 September Niblo's had arranged an impressive gala in which Féron sang in 'a delightful quintette' (Odell). This was followed by a short season of opera at the Bowery, organised by Hamblin, during which Féron sang with Mrs. Knight, Mrs. Hackett and Plumer. Odell thought that this combination exceeded that of the Park; but then the Park had Mrs. Austin, 'a glorious host in herself'.

On 4 October, at the Bowery, Féron duly repeated her

performance as Susanna, with Mrs. Knight as Cherubino and Plumer as Almaviva. Mrs. Hackett (contralto) did her best as the Countess. There was an after-piece called *Of Age To-Morrow*, with Féron as Maria. The review in *The Mirror* lamented that the orchestral accompaniments had been so bad as to ruin the best efforts of Mme. Féron. Odell suspected that the Bowery audiences did not really care for opera. All the same, the Signorina had performed before exceptional crowds.

The next so-called opera was *The Exile* (6 October) with Féron as Catherine. There followed *Guy Mannering*, with Féron as Lucy, and *The Quartetto*, with Féron as Mme. de Luceval. Feron's benefit was on 14 October, when she appeared as Lilla in *The Siege of Belgrade*. In the final months of 1830, she sang in at least two charity concerts in New York.

In 1831, apart from further concerts, Féron appeared in opera at the Chestnut Street Theatre in Philadelphia. She played in the Philadelphia *première* of *Tancredi* on 15 September and was in New York again in October to sing Maria in *Of Age To-Morrow*.

Following a concert for the New York Musical Fund at the City Hotel on 9 November 1831, Féron went to Cuba, where as 'the celebrated French singer' she gave concerts in two Havana theatres, the Principal and the Diorama. Before leaving Cuba, she had expressed her gratitude to the people of Havana by giving a charity performance in aid of the poor.

Féron and Mangeon continued their singing careers in the United States in 1832. Early in the year, Mangeon was at the Bowery taking parts such as Nell in *Two Strings to your Bow*, Lilla in *The Siege of Belgrade* (6 January) and Mrs. Pimpernel in *Everybody's Husband*. In March, when the theatre reopened after a closure, Mangeon played Maria in *Of Age To-Morrow* and Kathleen in *The Poor Soldier*. Although described as a vocalist of some merit, Mangeon did not make a favourable impression. A candid critic remarked that the airiness of her manner contrasted agreeably with the opposite quality of her form.

In September 1832, Féron was again at the Chestnut Street Theatre in Philadelphia. She is reported as having sung in *Masaniello*, which was in all probability Auber's *La Muette de Portici*, not Carafa's *Masaniello*. According to W. G. Armstrong, in *A Record of the Opera in Philadelphia*, Féron and Mrs. Austin were both very popular in the Quaker City at that period. However, most of the productions were the so-called ballad-plays. Operas were seldom sung as originally written. *Cinderella*, for example, would be a *pasticcio* of *Cenerentola*, *Armide*, *Maometto* and even *Guillaume Tell*.

1833 saw the last performances of both Madame Mangeon and Madame Féron in the United States. At a time when Shakespeare was alternating with opera, Mangeon re-appeared as Mrs. Pimpernel in *Everybody's Husband* (21 January). Then on 31 January the Park Theatre gave her a benefit. She played Thisbe in *Cenerentola*, with Féron in the name part, apparently for the first time. Féron's own final performances in New York appear to have been at concerts in Niblo's Garden between August and October 1833.

By now, it was obviously felt that the two ladies had had their day in America. As Odell remarked: 'How quickly these artists pass the prime of their popularity; who has even thought of Mme. Feron for a year past?' Yet in her day, Féron had shone with great brightness. Wemyss, writing in 1847, had this to say:

> 'This lady was decidedly the best English singer who ever visited the United States; although one who never played a successful engagement. Her appearance was not in her favour; her figure was too much *embonpoint* for an American eye; she was really fat, fair and past forty [sic]; but in the science of music, I doubt whether Malibran herself excelled her. The young ladies, who are taught to beat a tune upon the piano for the amusement of papa and mamma, could not appreciate the difficulty of her *cadenza*, or the study required to form a perfect singer: nay, they had the bad taste to laugh at some of the most beautiful and difficult passages, which she executed with such precision and brilliancy.
>
> 'The taste for opera (and even now it is more a fashion than a taste) had no existence then; *La Somnambula* [sic] and *Norma* had not become familiar to the ear; Mrs. Wood, Miss Sheriff, and Mrs. Seguin had not charmed all our fashionable ladies into ecstasies. The *prima donna* of a Neapolitan theatre was doomed to return home, mortified with her reception, with no very exalted opinion of the American taste for music.
>
> 'She declared this to be the country where mediocrity of talent was paid beyond its worth, but where excellence in music, painting or poetry, would pine and decay for want of patronage; and there is too much truth in this assertion.'

Perhaps, despite everything, Féron had made some contribution towards raising the standard of musical taste in America. Unhappily, though she was a lady-like actress, 'she lacked the graceful form, the face divine and the inexpressible charm of girlhood' which had rendered Malibran irresistible (Joseph Ireland).

By 1834, both Mangeon and Féron were back in London.

Mangeon then withdrew from the stage and is believed to have opened first a cigar-store then a millinery shop in Regent Street. Féron, on the other hand, actively pursued her singing career.

In London, she performed in several concerts between April and July, at Willis's Rooms in King Street, St. James, and in the Concert Room at the King's Theatre. She was on the bill with such leading singers as Clara Novello, Rubini, Curioni and De Begnis.

From this period, notices become somewhat fragmentary. By the Autumn of 1835, Féron was back in Italy and the AMZ reports that she sang in Schio. In the Summer of 1836, when Joséphine was in Milan, Féron made a successful appearance in Piacenza in *Il Barbiere di Siviglia*. The AMZ remarked on her fame in both Europe and America as a singer of variations. She had been truly in her element as Rosina and had caused amazement with the variations which she had sung at the pianoforte. She had been applauded throughout the opera. Féron had a final season in Padua in the Autumn of 1836; and at the *Teatro Re* in Milan, she took the title rôle in *Norma*, a performance which the AMZ preferred to pass over in silence.

When a singer is in her declining years, reports and reviews naturally become scarce and it is not until Féron returns to England that any noteworthy performances have come to light.

ELISABETH FERON'S LAST YEARS IN LONDON

In October 1840 a new theatre, the Princess's, had been opened in London and in December 1842 the stage manager there, H. I. Wallack, put on an English version of *La Sonnambula* in which Madame Féron had 'consented' to alternate with Mme. Sala in the part of Thérèse.

Féron remained with this company for some time. In February 1843, she had a part in a three-act 'fairy opera' called *Little Red Riding Hood* composed by her daughter Mary, Mrs. Gilbert A'Beckett. In the same season she also played Thérèse again. In July, Féron was billed as Claudine in a new English version of *La Gazza Ladra* and in September she appeared in the *Barber*, this time as Bertha.

Madame Féron was still one of the leading members of the cast when the new season opened at the Princess's on Monday 9 October 1843. On more than one occasion in 1843 and 1844, she took the part of Henrietta of France in *I Puritani*. There was a novelty on 23 November 1843 when a 'new and original drama, with music' called *Flower of Lucerne* gave Féron the rôle of Madame Duval. This work was by none other than the Charles Edward Horn with whom Féron had sung in America.

Princess's Theatre, 1840. Interior of Concert Hall showing the stage performance during a Promenade Concert.

(Photograph by Graham Brandon – By courtesy of The Trustees of the Theatre Museum, Victoria and Albert Museum.)

Son-in-law Gilbert A'Beckett had written a New Grand Musical Burlesque Spectacle called *Magic Mirror*, or *The Hall of Statues*, which was given no fewer than forty performances, but it is not clear whether Féron had any part. Her final appearances on the stage were perhaps in March and April 1844 when she once again played Thérèse and on the last night before Easter when she sang *Johnny came a'courting me* at a concert.

Meanwhile her son Augustus Harris, was firmly anchored in his career in the theatre. When he was married in February 1846, at St. Mary's Lambeth, to Maria Bone, his mother gave her consent, describing herself as Elizabeth Glossop, a widow and unmarried (though in fact Joseph Glossop was still alive).

The singer died on 9 May 1853 at 7, Pelham Crescent, Brompton, London. The cause of death was given as dropsy. Son Augustus, of 9, Pelham Place, was the informant. On the certificate he describes his mother as Elizabath Féron Glossop, widow of Joseph Glossop, gentleman. Her age is stated to have been fifty-five. If true, this would mean that she had been born in about 1798 and would have been only fourteen or fifteen when she married Glossop. Wemyss, who had been aware when writing in 1852 that Féron was then living in retirement in London, states in his *Chronology* that she had been born in 1793.

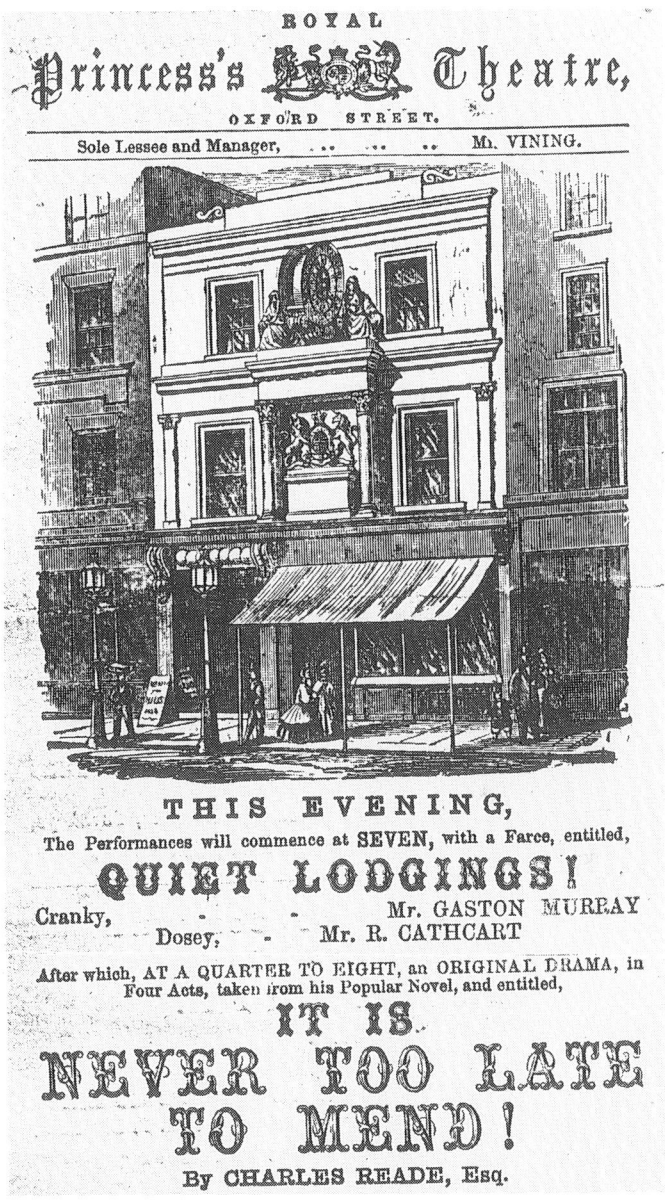

ROYAL

Princess's Theatre,

OXFORD STREET.

Sole Lessee and Manager, ... Mr. VINING.

THIS EVENING,

The Performances will commence at SEVEN, with a Farce, entitled,

QUIET LODGINGS!

Cranky, - - Mr. GASTON MURRAY

Dosey, - Mr. R. CATHCART

After which, AT A QUARTER TO EIGHT, an ORIGINAL DRAMA, in Four Acts, taken from his Popular Novel, and entitled,

IT IS

NEVER TOO LATE

TO MEND!

By CHARLES READE, Esq.

Exterior of the Princess's Theatre.

(By courtesy of The Trustees of the Theatre Museum, Victoria and Albert Museum.)

The descendants of Joseph and Elisabeth Glossop almost all had careers connected with the theatre and this story would not be complete without a brief note about them. This follows here, before the narrative returns to Emilie and the Emilie's venture in the United States.

Joseph and Elizabeth's daughters Frances Anne and Mary Anne were born in 1813 and 1815 respectively. Both had musical talent. Frances, a soprano, was a pupil of Braham's. Mary was a composer.

Braham had opened his new St. James's Theatre in King Street on 14 December 1835 with a 'new grand original operatic burletta' called *Agnes Sorel*. The libretto for this had been written by Gilbert A'Beckett, the versatile barrister and magistrate who had just become the husband of Mary Anne Glossop. Mary had composed the music and the title part was taken by her sister Frances.

The opera, if it may be so called, was not a success, but is memorable for being, it is believed, the first such work to have been composed by a woman. Frances, it seems, 'lacked the necessary power to sustain a position opposite Braham' and her contract was not renewed after the first season. All the same, she had received a favourable comment from *The Times* and had taken a curtain call along with Braham and the other male singer, Barker. She had been eclipsed by the gay and sylph-like Priscilla Horton, in the part of Louise, Agnes Sorel's attendant.

Frances marrried a gentleman by the name of Granville and is thought to have abandoned the theatre. She died in Paris in 1881.

Gilbert and Mary A'Beckett had two sons. Gilbert (1837 - 1891) was a playwright and Arthur William (born 1844) was a man of many parts who wrote *The A'Becketts of Punch* (1903) which is a source of first-hand information about the family.

As already indicated, Joseph and Elizabeth's late-born son Augustus Glossop Harris became an impresario of international repute. Augustus had three daughters, Maria and Nelly, who both became relatively well-known members of the theatrical profession, Patience, and two sons, Augustus and Charles.

It is his son who was to become Sir Augustus Harris, who did most to make a reality of what for grandfather Joseph had for the most part remained a dream. Frances Donaldson, in her *History of the Royal Opera House in the Twentieth Century*, has concluded that after Harris leased the theatre in 1888 one of the most important eras of opera in London began. Harris had succeeded in raising money, securing aristocratic patronage and recruiting such great singers as Melba, Jean De Reszke, Caruso, Emma Eames and Marcella Sembrich. Even so, it must be recorded that he owed his knighthood, not to his services to the theatre, but to the coincidence that he was Sheriff of the City of London on the occasion of a visit by the Emperor of Germany.

Seven members of the Glossop/Harris family are buried in three graves in Brompton Cemetery in the Fulham Road, London S.W.10.

The tomb of Joseph's son Augustus, who was buried on 25 April 1873, contains also the remains of his widow Maria (3 August 1892), his son Charles (8 February 1897), his married daughter Nelly Sedger (1 September 1897) and the unmarried daughter Patience Glossop (Harris) (1 January 1902).

Sir Augustus was buried separately, on 27 June 1896, as was his widow Florence, who had married a Terry as her second husband. She was interred on 10 September 1914.

Sir Augustus had had a daughter, Florence Nelly Glossop Harris, who became a leading actresss in Benson's company, which put on Shakespeare plays at the Theatre Royal in Brighton in 1915.

CHAPTER 44

Emilie with Mapleson in the United States and London, 1878-1879

NEW YORK (OCTOBER TO DECEMBER L878)

IN 1878, 'Colonel' James Henry Mapleson promoted his first Opera Season in the United States. His Company, billed as Her Majesty's Opera Company, opened at the Academy of Music in New York on 16 October. 'New York was to have this season what it had not had for several years – a fine opera company established with a considerable degree of security' (*Annals of the New York Stage*).

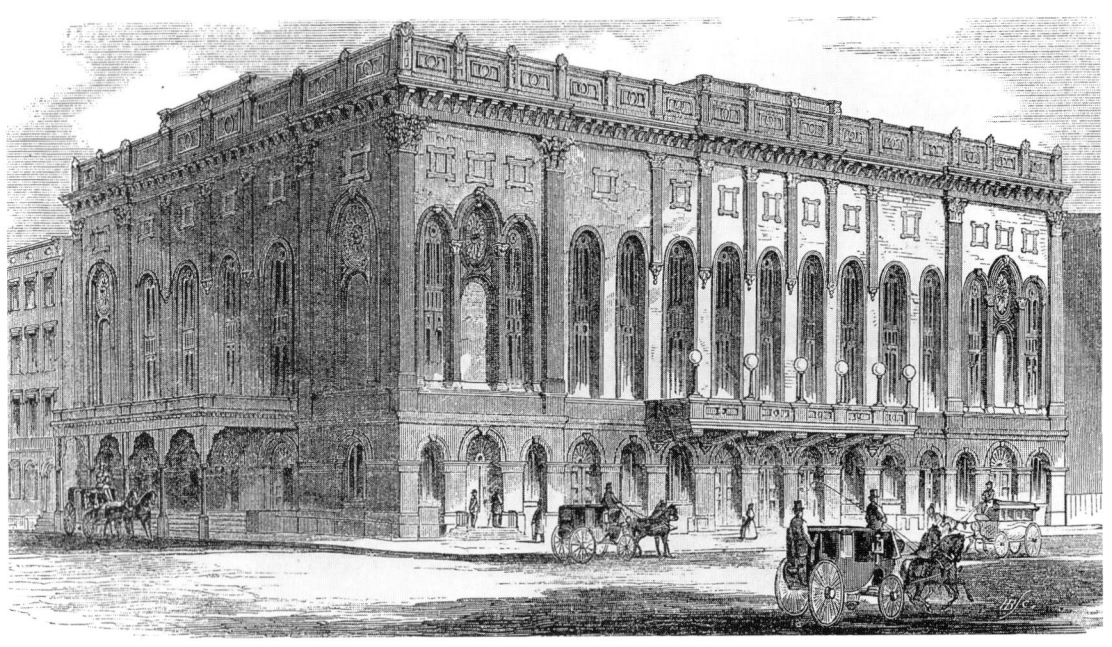

New York Academy of Music.
(By courtesy of The Harvard Theatre Collection.)

The conductor, Luigi Arditi, in '*My Reminiscences*', records that the opera party sailed from Queenstown in Ireland for New York on 25 September. The journey had been a splendid one, but in spite of the tolerably calm attitude of the sea, he and Mapleson were the only two who maintained steady sea-legs and never missed a meal.

356

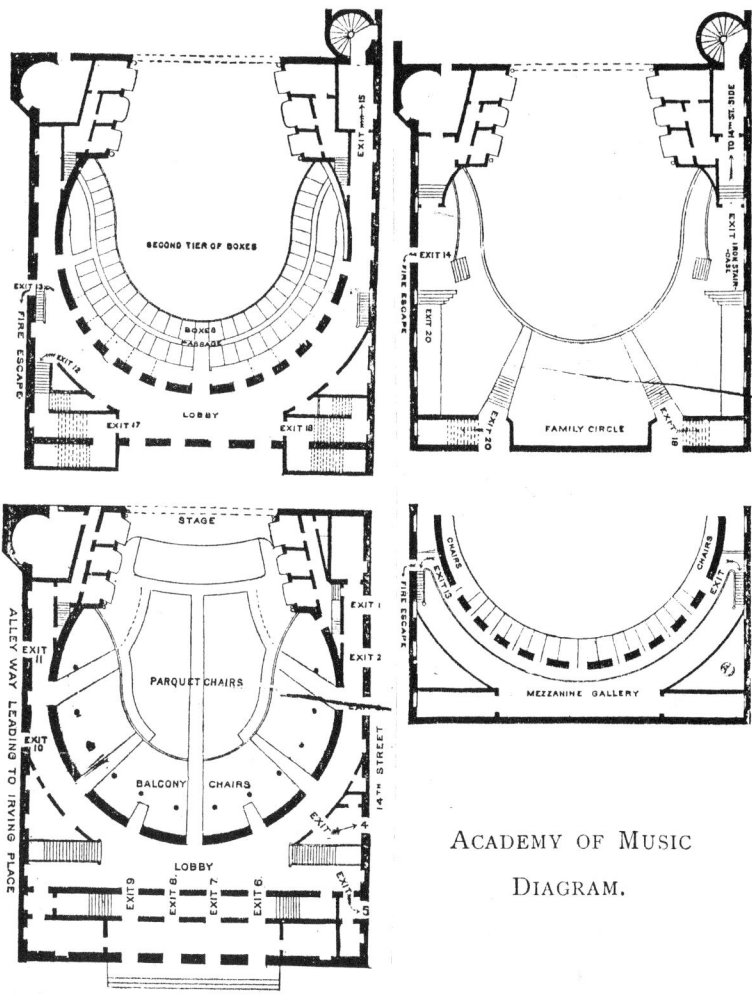

ACADEMY OF MUSIC
DIAGRAM.

Emilie was one of the party, and she was perhaps no better a sailor than we believe her mother to have been. Arditi has left us an intimate pen-picture of her. Madame Lablache, he wrote, was one of the most delightfully amusing women he had ever known and was a very important acquisition to the company.

> 'Always ready to sing, she never feigned indisposition for some trivial reason, or squabble in connection with her fellow artists, as several of the other singers were only too wont to do. In spite of our great intimacy (she is godmother to my boy [Gigi]), I feel the opportunity of telling a good story about her is so *à propos* at this moment that I am irresistibly tempted to draw a smile from my readers at her expense.'

'Mme. Lablache's great weakness was her desire to

spend money, and I must add that when she was in funds her generosity and kindness were proverbial. Her good-heartedness ran side by side with her extravagance and fondness for dress – which feelings often brought her into monetary scrapes. I remember how, on one occasion, a famous dressmaker [?Worth] sued her for the payment of a costly mantle she had chosen, and how, when the case came to court, she appeared in the witness-box, smiling and self-possessed, and at once gained everybody's sympathy by her affable manner.

'When [she was] asked to state her name, the judge, who had heard Madame Lablache sing in opera on the previous evening, of course recognised the eminent vocalist, and began to compliment her profusely on her voice and acting, telling her how much he had enjoyed the music etc. Hereupon they entered into a lively conversation, which had nothing whatever to do with the case; and to make a long story short, Mme. Lablache so entirely fascinated the judge that she not only gained the case with costs, but sailed triumphantly out of the court wearing, by the way, the identical cloak that had been the cause of the lawsuit'.

It would be rewarding to discover the official account of these apparently irregular proceedings and to learn whether the dressmaker went to appeal. Arditi gives no indication when or where the hearing took place.

It can be accepted that Emilie was a most useful and even irreplaceable member of Mapleson's Company, but she was not seen by this date as an incandescent star whose name on the billboards would of itself be enough to guarantee the success of the operatic enterprise. Odell described her as 'long a serviceable minor singer'. At forty-eight, she was regarded as no longer young, and youth tended to be at a premium in America. Gye's agent in Paris, B. Ullman, went so far as to describe Emilie in a letter to Mapleson as 'a good artist, but an old woman'. Furthermore, she was not a soprano and it was the soprano and the tenor who made the headlines.

And Mapleson needed some star material. He was repeatedly in debt and finding himself unable to advance money to his singers.

The Season opened with *La Traviata*. The audience 'was one of the largest, most fashionable and most critical ever gathered within the walls of the Academy; hundreds were turned away. New carpets had been laid in the corridors, a "sociable" restaurant had been established, the scenery was in excellent taste . . . and Luigi Arditi, of long ago, was conductor' (*The Herald*). In truth, all was not well. The plan had been to open with *La Sonnambula*, to introduce Etelka Gerster as the star, but she had fallen ill. Instead, Mapleson presented the New York girl, Minnie Hauk, who proved to be no more than a qualified success, as Violetta.

Emilie first came to notice on 18 October, as Marcellina in *Le Nozze di Figaro*. Minnie Hauk was the Cherubino. Partly owing to Gerster's continued absence and to the non-appearance of the 'luscious-voiced' Italo Campanini, the production was less brilliant than had been expected. However, by 21 October, when *Faust* was put on, 'pleasure reigned'. Campanini, in his mellow prime, was in the title rôle. Foli, 'a new bass', was Mephistopheles and Madame Lablache gave such a definitive performance that for long thereafter she was 'our only accepted Martha' (Odell).

Bizet's much-discussed opera *Carmen* was performed for the first time in New York on 23 October 1878. As Mercedes, Emilie was described variously as comparatively mediocre or as being good in the part, but this was only by contrast with the three chief singers who were outstanding in their rôles: Minnie Hauk in the part of Carmen which she had made her own in London; Giuseppe Del Puente as Escamillo and Campanini as 'a magnificent Don José'. *Carmen* was to prove a mainstay in Mapleson's repertory in America.

Emilie did not come thoroughly into her own until 24 December with the production of *Il Trovatore*. This caused a sensation. The *Daily Tribune* wrote that her Azucena was vivid and impressive in every line and gesture and rose in many passages to greatness:

> 'This picture of the old gipsy, savage and vengeful, tottering with decrepitude and fired with passion, is totally unlike the conventional Azucena, and as we watch it, the hackneyed text seems fresh again, and the well-worn music becomes new. The audience instantly perceived what a fine work of art it was, and Mme. Lablache was often interrupted by applause, and recalled again and again.'

Meanwhile, Emilie had done her duty as one of the Three Geni and, in the *Barber*, given an unimpeachable picture of the *duenna*, armed at every point, co-operating with the most amusing effect with Thierry's droll humour as Dr. Bartolo and Foli's sepulchral embodiment of Don Basilio (*New York Spirit of the Times*). On 23 December, when Etelka Gerster finally surfaced, to play Marguerite in *Faust*, Emilie was the Siebel.

Early in January 1879, Mapleson put on a highly-praised

performance of *Le Nozze di Figaro*. The *Daily Tribune* paid Emilie a pleasing compliment by saying that her acting in the small part of Marcellina ought to be held up to imitation as a study in the important art of doing little things well. Unfortunately the auditorium had not been full. The *Daily Tribune* lamented:

> 'If audiences at the opera were ruled less by rank and fashion and more by real love for music, we might be astonished that the performance last night was not witnessed by an overflowing house.'

Emilie went on to distinguish herself, in the New Year in Boston, by her performance as Cherubino. *Dwight's Journal of Music* singles this out in a generous tribute to Emilie's work as a whole:

> 'Madame Lablache, who has proved herself one of the most versatile and ever-ready artists of the troupe – having already harrowed up the feelings by her intense impersonation of Verdi's unlovely witch Azucena – made a very pleasing Cherubino, singing the arias finely (albeit transposed to a lower key, as were some of the other parts) encored after *Voi che sapete*, and entering with much spirit into all the pretty action and roguish by-play of the boy lover's part.'

Mapleson's first Season of opera in New York seems to have been generally regarded as an artistic success. Gerster, in particular, had received great public acclaim, especially in *Sonnambula* and *Lucia*. *Dwight's Journal* praised the Company for their rich resources, with even the secondary (but important) rôles being satisfactorily filled by excellent artists. Nevertheless, Mapleson had been beset by many difficulties. Minnie Hauk, jealous perhaps of Gerster, whose arrival had put her slightly in the shade, had refused to sing Pamina because she said that she did not know the part in Italian and had not time to learn it. (The part was taken by Mapleson's daughter-in-law Marie Rôze, who was making her *début* in New York during this Season). Then Mapleson ran foul of the Academy stockholders. Officers resigned, with Mapleson claiming that he was not receiving the promised financial support. With diplomatic tact, he gave a benefit for the stockholders on 26 December, but his disputes with the Academy were to persist for years to come.

At this period, operas were regularly followed by a ballet. Mapleson offered 'a new ballet divertissement, in one tableau, entitled *Les Papillons*, invented and arranged by Mme. Katti Lanner and numbering 60 artists.' It is obvious that dance performances on that scale added greatly to the expense of mounting an opera.

PROVINCIAL TOUR

From New York, Mapleson and his Company set out on one of the tours of provincial cities which were to become the pattern. In 1878-79, the itinerary included Boston (Boston Theatre), Chicago (Haverly's Theatre), St. Louis (Olympic Theatre), Cincinnati (Pike's Theater) and Philadelphia (Academy of Music). On tour, the Company would give a different opera every night, with two performances on Saturdays. On Sundays there was often a concert of sacred music.

Boston Theatre.
(By courtesy of NYPL:
*MBD (Uncat). Hauk, Minnie.)

According to the *New York Sun*, the performances in the provincial centres had been a pronounced success. 'As for the Chicago people, there seems to have been no bounds to their enthusiasm'. Often, in the Western cities, there had been standing room only, with many turned away. After *Carmen*, the favourite operas were *Lucia* and *Sonnambula*. *The Barber* was not very popular.

Carmen had been given its Boston *première*. In the cast were Mlles. Lablache and Robiati, representing the heroine's two gipsy friends. They had been 'excellent in their by-play and singing.' This Mlle. Lablache will be one of Emilie's two daughters, most probably Louise.

NEW YORK AGAIN

By 24 February 1879, the Company were back at the Academy of Music in New York, opening with Etelka Gerster in *Lucia*. Performances were given concurrently at the Brooklyn Academy of Music.

For this second part of his Season, Mapleson had added new works to his already extensive repertoire, making a total of twenty-six operas.

On 26 February, he ambitiously presented a version of *Lohengrin* in Italian, with Campanini in the name part, Gerster as Elsa and Emilie as Ortruda. The first performance was castigated by the *Herald* as almost an insult to American Wagnerites, or as a joke, though Campanini had admittedly made a most brilliant Lohengrin. Arditi, it was claimed, like most Italian conductors, had signally failed to give a sympathetic rendering of the orchestral score. This was not the first time that Mapleson's orchestra had been subjected to adverse criticism. Earlier, the *New York Tribune* had complained that though it played admirably, it was too small and Arditi needed to establish a better understanding with the singers and instrumentalists. 'There has been no representation of an opera yet this season without some brief yet serious musical contretemps'.

However, the subsequent performance of *Lohengrin*, on 4 March, was much more warmly appraised. The *Herald* considered that there had been improvements all round: the performance had been thoroughly artistic and therefore enjoyable. Emilie had a tendency to overact her part somewhat, but during the church scene 'she had displayed a grasp of the situation deserving of earnest recognition'. The *Tribune* said that Ortrud had found a superb representative in Mme. Lablache. The *New York Times* credited her with a memorable performance, and as the opera had been given without the cuts which had ruined its effect at the first representation, 'she had ample opportunity to show her pre-eminent abilities as a singer and an actress.' She had also proved, be it said, that she was still young enough to master a new rôle in a new genre of opera.

Another of Mapleson's innovations was *Ruy Blas* (14 March), an operatic version by Filippo Marchetti of Victor Hugo's romantic play of the same name. Mendelssohn's opera on this subject is better known, but Marchetti's music was described at the time as 'of a kind that appeals to every taste, as, while supplying plenty of melodies for the masses, the melodic beauty and originality of the phrases must commend themselves to every musician and connoisseur'. Emilie, in the part of Giovanna de la Cueva 'honestly earned the praise that was likewise bestowed upon her by an honestly critical and appreciative audience.'

During this second half of the Season, Emilie played both Martha and Siebel in *Faust*. The *New York Times* found her excellent as Siebel, but almost regretted her desertion of Martha, in which she was 'inimitable'. The reprise of *Trovatore* (1 April) led the *Spirit of the Times* to declare that Mme. Lablache 'may be said to have created the part of Azucena in this country'.

When the Season came to an end, the consensus was that Mapleson had done well. Arditi later recorded his view that this first Season in the States had been an eminently successful one, with Mapleson having at that time everything in his favour. The *St. Louis Musical Review* for February 1879 went into some detail. Colonel Mapleson, the paper asserted, had taught Americans a lesson in opera management which they sadly needed:

> 'The peculiarities of Italian opera in this country hitherto have been a high-priced and famous *prima donna*, with a wretchedly poor ensemble. The public have gone to opera to hear one or two singers, and in their adulation of the "stars" have tolerated the beggarly surroundings they have generally been treated to. Her Majesty's Opera Company is managed on a different plan; while the cast of the principal characters is remarkably strong, all of the surroundings are equally so. There are no "supes" at fifty cents per night who go on to swell the number of the chorus, and make a dozen singers look like thirty. All are singers, and good singers too. He does not bring six or eight instrumentalists to place among the ordinary theatrical orchestra, but a full orchestra well trained together and under the directorship of one of the ablest *maestri* living. He has given the people of this country the opportunity of hearing opera for the first time something after the manner in which it is done in European opera houses, and we thank him for it'.

The *Chicago Tribune* recorded its opinion that Mapleson's Season, considered in all its aspects, had been the finest Season Chicago had ever known, excelling even the famous ones of 1859 and 1865.

Similarly, Odell concluded that despite limitations here and there, Mapleson's Season had somehow brought back to New York 'the glorious visits of the Havana Opera Company' a quarter-century earlier. Mapleson's Company were certainly entitled to look back on this American tour with a sense of satisfaction.

Even financially, things seem to have turned out reasonably well. According to the *Herald*, the Colonel himself had actually made a profit of some $60,000 and no reports have been seen of artists not having been paid in the end.

The Company's next engagement was at Her Majesty's Theatre in London. They sailed from New York on Saturday 5 April 1879, after an early 12.30 matinée featuring *Sonnambula*. This was billed as the last performance of Etelka Gerster. According to the play-bill, the rôle of Teresa was to be played by Mlle. Lablache. This may indeed be one of Emilie's daughters, though it may well be an error for Madame Lablache herself who took the part on various occasions.

Several members of Mapleson's Company had not been above lending their names to advertisers in America. Arditi praised Mason and Hamlin's cabinet organs. Etelka Gerster, Marie Rôze and many others 'always used and highly recommended' Riker's American Face Powder (with its five tints, white, flesh, pink, brunette and yellow). The yellow was for evening, being particularly adapted to gaslight. No record has been seen of Emilie being named in this context.

LONDON

Mapleson's Summer Season in the Haymarket in London calls for little comment as far as Emilie is concerned. She was given her well-rehearsed parts as Teresa (*Sonnambula*), Martha (*Faust*), Mercedes (*Carmen*) and Marcellina (*Figaro*). In *Les Huguenots*, the rôle of Urbano was entrusted to Mme. Trebelli, who also sang Ortruda (*Lohengrin*), Maddalena (*Rigoletto*), Amneris (*Aïda*) and Siebel (*Faust*). The other main female singers were Etelka Gerster, Christine Nilsson, Minnie Hauk and Clara Louise Kellogg (as *Aïda*). The conducting was shared between Arditi, Michael Costa and Sainton.

Her Majesty's Theatre,

HAYMARKET.

—>•<—

Mr. MAPLESON has the honour to inform the Patrons of,

and Subscribers to,

Her Majesty's Opera,

That the Season will begin on

SATURDAY, 26th APRIL, 1879,

And the Arrangements as announced will be carried out as closely as circumstances will permit.

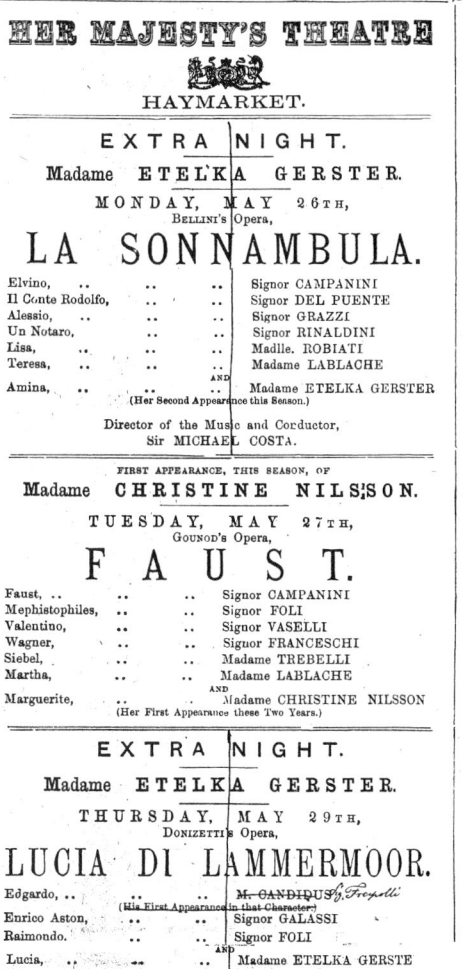

Notice for Mapleson's Season at Her Majesty's Theatre, London, (Spring 1879).

(By courtesy of NYPL (Music): *MBD (Uncat). Her Majesty's Theatre, Haymarket.

CHAPTER

45 Emilie in America, 1879-1883

MAPLESON and his company sailed for America, for another tour, on 25 September 1879 on board the *City of Berlin*. Arditi says that the Season did not open in such favourable circumstances as the previous year. This had been largely due to the absence of Etelka Gerster, who was too ill to leave Italy. In addition to Emilie, the Company included Miss Annie Louise Cary, 'a capital contralto, and a good actress to boot.' The American Miss Alwina Valleria was one of the leading sopranos, with Minnie Hauk, Mme. Emilie Ambré (a singer of Moorish extraction), Mme. Adini and Mlle. Marie Marimon. The principal male rôles were taken by Italo Campanini, Galassi, Aramburo, Del Puente and Foli.

Emilie's performances at the Academy of Music that Autumn generally received good notices. Though the *Daily Tribune* maintained that Siebel was a part for which her voice was manifestly unfit, the *New York Times* said that she had sung it with the taste which she always showed. As Azucena, she had not been up to the standard of the previous year, but had given a notable performance, careful and effective as usual and showing herself to be the admirable artist she was known to be.

IL TROVATORE
AN OPERA IN FOUR ACTS.
MUSIC BY VERDI.
DRAMATIS PERSONÆ.

MANRICO..............................SIGNOR ARAMBURO
IL CONTE DI LUNA...............SIGNOR DEL PUENTE
FERRANDO............................SIGNOR MONTI
AZUCENA...............................MME. LABLACHE
AND
LEONORA...............................MME. ADINI

Il Trovatore in New York (1879).
(From The Grand Italian Opera – Free Libretto.)

Miss Cary was billed to replace Emilie as the gipsy on 21 November and it had been Miss Cary who played Amneris in *Aïda* on 15 November, in a production which was acclaimed as a triumph both of staging and singing. Concurrently with the New York Season,

Emilie sang in *Rigoletto* and *La Sonnambula* at the Brooklyn Academy of Music. In *Rigoletto*, only 'Galassi of the ringing baritone' was singled out for praise.

In *Carmen*, Emilie was given her usual part as Mercedes and she played the Marchesa di Birkenfeld in Donizetti's *La Figlia del Reggimento*. In that sparkling work, 'the scene of the music lesson was admirably done, Mlle. Marimon's fun being well supported by the comical dignity of Madame Lablache' (*N. Y. Daily Tribune*). According to the *New York Times*, Emilie's singing and acting had been all that could be desired.

Mlle. Marimon had made her New York *début* on 3 December as Amina in *La Sonnambula* and Arditi says that she took the public by storm, just as Gerster had during the previous Season. Emilie was Teresa, the mother.

As was customary, members of Mapleson's Company took part in concerts, e.g. at the Chickering Hall. Rossini's *Stabat Mater* was a success on Sunday 16 November and was repeated the following Sunday. Emilie substituted for Cary in Rossini's *Messe Solennelle* on 14 December, apparently to general regret.

Boston paper showing Emilie in La Figlia del Reggimento.

(By courtesy of NYPL (Music) *MBD (Uncat) Boston Theatre - 1875-1914.)

367

The New York Season closed on 27 December 1879 with a farewell matinée of *Faust*. This was followed by a provincial tour. Arditi says that the Company had their greatest success in Baltimore, owing to the personal popularity there of Miss Valleria, who had been born in the town. Madame Ambré had proved to be 'a decided drug on the market'. On this tour, Emilie sang in *Rigoletto*, *Il Trovatore* and *Faust*.

Emilie in Faust at the New York Academy of Music, December 1879. (By courtesy of The NYPL (Music) – Mus.Red. *MBD (Uncat.) 19th Century programs (box 3).)

The Company returned briefly to New York after the provincial tour. It had been announced that the last appearance of Her Majesty's Opera Company prior to their departure for Europe would be on Thursday 25 March 1880 in *Carmen*. Emilie was billed as Mercedes. In the name part was Anna de Belocca, 'a contralto of much ability and possessed of great personal charm' (Arditi). With this success, Mapleson extended the Season and when *Sonnambula* was produced on 5 April it was Mademoiselle Lablache who was given the part of Teresa. Of Emilie's daughters, this was almost certainly Anna (Nina). There is a photograph, reproduced here, of Nina dated New York April 1880 which she gave to her friend Mlle. Corradi. Mapleson gave himself a benefit on 6 April.

Anna (Nina) Lablache as given to her dear friend Mlle. Corradi, New York, April 1880.
(By courtesy of The Bibliothèque de l' Opéra, Paris.)

The press had been airing some criticisms of the behaviour of the audiences. At the Academy, late arrivals were a problem. In *Aïda*,

'Signor Campanini had acted Rhadames with dignity, and sung his music with all his remarkable power and gracefulness. It is to be regretted that some of his most noticeable work comes in the beginning of the first act, and is therefore inevitably marred by the trampling of that large proportion of the audience who persist in arriving late, and disturb their neighbours while in pursuit of their seats. The beautiful aria *Celeste Aïda* was practically lost by the noise and confusion in the lower part of the house' (*NYT*).

Mapleson was urged to compel late comers to wait in the lobbies till the end of a scene.

Financially, it seems, this second tour had not been as successful as the first. At the Academy, the cheapest seats for the opera in 1879 (unreserved) cost 50 cents. The most expensive, for the parquet or balcony, were $3. Patrons could purchase elegant floral baskets of choice violets at the Bowery for $1. Tiffany and Co., as the sole agents, sold the opera-glasses of Voigtlander & Sohn, claiming that these excelled all others for abundance of light, scope of field and brilliancy of image.

It is clear that some at least of the members of Mapleson's Company remained in New York until the end of April 1880. A Grand Sacred Concert was given at the Academy of Music on Sunday 25 April. The star was the Hungarian pianist Rafael Joseffy, but by permission of Colonel Mapleson a number of members of Her Majesty's Opera Company took part. Among them were Emilie and Mlle. Lablache. This is believed to have been Emilie's daughter Louise, who was a contralto like her mother. On 30 April, Emilie sang at the benefit concert given for the impresario Max Strakosch, brother of Patti's brother-in-law Maurice Strakosch. The programme included the third act of *Trovatore*.

This Spring of 1880 is one of the rare periods when Emilie, her husband and her two grown-up daughters are known to have been together. The *New York Times* of 23 April reported that Monsieur Lablache (i.e. Nicolas) 'a Professor in the Paris Conservatoire' [sic], had come to New York to give singing lessons, aided by his wife. The *Boston World*, which also described Nicolas as a Professor of the Conservatoire, told its readers that he had been in charge of the principal opera houses in St. Petersburg, Havana and Cairo. In Cairo, it had indeed been 'under his direction that *Aïda* had been brought out [1871], and from which the representations since throughout Europe and America are only copies, that is, in the way of stage setting, properties etc.'

ACADEMY OF MUSIC.

THURSDAY, MARCH 25th, 1880,

Last appearance of Her Majesty's Opera Company, prior to their departure for Europe, when will be presented, BIZET'S OPERA,

CARMEN.

DON JOSE . . . . SIGNOR CAMPANINI
ESCAMILLO (Toreador) . . . . SIGNOR DEL PUENTE
IL DANCAIRO . . . . SIGNOR RINALDINI
ZUNIGA . . . . SIGNOR MONTI
MORALES . . . . SIGNOR GRAZZI
MICHAELA . . . . MLLE. ALWINA VALLERIA
PACQUITA . . . . MLLE. ROBIATI
MERCEDES . . . . MME. LABLACHE
CARMEN (a Gypsy) . . . . MLLE. ANNA DE BELOCCA

The incidental divertissement will be supported by Mlle. Adelaide and Mlle. Caroline Monti and the Corps de Ballet.

DIRECTOR OF THE MUSIC AND CONDUCTOR . . . SIGNOR ARDITI

BROOKLYN PRICES :

Parquet $2 50
Dress Circle 2 00
Family Circle 1 00
Gallery 50

General Admission, $1.50.

NIGHTLY PRICES OF ADMISSION, NEW YORK.

Parquette and Balcony (first three rows), ... $3.00
Balcony (other rows) 2.50
Family Circle, reserved 1.00
Family Circle, unreserved 50
General Admission 1.50

DOORS OPEN AT 7:30.   THE OPERA WILL COMMENCE AT 8.

DE BEAUPLAN'S GRAND FRENCH OPERA

While Louise Lablache had been with her mother in New York, her younger sister Anna had become a member of the French Opera Company in New Orleans formed by the impresario De Beauplan. After a four-month Season in New Orleans, this Company came to the Academy of Music in Brooklyn. On 21 April, they were billed to present Rossini's *Guillaume Tell*, with Mlle. Lablache as Edwige.

Detail is lacking about the activities of the Lablache family in America in the Summer of 1880. When it came to the 1880-1881 Season Emilie was not listed as a member of Her Majesty's Opera Company and in fact she and her two daughters had been engaged by De Beauplan to perform in New Orleans. Furthermore, Nicolas had been put in charge of the stage there as *premier régisseur*.

The De Beauplan Company performed in New Orleans at the *Théâtre de l'Opéra* from 8 November 1880 to 12 March 1881. The *Daily Picayune* congratulated De Beauplan on 'his successful re-inauguration of French opera in New Orleans.'

The Season had indeed opened with an essentially French work, Meyerbeer's *Robert le Diable*, 'familiar to all opera *habitués*, and especially to this public, before whom it has been sung during many seasons in the past, and at times by artists of the highest merit' (*Daily Picayune*). Anna, who is most frequently called Nina, had the soprano part of the Sicilian princess, Isabella. From this performance, we have an early description of Nina's voice and appearance. The *Daily Picayune*, referring to her as a *prima donna*, said that she was a very beautiful woman:

> 'She has grace of movement, and her voice is as sweet as a lute with never a break in her vocalization. She attempts nothing very arduous, but does her work with great consistency, and does it smoothly and well. There was a very hearty greeting for her, and her finer touches were all recognized and spontaneously rewarded.'

The *Nouvelle Orléans* wrote that she had a good voice and knew how to use it. *Dwight's Journal of Music* said that her voice was similar to Gerster's, only stronger. She was young and pretty.

Emilie's *début* in New Orleans was on 16 November 1880, as Azucena, when *Il Trovatore* billed as *Le Trouvère*, was put on in French. The *Daily Picayune* described her performance as a revelation:

> 'It is safe to say that, never in this city, was that rôle filled so well as it was last night. Time has dealt more than kindly with the lady's voice. Her acting and facial expressions are perfect, and ought to be studied and imitated by every would-be singer and actor.'

The next opera to be put on was *Faust*, with Emilie as Marthe. As was to be expected in the French atmosphere of New Orleans, the work was received with particular pleasure. The *Daily Picayun* wrote:

> 'It was quite refreshing after the late spell of Italian opera, to listen once more to the lovely strains of Gounod's *Faust*, in which the music is wedded to the libretto and not a succession of airs strung together without regard

to the action of the play or the meaning of the words. The test of good music is, that the more it is heard the better it is liked. Surely, the average Italian opera stands that test but poorly, while Gounod's *Faust* may be heard over and over again, and, at each hearing, new beauties discovered.'

As for Emilie, 'by her intelligent action, [she] made the secondary part of Marthe most interesting.'

Rigoletto, on 29 November, proved somewhat disappointing. Bad weather had affected the attendance and also seemed to have had a dampening influence on the performance. However:

'An interesting feature . . . was the *début* of M'lle de Méric [i.e. Louise]. She created a very good impression [as Madeleine] and, as far as can be judged by her short rôle, will prove a valuable acquisition to the troupe. She is the exact counterpart of what M'me Lablache, her mother, must have been twenty-five years ago – has the same tone of voice and facial expression, and the same style of acting. She is also quite pretty.'

Louise appeared next as Mercedes in *Carmen*.

On 2 December, the *Opéra Français* gave a performance of *Les Huguenots*. According to the *Nouvelle Orléans*, Nina Lablache had seemed to be prey to such an attack of fright that she all but lost her voice and could hardly even manage her recitative – a strange thing to have happened after her success in *Robert le Diable*.

In October, *L'Abeille* had given a preview of the names of the members of De Beauplan's Company. The lady singers were:

Mme. Emilie Ambré, 1re chanteuse en tout genre
Mlle. Del Prato, 1re chanteuse falcon [dramatic soprano]
Mme. Lablache, 1re chanteuse contralto
Mlle. Lablache, 1re chanteuse légère
Mme. de Méric, chanteuse contralto.

It is odd that one of Emilie's daughters should be described as Mme. de Méric. The object was presumably to distinguish Nina, the light soprano, from Louise, the contralto, but it would have been clearer if their first names had been given. Mme. Ambré was De Beauplan's wife.

On Sunday 23 January 1881, Emilie played the Marquise in *La Fille du Régiment*.

The musical director in De Beauplan's Opera Company was a Monsieur Momas. He had been welcomed on the first night as the old-time leader of the French Opera and greeted with hearty rounds of applause by his friends and admirers. On 31 January, a Grand Representation Extraordinary was given for his benefit. This took the form of a performance of *Paul et Virginie*, an opera based on the well-known story of love by Bernardin de St. Pierre. The music was by Victor Massé (1822-1884), chorus master of the Paris *Opéra* from 1860 to 1876. *Paul et Virginie* had had its *première* in Paris on 15 November 1867. 'How it ever survived its first performance is a mystery' (*Daily Picayune*). Rosenthal and Warrack describe it as Massé's most ambitious work, but have praise only for the short lyrical numbers which it contains. In New Orleans, Mme. Ambré took the part of Virginie, with a Monsieur Pellin as Paul. Emilie had the rôle of Meala, who is given a song in the first Act. As a whole, the *Daily Picayune* dismissed the work as being unsurpassed as a soporific. Only Mme. Ambré's delightful singing and chaste portrayal of Virginie had kept the audience in their seats. 'M'me Lablache's numerous admirers, who expected a finished rendition of the role of Meala . . . were disappointed. Neither her make-up nor her acting were equal to her former efforts.'

The Season in New Orleans ended with *Guillaume Tell* (8 February) and *Roméo et Juliette*. Emilie took, respectively, the parts of Edwige and Gertrude.

The new Opera-House in New Orleans.
(By courtesy of The Harvard Theatre Collection.)

According to J.G. de Baroncelli, who wrote an historical essay on the *Théâtre Français* in New Orleans, De Beauplan's 1880-1881 Season had proved to be one of the most brilliant since the founding of the Opera House in 1859. For that, the Lablache family can claim their share of credit.

It was one thing for a French opera company to be successful in New Orleans. It was quite another to expect French operas to attract audiences in the American cities in the North. So it was that De Beauplan took his Company on tour and failed. Cincinnati in March was followed by a fortnight in Chicago. In Philadelphia, in April, there were performances of *Les Huguenots, Faust* and *Le Trouvère* and Nina sang as a coloratura soprano in *Robert le Diable*. Then, in Brooklyn, the Company over-ambitiously put on such typically French operas as *La Juive, L'Africaine* and *Guillaume Tell*. Finally, in New York, attendances were so bad that De Beauplan went bankrupt. The swansong took place on 10 May when Campanini organised a concert at the Metropolitan Concert Hall in aid of 'the unfortunate singers from New Orleans'. Some of these unfortunates themselves, including Emilie and Louise, took part.

MAPLESON AGAIN

Meanwhile, Mapleson's 'delightful singers' had returned to New York at the beginning of March 1881, for their Spring Season. Though the cast as published did not include Emilie, she had become available with the demise of the De Beauplan Company and evidently sang in *Il Trovatore* on 16 May in a benefit performance for Campanini.

By the Autumn of 1881, Mapleson had formally withdrawn from the operatic scene in London, with the object of devoting his attention entirely to the United States. He had secured certain concessions from Gye, the manager of the newly-formed Covent Garden limited liability company, and Covent Garden was henceforth to be 'the recruiting house for his American season' (*Le Figaro*).

Before we leave 1881, it has to be recorded that James H. Cobley, who had married Louise Lablache in 1873, is registered in the Census Return for 1881 as being married, but living with only a housekeeper as the other resident at the address: 64, Clifton Hill, St. Marylebone, London. At the time, he is described as a commercial clerk, from Southwark. Whether or not there was a divorce, Louise subsequently became known as the wife of the Rumanian singer Ion Dimitrescu.

AMERICA 1881-1882

While, once again, the published list of the singers in Her Majesty's Opera Company in the United States for the 1881-1882 Season does not include Emilie's name, the Academy programme for the second night of the subscription (19 October 1881) stated that the part of Mercedes in *Carmen* would be played by Madame Lablache. Moreover, it is abundantly clear that Emilie was singing with Mapleson's Company in late March.

OPERA SEASON, 1880–81,

OF

HER MAJESTY'S OPERA COMPANY

IN THE UNITED STATES.

SOPRANI.

Madame ETELKA GERSTER,
Mademoiselle ALWINA VALLERIA,
Madame MARIE LOUISE SWIFT,
Mademoiselle BIANCA MONTESINI,
(Of the Licée of Barcelona, Her First Appearance.)
Mademoiselle ISIDORA MARTINEZ.
Mademoiselle VALERGA,

AND

Mademoiselle LORENZINI-GIANOLI,
(Of the principal Theatres in Italy, Her First Appearance.)

CONTRALTI.

Mademoiselle ANNA DE BELOCCA,
Mademoiselle RICCI,

AND

Miss ANNIE LOUISE CARY.

TENORI.

Signor RAVELLI,
(His First Appearance.)
Signor RUNCIO,
Signor LAZZARINI,
Signor RINALDINI,
Signor GRAZZI,

AND

Signor CAMPANINI.

BARITONI.

Signor DEL PUENTE,
Signor BELLATI,
(His First Appearance,)

AND

Signor GALASSI.

BASSI.

Signor MONTI,
Signor ORDINAS,
(His First Appearance,)
Signor BALDASSARE CORSINI,
(His First Appearance,)

AND

Signor FRANCO NOVARA,
(His First Appearance.)
PREMIERE DANSEUSE,
Mme. MALVINA CAVALLAZZI.

THE CHORUS

Has been placed under the charge of
Signor ZARINI,
(Chorus Master of La Scala, Milan.)

Director of the Music and Conductor,
Signor ARDITI,
Who has been specially engaged.

The Notice for the 1880-1881 Opera Season in America which omits Emilie's name.

(By courtesy of The Museum of the City of New York – Theatre Collection.)

In *Aïda*, on 25 March, Emilie played Amneris and was described as a real artist 'though no longer young'. She was then billed to make on 3 April 'her second appearance in two years' as Azucena. A newspaper cutting in the New York Public Library contains the following illuminating critique:

'The Azucena of Mme. Lablache has long been known as one of the finest pieces of combined vocal and dramatic effect ever witnessed on the New York stage. Spite of the evident signs of wear in her voice, she sings the music admirably well, with broad, bold phrasing, and a fine color and pathos, which are as refreshing as rare. Dramatically speaking, it would be hard to praise the impersonation too highly. The perfected art with which Mme. Lablache brings out all the subtle and contrasting shades of this remarkable creation - the alternating craftiness, treachery, hate, affection, terror and vengeful malice of the rôle - make the whole picture really a triumph of creative force'.

More succinctly, she was also described as 'noble in style, if not fresh in voice.'

ACADEMY OF MUSIC.

◄•••►

Farewell Performances at Cheap Prices.

◄•••►

Monday, April 17th, 1882,
WAGNER'S OPERA,

LOHENGRIN.

Lohengrin . . . . Signor CAMPANINI
Telramondo . . . . Signor GALASSI
L'Araldo del Re. . . . . Signor MONTI
Enrico . . . . Signor NOVARA
Ortruda . . . . Mme. LABLACHE
AND
Elsa . . . . Mlle. MINNIE HAUK

Director of the Music and Conductor . . . . Signor ARDIT

POPULAR PRICES.

Boxes to hold Four Persons, $8, $10 and $12 (according to Location).
Parquet and Balcony $2.00
Mezzanine box seats...................................... .... 1.50
General Admission 1.00
Family Circle, (the whole thrown open to the public)............. 50

Academy of Music - Lohengrin.

(By courtesy of The New York Historical Society - The New York Academy of Music Clipping File.)

Carmen was staged at the Academy in Brooklyn on 13 April, when Emilie substituted for Mlle. Kalas as Mercedes. This, according to the *Eagle*, was an improvement. Later in the month, she was billed to re-appear as Ortruda in *Lohengrin*.

According to Odell, the first five weeks of the Season had been successful, with few substitutions and with even a fine revival of *L'Africaine*. Once again, Arditi had conducted. However, by mid-April 'farewell' performances were being offered, at cheap prices (Parquet and balcony $2). *Aïda*, on 20 April, had been severely hampered by the illness of both Ravelli and Emilie, who was replaced by Mlle. Cobrianchi. The following evening in *Carmen*, when Ida Valerga was indisposed, Emilie did her best to take the parts of both Frasquita and Mercedes. When Mapleson took his benefit on 28 April, Emilie sang in the garden scene from *Faust* and she duly performed in *Il Trovatore* at the Grand Farewell of the Opera Season on 10 May. After that, it only remained for a benefit concert to be given for Emilie and this was held at the Chickering Hall on 20 May, with Italo Campanini singing and directing.

In June 1882, Louise was at the *Teatro Nacional* in Buenos Aires, singing in *Faust*, *Rigoletto* and *Lucrezia Borgia*.

INTERLUDE IN ITALY

Although Emilie was by now making the most of her career in America, she came back to Europe in 1882 and took a major part in the Autumn in a production of *Il Trovatore* at the *Teatro Regio* in Parma. This was in a special Season organised by the conductor Cleofonte Campanini to erect a monument to the patriot Garibaldi. Four performances of *Trovatore* were given, Emilie being joined by Adalgisa Gabbi, Italo Campanini, Leone Ghiraldini and Lodovico Contini. Emilie had given rousing renditions and the official record describes the production of *Il Trovatore* as 'excellent'. The *Gazzetta di Parma* had spoken of a veritable artistic triumph. The Campanini brothers, born in Parma and products of the Parma Conservatory, were the city's heroes, but Emilie was also claimed as a citizen. She had certainly spent some of her childhood there and her step-father Timoleone Alexander was a *Parmegiano*. The *Gazzetta* recorded that Emilie had been given the warmest of welcomes, being immediately recognised by the audience as a conscientious and highly intelligent artist. Such a fine performance of Azucena had never before been seen in Parma. Emilie had been repeatedly interrupted by applause and was called before the curtain to receive a rich bouquet of flowers.

AMERICA 1882-1883

When Mapleson's Company returned to the United States in October 1882, Emilie was once more on the official list of his singers. Arditi was again directing and conducting. The attention of the public was now concentrated on Adelina Patti, whom Mapleson paid $4,500 per performance, including the services of her husband Nicolini when he sang. There was a 'Patti boom' in America, but Mapleson's success also owed much to his strong supporting cast which, besides Emilie, included Fürsch-Madi, Valleria, Minnie Hauk, Albani, Scalchi, Campanini, Ravelli, Galassi and Del Puente, all but one of whom have already appeared in this narrative.

Klein describes this Mapleson tour as prolonged and successful. There seems to be nothing new to say about Emilie's performances. The tour ended with an operatic festival in Cincinnati, during which Patti appeared in *Aïda*, *La Traviata*, *Semiramide* and *Don Giovanni*.

ANOTHER ITALIAN INTERLUDE

It is recorded in the Asti paper *Il Cittadino* that on 3 November 1883 'Demerik' took the part of Siebel in a performance of *Faust* at the *Teatro Alfieri* in Asti, which is a town lying to the South-East of Turin. There have been suggestions that this was Emilie, but the review in the paper speaks of the singer being a pretty young *débutante*. She had sung effectively and, with study, should have a promising career before her. This description in no way fits Emilie at this date and must surely refer to Louise.

Mademoiselle Louise Lablache.
(By courtesy of The Harvard Theatre Collection.)

CHAPTER
46

Emilie deserts Mapleson for Abbey, *1883-1884*

THE name of Madame Lablache, with that of Signor Del Puente, duly figured in the list of singers which Mapleson published for his 1883-1884 Season at the Academy. At the head of the list, once again, stood the name of Adelina Patti. She was his star and Mapleson was prepared to use almost any means to retain her.

However, 1883 was the year when the Colonel was abruptly faced with stiff competition from the American impresario Henry Eugene Abbey (1846-1896), the first manager of the new Metropolitan Opera House in New York. Abbey, 'like other entrepreneurs of the day, showed no hesitation in raiding the ranks of the opposition.' He indeed succeeded in depleting Mapleson's ranks, though not in enticing Patti away. Mapleson, for his part, managed to recruit Etelka Gerster and she enjoyed a triumph at the Academy in *La Sonnambula.*

In his Memoirs, Mapleson complains as follows:

> 'Prior to the commencement of my season, I found on perusing Mr. Abbey's list the names of Sign. Del Puente, of Mdme. Lablache, of my stage-manager Mr. Parry, and a good many of the choristers, all of whom were under formal engagement to me.
>
> 'It is true that I did not care much for the services of these people [sic], but I could not allow them to defy me by breaking their contracts. I consequently applied for an injunction against each, which was duly granted, restraining them from giving their services in any other place than where I by writing directed.
>
> 'Arguments were heard the following day before Judge O'Gorman, on my motion to confirm the injunction which I had obtained against Signor Del Puente and Madame Lablache, who were announced to sing the opening night at the new Metropolitan Opera House'.

Thus that historic opening night, Monday 22 October 1883, saw the Met's *première* of Gounod's *Faust*, in Italian, without Emilie.

However, the rôle of Martha was taken by her daughter Louise, who had also been named in Abbey's list. Mlle. Louise Lablache was said to have 'kindly consented to assume the part at short notice – her first appearance [in New York.' According to the *Annals*, she did her work cleverly, but the *New York Times* said that the young and inexperienced singer had proved a feeble representative of Martha. Del Puente, it seems, had been prepared to pay Fcs.15,000 to abrogate his contract with Mapleson and he is billed as Valentino in the programme for that famous night.

When the Metropolitan Opera produced *Il Trovatore* for the first time, on 26 October, Emilie's star rôle of Azucena was entrusted to Zélia Trebelli (1838-1892), the French mezzo-soprano who had made her *début* in Madrid in 1859 and had had the satisfaction of being compared, in Germany, to Alboni. However, Emilie shortly afterwards succeeded in making her peace with Mapleson, though without returning to his fold. It is not easy to determine what her motives for defecting had been. Ambition, perhaps, to be a member of the new Company in the prestigious new Opera House. Or, indeed, the higher salaries which Abbey offered. Be that as it may, by 5 November she was singing as Flora in the Met's *première* of *La Traviata* and on 9 November she had duly replaced Louise as Martha. The *Star* commented that Abbey had snatched Mme. Lablache from out of the jaws of "Colonel" Mapleson: she, by her thorough art, had raised to importance the comparatively insignificant part of Martha and proved that the Colonel had lost a really great singer. Emilie's name duly disappeared from the revised list of the members of Her Majesty's Opera Company in the United States.

After Emilie had played Teresa in the Met's *première* of *La Sonnambula* (14 November), the *Morning Journal* remarked that it was because Mr. Abbey did all things well that he had chosen an artist of her respectability [sic] for such a small part, one usually assigned to advanced chorus singers. Certainly Abbey had collected an extremely strong team. He had Sembrich, Valleria, Fürsch-Madi, Christine Nilsson, Campanini, Del Puente, Novara and Malvina Cavalazzi. Campanini is credited with having played a part in Abbey's recruitment of Emilie and this seems inherently plausible.

The first part of the Season at the Met continued until 24 December 1883. There is a conflict of evidence as to who sang the Countess in *Rigoletto* on 16 November – the Met. programme cites Mme. Lablache, while the *Annals* say that it was Genetti – but it seems certain that Emilie was the Berta in the *Barber* on 23 November and 14 December. Del Puente played Figaro, with Marcella Sembrich as a truly delightful Rosina. On 28 November in *Don Giovanni*, Nilsson had been 'possibly the best Elvira ever heard in the U.S.A.'

Yet all was not well, either with Mapleson or with Abbey. Even the best performances were failing to attract sufficient paying audiences. The truth was that the rivalry between the two impresarios had overstrained the resources of both. First nights apart, neither opera house ever played to a capacity audience. Mapleson had the support of the aristocracy of old wealth, whereas Abbey relied mainly on the 'new money'. Abbey was enabled to pay higher salaries and this often proved more compelling than loyalty.

All in all, the opening Season at the Met was considered to have been an artistic success. Emilie can be credited with having played a modest but not insignificant part in an opera season of unusual brilliance. Some memorable performances had been given. The shapely Marcella Sembrich had made her New York *début* in *Lucia di Lammermoor* (24 October) and had become an immediate favourite with connoisseurs and public alike. Madame Fürsch-Madi was acclaimed as the finest Donna Anna since Mme. Parepa-Rosa. The orchestra, according to Eisler, 'had never been excelled for precision and nicety of shading.' This was a tribute to Abbey's conductor, Auguste Vianesi (1837-1908), who had earlier been employed by Mapleson.

Immediately after Christmas, the Metropolitan Opera Company had a fortnight in Boston, Massachusetts. Emilie played Martha in *Faust* and appeared, as previously in New York, in *La Traviata* (31 December) and *Il Barbiere* (2 January 1884). It is an open question whether it was Emilie or Imogene Forti who took the part of Teresa in the performance of *La Sonnambula* which had been given on 29 December. In the Boston *première* of *Carmen* (5 January), Louise played Mercedes and Trebelli made a sensation in the name part, with her phenomenal voice. *Carmen* was repeated in Brooklyn and then came in triumph to the Met itself on 9 January. In Boston, Eaton notes, audiences have always been hard to please, both by temperament and taste. Abbey had been able to provide singers who were well liked there. Nilsson was still much in vogue and Italo Campanini was the most admired Faust of the time. Sofia Scalchi was unrivalled as Siebel and Del Puente was a popular baritone. Sembrich had a brilliant voice matched by a superb technique and, not least, perhaps, Madame Lablache had 'proved to Bostonians that she lacked nothing of perfection.'

In the course of their opera season in New York and Boston, Abbey's Company gave ten concerts. Emilie sang in three and Louise in seven. Their choice of offerings gives an indication of the taste of the American audiences of the period. Emilie's solos were *Ah, mon fils* from *Le Prophète* and excerpts from Rossini's *Stabat* and *Petite Messe Solennelle*. Louise sang *Nobles Seigneurs* from *Les Huguenots*, *Una voce poco fa* from the *Barber*, *Gentille fillette* from *Le Pardon de Ploërmel*, *Il segreto* from *Lucrezia Borgia*, *Comin' through the rye* and *Dieu qu'il la fait* (Sanzay). Mother and daughter joined with Valleria on 9 December to sing *Le faccio un' inchino* from *Il Matrimonio Segreto*, Louise took part in the quartet *O sommo Carlo* from *Ernani*.

The provincial tour which followed the operas began in snowbound Philadelphia. Emilie and Louise both appeared in *Carmen* and in a matinée on 19 January Emilie took over from Scalchi as Nancy in Flotow's *Marta*.

Next came Chicago. From 21 January, when the Season opened with *Faust*, that city was to undergo a hectic fortnight of music, with concurrent performances by the companies of both Abbey and Mapleson. The public were bewildered by being confronted simultaneously 'with the most famed of the world's sopranos.' Abbey had Nilsson. Mapleson, in addition to Patti, had Gerster, who was well loved in Chicago, but his ensembles were weak. Similarly, Abbey was accused of having a company top-heavy with expensive artists and of using great names as a cover for shabbily mounted and carelessly-produced, worn-out operas. It was the Italian repertoire which was generally considered to be 'old hat', but in January 1884 gales and sleet had played their part in keeping people away. As between Abbey and Mapleson in Chicago, Eaton's conclusion was that at the end of the tournament both sides had lost.

In St. Louis, Missouri, which was the next stop, Louise had an unexpected break. A performance of Ponchielli's *La Gioconda* had been billed for 8 February, with Fürsch-Madi as Laura, but she succumbed to illness just the day before. With some misgivings, Abbey and his associate, the Czech impresario Maurice Grau, decided to give young Louise the assignment. According to Eaton, because she was 'barely eighteen' her mother's formal consent was necessary. Emilie freely gave it. Then, through all the performances, the devoted mother stood in the wings, mouthing the words at Louise, calling out directions, even singing along with her daughter.

Actually, Louise must have been well over twenty-five at the time so if Emilie's consent was really required it must have been for some other reason.

The following day, Fürsch-Madi was still too ill to appear, as billed, in the part of Donna Anna. 'So', writes Eaton, 'one of the Lablaches was called on to meet an even more severe test. Whether Emily or Louise was chosen . . . is not clear, but it seems likely that the mother assumed the task. Versatile and obliging, the contralto had come to the rescue in a similar emergency years before, as Arditi relates in his memoirs. Extravagant clothes were Emilie's weakness. When she stepped into the earlier *Don Giovanni* performance, she wore her own costly dress. As her scenes with Don Ottavio progressed, she felt grave anxiety for the fate of her gown, for Brignoli, the tenor, afflicted his colleagues with his habit of constant expectoration. During the trio of the maskers, Emily was heard to say: "*Voyons, mon cher, ne pourriez-vous pas une fois par hasard, cracher sur la robe de Donna Elvira?*" (The *Annals* confirm that in St. Louis Emilie played Donna Anna).

The wretched weather had persisted and Abbey failed to attract full houses in St. Louis. The lessee of the Olympic Theatre there said that both Mapleson and Abbey were losing money, but Abbey had the worst of it. 'He pays no attention, but keeps on giving the country better opera than it ever had before'.

Abbey had reason to hope for better fortune in Cincinnati (11-23 February), where a well-organised civic committee had offered a $50,000 guarantee. Cincinnati boasted a high degree of culture, more lovers of classical music than many cities twice the size and a Music Hall with graceful proportions and remarkable acoustics. The Metropolitan Opera almost always included the Ohio city in their tours.

Unfortunately, this 1884 visit coincided with very serious floods and even the last-minute and deeply resented decision by Mapleson to cancel his Cincinnati contract was only enough to give Abbey a brief shot in the arm.

There is some uncertainty about the rôles played by Emilie and Louise, but it seems probable that Emilie was the Martha in *Faust* and the Teresa in *La Sonnambula*. Abbey organised a matinée Gala Performance for flood relief on 17 February. Scalchi, Trebelli and Emilie, 'with their different timbres', sang in unison the half-dozen high As required from Ortrud in *Lohengrin*. As solos, Emilie offered *Fac ut portem* and Louise gave a rendering of *Nobles Seigneurs*.

The *Cincinnati Enquirer* had declared that 'Italian opera does not pay and cannot be made to pay in America.' Certainly its heyday was over, but Abbey took his Company on to Washington D.C. (where the public thought the ticket prices too high) and then to Baltimore, Maryland.

The Theatre at Cincinatti. Ohio.
(By courtesy of The Harvard Theatre Collection.)

At Baltimore's Academy of Music, Eaton records, Sembrich 'created the usual furor, but only Nilsson brought out an audience'. Scalchi caused trouble by going off to New York, with her costumes, declaring that she had a reputation to maintain in Baltimore and was not going to sing 'any such picayune rôle as Siebel'. Since she had sung that part many times before, the excuse was somewhat transparent. Louise stepped into the breach (1 March). Emilie played Martha.

NEW YORK AGAIN

Programmes for the Spring Season in New York in 1884 (10 March – 21 April) have not been preserved in the Metropolitan archives,

385

but the *Annals* give a fairly comprehensive list derived from newspaper reviews. Both Emilie and Louise were fairly active. They sang together, as Marthe and Siebel respectively, at a matinée performance of *Faust* on 15 March, with the tenor Joseph-Amédée-Victor Capoul (1839-1924) in the name part. Louise, having played Laura in *La Gioconda* (29 March), replaced Forti as Annina in *La Traviata* on 31 March. Emilie was the Azucena on 9 April and, according to the *Annals*, took the part of Donna Elvira the following night, vice Nilsson, who was sick. This is an extreme example of Emilie's versatility and must have involved a radical transposition of the music. At the Good Friday sacred concert on 11 April, Emilie sang *O Salutaris* and *Crucifixus* from Rossini's *Messe Solennelle*.

Academy of Music – Baltimore, Maryland.
(By courtesy of The Harvard Theatre Collection.)

Outside New York, Abbey's Company gave performances in Philadelphia from 14 - 19 April. These included the Met's local *première* of Gounod's *Roméo et Juliette* in which Emilie had the rôle of

Gertrude and Louise played Stéphano, Romeo's page. Italo Campanini and Sembrich were in the name parts and Vianesi conducted.

The Company gave a farewell Gala Performance at the Metropolitan Opera House on 21 April, but it seems from the *Annals* that neither Emilie nor Louise took part. The Gala was memorable for including, with the excerpts from operas, the Trial Scene from *The Merchant of Venice* with Ellen Terry as Portia.

CHAPTER
47

Emilie back with Mapleson: Italian opera loses popularity, 1884-1886

IT may well be that it became Emilie's custom to spend her Summers in Europe, but no record has so far been traced of her movements in the Summer of 1884. By the Autumn she was back in the United States. The name of Madame Lablache appears in at least one of the published lists of the singers in Her Majesty's Opera Company for the New York Season 1884 – 1885 at the Academy of Music. So Emilie had returned to Mapleson. However, no evidence has been discovered of her participation in any of the operas which the Company produced. This was the Season when the premature announcement was made that Patti would be making her farewell appearance in the United States. At the top of the list of Mapleson's tenors was a new name, that of Signor Cardinali. According to the *New York Herald*, Cardinali, a Sicilian, was as handsome as Apollo. As Manrico in *Il Trovatore* 'his youth and passion had carried all before it.' There was also a new baritone, Signor de Anna, whose powerful and resonant voice made him an instant success.

Emilie is recorded as having been billed to sing in a concert on 30 November 1884. This was at The Casino, the home of operetta, where according to Odell members of Mapleson's Company appeared in concerts in late 1884.

In 1884-85, Anna Lablache (Nina) was at the *Liceo* in Barcelona as 'comprimaria', or junior lead. Louise, for her part, had left America by the end of 1884 and was performing at the *Théâtre Italien* in Paris. On 15 October, she sang there in a charity concert for the families of cholera victims. This had been notable for the Paris début of Marcella Sembrich. On 16 December, Louise took the part of Zuléma in an Italian version of the opera *Aben-Hamet* by the French composer Théodore Dubois (1837-1924). Described as a *débutante*, Louise replaced Mme. Trebelli, at short notice. Trebelli had fled from Paris for fear of the cholera.

Aben-Hamet is a drama of the conflict between love and faith, Moslem and Christian, and takes place in the grandiose setting of the Alhambra in Granada. Zuléma is the mother of the Moslem hero, Aben-Hamet, who falls in love with the daughter of the Christian Governor. *Le Figaro* (Auguste Vitu) praised Mlle. Lablache, saying that she had the voice of an Italian contralto, sonorous and sweet in the lower registers. The reviewer added that the singer had designed her rich Moorish costume herself. She had seemingly inherited her mother's interest in fine clothes. *Le Menestrel* said that Louise had a pretty voice, but it needed more control. She had been made up to look more like the hero's daughter than his mother. This suggests a touch of vanity alien to Emilie's approach to the part of the gipsy Azucena.

THÉATRE ITALIEN

MERCREDI 15 OCTOBRE 1884, à 8 heures très précises

Concert-Festival

Au Bénéfice des Familles des Victimes du Choléra de France et d'Italie

SOUS LE PATRONAGE DE

M. LE MINISTRE DE L'INTÉRIEUR & DE M. LE MINISTRE D'ITALIE

PROGRAMME

Ouverture des *VÉPRES SICILIENNES* . . . . VERDI	LUCIA DE LAMMERMOOR (Scène de la Folie) . . DONIZETTI
ORCHESTRE du Théâtre, sous la direction de **M. CONTI.**	**M**me **MARCELLA SEMBRICH.**
La *VERGINE DI SUNAM*. . . . . RICORDI	Solo de Flûte par M. GÉNIN.
Les CHŒURS du Théâtre, sous la direction de	MACBETH (Scène du Somnambulisme) . . . . . . SHAKESPEARE
M. LOMBARDI.	**M**me **RISTORI.**
Sérénade de la *DAMNATION de FAUST* . . . . BERLIOZ	FANTAISIE . . . . SIVORI
M. LAUWERS.	M. SIVORI.
Brindisi de *LUCREZIA* . . . . DONIZETTI	Air du *BARBIERE* . . . . ROSSINI
M**lle** LOUISE LABLACHE.	M. DELLE SEDIE.
AIR	Danse des Heures, de *GIOCONDA* . . . . PONCHIELLI
M**me** TREMELLI.	ORCHESTRE, sous la direction de M. GIALDINI.
Air de *MEFISTOFELE*. . . . . BOITO	LA MUSICA PROIBITA. . . . . GASTALDON
M**lle** CÉCILE RITTER.	M. NOUVELLI.
FRANCESCA DI RIMINI . . . . DANTE	MONOLOGUE . . . .
M**me** RISTORI.	M. COQUELIN CADET.
LA FARANDOLE. { Les Tambourinaires, Sylvine. La Farandole fantastique } DUBOIS	*Airs de Danse variés, pour instruments à cordes* . . . . . SALVAYRE
ORCHESTRE sous la direction de l'AUTEUR.	ORCHESTRE, sous la direction de l'AUTEUR.
DANSE TCHERKESSE, pour deux pianos . . . . . . RITTER	Air des *SAISONS*. . . . . VICTOR MASSÉ
MM. THÉODORE RITTER et KOWALSKI.	M**lle** LINA BELL.
LIVRE III, CHAPITRE IER, Comédie en un acte. . . EUG. PIERRON	*LA MUETTE* (Prière) . . . . AUBER
M. COQUELIN AINÉ, M. FEBVRE, M**lle** BARTET.	Les CHŒURS du Théâtre, sous la direction de
Air et Duo de *POLIUTTO*. . . . . DONIZETTI	M. LOMBARDI.
M. TAMBERLICK et M**me** RITA SONNIERI.	2me SOLO DE CONCERT . . . . ARBAN
a. Sérénade Hongroise . . . . } JONGIÈRES	MM. FANTHOUX, DAULIN, DUCLAUD, PETIT
b. Polonaise de *DIMITRI* . . . . }	et SABATHIER, sous la direction de M. ARBAN.
ORCHESTRE, sous la direction de l'AUTEUR.	MARCHE. . . . .
	ORCHESTRE, sous la direction de **M. CONTI.**

Le Piano sera tenu par M. MANGIN.

10 81 28 — Typ. Morris père et fils,   Rue Amelot, 64, Paris.

Concert-Festival.

(By courtesy of the Bibliothèque de l'Opéra.)

Aben-Hamet was a success, but a repeat performance planned for 27 December had to be cancelled because Louise had an attack of jaundice. Then the impresario, Victor Maurel, who also played the name part, found himself in financial difficulties and was obliged to abandon his enterprise. Louise must have been reminded of the fate of the other French impresario with whom her career had been bound up: De Beauplan.

Emilie, meanwhile, remained with Mapleson, who, after a brilliant fortnight at the French Opera House in New Orleans, somewhat unexpectedly returned to London in the Summer of 1885 to give a short Season of Italian opera at Covent Garden. This was to have opened on 16 June, but had to be postponed until 20 June owing, it was stated, to the sudden indisposition of Madame Patti, who was to sing Violetta in *La Traviata*.

At this period, Italian opera was not in vogue. *The Times* gave Mapleson's project a very lukewarm reception. 'The short season of Italian opera at Covent Garden . . . marks a stage in the decline and fall of that time-honoured institution which we have frequently anticipated. The patrons of Italian opera have long ceased to take much interest in the music that is sung; they care only for the singers; and among the singers chiefly for Madame Patti. That Italian opera without Madame Patti is impossible everyone knows; whether it is possible with her, taking into account the terms which the great *prima donna*, conscious of her worth, thinks it right to demand, is a question which the present season must decide.' A daunting scenario indeed for a singer in the old Italian tradition such as Emilie, who was by then fifty-five.

Naturally enough, Emilie was not any longer being selected for many major rôles, but she continued to give excellent performances in important secondary parts such as Berta (*Il Barbiere*), Martha (*Faust*), Mercedes (*Carmen*), Flora (*La Traviata*) and the Contessa in *Rigoletto*.

Reviewing the *Barber*, which had been attended by the Prince and Princess of Wales and Prince Albert Victor, the *Globe* wrote that with the exception of Del Puente as Figaro and Madame Lablache (Berta), the cast was scarcely worthy to co-operate with Patti. In the opinion of the *Daily News*, Emilie had filled the part of Berta well and, in *Faust*, had played Martha 'with customary point'.

This was the Season when Patti attempted the title rôle in *Carmen*. It was the first time that she had played the gipsy part on any stage and it had apparently cost her three years of patient study. Alas, the attempt proved to be 'the one decisive disappointment of her career' (Klein). Emilie appeared as Mercedes.

FAREWELL MATINEE, SATURDAY, JAN. 16th,
Mlle. ALMA FOHSTROM,
MARTHA

Lionello	Signor RAVELLI
Plunketto	Signor CHERUBINI
Tristano	Signor CARACCIOLO
Nancy (Her original character)	Mme. LABLACHE

— AND —

Martha (Lady Henrietta)	Mlle. ALMA FOHSTROM
Director of Music and Conductor	Signor ARDITI

Emilie at the Boston Theatre,
January 1886.
(By courtesy of the NYPL (Music)
*MBD. (Uncat) Boston Theatre.)

Mapleson put on the first performance of *Il Flauto Magico* which Her Majesty's Opera Company had staged for six years and Emilie sang with Mlles. Bauermeister and Justine Macvity as one of the three Geni.

On the final night of the London Season, there was a celebration in honour of Patti's twenty-fifth annual engagement at the Royal Italian Opera. This took place after a performance of *Il Trovatore*, distinguished by the most magnificent rendering of the part of Leonora that Patti's biographer Klein could recall. Was Emilie the Azucena? Arditi had conducted and received his usual meed of praise.

During this Summer of 1885, Mapleson had tried under the cloak of his son Charles to put his operas on at the Met. This failed. Instead, he announced himself as the Sole Lessee snd Director of the Academy of Music and introduced his 1885-86 Opera Season with a characteristic example of his public-relations style:

> 'In no country in the world is music more appreciated than in the United States. In no country has the art so rapidly extended itself, and by no people have its beneficial effects been so powerfully demonstrated as by the American public. Through the liberality of the Stockholders, during the recess the Academy of Music has been entirely redecorated, re-furnished, altered and improved throughout, at very great expense, thus rendering the "Old Home of Music" one of the most attractive Opera Houses in the world. Since the close of the last season the Director has visited most of the continental cities, and trusts the artistic selection he has made will meet with the approbation of his friends and supporters. He therefore confidently enters upon the Eighth Year of his Management in this country (and Twenty-seventh of his operatic career) feeling assured that sufficient admirers will always be found of the delightful melodies of Mozart, Rossini, Bellini, Donizetti, Verdi, Gounod, etc., etc., interpreted by the most competent artistes available in the acknowledged language of music.'

It was clear from this that the emphasis would be on the Italian school.

Having been deserted by Patti, Mapleson announced that he had abolished the star system and in order to lend variety to the repertoire, he was contemplating two novelties: Vincent Wallace's opera *Maritana*, for its first showing on the 'Italian' stage, and Massenet's *Manon*, which would be given its American *première*. Mapleson stated that he had secured the sole right of representation for *Manon*, for which the composer had made several important alterations and additions.

Mapleson declared that his aim was to make Italian opera 'truly the music for the people'. However, the truth was that public taste had changed. Perhaps the phrase 'feeling that sufficient admirers will always be found' had betrayed a nagging doubt. Be that as it may, 'everything went wrong.' The American tour of 1885-86 led to Mapleson's bankruptcy and he was never again able to mount a season of the first rank in the United States. One of his problems, apart from the growing indifference to the old repertoire (except when Patti was singing) was that he did not find adequate space and time for his rehearsals.

The Season was billed to open on Monday evening, 2 November 1885. As usual, Arditi was to be the Director of Music and Conductor and there was to be a ballet with Mme. Malvina Cavalazzi as the *première danseuse*. The list of singers included Madame Lablache and Mlle. de Méric (probably Louise Lablache).

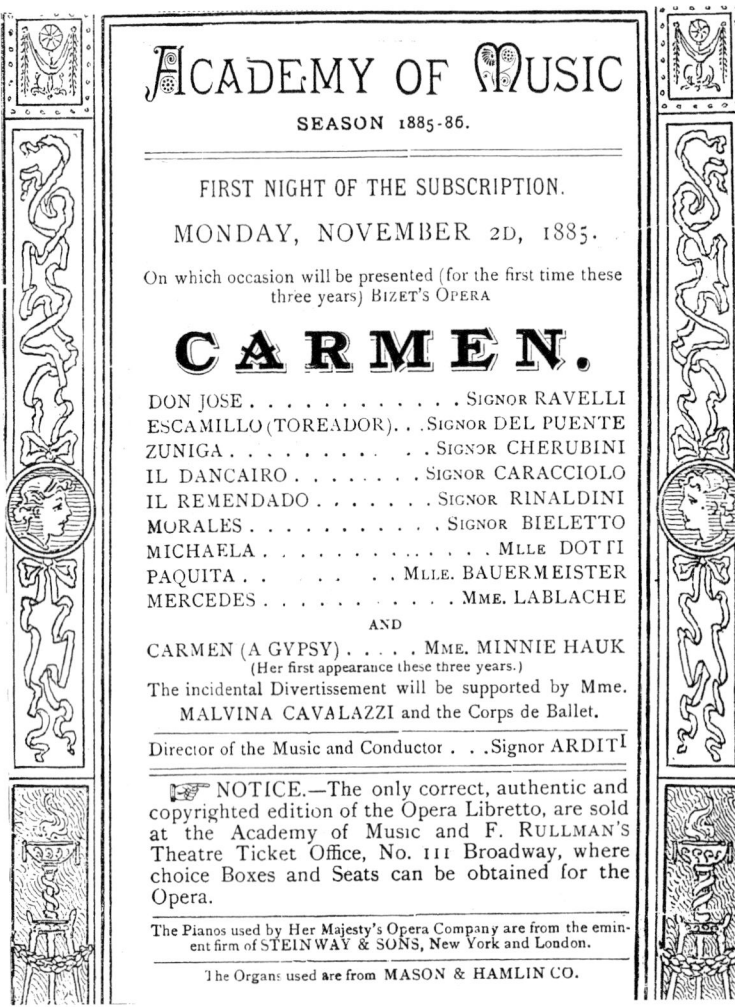

The opening night at Mapleson's 1885-1886 Season.

(By courtesy of the NYPL.)

The first night was devoted to *Carmen* 'for the first time these three years', with Minnie Hauk in the name part which was one of her most celebrated rôles. Emilie played Mercedes. *Il Trovatore* followed, with Emilie as Azucena. As the *New York Times* said, Madame Lablache 'embodied Azucena'. However, her portrayal 'will not be remembered for the quality of the vocalist's tones, and she sometimes lays herself open to reproach by a tendency to excessive emphasis in the delivery of particularly dramatic passages, but as a varied, forceful, and suggestive delineation of the gipsy, the effort is second to none recalled in connection with the lyric stage. In a dramatic sense, indeed, the Azucena of the occasion was, as heretofore, one of the very best that New York audiences have looked upon since the original production of *Il Trovatore*' [May 1855]. The Leonore was 'the charming Russian soprano from the Paris Opéra' Mlle. Félia Litvinova (1860-1936), famous for her portrayal of Gluck's Alceste.

So far, all seemed to be going well enough. After the production of *Lucia di Lammermoor* (9 November), the *New York Times* opined that the obviously genuine enthusiasm of the audience indicated that the public's fondness for Italian opera was 'not quite as extinct as a small but noisy fraction of the community would have us believe'. The directors of the Academy were rumoured to be dissatisfied with Mapleson because he had not engaged Patti or Gerster, but there were those who thought that the performances as a whole were more artistically enjoyable than they had been in the era of the expensive stars. They deserved the fullest appreciation of the musical public in New York.

Unfortunately, there was an inexorable trend against what was perceived to be the artificiality of the Italian tradition. Reduced prices were in force by 20 November when Mapleson put on Auber's fifty-year-old comic opera *Fra Diavolo*. The libretto of this work, by Scribe, concerns a famous Robin-Hood-like character from the Naples area, masquerading as a Marquis, who involves a girl in one of his robberies, then absolves her of blame and reunites her with her lover. The *Herald* said that the performance had been a most brilliant success. Emilie played Pamela, the wife of the wealthy English traveller Milord Cockburn (or Koburg), 'with irrestible humour, as the accomplished artist which she is.' The tenor Ravelli was in the name-part as the bandit chief and the rôle of Zerlina, the innkeeper's daughter, was taken by Mlle. Alma Fohström.

After *La Sonnambula* (13 November), in which Emilie was Teresa, *Fra Diavolo* seems to have come as welcome light relief. The *Star* praised the Company's bright and amusing performance and rejoiced at the return of a typical specimen of 'real *opéra comique*', a genre which had been replaced on the one hand by more serious works and on the other by *opéra bouffe*. *Fra Diavolo* was so seldom given that it had almost the charm of novelty and the performance had

Mme. Lablache proved herself once more the accomplished artist that she is in the part of Lady Coburg. She performed it with irresistible humor and lent valuable aid in the concerted music.

Signor Del Puente, the ever welcome artist, was admirable as Beppo, and excruciatingly funny, and Signor Caraccioli's portrayal of Lord Coburg was worthy of much praise Signor Cherubini was very amusing as Giacomo.

The divertissement by Mme. Cavalazzi and the ballet was an elaborate and beautiful one.

The orchestra was in excellent form and the opera was a most brilliant success.—*N. Y. Herald*.

been a shining example of the art of giving equal significance to the musical and comical elements of an opera of this kind. Del Puente and Cherubini had succeeded in raising much laughter, while skilfully avoiding being mistaken for clowns.

The *Daily Telegraph* declared that the audience had rarely been dismissed from the Academy in such delightful humour. 'It is scarcely possible to imagine a more satisfactory performance of Auber's ever-fresh and delightful *Fra Diavolo*. It is in the interpretation of such works as this that Col. Mapleson's company is seen to greatest advantage, and it is to this class of opera that [he] should give most attention.'

Maritana was also acclaimed as a success. This is a romantic tale, not without humour, set in Madrid and featuring swashbuckling noblemen and a beautiful *gitana*. At the time of the New York production, 'both the story and the score . . . were well known to the frequenters of the theatre and the concert room.' The Italian version had gone down well. 'It had been an uncommon treat' to listen to 'solo and concerted pieces, full of gentle feeling, brightness or martial rhythm, sung by voices which are seldom if ever heard in English playhouses, and with the art of which the secret has not yet been wrested from Italian teachers and performers' (*New York Times*). In the mezzo-soprano part of the Marchese di Montefiore, Emilie 'had done excellent work'.

Emilie also received favourable critical review for her performance in *Manon* as Javotte, one of the actresses. Massenet's opera was given on 23 December for Mapleson's annual benefit. Minnie Hauk was Manon and Giannini Des Grieux.

Against these apparent successes of Mapleson's efforts, must however be set the opinion of the respected Odell. As he saw it, 'The fading glory of the famous Academy finally died out . . . . Fashion now patronised the Met. Mapleson had came back with the singer Minnie Hauk, and the opera *Carmen*, which had helped to establish him in 1878-79, but 1885 was not 1878 and by contrast with the operas at the Met 'Mapleson's second offering was antiquated to a degree.' With Del Puente and 'the respected' Madame Lablache, the cast of the 'venerable' *Trovatore* had surely been worthy, but it was of the second rank and that was not enough. In *Lucia*, Mlle. Fohström had not been able to eclipse the memory of Patti, Gerster and Sembrich.

During this New York Season, Emilie had also played Marthe in *Faust* and taken part in performances in New Haven (*Carmen*) and Brooklyn (*Carmen*, *Fra Diavolo*, *Maritana* and *Faust*). She was on the programme for all these productions except for the Brooklyn *Carmen*, when Mercedes was played by Jane De Vigne.

Brooklyn, it seems, had come to the rescue of Mapleson and his

Academy of Music.
GRAND SACRED
AND
Instrumental Concert
(THE ONLY ONE)
Sunday Evening, Nov. 29, 1885

PRINCIPAL ARTISTS.
Mme. Minnie Hauk,
Mlle. Litvinoff,
Mlle. Dotti.
Mme. Lablache
AND
Mlle. Fohström.
Signor Giannini
AND
Signor Ravelli.
Signor De Anna
AND
Signor Del Puente.
Signor Caracciolo,
Signor Vetta
AND
Signor Cherubini.

Emilie in a Sacred Concert, November 1885.

(By courtesy of The Museum of the City of New York – Theatre Collection. Academy of Music Folder. (Arch Mrs J.D.W. Pe Hz 1962.)

company. When describing their *Faust* there (22 December), Odell referred to them as homeless: 'Poor Mapleson and poor singers, apparently lost to patronage in Manhattan'. Similarly, the Mapleson forces at the Academy were portrayed as struggling against an indifferent public when some of their members, including Louise, gave a concert at the Casino on 15 November. Louise found employment in December by singing in *The Black Hussar* at the Star Theatre in December and again at the Park Theatre in Brooklyn in February 1886.

Park Theatre, Brooklyn.
(By courtesy of The Harvard Theatre Collection.)

The Black Hussar is an English version of a comic opera *Der Feldprediger* [*The Army Chaplain*] by the Austrian composer Karl Millöcker (1842-1899), known for his melodious Viennese music. Louise had the part of the pretty daughter of the burgomaster, wooed by the hussar captain disguised as an Army chaplain.

Mapleson set out on his American provincial tour in January and it lasted until May. He visited over twenty cities and went as far afield as San Francisco, Salt Lake City and Louisville. For the tour, he had re-engaged Nordica.

Emilie naturally played many of the rôles in which she had appeared in New York, but she is also recorded as having taken the part of Frédéric in *Mignon*, by Ambroïse Thomas (1811-1896), Nancy in *Marta*, Siebel in *Faust* and Flora in *La Traviata*. More surprisingly, she was cast as Donna Elvira in *Don Giovanni* in St. Paul (26 February 1886).

For some of the time at least, Louise was with her mother. Louise took the part of Javotte in *Manon* in Detroit (12 May 1886) while Emilie played the other actress, Rosette. 'Mlle. de Méric' was billed as Marthe in *Faust* in Chicago in May.

However, Louise had also been engaged by the *Opéra Comique* Company run by Colonel McCaull. In March that Company had been at the Boston Theatre, where Louise once again played the burgomaster's daughter, Minna. Mlle. Lablache 'was in excellent voice and sang the charming numbers assigned to her rôle with most acceptable effect, especially the French chanson opening the third act.' It had been at the Boston Theatre that Mapleson had begun his 1866 provincial tour and he gave the Bostonians their first performances of both *Manon* and *Maritana*.

The 1885-1886 Season proved to be the last American Season for Arditi as well as for Mapleson. The conductor had fallen ill with pneumonia in the course of the tour and his place had been taken by his assistant Oreste Bimboni. Arditi came back to the podium in Cheyenne, for *Carmen*, on 16 March 1886.

There had been some hope that performances in San Francisco would restore Mapleson's fortunes, but this was disappointed. There were disputes over the payment of salaries which led to De Anna leaving the Company and to a lawsuit between Mapleson and Ravelli. In Chicago, in May, the orchestra went on strike, claiming that they had had no payment for three weeks. To make matters worse, the city itself was in turmoil, with riots and bomb explosions, an atmosphere most inimical to the success of opera.

The disappointing tour at an end, Mapleson and his troupe boarded ship for Europe.

The final years of a singer's career, when the best days are over, can only be a somewhat melancholy catalogue of minor rôles and so it was for Emilie after about 1886. Furthermore, her inevitable decline coincided with a general warning of interest in the kind of opera in which she had excelled. Gradually, Emilie was handing the baton to Louise who, despite her abilities and charm, did not attain to her mother's standard.

48 *Mapleson refuses to abandon Italian opera, 1886-1888*

1886

FOR the 1886-1887 Season in America, Louise had joined the Boston Ideal Company and sang in *L' Elisir d' Amore*.

Emilie remained with Mapleson in England and was the Berta in a celebrated performance of the *Barber* at Drury Lane in July. This was a benefit for Mapleson and it had been announced that Madame Adelina Patti, as Rosina, would make 'her only appearance in Opera this season'. Patti and Nicolini had been married on 9 June, by the French Consul in Swansea. Henry Abbey had been present at the subsequent religious ceremony at the Parish Church in the village of Ystradgynlais.

In the Autumn, Mapleson and Arditi took the Italian Opera to Ireland again. The Company had twelve nights at the Gaiety Theatre in Dublin, in September, when Emilie had a part in most of the productions: *Il Barbiere* (Berta), *Faust* (Martha) and *La Sonnambula* (Teresa). On less familiar ground, she took the part of Frédéric in *Mignon*.

Cork was given a week from 4 – 9 October. Emilie appeared as Flora in *La Traviata* and Teresa in *La Sonnambula*.

1887

The indefatigable Mapleson opened an early Season of Italian Opera at Covent Garden in March 1887 with the announcement that prices would be reduced by half. They would range from 10/6d for the stalls, 5s. for the pit, to 2/6d for the amphitheatre and one shilling for the gallery. The impresario undertook that the orchestra would be kept up to its usual standard of efficiency, but under Vianesi, Logheder and Li Calsi in place of Arditi. Most of the members of the Company had previously sung with Mapleson either in America or Britain and one of these was indeed Madame de Méric Lablache. She was by this time in her fifty-seventh year and had been performing for some forty years on the stage. One may certainly believe that she was devoted to her art, but it seems also more than likely that she was in need of the money. Even after her marriage, she had never been one of the many singers who abandoned their careers and settled for the normal life of a nineteenth-century matron.

It was not only in the United States that Italian opera was falling out of favour, as Mapleson's pricing policy implied. The Season had opened with *La Traviata* and this was roundly condemned, despite the attraction of the *début* of Mlle. Nordica, the American soprano, as Violetta. Emilie was Flora Belvoix.. The *Daily Telegraph* wrote that the cast, with Mlle. Bauermeister, Signor Ciampi, Signor Del Puente, Signor Rinaldini and Madame Lablache had been 'one of so many links with the past' which 'imparted a certain flavour of antiquity, the value of which depends on circumstances.'

It was the 'less hackneyed operas', *Carmen*, *Faust* and *Fra Diavolo* which attracted the best houses. In *Carmen*, the re-appearance after three years of Minnie Hauk was welcomed. The part of Mercedes was taken on 23 April by Emilie and on 28 May by Louise. Thus the two contralto singers were able to alternate. In *Faust*, Emilie 'once more proved herself the best of all representatives of Martha; her finished acting and excellent vocalisation lent importance to the part, and she did good service in the fine quartette of Act III.' As the travelling Englishwoman Lady Koburg, in *Fra Diavolo*, her impersonation had been most comical. However, one critic declared that though she acted well, the music did not suit her and it was only in the concerted ensembles that her voice told. The *Musical World* commented that Madame Lablache sang cleverly, but in a somewhat worn voice.

Emilie proved able to demonstrate that she was not too old to take on a new rôle: after a Maddalena and Teresa, she played with success the part of the old crone Tavena in Gounod's *Mirella*, the opera based on the poem *Mireille* by the Provençal poet Mistral. As Teresa, Emilie had once again shown 'how much may be made, by clever artists, of small opportunities'. In *Mirella*, as the reputed 'wise woman', she had sung the music well and 'produced a great effect by her delivery of the *canzone La stagione arriva*.' This had been extremely well received and heartily encored. Later, Emilie played Edwige in *Tell* and Gertrude in *Roméo et Juliette*. In April, she had taken part in an Opera Concert at the Royal Albert Hall, singing, however, only in concerted pieces.

Augustus Harris, meanwhile, staged in 1887 his sensational first Grand Opera Season at Drury Lane. On the opening night, Jean De Reszke (1850-1925) had triumphed as the hero Radamès in *Aïda*. As Frances Donaldson has pointed out in *The Royal Opera House in the Twentieth Century*, Harris was astute enough to be able to secure the

Emilie at Covent Garden in 1887.
(By courtesy of The Theatre Museum, Victoria and Albert Museum.)

three things most necessary for success in operatic ventures at the end of the nineteenth century: financial backing, aristocratic patronage and artistic talent. Already in 1887 he had recruited the De Reszke brothers, Victor Maurel (1848-1923), Minnie Hauk, Mattia Battistini (1856-1928), the *bel canto* operatic baritone, and Lillian Nordica.

Both Emilie and Louise were members of Mapleson's company which, with Arditi conducting, gave twelve nights of Italian opera at the Gaiety Theatre in Dublin in the Autumn of 1887. There was apparently some disappointment that at rather short notice Emilie had replaced Madame Trebelli as Azucena, but 'Mdme. Lablache . . . is an old Dublin favourite, always welcome, and always deserving of the kindliest greeting . . . . Suffice it to say that she sang and acted the part, with which her name is so intimately associated, with all her familiar and intense dramatic force, vast artistic judgment, and with a vocal power and skill little, if at all, impaired. She was most warmly received, and throughout the opera, but especially in the third and last acts, her fervent and effective performances gained great applause' (*Freeman's Journal*).

Louise, in the early part of 1887, was once again at the Boston Theatre, again with the Ideal Opera Company. In general, she was playing parts which had previously been associated with her mother, such as Lady Pamela in *Fra Diavolo* and Nancy in Flotow's *Marta*. However, she broke new ground in the rôle of Ulrica in a three-act opera called *Victor, the Bluestocking*, by Bernicat.

Boston Theatre.
(By courtesy of The Harvard Theatre Collection.)

One of the *prime donne* in the Ideal Opera Company was the American soprano Mlle. Zélie De Lussan. She was to be engaged by Augustus Harris for his first Covent Garden Season in 1888 and to join Carl Rosa from 1890 to 1910. She became a famous Carmen, Zerlina, Mignon, Cherubino and Nedda (Rosenthal and Warrack).

In his Memoirs, Mapleson speaks of being 'back in the old country' in 1887, with plans for an extended provincial tour, beginning in the Autumn. Both Emilie and Louise had been engaged.

'Unfortunately', declared the *Freeman's Journal*, in Dublin, 'it had come to be almost an accepted fact that Italian opera was dead.' So Mapleson's company faced an uphill task; but he persevered.

In Dublin, he opened with *Carmen* (10 October 1887). This was a good choice. In Minnie Hauk he had 'an ideal Carmen' and she was well remembered for first having made the opera popular in the city. Louise, as Mercedes, had 'deserved a word of special recognition.' The *Freeman's Journal* went to the length of saying that the 'singularly equal' performance of *Carmen* had far and away transcended any representation of the opera that had ever been given in Dublin.

Emilie and Louise appeared together in *Faust* on 13 October. The *Journal* praised Emilie for having sung and acted artistically as Martha. For the part of Siebel, the name in the programme had been Mlle. Medori, 'but most of those present recognised, or fancied they recognised, in the young artiste who appeared Mdlle. Lablache, and naturally assumed that either Medori was a name assumed by her for the occasion [!] or that the programme was wrong. However that may be, the artiste deserves to be congratulated on her careful and most creditable performance.' On 14 October, *Figaro* was put on and Emilie had deserved 'passing mention for careful performance' as Marcellina.

The appearance of Arditi on the podium had also helped to give the Season a good start in Dublin. 'A few of his admirers' took the opportunity to make him the present of an elegant baton.

From Dublin the Company returned to England, to the Theatre Royal at Nottingham, where they played from 17 – 19 November. Emilie's one appearance was as Azucena. As the *Nottingham Daily Guardian* said, it was indeed late in the day to say much in praise of Madame Lablache in that part. 'She is experienced alike as an actress and singer, and endows the character of the gipsy with more than ordinary significance. Again and again she was vociferously applauded.' It must have helped her throughout that she had her old friend Arditi conducting. However, by this date younger performers were inevitably the ones in the headlines. Mlle. Louise Dotti, who had apparently made her *début* in Nottingham, played Leonora in

Trovatore and Donna Anna in *Don Giovanni*. Minnie Hauk took the parts of Carmen and Zerlina.

The *Daily Guardian* reported that Mapleson had one of the strongest and most competent companies that had ever ventured upon a tour of the provinces. In Nottingham he had been so greatly delighted that he intended, at a future day, to pay the city a return visit and to stay for a week. Mapleson, however, was ever one to whistle to keep up his spirits.

From Nottingham the Company moved to the Prince's Theatre in Bristol (9 – 10 December), where they gave performances of *Don Giovanni*, *Faust* and *Il Trovatore*.

The *Bristol Times and Mirror* complimented Mapleson on having 'wisely discarded the vicious "star" system . . . and gone for what may be styled "the good all round system",' thus 'enabling him to give really good representations of operatic works in Italian at prices which are after all not prohibitive.' Yet to what avail if the public did not want Italian opera anyway? 'Ten years had elapsed since Italian opera had been heard in our midst. The majority of us would have none of it and after last week's experience we should imagine many decades will pass over before it is heard here again.'

Faust might not have been put on in Italian in Bristol for ten years, but the popularity of this opera was 'pre-eminent with English metropolitan and provincial audiences' and it had been given several times in the city in English, by the Carl Rosa Company during their annual visits. The performance by Mapleson's Company was described by the *Times and Mirror* as a most excellent one, with Petrovich as Faust and Abramoff as Mephistopheles. As Martha, 'her original part', Madame Lablache had again shown that it was a question whether any other artist could fill the rôle as she did.

The performance of *Il Trovatore* would have been memorable, the *Times and Mirror* wrote, for Emilie's efforts alone. Veteran artiste that she was [at fifty-seven], she had sung with a volume of tone that was truly astonishing. Her interview with the Count di Luna had been so splendidly given that the audience had enthusiastically and deservedly recalled her.

Mapleson's provincial tour in the Autumn of 1877 had had a certain *succès d'estime*, but it had failed financially. His Company had played to full houses in Dublin alone. Receipts in such places as Liverpool and Bradford were said to have been nil. The impresario himself claimed that his performances had been admirably given 'but . . . inferior English opera seemed now to be preferred to my grand Italian opera.' Perhaps, with hindsight, the most remarkable thing is that such an exotic art form as Italian opera should have held the stage for so long in almost every corner of the British Isles.

49 *Augustus Harris takes over, 1888*

MAPLESON'S season at Covent Garden in 1887 had been followed by the one at Drury Lane managed by Augustus Harris. It was an open secret that that venture had cost Harris a great deal of money, but that had not prevented him from finding sponsors for a programme of opera at Covent Garden in 1888. After the Summer Season in London, Harris took his Covent Garden Company on tour.

Louise had played her modest part in the success at the Garden and Emilie was with the Company in the provinces.

On 15 May, at Covent Garden, Nordica had the title rôle in *Carmen*, 'ably supported by Mesd. Bauermeister and Louise Lablache [Mercedes] (*The Times*).' Taste in opera at the period may be inferred by the following comment from *The Times*: 'After the unmitigated dulness of *Lucrezia Borgia* [14 May], the sparkle and brilliancy of *Carmen* . . . was a perfect relief, and a very large audience, including once more the Prince and Princess of Wales, testified to the un-diminished popularity of Bizet's masterpiece. Of the general efficiency of the performance it would be difficult to speak too highly.'

If only in parenthesis, it must be noted that this was the Season when Nellie Melba made her London *début*, in *Lucia di Lammermoor*, and the *Athenaeum* declared that she would never be a great artist.

Louise was given the part of Lady Koburg in *Fra Diavolo* (20 June). The *Athenaeum* offered a word of thanks to Mr. Harris for mounting this opera, 'ill suited as it is to the Italian stage,' because Auber's delightful works were so rarely heard. The performance had been creditable, if hardly first rate in all departments, but 'Louise Lablache gave a praiseworthy rendering of the part of Lady Koburg.' The *Illustrated London News* also praised Louise and the *Musical World* said that she had sung with more than usual effectiveness.

A highlight of the Season had been *Guglielmo Tell*. The *Athenaeum* regarded this as one of Harris's most creditable achievements and rejoiced that the reign of the *prima donna* was, at least temporarily, at an end. Lassalle and Prévost had been superb as Tell and Arnold and admirable service had been rendered in small parts by Mdlles. Bauermeister and Lablache (Edwige) and by

Monsieur Edouard de Reszke (Walter).

The *Illustrated London News*, in its review of what it described as a remarkable season, noted that Louise had won favour in the less important parts. These had included one of the three Geni in *Il Flauto Magico* and Maddalena in *Rigoletto*. Aside from opera, Louise took part in a concert in the St. James's Hall on 4 July, when she appeared with Albani, Edouard De Reszke, Nordica, Del Puente and others.

The provincial tour appears to have started in Ireland. The Harris Company from Covent Garden were billed in the *Cork Daily Herald* to give six performances of Italian opera in the city from 30 October to 3 November 1888. Madame Demeric-Lablache was among the 'distinguished artistes'. Arditi was to conduct. The first contralto was Madame Scalchi, but Emilie was given Flora in *La Traviata* and the part of one of the three Geni in *Il Flauto Magico*.

Next, in Dublin, at the Gaiety Theatre, Emilie was billed to appear not only in *Faust* (Martha), but in *Lohengrin* and *Il Flauto Magico*.

From Ireland, Harris took his Royal Italian Opera Company for a week to the Royal Court Theatre in Liverpool (19 -24 November). He boasted that notwithstanding the enormous cost, he had engaged the artistes who were the rage of the London Season. The Liverpool papers gave him the warmest of welcomes. The *Daily Post* said that Liverpool had not had so distinguished a company for many years. It would be an event of the greatest interest to hear them render such masterpieces as *Aïda*, *Ernani* and *The Huguenots* – grand operas that were seldom heard outside Paris or Vienna.

Aïda was new to Liverpool. The house was by no means full. The attendance at *Ernani* was described by a correspondent to the *Liverpool Echo* as a disgrace to the inhabitants of the second city of the Empire. The fault did not lie with the performers. They were the *crème de la crème* of the artistes of the day. It was the taste of the public, who had flocked to *The Yeomen of the Guard*.

There seems little doubt that artistically the productions were of a high order. Indeed, in musical circles in Liverpool comparisons were made with 'the great Italian Company' which had performed at the opening of the Alexandra Theatre twenty years earlier. According to the *Echo*, there were some old playgoers who had ventured to assert that even those palmy days did not equal in the general ensemble of quality the presentations of the modern company. This may have owed something to the grandeur of the *mise-en-scène* which Harris was able to produce, but his choruses and orchestra were also highly regarded. All the same, Arditi came in for some adverse comment. There were well-founded complaints about excessively long intervals between acts. Arditi apparently 'thought nothing of discussing matters between acts . . . forgetting that Liverpool . . . as regards trains and busses was not London'.

As for Emilie, she was the usual standby as Azucena, but also undertook 'the exceedingly exigent music of Ortruda [in *Lohengrin*] with much artistic success.'

Harris was reported to have lost £750 on the week, but the theatre had been crowded for the last three nights and he was advised that if he were to return he could recoup his losses. He promptly did so (11 – 12 December), this time at the Royal Alexandra Theatre. Emilie appeared as Flora in the matinée performance of *La Traviata*.

Final appearances, 1889-1894

IN the Summer of 1889, when Harris collaborated with Carl Rosa to mount productions of opera at Covent Garden, their prospectus included the name of Louise Lablache, contralto. Emilie was not listed, but it would seem from various reports that she may well have been in the cast from time to time. There are references to 'Madame Lablache' which have been taken to mean either Emilie or Louise.

In June, in *Guglielmo Tell*, Mlle. Bauermeister and Madame Lablache, respectively, were the son and wife of Tell and 'contributed to the general effect of the performance.' Madame Lablache was named in the advertisement for Gounod's *Roméo and Juliette* as playing Gertrude, with Jean De Reszke as Romeo and Melba as Juliet. Critics spoke of the parts being strongly cast, with Madame Lablache as an efficient Gertrude. Klein says that the performance of the opera, in the original French, had been highly successful and had attracted crowded audiences throughout the Season.

Louise was in the cast at Covent Garden again in 1890. So was her second husband, the Rumanian tenor Ion Dimitrescu. On 10 November, in *Rigoletto*, Louise played Maddalena and Dimitrescu the Duke. The opera had only two performances, but *The Times* had described Louise as a sprightly and efficient Maddalena. Dimitrescu, too, had made a favourable impression, 'having a moderately powerful voice with an agreeable quality', though he indulged in far too much vibrato. Dimitrescu also sang in *Lucia* (Edgardo) and *La Gioconda* (Enzo).

The name of Louise does not feature in the Covent Garden lists after 1890. By early in 1891 she had joined the Carl Rosa Opera Company. According to the *Liverpool Mercury*, her first appearance with that Company was at the Royal Court Theatre in Liverpool on Friday, 16 January 1891, in the name part of Mignon. She then played Carmen. This was to a very full house and 'the new aspirant to high tragic fame was in many respects effective, and was very heartily received' (*Liverpool Echo*). From Liverpool, the company proceeded to Manchester, Glasgow and Edinburgh. Then in the summer, a Season started in Cork (10 – 15 August) and went on to Dublin, Belfast, Manchester, Birmingham, Leeds and Newcastle, followed by a return to Edinburgh (23 November – 5 December

1891), Liverpool, Manchester and other cities. An unidentified press report had stated that Mlle. Louise Lablache had won great favour in America: she made skilful use of a fine mezzo-soprano voice and was an accomplished and attractive actress. There is some evidence, unconfirmed, that Emilie too may have been for a time with Carl Rosa. With Dimitrescu, Louise sang Amneris in performances of *Aïda* given in Manchester, Liverpool, Glasgow and Edinburgh in February – May 1892.

Dimitrescu had remained at Covent Garden for a second year. In the Summer of 1892, he seems to have made a moderate success as Don Ottavio and to have done very well as Radamès, giving 'a most creditable rendering of *Celest' Aïda*'.

NEW YORK (1893 – 1894)

In 1893, when Emilie was already well over sixty, she went back to sing in the United States. She had again been engaged at the Metropolitan Opera House in New York by Henry Abbey and his associate Maurice Grau. Bevignani was one of the principal conductors. There had been no operas at the Met in 1892-1893 because of a fire.

Not surprisingly, Emilie seems by this time to have served mainly as an understudy. On 31 January 1894 she had 'come out of an historical past' to play 'a still inimitably funny' Marcellina in *Figaro*. This had been in lieu of the indisposed Bauermeister. Similarly, she had taken Bauermeister's place as Martha in *Faust* (2 February) with Campanini in the name part, Eames as Marguerite, Edouard De Reszke as Mephistopheles and Scalchi as Siebel. According to Odell, Campanini sang beautifully, though with much diminished powers. Regrettably, Madame Lablache had strayed at times from the pitch.

Contemporary reports make it clear that at this period Emilie was taking pupils in New York. She herself also sang in several concerts. In November 1893, the impresario and composer Walter Damrosch (1862-1950) had begun a series of Sunday evening concerts at the fine Carnegie Music Hall. Emilie took part in a charity concert which Damrosch gave in March 1894 for the benefit of the Mothers' Home of the Sisters of Miséricorde. Odell, with scant gallantry, remarked that the soloists themselves may have needed some pity – 'Martha Miner, the ageing Mme. Lablache.' On 24 April, Emilie gave a Grand Operatic Concert which seems to have been her last appearance in America. The first part of the programme was contributed by a dozen of her female pupils, who reportedly acquitted themselves in a creditable manner. The concert had been postponed twice and some of the leading singers had not been able to appear, but Emilie herself and Nordica both sang. The audience had not been large, but it was appreciative.

Sadly, Emilie had outlived her reputation in New York. The last word has to be with Odell: 'Campanini, Galassi. Del Pu[en]te, Mme. Lablache, towers of strength 12 years previously in the Mapleson opera – why were they lingering, with impaired voices, on these shores?'

Emilie Glossop had had a very long singing career, marked by as many successes as setbacks. She had striven to maintain the highest standards in both singing and acting. She had held her own with the greatest singers of her time and could claim, at her best, to be numbered among them. Yet posterity has heard little of her and her name is to be found in few of the biographical dictionaries. Perhaps the above story may help to put her life into better perspective. However, let others speak the last words.

Ferrari, in his account of performances in Parma, devotes a paragraph to Madame de Méric Lablache. She was, he says, a *figlia dell'arte*, who had a famous singer as her mother. She had studied music in Bologna under the great Rossini, then continued her musical education in Paris. She had performed at the principal theatres in Europe and America, in the company of famous singers, and always with the happiest of results. She had had the honour of being numbered among singers at several Courts, and the Czar of Russia had conferred on her one of his seven orders of merit. She was a singer of the old school, the school of true singers, but though she had begun her brilliant career with the works of Rossini she had been able to pass on to the variety of operatic styles which followed and gain further laurels.

Finally, Joseph Bennett, in his *Forty Years of Music*, had this to say: ' . . . Mapleson at last died [14 November 1901]. I attended his funeral in Highgate Cemetery [in North London], and found myself one of a very small company. A few of his old chorus people, faithful to the end, stood around the grave, but of all the artists who had served under him only Madame De Meric Lablache had the grace to put in an appearance. I cried "shame" at the time; I repeat it now.'

Yet when and where did Emilie herself die? And when and where, indeed, did Nicolas Lablache die? At the time of writing, despite diligent research, the author has not solved these two mysteries. All that can be said with virtual certainty is that they were both dead when their daughter Anna died in Paris in 1906, as stated on her death certifcate. The date and place of death of Louise also remains to be discovered.

Postscript

APPENDIX A

OPERAS WRITTEN FOR JOSÉPHINE AND TIMOLEONE

According to records received from Ravenna, seven operas were written for Joséphine de Méric and four for Timoleone Alexander. These were:

FOR JOSÉPHINE

Gli Avventurieri, by Giacomo Cordella
(performed at La Canobbiana 6 September 1825)

Giulietta e Romeo, by Nicola Vaccai
(La Canobbiana 31 October 1825)

Un'Avventura di Scaramuccia, by Luigi Ricci
(La Scala 8 March 1834)

La Casa disabitata, by Lauro Rossi
(La Scala 16 August 1834)

Il Posto abbandonato, by Bazzoni
(Sao Carlos, Lisbon, September 1835)

Don Chisciotto, by Alberto Mazzucato
(La Canobbiana 26 April 1836)

I tre Mariti, by Bazzoni
(La Canobbiana 24 June 1836)

FOR TIMOLEONE

Gli Sposi fuggitivi, by Luigi Carlini
(Teatro Nuovo, Naples, 1828)

Il supposto Marito, by Vincentino Fioravanti
(Teatro Nuovo, Naples, 1828)

Colombo, by the brothers Ricci
(Teatro Ducale, Parma, 27 June 1829)

La Vedova del Bengala, by A. Pellegrini
(Teatro Ducale, Como, 1835)

APPENDIX B

POEMS TO JOSÉPHINE IN RAVENNA

To Giuseppina Demery who in the Spring of 1837 delighted Ravenna with the sweetness of her song,
Some admirers offer these verses on the evening of her benefit performance.

When Saturn, in his still unsullied reign,
made golden the age, then Philosophy dwelt in
joyful companionship with the Muses
and Truth sang in the sweetest of tones to the hearts of men.

But the gold turned into iron and words of deceit
fell from the lips of the Poets; now tainted and murky,
that sacred source which once gushed forth in such purity
has been trampled under the hooves of iron steeds.

The iron has held its grip and all that we Italians
hear now are senseless rhymings; the crowd applauds, for
in our time few hearts still respond to the wisdom of old.

O Lady, o new Euterpe, you who achieve so much by
your voice alone, what praise would not be yours if you
were granted noble verse to sing?

This tribute of praise is offered to Giuseppina de Méric, *prima donna assoluta* at the *Teatro Comunale* at Ravenna, at her benefit performance on the evening of 30 May 1837.

Who shall not praise you, Lady,
for your signal merit both in nature and art?
Yet who has the wings to scale the heights
to do justice to your worth?

No human breast harbours so much pain
as not to be assuaged if it will yield itself,
however briefly, to your dulcet strains;

We need none but you
to feel what bliss is granted to us mortals:
you who by your inspired singing
can evoke in every heart now joy, now tears.

just as the court of heaven is transported
by the music of the ethereal spheres
when Jove's shafts of sunlight strike the earth below.

APPENDIX C

JOSÉPHINE'S DESCENDANTS

As far as is known, Joséphine and Joseph Glossop had the one child, Emilie. As the wife of Nicolas Lablache, second son of Luigi Lablache, Emilie had three children: Louise, Henri and Anna (Nina). The daughters both followed their mother to make careers on the operatic stage.

Louise, a contralto like Emilie, married firstly James Hamilton Cobley (c. 1847 - 1905), a London businessman. Her second husband was the Rumanian tenor Ion [John] Dimitrescu (b. 1860), who had a distinguished career in opera in many European cities and in South America. He was much admired in lyric and dramatic rôles, especially as Raoul and Vasco, and has been compared with Tamberlik. He had two seasons in London. Dimitrescu committed suicide in Hove in 1913, having first shot his dog, a shaved and trimmed black French poodle. He left a note saying: "Please do bury me with my dog; he is my only friend." The County Coroner's Report has not survived, but the *East Sussex News* of Friday 14 March 1913 contained the following notice: 'Louise Dimitrescu, a teacher of singing, whose professional name is Labache [sic], said her husband was an opera singer, 46 years of age, and was a native of Bucharest. He had been a professional singer for 25 years, and had been decorated by the King of Roumania. Three years ago he lost in one day a fortune of £60,000 from investments, chiefly in timber. Coming to England, he failed to obtain more than one or two engagements. He had threatened to commit suicide. Witness gave him her last shilling on the morning of the day of his death. She herself had been ill and in a nursing home.' The report went on to state that only three halfpence in money and the letter had been found on him. The doctor said that the death had been instantaneous, the bullet piercing the heart. (Such was the sad outcome, in a Sussex seaside resort, of two international operatic careers).

A Mara Dimitrescu, presumed (though without evidence) to be a daughter of Dimitrescu (?by Louise) was also a singer. She is recorded as having performed at the *Teatro Bellini* in Naples from October to December 1898, in *La Traviata*, *Ballo in Maschera* and *I Puritani*. In *Ballo*, she had the part of the page, Oscar, so was probably a soprano.

Little has come to light about Henri. He seems to have settled in London as a businessman. He signed as the informant when the death of Joséphine was certified in London in 1877.

Anna was a soprano. She married Athanase Georges Nicolopulo, but they were divorced. Anna died in somewhat straitened circumstances in Paris in 1906.

To return to Louise: by her marriage to James Cobley, she had a daughter, also named Louise. Louise Cobley married firstly a man named Russ, about whom nothing has been traced. Her second husband was William James Parkinson Smith and one of their sons was Norman Parkinson Smith (1913-1990), famous as the photographer Norman Parkinson.

Near Joséphine's tomb in the Kensal Green Cemetery is the grave of Settimio Alexander. The signature S. Alexandre appears on the Church Register at the marriage of Emilie to Nicolas Lablache. This Settimio, who is presumed to have been Joséphine's son by Timoleone Alexander, died in Hampstead, London, in May 1890. He was described on the death certificate as a professor of languages. It is not known whether he married.

DESCENDANTS OF JOSÉPHINE'S BROTHERS

Joséphine had an unmarried sister, Sophie, and three brothers.

The eldest brother, Hector Alexandre (1804 - ?) was in the French Army and served at one period as *maréchal des logis* with the *8e régiment de chasseurs à cheval*, later becoming a banker in Paris. He claimed the patronymic 'de Méric de Gardebosc'. Hector married Marie Louise Prévost and they had a son, Louis Philippe (1832 - 1897). Louis Philippe married Louise Nargeot, daughter of the composer Pierre Julien Nargeot. They apparently had no children, so the senior de Méric line from Joseph died out. Hector and his son had remained in France.

Jacques Eugène (1809 - 1875), the second brother, emigrated to Ireland, where he became Professor of French Literature at the Alexandra College in Dublin. As a respected local resident, Jacques Eugène was appointed *chancelier* and later Vice-Consul at the French Consulate in Dublin. He was a devout member of the Protestant *Eglise Chrétienne Réformée de France*. He married Rosalie d'Arenberg (or Abeltshauser) from another French family which had emigrated from Strasbourg.

Jacques Eugène and his wife had two daughters and a son, Eugène Victor (1847 - 1911). This son, having been born on British soil, had British nationality and joined the Royal Navy, as a surgeon. In 1869 he was stationed in the Far East and was present at Hakodate, in the North Island of Japan, where he witnessed the final battle in the civil war which marked the downfall of the Tokugawa Shogunate. He was able to assist in the treatment of the wounded on both sides, especially as the foreign language which his Japanese counterparts spoke was French. The young surgeon-lieutenant was presented with two magnificent pieces of lacquer-work in recognition of his services.

Eugène Victor married Mary Clifton Coucher. They settled in Weymouth, Dorset, and had two sons. The elder, Martin John Coucher de Méric (1887 - 1943), also joined the Royal Navy and rose to the rank of Rear-Admiral. He died at his desk in the Admiralty during the Second World War. Admiral de Méric married Carmen Pengilly, eldest daughter of Sir Alexander and Lady Pengilly of Weymouth. Sir Alexander was the leading solicitor in the town and a pillar of the Conservative Party.

Admiral de Méric and his wife had a daughter and a son. The daughter, Yvonne (1916 - 1991), was a W.R.N.S. officer in the war and she became the wife of the author. The son, Lieutenant-Commander Martin Alexander ('Tony') de Méric, RN (retd), married Priscilla Fry and they have a son, Nicholas, who has married and had a son to continue the sole remaining male line from Joseph Bonnaud de Méric of Strasbourg.

Eugène Victor's second son, Victor Eugène, had married but had no sons.

Joséphine's third brother, Jean Jacques Victor M.D., F.R.C.S. (1811 - 1876), studied medicine in Dublin and Glasgow and made his career in London, where he achieved distinction as President of the Medical Society. He was an authority on venereal diseases. Jean Jacques Victor married Sarah née Hardwick, widow of Joseph Chitty, the last of the Special Pleaders. They had a son Henry (1849 - 1919), who was also a medical doctor, and a daughter, but no male de Méric descendants. The daughter Julia became Mrs. George Sampson. She died in Boulogne. The two doctors are buried in the cemetery at Kensal Green.

DESCENDANTS OF ELIZABETH FERON AND JOSEPH GLOSSOP

Of the daughters of Elizabeth Féron and Joseph Glossop little has been traced about the eldest, Frances (born in 1813), except that she married a Granville and died a widow in Montmartre, Paris in 1881. The second daughter, Mary (born in 1815), composed operas and is thought to have been the first British woman to have done so. She married Gilbert Abbott A'Beckett (1811 - 1856), a barrister who became a metropolitan police-magistrate in London. Gilbert was well known as a writer for *Punch* and *The Times* and as the author of books such as the *Comic Histories of England and Rome*. The A'Becketts had a son, Arthur, who was also a writer. He was the author of *Green-room Recollections* (1896) and *The A'Becketts of Punch* (1903).

It is common knowledge that the most famous descendants of Elizabeth Féron and Joseph Glossop are their son Augustus Glossop Harris (1825 - 1873) and his son who became Sir Augustus Glossop Harris (1852 - 1896). Both have appeared from time to time in the pages of this book, but another tome would be required to do justice to their careers. Each, it may truly be said, had been able to fulfil much of what for Joseph had been only dreams. Both had achieved great success as impresarios. Augustus the first was also a playwright who wrote successful dramas in collaboration with others such as Henry Pettit. For father and son, let Herman Klein leave us with his description of the scene in August 1891 when Sir Augustus and Lady Harris arrived as guests at Patti's Welsh castle, *Craig-y-Nos*. 'Sir Augustus was in great spirits. That industrious and versatile individual who that year filled the triple rôles of Sheriff of London, impresario of the Royal Opera at Covent Garden and manager of Drury Lane Theatre, had just received his knighthood . . . Adelina Patti had known him from childhood, when his father brought him, as a small boy, to stand in the wings and listen to an opera at Covent Garden. They were the best of friends'.

Two of the sisters of Sir Augustus, Maria and Nelly, were actresses. So was his daughter Florence Nelly Glossop Harris. His widow, Florence née Rendle, married the actor Edward Terry. Thus, from Elizabeth and Joseph Glossop onward, the stage had remained in the blood.

Many of the Glossop Harris graves are in the Brompton Cemetery, London S.W.10.

DESCENDANTS OF LUIGI LABLACHE OTHER THAN THROUGH HIS SON NICOLAS

Luigi Lablache had a large family. His eldest son, Frédéric (1815 - 1887) was also s singer of international repute. Frédéric married the English actress Frances Wilton, professionally known as Fanny Wyndham, and settled in London. They had two daughters, Thérèse and Fanny, and a son Louis (1850 - 1914).

Thérèse married the Austrian bass Johann Rokitansky. Fanny died unmarried.

Louis married Jane Breadon, known professionally as Jane Emmerson. Their younger daughter, Eliza Frederika Charlotte, became the mother of the famous actor Stewart Granger (actually James Lablache Stewart). The elder daughter, Frances Maud Thérèse, was the grandmother of Mrs. Clarissa Lablache Cheer, founder of the Lablache Society in California.

Luigi's son Dominique was an artillery officer in the French Army who served in the Crimean War. He was a *chevalier de la Légion d'honneur*. He married Marie Battu, a singer. They apparently had no children. Dominique was buried at Père Lachaise.

Luigi's eldest daughter, Marie Isabelle (1831 - 1881) was a talented amateur singer and by all accounts a beauty. She married the Belgian Baron Ernest de Caters.

Daughter Francesca married twice. Her first husband was François Bouchot. Her second was Sigismund Thalberg (1812 - 1870), the celebrated Austrian musician.

Daughter Marianne married Henry Singer. One of their descendants is Madame Ba-lsan, living near Paris, who has most kindly provided invaluable material about the Lablache family.

There are Lablache mausolea at Maisons-sur-Seine in France. Frédéric and his family are interred at Kensal Green.

APPENDIX D
LONDON RESIDENCES

The residences of the Lablache and de Méric families which settled in London were close together in the Marylebone area. Some of their colleagues also lived in that district.

Frédéric Lablache favoured Albany Street. He was at No. 21 in 1848, at No. 149 in 1852 and at No. 51 from 1866 until he died in 1877. His son Luigi (Louis) remained there until his death in December 1914.

The doctor Jean Jacques Victor de Méric was living at No. 39, Upper Baker Street in 1852 and then moved to Brook Street (Nos. 17 and 52).

In 1856, Gilbert A'Beckett's address was 82 Baker Street.

Arditi took a house at No. 41 Albany Street in 1866. Later, he was on the South coast at Hove, where he died, aged eighty, in 1903.

APPENDIX E
OPERATIC CAREERS OF LOUISE LABLACHE AND ION DIMITRESCU

By courtesy of Mr. Tom Kaufman, two lists follow giving chronologies of the operatic careers of Louise Lablache and her husband Ion Dimitrescu. The asterisks on the Tables indicate where the pair were singing together.

DIMITRESCU

	WINTER	SPRING	SUMMER	AUTUMN
1885				Bucharest
1886	Bucharest			Bucharest
1887	Bucharest			
1888		Milan		Melbourne*
1889	Sydney*			
1890		Trieste	Athens	London*
1891	U.K.tour*	U.K Tour*		U.K. Tour*
1892	U.K. Tour*	U.K. Tour,* London		Warsaw
1893	Modena, Kharkov*			
1894	Moscow	Kiev,* Kazan		

1895	Iasi			Kharkov
1896	Kharkov, Kiev	Fiume		Milan
1897	Ferrara, Parma	Santiago	Santiago	
1898	Palermo		Rio	
1899	Piacenza	Seville		Bucharest
1900	Bucharest			
1901	Lisbon		Rio	Sao Paulo
1902	Naples			Warsaw
1903		Trieste		
1904				
1905		Genoa		
1906				
1907				
1908				
1909				Ecuador, Lima
1910	Lima			
1911				

Louise Lablache

1880				New Orleans
1881	New Orleans	U.S. tour		
1882		Buenos Aires	Buenos Aires	
1883				New York
1884	New York	U.S. Tour		
1885		London		
1886				U.S. Tour
1887	U.S. Tour	London		
1888		London	London	Melbourne*
1889	Sydney*	(London)		
1890				London*
1891	U.K. Tour*	U.K.Tour*		U.K. Tour*
1892	U.K. Tour*	U.K. Tour*		
1893	Modena, Kharkov			
1894		Kiev*		
1894		Kiev *		

Acknowledgements

My debt of gratitude to individuals and institutions is boundless. High on the list must be the editors and publishers, for whom nothing could be too much trouble. I am particularly beholden to Cintia Stammers and Sue Wilson.

Several of the individuals have helped me so much that they deserve to be thanked as major collaborators. These include Mr. Brian Meringo, Mr. Tom Kaufman, Dr. Robert Cammarota, Mrs. Clarissa Lablache Cheer and Miss Valentina Mironova. I am also profoundly grateful for invaluable assistance from the following:

Dr. Girvice Archer, jnr.
Madame Aubin.
Madame Balsan
Dr. Domenico Berardi
Ms. Eithne Cavanagh
Mrs. Chandler
Signor Ermanno Comuzio
Mr. John F. Cone
Monsieur J. Descheemaeker
Captain G. B. Glossop, R.M.
Monsieur Y. du Guerny

Dr. Jacques Heran
Mr. Trevor Higgins
Pasteur Koch
Dr. K. J. Kutsch
Mr. Bernard Levin
Mrs. Nesta Macdonald
Miss Pamela Marshall
Signor Gino Missiroli
Signor Gaspare Nello Vetro
Signora Barbara Pasquini
Madame Pérès

Mr. Henry Pleasants
Judge Henry Pownall
Prof. Paolo Rigoli
Mr. John Rosselli
Mrs. Joseph Senior
Mr. and Mrs. Norman Singleton
Mrs. Frank Spooner
Mr. Robert Tuggle
Signor Gaspare Nello Vetro
The Venerable George Westwell

Finally but not least I most warmly thank my own family: my late wife, my two sons and my two sisters and my brother-in-law.

Every effort has been made to contact the copyright holders of all articles, playbills, illustrations and advertisements: the publishers apologize for any omissions and will be pleased to make the necessary arrangements at the first opportunity.

The public and private bodies to whom I am profoundly grateful for their co-operation in my research include the following:

Austria

The Austrian Embassy, London
Oesterreichische Nationalbibliothek

France

Archives de l'Armée, Vincennes
Archives du Conservatoire National de Musique, Paris
Archives Départementales, Bas-Rhin
Archives de l'Etat Civil, Paris
Archives Municipales, Boulogne-sur-Mer
Archives Municipales, Paris
Archives Municipales, Strasbourg
Archives Nationales, Paris
Archives Nationales, Versailles
Bibliothèque de l'Arsenal, Paris
Bibliothèque Historique de la Ville de Paris
Bibliothèque Nationale, Paris
Bibliothèque Nationale, Versailles
Bibliothèque de l'Opéra, Paris
Bibliothèque Universitaire, Strasbourg
The Cemetery at Maisons-Lafitte
Conservatoire National de Musique, Paris
L'Eglise St. Pierre le Jeune, Strasbourg
L'Evêché à Versailles
Mairie du 8e Arrondisement, Paris
Mormon Research Center, Paris

Ministère des Affaires Etrangères
Musée Condé
Opéra du Bas Rhin, Strasbourg
Société Historique d'Auteuil et de Passy
Théâtre Municipal de Strasbourg

Germany

Akademie der Künste, Berlin
Bayerisches Hauptstaatsarchiv, Munich
British Consulate-General, Berlin
British Consulate-General, Munich
Deutsche Staatsoper, Berlin

Ireland

Cork City Library
Dublin Public Libraries
The National Library of Ireland
Orfig an Ard-Chlàrai theora, Dublin

Italy

Accademia Nazionale di Santa Cecilia, Rome
The Archivio di Stato in: Asti, Belluno, Bergamo, Bologna, Como, Fiorenze, Livorno, Lucca, Mantua, Modena, Napoli, Padua, Palermo, Piacenza, Ravenna, Rovigo, Treviso, Trieste, Torino, Venezia, Verona and Vicenza.
Archivio Storico Civico e Biblioteca Trivulziana, Milan

413

Archivio Storico del Comune di Ravenna
Biblioteca "Carlo Bonetta", Pavia
Biblioteca Centrale, Palermo
Biblioteca Civica Angelo Mai, Bergamo
Biblioteca Civica Bertoliana, Vicenza
Biblioteca Civica, Cuneo
Biblioteca Classense, Ravenna
Biblioteca Consorziale Astense
Biblioteca Nazionale Centrale, Rome
British Consulate-General, Naples
Centro Internazionale di Ricerca sui Periodi Musici, Parma
Città di Feltre (Ufficio Musei)
Civica Raccolta delle Stampe A. Bertarelli, Milan
Civiche Raccolte d'Arte, Milan
Civici Musei di Storia ed Arte, Trieste
Civico Museo Teatrale "C Schmidl", Trieste
E. A. Teatro Comunale dell'Opera di Genova
E. A. Teatro La Fenice, Venice
Fondo Dono Pellegrini, Lucca
The Foreign Cemetery, Florence.
Museo Teatrale alla Scala, Milan
Società Palchettisti del Teatro Sociale di Como

Portugal
Real Teatro de S. Carlos, Lisbon

Russia
British Embassy, Moscow
Ministry of Culture, Moscow (State Central Theatrical Library)

Spain
Biblioteca Nacional, Madrid
British Embassy, Madrid

United Kingdom
Archbishop's House, Westminster Cathedral
The Archive Office, Covent Garden
Basingstoke Public Library
The British Library (with the Newspaper Library, Colindale)
The British Museum

The Cemeteries at Brompton, Highgate and Kensal Green
The Central Libraries at Bath, Birmingham, Bristol, Edinburgh, Leeds,
Manchester, Newcastle-upon-Tyne, Northampton and Norwich
Cheltenham Art Gallery and Museums
The Community Leisure Department, County of Avon
The County Record Office, Lewes, Sussex East Sussex and Wiltshire Record Office
The Genealogical Society
The General Register Office
The Greater London Record Office
The Guildhall Library
The John Rylands University Library, Manchester
Lambeth Palace Library
Leeds Leisure Services
The Library of the Foreign and Commonwealth Office
The Library of the United Oxford and Cambridge University Club
Liverpool Record Office
The London Library
The Mitchell Library, Glasgow
The Music Library, University of London
Nottingham County Library
The Public Record Office
The Royal Library, Windsor Castle
The Royal Pavilion Art Gallery and Museum, Brighton
The Society for Theatre Resarch
The Theatre Museum
Tyne and Wear Archives Services
The Victoria Library, Westminster

United States of America
Academy of Music, New York
Dramatic Museum Collection, Columbia University
Harvard Theatre Collection, Harvard College
Metropolitan Opera Archives
New York Historical Society
New York Public Library
State Museum, Louisiana
Theatre Collection, Museum of the City of New York
University of Texas at Austin

Bibliography

A'Beckett, Arthur William *Green-room Recollections*, Bristol 1896

A'Beckett, Arthur William *The A'Becketts of Punch*, 1903

Agosteo, P. *Cronistoria del Teatro Fraschise* [Pavia] 1773-1899

Albani, Emma *Forty Years of Song*, Mills & Boon 1911.

Almanach Royal et Impérial, Paris

Almanach des Spectacles, par K et Z, Paris 1818-1819

Amadei, Giuseppe *I 150 Anni del Sociale nella Storia dei Teatri di Mantova*, Mantua 1873

Arditi, Luigi *My Reminiscences*, Da Capo Press, New York 1977

Armstrong, W.G. *A Record of Opera in Philadelphia*, Philadelphia 1884

Army Lists, London

Ashbrook, William *Donizetti*, Cassell, London 1965

Baroncelli, J.G. de *Le Théâtre-Français à la Nlle. Orléans: Essai Historique*, New Orleans, Muller,1906

Beale, Willert *The Light of Other Days* (2 vols) London, 1890

Becker, Heinz and Gudrun *Giacomo Meyerbeer: A Life in Letters*, London, 1989

Benevides, Francisco da Fonseca *O Real Theatro de S. Carlos de Lisboa*, Lisbon, 1883

Bennett, Joseph *Forty Years of Music 1865-1905*, London, Methuen, 1908

Bibliographie Universelle, Paris

Bignani, Luigi *Cronologia di tutti gli Spettacoli . . . nel gran teatro communale di Bologna 1763-1880*, Bologna,1880

Boase, Frederic *Modern English Biography*, Truro 1892-1908.

Bottuna, Giuseppe Carlo *Storia Aneddotica Documentata del Teatro Comunale di Trieste 1801-1884*, Trieste, 1885

Brunelli, Bruno *I Teatri di Padova*, Padua, 1921

Bunce, J.H. *A History of the Birmingham General Hospital and the Musical Festivals*, 1873

Cambiasi, Pompeo *Rappresentazione . . . nelle reali teatri di Milano 1778-1872*

Castil-Blaze, F.H.J. *L'Opéra Italien de 1548-1856*, Paris 1856

Castil-Blaze, F.H.J. *L'Académie Impériale de Musique de 1645 à 1855*, Paris 1855

Cervetti, Valerio *Dietro il Sipario*, Teatro Regio, Parma 1881-1898

Chernyshevsky, Nicolai *What to do?* (in Russian), 1906.

Chorley, Henry F. *Thirty Years' Musical Recollections*, Hurst & Blackett, London 1872

Christiansen, Rupert (ed.) *The Grand Obsession: An Anthology of Opera*, Collins 1988

Clayton, E.C. *Queens of Song*, London 1863

Clément, F. and Larousse, P. *Dictionnaire Lyrique ou Histoire des Opéras*, Paris 1905

Cone, John Frederick *First Rival of the Metropolitan Opera*, New York 1983

Cox, Rev. T. C. *Musical Recollections of the Last Half Century*, London 1872

Dale, Antony *The Theatre Royal*, Brighton, Oriel Press 1980

Davis, Ronald L. *A History of Opera in the American West*, 1965

Deck, Pantaléon *Histoire du Théâtre Français à Strasbourg 1681-1830*, Ed. Le Roux et Cie, Strasbourg-Paris

de Méric, Blanche *Genealogical research* (unpubl. Ms)

Derwent, Lord *Rossini and some forgotten Nightingales*, Duckworth, London 1934

Dobbs, Brian *Drury Lane 1663-1971*, Cassell, London 1972

Donaldson, Frances *The Royal Opera House in the Twentieth Century*, Weidenfeld & Nicolson 1988

Duncan, Barry *The St. James's Theatre 1835-1957*, Barrie & Rockliff 1964

Durham, Weldon B. (ed.) *American Theatre Companies 1749-1887*, Greenwood Press, New York 1986

Dwight's Journal of Music, Boston, Massachusetts 1851-1881

Eaton, Quaintance *Opera Caravan: The Metropolitan on Tour 1883-1956*, Da Capo Press, New York 1957

Ebers, John *Seven Years of the King's Theatre*, London 1828

Eisler, E. *The Metropolitan Opera: The First 25 Years*, (1984)

Ferrari, Paolo Emilio *Spettacoli drammatico-musicali e coreografici in Parma dell'anno 1628 all'anno 1883*, Parma 1884

Ferrarini *Teatrale Ottocentesca*, Parma 1978

Fétis, F. Joseph *Biographie Universelle des Musiciens*, Paris 1835-1844

Forbes, Elizabeth *Mario and Grisi*, Victor Gollancz 1985

Forlani, M. Giovanna *Il teatro municipale di Piacenza 1804-1984*, Piacenza 1985

Foster, Myles Birket *The History of the Philharmonic Society of London 1813-1912*, The Bodley Head 1912

Foster's *Hand-List of Men-at-the-Bar*, Reeves & Turner 1885

Frassoni, Edilio *Due Secoli di Lirica in Genova*, Genoa 1980, 2 vols.

Fulcher, Jane F. *The Nation's Image: French Grand Opera as Politics and Politicized Art*, Cambridge University Press 1987

Gattey, Charles Neilson *Queens of Song*, Barrie & Jenkins 1979

Gatti, C. *Il Teatro alla Scala*, (1964) 2 vols.

Gerson, Robert A. *Music in Philadelphia*, Greenwood Press, Westport, Connecticut 1970

Gipson, Richard McCandless *The Life of Emma Thursby*, New York Historical Society 1940

Groves *Dictionary of Music* 1880

Hall, Lillian Arvilla *Catalogue of Dramatic Portraits in the Theatre Collection of the Harvard College Library*

Hartnoll, Phyllis (ed.) *The Concise Companion to the Theatre*, Omega Books 1988

Hayes, Richard *Irish Swordsmen of France*, M.H.Gill & Son Ltd., Dublin 1934

Howard, Diana (compiler) *Directory of Theatre Resources*, The Society for Theatre Research 1986

Ireland, Joseph. *Records of the New York Stage from 1750 to 1800* (2 vols), Morrell 1866-1867

Ivanov, M. *History of the Resident Italian Theatre in St. Petersburg* (Vols I & II), St. Petersburg 1895 (in Russian)

Johnson, Claudia D. and Vernon E. *Nineteenth-Century Theatrical Memoirs*, Greenwood Press, Westport, Ct. 1982

Kaufman, T. G. *Italian Performances in Vienna 1835- 1859*, Donizetti Society Journal 4, London 1980

Kaufman, T. G. *Verdi and his Major Contemporaries*, Garland Publishing Inc., 1990

Kennedy, Michael *The Concise Dictionary of Music*, Omega Books 1988

Klein, Hermann *The Reign of Patti*, T. Fisher Unwin, London 1920

Klein Hermann *Thirty Years of Musical Life in London*, New York, 1903

Kmen, Henry A. *Music in New Orleans 1791-1841*, Louisiana State University, 1966

Kobbé, Gustave *Complete Opera Book*, Putnam, 1954

Kolodin, Irving *The Story of the Metropolitan Opera 1883-1950*, New York, 1953

Krehbiel, Henry Edward *Chapters of Opera (The Lyric Drama in New York)*, Da Capo Press, New York, 1980

Kuhe, Wilhelm *My Musical Recollections*, London, 1896

Legouvé, Ernest *Souvenirs Biographiques*, Paris, 1893

Levey, R.M. and O'Rourke, J. *Annals of the Theatre Royal*, Dublin 1821-1880, Dublin 1880

Levin, Bernard *Conducted Tour*

Loewenberg, Alfred *Annals of Opera 1597-1940*, 1943.

Lumley, Benjamin *Reminiscences of the Opera*, London, 1864

Madeira, Louis C. *Annals of Music in Philadelphia* [etc] 1820-1858, Ed. Philip H. Goepp, Philadelphia Lippincott, 1896

Mancini R. and Rouveroux J.J. *Guide de l'Opéra*, Librairie Arthème Fayard, 1989

Mander, Raymond and Mitchenson, Joe *The Theatres of London*, Rupert Hart-Davis, 1961

Mapleson, J.H. *The Mapleson Memoirs 1848-1888*, Remington, London, 1888

Mattfeld, Julius *A Hundred Years of Grand Opera in New York 1825-1925*, NYPL New York, 1927

Merli, Domenico *Diario Lucchese dal 1761 al 1829*, Lucca

Mendel, Hermann *Musikalisches Conversations-Lexicon*, (1873)

Meyerbeer, Giacomo *Briefwechsel und Tagebücher*, ed. Heinz Becker, Verlag Walter de Gruyter and Co., Berlin

Moscheles' Leben, Herausgegeben von seiner Frau, Leipzig, 1872

Nalbach, Daniel *The King's Theatre 1704-1867*, The Society for Theatre Research, London, 1972

Nello Vetro, Gaspare *Le Voci del Ducato* (1982)

Nello Vetro, Gaspare *Cronaca degli spettacoli lirici del Teatro Regio di Parma*

O'Callaghan, J.C. *History of the Irish Brigade in the Service of France*, Glasgow, 1870

Odell, George C.D. *Annals of the New York Stage*, Columbia University Press, New York 1942 (and revisions)

[Padua] *I Teatri di Padova*

Pearse and Heard *The Romance of a Great Singer* [Mario] London, 1910

Piretti, G. *Carte varie riguardanti le Stagione Teatrali in Bergamo*, Biblioteca Civica Angelo Mai, Bergamo

Pleasants, Henry *The Great Singers*, Gollancz, London, 1967

Radiciotti, Giuseppe *Teatro, Musica e Musicisti in Sinigaglia*, 1893

Ramirez, Serafin *La Habana Artistica: Apuntes Historicos*, Havana, 1891

Ravaldini, G. *Spettacoli nei Teatri e in altri Luoghi di Ravenna 1555-1977*, Bologna 1978

Rosenthal, H. *Two Centuries of Opera at Covent Garden*, Putnam, London, 1958

416

Rosenthal, H. and Warrach, J. *Concise Oxford Dictionary* of Opera, Oxford University Press 1964

Rosselli, John *The Opera Industry in Italy from Cimarosa to Verdi*, C.U.P. 1984

Sadie, Stanley (ed.) *History of Opera*, Macmillan, 1989

Sadie, Stanley (ed.) *The New Grove Dictionary of Opera*, 1992

Saint, Andrew et al, *A History of the Royal Opera House, Covent Garden. 1732-1982*, The Royal Opera House 1982.

Salichet, Léon *Histoire de Maisons-Laffitte*, (1892)

Saxe-Wyndham, H. *Annals of Covent Garden*, (1905, 2 vols)

Schierer, Fernand *L'Hôpital Militaire Gaujot de Strasbourg*, (1955)

Seltsam, William *Metropolitan Opera Annals*, New York, (with unpublished revisions), H.W. Wilson & Co. 1947

Shaw, G.B. *Shaw's Music*, Bodley Head, 1981

Shockley, Martin Staples *A History of the Theatre in Richmond, Virginia, 1819-1838*, Ph.D diss. Univ. of N. Carolina, Chapel Hill, 1938 (2 vols)

Stendhal *Life of Rossini*, Paris 1922 and trans. by Richard Coe, John Calder, London, 1956

Stephens, J.L. *Incidents of Travel in Greece, Turkey, Russia and Poland*, Richard Griffin & Co. London and Glasgow (no date)

Stoutamire, Albert *Music of the Old South*, Farleigh Dickinson University Press, 1972

Strohl, P. *Manuel du Commerce etc. de la Ville de Strasbourg* (1824)

Tiby, O. *Il Real Teatro Carolino e l'Ottocento Musicale Palermitano*, Florence 1957

Tintori, Giampiero *La Scala, Cronologia completa*, Milan, 1964

Toye, Francis *Italian Opera*, Max Parrish, London, 1952

Traniello, L. *Il Teatro Sociale di Rovigo*, Minelliana, Rovigo, 1970

Valabrègue *Etat du Théâtre Royal Italien depuis la Direction de Madame Catalani*, Paris, 1818

Virella, F. Casañes *La Opera en Barcelona*, 1888

Wearing, J.P. *The London Stage 1890-1899* (Vol I), Scarecrow Press, Metuchen, N.J. 1976

Weaver, William *The Golden Century of Italian Opera*, Thames and Hudson, 1980.

Weinstock, H. *Vincenzo Bellini: His Life and his Operas*, Weidenfeld & Nicolson, 1971

Weinstock, H. *Donizetti and the World of Opera in Italy, Paris and Vienna in the First Half of the Nineteenth Century*, Methuen, London, 1964

Wemyss, Francis Courtney *Twenty-Six Years of the Life of an Actor and Manager* (2 vols), New York, 1847

Wemyss' Chronology of the American Stage from 1752 to 1852, Taylor, New York, 1852

Widen, Gustav *Lablache*, Göteborg, 1897

Winston, James *Drury Lane Journal 1819-1827*, Ed. Nelson and Cross, The Society for Theatre Research, London, 1974

Wood, William B. *Personal Recollections of the Stage*, Philadelphia, 1855

Yakhontov, A.N. *St. Petersburg Italian Opera in the 1840s*

NEWSPAPERS AND PERIODICALS

Austria
Allgemeine Theaterzeitung, Vienna
Gazette Musicale de Vienne
Wiener Conversationsblatt

France
L'Art Musical
The Boulogne Gazette
The Boulogne Messenger
The Boulogne Times and Visitors' List
Le Corsaire
Le Courrier du Bas-Rhin
Le Figaro
La France Musicale
Galignani's Messenger
La Gazette des Tribunaux, Paris
La Gazette des Etrangers
La Gironde, Bordeaux
L'Illustration
Le Journal des Débats
Le Journal de Paris
Le Menestrel
Le Nouveau Journal de Paris
La Quotidienne
La Revue et Gazette Musicale de Paris
Le Sémaphore, Marseille

Germany
Allgemeine Musikalische Zeitung
Berlinische Nachrichten
La Gazette Musicale, Berlin
L'Illustration de Bade
Le Mercure de Bade
Neue Frankfurter Zeitung

Ireland
The Freeman's Journal, Dublin
The Irish Times

Italy

L'Armonia, Florence
Gazzetta Musicale di Firenze
Gazzetta Privilegiata di Milano
Gazzetta Privilegiata di Venezia
Giornale Officiale di Palermo
I Teatri, Milan
Teatri, Arte e Litteratura, Bologna
Il Telegrafo Siciliano
Il Vapore, Palermo

Portugal

Gazeta de Lisboa

Russia

The Contemporary
The Italian Opera in St. Petersburg
Le Journal de St. Pétersbourg
Le Journal des Théâtres et de Musique
The Northern Bee
The Russian Artistic Bulletin

Spain

Iberia, Madrid

United Kingdom

La Belle Assemblée
The Court Journal
The Illustrated London News
The Illustrated Sporting and Dramatic News
The Morning Advertiser
The Morning Chronicle
The Morning Post
The Observer
The Sunday Times
The Times
The Annual Register
The Athenaeum
The Atlas
Fraser's Magazine
The Globe
The Guardian and Public Register
The Harmonicon
The London Literary Gazette
The Musical Times
The Musical World
The New Monthly Magazine
The Spectator
The Theatrical Inquisitor
The Aberdeen Herald
Aris's Birmingham Gazette
The Bath Chronicle
The Birmingham Daily Gazette
The Birmingham and General Advertiser
The Birmingham Journal
The Bradford Daily Telegraph

The Brighton Argus
The Brighton Gazette
The Bristol Times and Mirror
The Daily Post, Liverpool
The Dumfries Standard
The East Sussex News
The Evening Courant, Edinburgh
The Glasgow Herald
The Hampshire Independent
The Hull and North Lincolnshire Times
The Leeds Intelligencer
The Leeds Mercury
The Liverpool Echo
The Liverpool Mercury
The Manchester Courier
The Manchester Daily Examiner and Times
The Manchester Guardian
The Newcastle Courant
The Newcastle Weekly Chronicle
The Northampton Mercury
The North British Daily Mail, Glasgow
The Northern Whig, Belfast
The Nottingham Journal
The Norwich Chronicle
The Portsmouth Times and Naval Gazette
The Scotsman
The Ulsterman, Belfast
The Wiltshire County Mirror
The Yorkshire Post

The United States of America

L'Abeille, New Orleans
The Albion
The Boston Herald
The Brooklyn Daily Eagle
The Daily Picayune, New Orleans
The New York Clipper
The New York Daily Tribune
The New York Times
La Nouvelle Orléans
The Quarterly Musical Magazine and Review
Répertoire International de la Presse Musicale, (University of Maryland)
The World

Index

Bedford, Mrs. 95

Beethoven, Ludwig van 28, 41, 208, 328

Begrez, Pierre (Ignace) 127

Belfast News Letter 336-7, 339-40

Belfast, Northern Ireland 336, 339-40, 405

    Theatre Royal 336

    Ulster Hall 337, 340

Belgians, King of the 239

Belgioioso, Prince 188

Belgrave Square, London 315

Belisario 184

Bella figlia 298

Bellchambers, Miss 153

Belle Assemblée, La 96, 343

Bellini, Vincenzo 146, 149-50, 152, 155, 157, 168, 174-5, 182, 184, 186, 335, 391

Belluno, Italy 186

Bendazzi, Luigia 243, 249, 252

Benedict, Madame 236

Benedict, (Sir) Julius 236, 300, 317-8, 328

Benedictus 208

Bennett, James 151

Bennett, Joseph 294, 407

Benson's Company 355

Berg, Herr 20

Bergamo, Italy 171-2

    Biblioteca Civica Angelo Mai 171

    Teatro della Nobile Società 171-2

Berlin, Prussia 57, 121, 166-8, 213, 329

    Königsstädtische Theater 166

    Berlinische Nachrichten (BN) 166-8

Bernicat, Firmin 399

Berri, Marie-Caroline, Duchesse de

Bertrand, Aline 68

Bertrand, Ida 213, 239

Bettelheim, Karoline 323

Bettini, Alessandro 248, 252, 259-61, 324, 330, 340

Bettini, Geremia 244, 261, 273, 275, 283, 285

    (*Note:* There may be confusion between the above two as several references refer only to Signor Bettini)

Bettini, Madame (*see* Trebelli)

Betts, Miss 140

Bevignani, Enrico 320, 323, 406

Bianca e Falliero 170, 188

Biblioteca Civica Angelo Mai, Bergamo (*see* Bergamo)

Bigottini, Mlle. 32, 35

Biletto, Signor 229

Bimboni, Oreste 396

Biondini, Signor 65-6

Biricchino di Parigi, Il 212

Birmingham, England 206, 405

    Central Library 207

    A History of the Birmingham General Hospital and the Musical Festivals 207

    General Hospital 206

    Musical Festival 206-9

    Town Hall 206-7

Birnie, Sir Richard 54

Bishop (née Rivière), Mrs. Henry 111

Bishop, (Sir) Henry 134, 151, 205

Bizet, Georges 359, 402

Black Hussar, The 395

Blagrove, Mr. 160

Blangini, Felice 25

Blasis, Mlle (*see* De Blasis)

Bloomsbury, London 190

Boccabadati, Luigia 138-9

Bochsa, Robert-Nicholas-Charles 129

Boieldieu, François-Adrien de 34

Boissy d'Anglas, rue (Paris) 190

Bologna, Italy 57, 74, 185, 193, 407

    Gran Teatro Comunale 185

Bolshoi (Grand) *Theatre*, St.Petersburg (*see* St. Petersburg)

Bonasegla, Mlle. 20

Bone, Maria (*see* Glossop-Harris, Maria)

Bonfigli, Lorenzo 185

Bonnaud (*see* de Méric)

Bonsoir, Monsieur Pantalon 239

Booth, Junius Brutus 44

Bordeaux, France 330

    Grande Salle Franklin 330

Bordogni, Marco 25, 30, 34, 37, 39, 93

Borghi-Mamo, Adélaïde 245, 249, 252, 258, 264-5, 271, 280-1

Borgognio, Signora 233

Boronowski, Count 71

Bosio, Angelina 197, 254-5, 259, 261, 263, 267-8

Bossi, Signor 294, 306, 312, 315

Boston Ideal Opera Company 397, 399, 400

Boston World 370

Boston, Massachusetts, U.S.A. 360-2, 382-3

    Boston Theater 361, 396, 399

Bottari, Giovanni 68? 71

Bouché, Monsieur 270-1, 280

Bouchot, François 411

Boulogne, France 229, 272, 410

    Hôtel du Nord 272

    Hôtel Impérial 272

    Hôtel Royal 272

Bourse, La, Paris (*see* Paris)

Bowery Theater, New York (*see* New York)

Bow Street, London 54

Boyle, Mr. 347

Bozzetti, Signor 240

Bradford, England 342, 401

Braham, John 95-6, 136-7, 144, 343, 354

Brambilla, Marietta 165-6

441